INTRODUCTION TO RURAL SETTLEMENTS

REVISED AND ENLARGED EDITION

By the Same Author

1. Frontiers in Migration Analysis
2. Introductory Methods in Population Analysis
3. Land Utilisation: Theory and Practice
4. Patterns of Regional Geography: An International Perspective (in 3 Volumes)
5. Recent Trends and Concepts in Geography (in 3 volumes)
6. Statistics for Geographers and Social Scientists (Revised and Enlarged)
7. Systems of Rural Settlements in Developing Countries
8. Urban Geography: A Textbook

About the Author

Dr. R. B. Mandal born on 7.5.1948 in Kharsam village of Darbhanga district, Bihar. He passed M.A. (1968) and Ph.D. (1973) from Patna University. He taught in the Universities of Patna, Dar es Salaam (Tanzania) and Bhagalpur since 1973. Uptil now Dr. Mandal has written and edited more than 20 books on different levels in geography. He has also successfully supervised 12 Ph.D. thesis and published more than 50 research papers in different journals of India and abroad. His current interest is on urban studies, wetlands, aerial photograph and remote sensing besides project appraisal through cost-benefit analysis. He edits a bi-annual journal entitled 'East West Geographer' since 1990. At present Dr. Mandal is a University Professor of Geography in Tilka Manjhi Bhagalpur. University and teaching at the Post-Graduate Centre of R.D & D.J. College, Munger.

INTRODUCTION TO RURAL SETTLEMENTS

(Revised and Enlarged Edition)

R. B. MANDAL
Department of Geography
R.D & D.J. College
Munger (India)

CONCEPT PUBLISHING COMPANY, NEW DELHI- 110059

ISBN 81-7022-813-1 (PB)

First Published 1979

Second Revised and Enlarged Edition 2001

Published and Printed by
Ashok Kumar Mittal
Concept Publishing Company
A/15-16, Commercial Block, Mohan Garden,
NEW DELHI - 110059

Phones: 5648039, 5649024

Fax : 091-11-5648053

E-mail: publishing@conceptpub.com

PREFACE TO FIRST EDITION

Rural Settlement geography is a recently developed branch of human geography. Settlement as the primary residence of human society should be in the forefront of research in geography. Such studies are necessary for determining various aspects and problems associated with the cultural geography of the country without which we cannot hope to achieve optimum social conditions for development and progress.

Bihar Plain has a long cultural and historical background; it is significant not only for its physical and economic aspects but also for its population of over 40 million people. It is marked by great regional variations in the form, type and pattern of rural settlements and housing conditions. The area is susceptible to recurrent floods and thousands of rural settlements are swamped or washed away annually. However, the scene is now changing for the better on account of the construction of embankments and reclamation of marshy lands. The problem has become complex because more than 80 per cent of the population of the region resides in rural settlements. The pressure of the growth of population is increasing upon them every day, thereby leading to numerous problems like transport, sanitation and others. Yet neither the academicians nor the planners have taken up the problems of rural inhabitants in earnest.

In the prevalent circumstances and conditions the study of the rural settlements of the Bihar Plain assumes added significance. It may lead to the recognition of various factors associated with rural settlements. A statistical rather than descriptive approach is the forte of the present study.

The author is extremely grateful to P. Dayal, M.A. (Alig.) Ph.D. (London), Professor and Head of the Department of Geography, Patna University, not only for providing the opportunity to work on the present topic, but also for his kind inspiration and ready guidance.

Grateful thanks are also due to L.N. Ram, Ph.D., (Pat.) Reader in the Department of Geography, Patna University, who as a supervisor presided over the destiny of this work at every stage.

The author expresses his obligation for the valuable suggestions of Professor G. Jordan, Chairman of North Texas University and Professor Kirk H. Stone of the University of Georgia.

The views expressed in the following pages are entirely those of the author and constructive criticisms and suggestions from scholars as well as from the learned readers are invited for the modification of this book in its future editions.

Munger
5-5-1978

R.B. MANDAL

PREFACE TO THE SECOND EDITION

In rural areas the aggregate of houses for the purpose of agricultural operations, storage of grains and tethering cattle is known as rural settlements. It is a vulnerable branch of human geography which deals with rural population pressure, culture and housing facilities, rural economic activities and rural environmental conditions available for people's living. This provides safety from rigours of climate, flood and rowdy elements in the odd hours.

Human being obtains food, clothing and settlements with the help of their technological know how from the land and the surrounding environment. They work under natural environment and use natural resources to get a certain type of shelter, food and clothing. Hence, shelter has a dominant impact on the built environment while at the same time its characteristics are influenced by the natural environment. Human settlements can influence the environment by consumption of natural resources, adding physical elements to the environment, and acting as an intermediary between human being and the nature.

The form of human settlements generally determine social requirements and the physical environments as origin of settlements took place near cross roads, houses of landlords and hermits which starts depleting natural resources and its metabolic process pollute the land, air and water at the same time, because all these are related with the process of feedback mechanism. Hence, the productivity of land, labour and metabolic processes of settlements determine the environmental conditions for human comfort. This book will highlight some of these points through macro, meso and micro level analysis.

In different parts of India the systems of rural settlements are quite different with reference to its type, patterns, housing conditions and availability of service centres. Besides these, the description of models, quantitative techniques, GIS, regional patterns, central place studies and rural environment also find a suitable place in this book.

Systems of rural settlements find discussions regarding variations of living conditions in different parts of India i.e. in Kerala the rural settlements are surrounded by coconut trees, in Assam the hutments are surrounded by betelnut trees and bamboo grooves, in West Bengal settlements are located on the side of small wetland and banana grooves, in north-eastern Bihar due to annual havoc of flood hutments of grass and leaves are found on longitudinal embankment but in the deserts of Rajasthan the flat roof houses are preferred in comparison with gabled roof of Meghalaya.

The types of rural settlements in India are compact in northern plain, semi-compact in Madhya Pradesh and Assam Valley, semi-sprinkled in Peninsular India and flood affected areas. Sprinkled and dispersed rural settlements are typical feature of forested areas of western ghat, Jammu and Kashmir and desert areas of Rajasthan where settlement siting is selective either on slope or oasis. Patterns of rural settlements determine the shape, size and structure of rural settlements such as square, rectangular, circular, pentagon, hexagon and octagon in shape. All these are the reflections of siting condition, environmental situation and ground water level.

Housing conditions vary in rural areas in terms of materials of wall and roof, housing designs and availability of rainfall. Income variations have also played an effective role in housing differentiations. Recently, it has been found that pucca houses with RCC roofs are increasing in number due to high income potential of people living in rural areas.

Rural service centres are prolific in rural areas especially on cross-roads. This has happened due to rapid growth of population and increased unemployment situation. Rural service centres are growth foci on which the health centre, shops of medicene, fertilizer, grocery shops, banking facility, blacksmiths shop, shoe menders shops, studio, laundary and barbars saloon are located. They act as central places of the area where the convergence of roads and railways find place along with administrative nuclei and aggregate of commercial establishments.

The models of rural settlements are abstractions of real world situations found in the area. It covers the models of Udo, Doxiadis, Von-Thunen, Haggerstand, R.B. Mandal and others. Quantitative techniques have been applied from literatures collected from different journals. These are related to size, spacing, circularity, centrality and finding relationship in between different variables.

Geographical Information system is entirely based on computer generated data regarding type areas of rural settlements from satellite imageries or it may be graph theory or matrix algebra and the allied items prepared on computer.

Regional patterns of rural settlements prepared by considering types and patterns of rural settlements based on ceive method. This may be compact rural settlements with pucca houses and high population density or dispersed rural settlements with hutments of grass-leaves and sparse population density.

In this book Central Place study has been designed by considering methods of Christaller (1933) and he believes in the preparation of service centres network based on transportation, administrative and commercial activities as hexagonal lattices. This has been considered to be most efficient planning of rural areas for providing equitable amount of services to the rural inhabitants.

This book has been written for the students of Indian Universities according to the syllabus and changed environmental conditions of the Indian society. I am highly thankful to my teachers Prof. P. Dayal, Prof. L.N. Ram, Prof. V.N.P. Sinha and Prof. B. Thakur for teaching me about rural settlements. I am also thankful to Dr. R.B. Singh, University of Delhi who helped me in adding GIS in this book.

I hope the students and teachers will find this suitable as Text-book. Constructive criticisms and suggestions are invited for further modification of this book.

R.B. MANDAL
University Prof. of Geography,
R.D. & D.J. College
Munger

CONTENTS

CONTENTS

LIST OF FIGURES

LIST OF TABLES

1

INTRODUCTION TO RURAL SETTLEMENT

Rural Settlement Geography and Urban Settlement Geography are the two areas that constitute the discipline of Settlement Geography which itself is a recent branch of Human Geography. Settlement geography is the study of the form of the cultural landscape.[1] It is a science of systematic enquiry of occupancy features distributed over space with differentiation in relation to man. The minutest detail of the distribution of population manifests itself in the form of grouping of houses scattered at places and agglomerated at others. Siedlungs Geographie[2] is a German word that represents the concept of settlement geography and it means the cultural landscape developed by man in the process of occupancy. Doxiadis,[3] the architect of the capital city of Islamabad in Pakistan, used the Greek word Ekistics which again means the science of settlement.

Rural settlement, as man's living and functional space, dots the countryside since prehistoric times and forms an integral part of human life. A rural settlement, as the point of origin and primary residence of human society, is the linking thread and life blood of all geographical studies. Therefore, the consideration of settlement runs like a thread through almost the whole fabric of geographic thought.[4]

Rural settlement is the mainstay of human society throughout the world. It is the topographic expression of houses and highways as the home of man for safeguarding against environmental hazards. In such a situation the areas having fertile land and free from environmental dangers have dense population, compact rural settlements and central places with more confined hinterlands due to inter competition whereas areas having infertile land and less safety from environment have given rise to low population density, scattered human settlements and central places having wider zones of influence especially in flood plains and forest margines.

In any settlement whether rural or urban houses act as the flesh and highways as the circulatory system for the movement of human being. In this way, the study of rural settlement as the place of residence, concentration of services, nodes of transportation lines on growth points, growth centres and growth poles and their integral part houses in spatial integrated planning should be considered pivotal in any scheme of regional development and planning.

The location and functions of human habitation on the earth surface are the outcome of human behaviour in a particular geographical environment in relation to houses and highways. Whereever, the location of houses are systematic on beautiful sites and protective spaces it increases the accessibility and efficiency of work performance, and releases valuable bariland for the production of fruits, vegetables and food crops. In cases where growth and development are haphazard it decreases human effort, and accessibility and makes living uncomfort-able and leads to insanitary and vice of the underworld. Hence, systematic living is the sign of good environmental conditions, whereas the zig-zag fashion of roads and congested huddled houses are indications of environmental pollution, unscientific living and the development of slums.

Rural development is a highly complex socio-economic process which must take place over an extended time period; rural development must aim at helping the entire population, not merely agricultural producers, the integration process must focus on a minimum number of factors in order to meet major needs; and rural development projects must make provision for, and encourage the development of local institutions rather than relying on government institutions.

The Asian Institute of Technology (AIT) in Bangkok, Thailand, explained in the plan of operations for its new division: "The human settlements approach focuses on the spatial units of society–its regions, cities, villages and communities-as the appropriate units for the implementation of social and economic development. This approach aims at reaching all people, particularly those now being neglected, and bring them into the orbit of improvement and advancement"

The programme itself is already in progress. It has three main goals: (1) educating high-quality manpower for human settlement planning, development, management and education; (2) research in human settlements in the Asia region; and (3) dissemination of information.

The objective of this study is to highlight the spatial organization of rural settlements and service centres in India in its totality and suggest some measures for its planning, particularly with a view to checking the present situation of haphazard natural growth to allow utilization of available limited amount of natural resources. In brief the following are the objectives of this study into rural settlement planning:

(a) Maintenance of social equality, security and increase of protected living space.
(b) Provision of habitable residential houses to each family and estimation of its shortage.
(c) Best possible utilization of available limited resources of land and infrastructure facilities.
(d) Provision of a decent living to the ever-increasing population based on fixed and finite limited resources.
(e) Safety from the rigours of climatic hazards and communicable diseases.
(f) Increasing the accessibility, approachability and provision of highways and service facilities through growth points, growth centres and growth poles in a systematic manner.

Many European and other scholars have contributed substantially to this branch of geographical knowledge. Ritter (1779-1859) is the pioneer of the geographical study of rural settlement. But the history of systematic study of rural settlement goes back to the twenties of the present century when scholars like Paul Vidal de la Blache, Aurousseau, Ahlmann, Demangeon, Brunhes and others started laying foundations of the branches of settlement geography. The establishment of the Commission on Types of Rural Habitation[5] under the auspices of the International Geographical Union, however, is a landmark in making definite beginning in the study of rural settlement geography. Its first report published in 1928 which aroused much interest among geographers.[6] But the science of human settlement still continues to be in an experimental stage. Despite numerous studies made in many parts of the world, no general law has been formulated so far which could be universally applicable and is 'comparable to the principles of location in industrial geography and nationalism in political geography.[7] Besides, the geographical, economic, and social conditions obtaining in India are very different from those found in Europe or Americas. The present study, therefore, may open up new avenues for the study of settlements under Indian conditions and may also indicate a few principles applicable, if not universally, at least to the places where favourable geographical conditions obtaining in India.

Purpose of Settlement

The main purpose of settlement is to provide shelter to the human being. After wholeday work in the fields, farms, barns and factories- settlement provides a home to take rest whenever it is needed. Settlement is a congregation of houses. In one settlement the people of one occupation/different occupations reside in a congenial manner.

The purposes of a settlement are as follows.

(a) a place to take rest,
(b) protections from enemies,
(c) safeguard from wild beasts,
(d) store house of resources for future use,
(e) a place to run occupational activities i.e. household work, dairy, livestock rearing, running a shop besides schools, theatre ground and a community hall,
(f) it serve the purpose of social, political and cultural activities.

It reveals that a settlement serves many purposes and its built space varies accordingly. For example, one can run a motel in a small room on a roadside whereas for a dairy farm or high school a big space is required.

Scope and Objectives of Study

Rural settlement means the totality of human community in rural areas with all the social, material, organisational, spiritual and cultural elements that sustain a community. These elements may be spelt out in terms of physical requirements for housing work, energy supply, transport, communication, water availability and sanitation besides services for education, health, protection and welfare, systems of territorial organisation, government, law and economic management; and cultural facilities for art, recreation, leisure, etc. along with factors like ever increasing population, migration from rural to urban areas, demand of habitations for rehabilitation of displaced persons, etc. The problem of rural settlement is further widened its scope and requires an integrated approach for its solution.

Permanent settlement is a distinct phase of civilized life. The nomadic and semi-nomadic people of early prehistoric times led an unsettled life. They depended for their livelihood on hunting and fishing etc., wherein permanent settlement was unthinkable. A change in the pattern of life from that of the constant wandering to one with permanent agriculture on a fixed piece of land marks the origin of the settled life. The character and pattern of settlements in any region are very intimately linked with the organization and practice of agriculture, its historic evolution and the cultural advancement of people inhabiting in the area.

Habitations, like any other cultural trait, evolve through both time and space. They, inevitably, carry within themselves some hidden characteristic elements of spatio-temporal dimensions. Hence, they provide us with one of the most readily available forms of synthesis, the temporarily changing patterns of the inter-regional and intra-regional character of the cultural landscape. As settlements have an enormous range of variations in terms of their attributes inhabitants of the area. They also vary with the physical and cultural elements of an area. All of them could be closely linked to give character of diverse nature.

While natural resources and economic development are integral parts of the establishment and growth of human settlements, other associated factors are elements of cultural geography, cultural history, cultural processes, cultural ecology and cultural areas as well as locally significant factors like typology, distribution, variations, integration and area characterization.[8] The study of rural settlements has great significance, especially in the field of analytical study of the distributional pattern of population, with special reference to size and spacing of rural settlements.[9]

The arrangement of houses and highways in relation to man engaged in agricultural operations is known as rural settlement. It may be permanent, temporary, residence, store house, cattle kral and a tiny hutment.

Rural settlement are the topographic expression of the groupings and arrangement of the two fundamental elements of human geography, houses and highways*[10] *in the rural environment. Settlement geography, therefore, deals with the facilities built in the process of human occupance of land. Their nature and distribution are related on the one hand to the mode of human living and on the other to such physical factors as water supply, slope, forest and marshy lands. The external form of the settlement reflect the architectural style of the time, culture and region in which they evolved. Their distributional pattern is distinguishable in the landscape. Once created they may outlive both the cultural processes of the time and the function for which they were originally designed. For these reasons they reflect changes in human occupance of the land and may also exhibit relict expressions of the past cultural landscape.

A settlement is an organized colony of human being, including the building in which they live or work and the tracks or streets over which their movements take place.[11] The centre of interest in settlement geography is the built-up structure and its relation to the environment. In the beginning, these settlement features bear simpler forms and relationship with the environment but with the growth of civilization and technical knowledge, the degree of variability in their size and the complexity of their relationship becomes overwhelmingly greater.

Generally, individual buildings and other facilities are grouped in permanent clusters at nodal points in a settlement. These groups range from a simple cluster of farm house to most complex cultural organisms. Thus settlement geography includes not only the present buildings grouped around agricultural fields, but also the temporary camp of the nomadic herder, running the scale from hamlet to village, to town, to city, to metropolis and to ecumonopolis of total world urbanization.

Geographers consider rural settlement as man-made habitat on the rural landscape, based on primary occupations such as agriculture, forestry, mining, fishing, hunting, etc. which flourish on local resources. They examine the settlement features such as buildings and their architectural styles, roads, and lanes, in order to distinguish new categories and patterns and determine their functional relationships. Thus the size, spacing, form and functions of rural settlements and their origin are essentials of the subject matter. Their regional variations are mostly dependent on the sequential growth of their morphology and the social and economic structure of the society they represent and serve.

Geographers study settlement units and their distributional patterns for analysing the sequence of change in the cultural landscape. The character and layout of buildings, roads and fields and their arrangement for business, worship and recreation varies according to the merit of place and time on the one hand and tradition, technical knowledge and necessity on the other.

Rural settlement planning involves remodelling of existing villages with planned streets, restructuring the facilities and the removal of slums and squatters in order to provide prosperous life and descent living conditions to the rural people.

One should restrict himself for using barren and wetlands for the construction of houses by way of proper reclamation measures. The study about warehouses and residential houses essentially come under settlement ensemble along with cattleshed, temporary camp and the industrial and commercial centres located in the rural areas. Most of the farm houses kral's herders camp, military bases, railway junction, bus depot, administrative centres, Block offices, rural markets, schools, colleges and religious places come under the subject matter of rural settlement study.

Recently, the integrated rural development has gathered momentum for the planners and politicians but this concept has not got 100 per cent success in any part of the world. Nowadays, the sustainable development has gathered momentum due to lack of resources and protect our environment for the future generations.

Buildings and transport routes form the fixed elements of landscape and they continue as relict features even after the way of living, they represent, is changed. In India several ancient temples have been converted into mosques on the same foundations. e.g. Babri Mosque in Ayodhya which is no longer remain. New towns have came up on the ruins of the old ones or in their close proximity. Rebuilding of old sites were common during the Muslim period, and even in the British period civil-lines and cantonments were sometimes developed as twins to the older Indian settlements. The ruins of rural settlements of the past still survive as mounds even in the centre of new settlements, often bearing the same name. Such settlement sites in a region exhibit the nature and pattern of the ancient settlements and show details of the lines of migration of certain ethnic groups. One reason why the old and the new settlements are found closely associated is the lack of higher building sites in which the plain lands are subject to recurrent floods. The newer settlements naturally tend to gravitate towards the higher level grounds selected by the earlier settlers perhaps for the identical considerations.

The functional analysis of settlements has added new significance to the modern social, economic and political layout and organisations. Functions performed by different elements of the settlement impart distinctive shape and form to it. They also affect spatial distribution of landuse inside the settlement. The Indian village as a self-sufficient unit may be distinguished in different cases by the spire of the temple located centrally or by the house of the landlord or by the central block of residents belonging to the higher castes, surrounded by the peripheral circle of agricultural labourers and artisans. In different economic and cultural regions, the grouping of different buildings around the cultivable land takes place according to the needs of the area. The community has its distinctive religious sites, temples, mosque and churches, educational and recreational institutions and other features according to the needs and tradition of local people. The analysis of functions also covers the broad landuse patterns, nature of the occupational structure and other aspects related to institutional framework of a settlement.

Thus the functional analysis of rural settlements made no emphasis. In any programme of rural development it is of paramount importance to know the distributional pattern and type of services, the number and functional inter-relationships of the services areas, the occupational structure of jobs and the functional segregation of landuse in various settlements. The study of functional aspects, however, is of recent origin.

The problem of an economist is to analyse the vacant marginal or submarginal lands to determine the possibilities of their economic utilization. Similarly, a geographer approaches the pioneer fringe to know the potentiality of new settlements. 'The pioneer fringe is a laboratory of exceptional scientific work because there human intelligence is pitted against extreme or unusual environmental conditions.'[12] These conditions may have applied to the earlier settlers in India. Today, however, the region is extremely amenable to human occupance owing to its warm humid climate and a fertile alluvial land. It is densely settled, although most of the area is rural and the clusters have not developed into large towns. Isha Bowmen has remarked that 'city geography is at one end of the scale of settlement, pioneering at the other'.[13] The growth of cities has not been possible owing to economic backwardness. In India the rural settlement study falls in between these two extremes.

Concepts of Rural Settlement Geography

The concepts of settlement geography include the spatial arrangement of houses in relation to transportation lines, industrial locations, agricultural operations, utilization of land, ranching of cattle, technical know-how through educational institutions, defence from thieves and hazards of climate, etc., all for the welfare of human society. These are directed towards the understanding of the variable traits of places, the causes of their location, consequences and above all, their interactions with physical and cultural parameters. Settlement study is, therefore, multi-disciplinary in nature where geographers study the spatial arrangement of habitations, sociologists focus attention on social groups, economists study its optimum location for economic gains, while planner's interest centre round the best environmental conditions in it.

The concepts of settlement study are basically related to the following:

(a) The use of natural resources i.e., environment, soil, space, time, energy, goods, techniques, money, information and other resources for the best location and distribution of human habitation in rural areas;
(b) The colonization, spread and competition, density, change and dynamic of rural settlements depend upon the economic conditions, history of land occupancy and availability of food in any region;
(c) The attributes of clan settlements, types, morphology, materials of wall and roof, facilities of professional service and the transformation of rural settlements into urban settlements play an important role in the growth and development of rural settlements themselves;
(d) Settlements on a particular place and time provide an opportunity to make the best use of available resources for the construction of houses, production of food, shelter from rigours of climate and defence from thieves and wild beasts, and
(e) Planned development of rural settlement is necessary for regional economic development and welfare of rural people.

The settlement evolved only with the use of resources available locally according to the sources of information of a person and the society. The concept of evolution of rural settlement also includes the colonization, spread and competition of different clan groups in the process of origin and growth of rural settlement. Generally, settlement originated on higher level ground amidst fertile agricultural fields where water supply is plentiful and life is secure. In this way, rural settlements originated with the emergence of permanent agriculture. The enfighting of plundering hordes, migration of clan groups and the succession of one political power after the other, during historic times, led to the evolution of settlements of varied nature with respect to monumental designs, architectural styles of the time, place names, territorial organization and the union of clan groups into rural settlements.

The concepts of density and distribution of population are correlated and their studies are not possible in isolation. The high density of settlements has been found to depend upon agricultural prosperity and suitability of the region for human settlements since historic times. On the other hand, the distribution of settlements may indicate the agglomeration or dispersion of settlements in a particular ecological condition. This gives an idea of types of rural settlements in which the compact, semi-compact, semi-sprinkled and sprinkled settlement forms are generally observed in a regional analysis of Indian rural settlements.

The concepts of size and spacing of rural settlements are again correlated and interdependent upon each other. In areas with large size settlements, their spacing is abnormally high while in areas with small settlements the spacing is very close, except for the hilly, forested and flood affected areas.

The concepts of pattern and process of village morphology include the measurement of shape of rural settlements variant from the circle. identification of external shape of settlements from a birds-eye view and internal layout of streets and lanes.

In the concept of house types, the regional variation of houses in relation to the material of wall, roof, construction method, architectural style, cost involved and placing of courtyard, inner verandah, eavesline, female apartment and male apartments are important aspects of consideration. The density of houses, occupancy rate, and demand and shortage of houses are also the subject matter of this study.

The concept of regional patterns of rural settlements includes the regional conditions of their density, as also residential houses, settlement types and other elements of settlements in totality.

The concept of rural service centre includes the primary, secondary and tertiary service centres. The concepts of urban centres, centres of trade and commerce and central place hierarchy all come under the category of service centres. The centres which provide goods and services to their zone of influence are known as service centres. The functions which are performed by a centre for the hinterland are known as central functions, while the functions centred in urban areas are called nodal functions.

The concept of hierarchy of service centres ranges from a roadside settlement to a megalopolis, fabroblast and sacroma settlements. A roadside settlement is an isolated house of a motel or a petrol pump station or an eating place for passers bye. In India, roadside settlement is a common feature especially a betel shop. A hamlet is larger than a roadside settlement and this includes some residential houses besides commercial establishments. A village is larger than a hamlet with varied function of agriculture, residence, craftmenship and commerce.

A town is a settlement with marked tertiary functions, daily retail market, large population size, development of educational institutions, industries, hospital, telephone exchange, wholesale market, etc. When a town has reached the stage of 100,000 population that is known as a city. When several industrial cities coalesce physically and economically, even if they are politically independent they are known as conurbation.

The term metropolis is applied to such a city which has a population of 1,00,000. This is also known as a millionaire city. When several conurbations and metropolises coalesce the term megalopolis is applied to such a contiguous urban area. Such a megalopolis is discernible on the eastern sea coast of United States.

The term fabroblast and sacroma settlements are generally applied to the highly congested and overcrowded urban places. Similarly, the term growth centres and growth poles are applied in India to developing service centres like small towns and developed service centres like state capitals respectively.

Locational decisions are generally taken in recent times, on the basis of locational relationships of rural settlements which reflect an ordered adjustment to the factor of distance. The concept of the rural settlement system may be seen as an adjustment to a combination of physical, biological and cultural inputs, so that a change in one or more inputs may be expected to lead to a readjustment within the system. When the chronological relationship of different grades of settlements is applied with certain logical principle, it is called system analysis. A system generally works with the process of feedback mechanism, whether be it a close or open system. In 1976 R. L. Singh has given a call to social scientists to find out 'national settlement system' for Indian settlements.

There are some common concepts in settlement geography which have linked the rural and the urban settlements together in a single unifying bond. The separation of rural from urban studies may be permissible in geographical work, but it should not stand as a barrier between the two. For example, it is not possible to analyse the service centres purely as rural phenomenon; they should preferably be studied in close association with the urban studies. One effect of such studies is the central place anslysis, an important concept in settlement geography devised by Christaller in 1933.[14] The geometric figures drawn up by him, as well as by several other geographers recently, give expression to the theoretical spacing of central places of different ranks in an area of evenly distributed rural settlements. For such studies, therefore, it is essential to exceed the realm of rural settlement geography in order to appreciate and do justice to the subject.

Relationship to other Branches of Geography

The subject of rural settlement is associated with that of regional economy, particularly in the fields of land-utilization, and transport network. In land utilization, settlements are included in the category of land not available for cultivation. The spatial arrangement of habitations has a vital bearing on the existing patterns and the future planning for better landuse. The relationship between transport network and settlements can be considered as the cause and effect of each other. This relationship is increasing with the slow change in subsistence economy due to regional inter-dependence and market location. The increasing volume of both freight and passenger traffic results in considerable changes in the settlement network, particularly, in its systematic hierarchy.

Rural settlements are also related to population geography, both in its historical and functional perspectives. The settlement site is pivotal to all branches of geography, because the house is a fundamental concept in human geography. It is the link between man and the land, and serves not only as a shelter or a place of residence, but also as a place of work. A settlement is a fixed element of the cultural landscape, while population is a dynamic element on it. Geography is primarily concerned with the distribution and spatial patterns of these phenomena. The settlement map of any region gives the most meaningful picture of population distribution for at least a considerable part of the earth's surface.

Settlements and historical geography are genetically similar in their approach. The study of the evolution of settlement is profitable in determining their origin and development of morphology. Whatever interpretation a geographer may give of the present form or pattern, it must be considered in terms of the processes at work which generated them. Historical geography should be studied in terms of the past distributions and settlement changes. The significance of place names in examining historical geography is, therefore, obvious as they help to identify various groups of settlers and their culture in the past.

The study of settlements as a permanent element of the landscape is most important for the purpose of terrain evaluation in military geography. Settlement features are also included in tactical and strategic studies of modern warfare as expressed in road patterns and their focal points.

Highways are the fundamental concepts in settlement geography which provide a common link with other branches of geography. As a matter of fact the study of transportation cuts across all fields of human geography. A settlement can be visualised as an arrangement of houses and highways, but the link between settlements is provided by transport routes. Any change in the modes of transport, therefore, has an influence over the settlement pattern of an area. In regions having ancient civilized culture, the patterns of transport routes are often guided by the location of settlements. These patterns have been constantly changing from the days of bullock carts to jet planes, and have, in turn, influenced the morphology and character of the settlement they served.

Rural settlements are primarily agricultural in character. Hence settlements are intimately related with field patterns, and any change in landuse pattern would affect the settlement pattern. Similarly, the regional distribution of rural settlements has some relationship with the regional distribution of crop combination and agricultural practices. Agricultural geography on the other hand, be incomplete if it did not take into consideration settlements as focal points for the marketing of agricultural produce as well as a source of labour for all agricultural operations.

Rural settlement geography, thus has a number of aspects related, to human geography and includes a large number of topics such as house types and patterns, morphology, functions, spatial distribution, and rural-urban relationships. These must all be examined thoroughly in order to appreciate and understand this vast and distinct subject.

Settlement geography thrived on methods developed in economics, biology, mathematics, statistics and social sciences. A settlement geographer need to be a combination of historian, cartographer, artist, market researcher, sociologist and statistician. His work is to assess building, streets, inhabitants, functions performed by community besides mapping, correlation and interpretation of comparative studies, etc.

In the present study a systematic approach has been applied and a balanced geographical account of the rural settlements in India developed on a firm statistical base, has been given. Certain specific rural-urban relationships have been determined and the complex settlement unit has been broken down to its formal or basic geographical units. While a large number of techniques have been applied to the preparation of maps and diagrams, the choropleth and isopleth techniques are most frequently used. Several maps have been drawn to illustrate the results of various statistical techniques applied to analyse and properly interpret the available data.

The data has been collected from a number of source which include both published literature, census data, unpublished data from official sources, field investigation and statistical analysis of relevant data. An attempt has been made to analyse and interpret this data scientifically and objectively by applying suitable statistical and cartographic techniques. The hierarchical and functional studies of the rural settlements made on the basis of the theoretical models which should be useful in regional planning and the preparation of rural development schemes.

Current Trends and Future Tasks

The establishment of settlement reflects the Art of Man in Nature's setting, was delightfully brought to us by P. Vidal de la Blache at the beginning of this century. The settlements are accretions of houses in time is well revealed in human history from the pre-Harappan sites, Vedic literature and ancient, medieval and modern historical sources.[15] The common feature in the evolution of all human settlements is the need of a human group to settle down, to stabilise itself against inclement weather through occupance of the surrounding land which could ensure social cohesion and progress towards political and economic betterment, with a continuously evolving technology to assist. The dichotomy between urban and rural settlements, is not supported by any historical evidence. The town stemmed out of a village acquired all the characteristics of a city. In the pre-colonial and pre-industrial landscapes of India, there does not appear to have been the sharp contrast between the city and the village. The cities and towns of ancient and medieval India functioned more as prima inter pares and less as dominating and often exploiting nodes in the regions as they developed recently.[16]

Clearly, it was the impact of European colonialism with its emphasis on commercial crops, railways, roads and exporting centres like Mumbai, Calcutta and Chennai, that created the present dichotomy. Modern industrialisation had a much stronger influence on what was already a changing landscape of the early colonial era. The nature of this impact of Western colonialism, science and technology on the Indian regions and their settlements-urban and rural–does not seem to have been studied so far, though beginnings have been made.[17] It is important to note that whereas the imprint of modern technology on the terrain was drastic enough in the Western countries, it came out of the changing regional milieu where mechanical transport and factories were a part of the rapidly transforming landscape. In India, this change came almost as a 'transplant', with port and commercial cities becoming strong nodes of industrialisation and the countryside, under commercial cropping, being strongly tied up with the cities through the improved roads and new railways, all gravitating to the three colonial cities. The landscape features of the Western technology were superimposed on the earlier pre-industrial landscape of largely self-sufficient villages, market towns and capital cities with the minimum necessary administrative and economic links. The contrast between these two interfaces one westernised and aggressive and the other indigenously evolved, stable, yet weakened and submissive, continues to produce urbanised nodes and metropolitan areas on the one hand and the sluggish agrarian regions and the far more backward tribal hill regions of tribal settlement on the other.

Trends in Indian Settlement Studies

During the last forty years substantial work has been done in the field of Indian settlement Geography, accompanied by the development of sub-fields of urban and rural settlements geography.[18] A further sub-division in each of these two sub-fields is in evidence. Locational, structural and functional aspects received major attention to begin with; much of this was descriptive with hardly any attempt to link these aspects with general trends and theory building. The impact of Christaller began to be felt by the early 1950's,[19] with a subsequent rapid spread in nearly all research institutions. It could be safe to say that the majority of geography departments in India are involved in studies of settlement hierarchies and testing the Rank-size Rule. Some institutions, very desirably, link up this aspect of settlement Geography with Regional Planning and Development.[20]

Western Concepts and the Eastern Scene

It may be said that research in the geography of Indian settlements has followed, by and large, the application of Western concepts and techniques, without much critical examination as to whether these are apt or need any modification in our context. This is reflected in the simplistic phase of rural and urban settlements–their sites and morphology–with hardly any concern for the social and economic factors which condition the behavioural patterns of the residential community. These, studies are apparently static in nature, followed by a rather lively concern over identifying spatial organization. "Umland" studies formed a particular aspect initiated by L.D. Stamp.[21] These cartographic approaches become considerably strengthened with the application of Quantitative Methods, and thanks to the close association of studies in urban geography and those in Regional Planning and Development, studies of settlements as functioning systems over a terrain, open out a new and rewarding field in Settlement Geography. The initial phase in the study of settlement systems, is based on the initial hypothesis that: (i) the settlement cannot exist or function in isolation, it exists and functions in space, (ii) as a unit in a constellation of other villages, towns and cities, and (iii) that many attributes-demographic, social, economic of each settlement are capable of revealing the city's role in the system in a given region-large or small. The inadequacy of this approach of inferring linkages and hierarchies from individual settlement data has been recognised recently and the next step in research tends to get at grips with 'flow' data relating to movement of persons and goods between two settlement points. The concept of a settlement 'system', revealed on a map as an arrangement on terrain and operating as a circulation of men and material, thus, merits further research relating to the various regions of India. This is mainly because such studies seem to hold some clues in well-directed and purposeful regional planning.

Today settlement Geography in India appears to be overtied with Western concepts such as Christaller's hexagonal hierarchies, Losch's economic landscape. Zipf's Rank size Rule and, more recently, the Growth Pole strategy for regional development.[22] Some significant work is noticeable, but much of the rest has gone to test an empirical fit, but without deriving meaningful results.

Current Perspective

Geographers should take a closer view of the problems of rural settlements and apply only those techniques that are likely to yield meaningful results. A good deal of work on the internal social structure of the Indian village has been done[23] but there is a greater need to understand the social integuments that make the village–an aspect which came out powerfully in the newly settled communities whose older villages were submerged by the Tilaiya, Maithon & Jayakwadi dam on the Damodar and Godavari rivers. Though the displaced families were allotted their new sites on a random basis, after two or three years it became clear that many householders had exchanged their sites so that they could reside in their own 'caste-shell'. The planning of new rural settlement will have to take into account this aspect of social zoning which will disappear only with education and economic uplift.[24]

The hierarchy of settlement and the Growth Pole strategy when applied to the Indian conditions is simply not effective. They assume that the countryside is well developed and has the necessary 'demand' factor operating. This may be so in developed countries but it is not true in India; especially in flood prone, drought prone, tribal and hilly areas. The Growth Pole strategy is itself being questioned in France where the disparities between rural and urban regions are not wide. It defeats one's reasoning as to how a Growth Pole endowed with all the inputs can generate the economy of rural India that is backward and impoverished.[25]

The development of rural settlements in India will emerge through the long and hard way of regeneration of the countryside, than by a Growth Pole strategy of endowing some nodes with economic inputs and hoping that these would have 'spread-effect' on the countryside. Thus it would be rewarding to examine the Christaller approach from the base to the apex. This is possible in the green revolution regions of the Punjab-Haryana and the deltaic regions of the Godavari, Krishna and Cauveri rivers. It is necessary to assess first the economic level of these regions then interpret the available settlement hierarchy on this basis. It is very likely that such a study may give us a better clue to the understanding of settlement hierarchies in backward regions, their role in the regional development and the ways in which the hierarchy can be modified for a better socio-economic development of the region.

The Study of Environment

The environmental study is the recent sub-field of rural settlement study for sustainable and sound development of our economy. The exploration of our rural environment is essential to bring us to the reality of the Indian scene. The problems of rural settlements are unemployment, housing shortage, lack of proper drainage, pavements stoney houses to the ring of cattle in the close proximity besides safe drinking water supply and the barriers of religion and caste. How does each section of the village community-farmers, landless labourers, shepherds and artisans-function in relation to the land they have? How does a family unit in each section live in relation to its resources? How does a farmer view the agricultural innovations that he has been encouraged to adopt? Where he has the resources, the aptitude and the outlook will change? How much of his labour comes from the rural family?

An answer to all these questions have a common geographical base-man's reaction as member of a rural social group to his environment. This is so because a rural settlement–especially the Indian settlement with its long historical and cultural evolution—cannot be explained merely by its geometrical pattern or form, by the statistics of its work force as a functional index, or by its external relationship to the hinterland. It should be explained by living response to nature's environment; with the settlers forming a resident community which is endowed with a cultural heritage, economic assets and a future full of environmental challenge.

REFERENCES

1. T.G. Jordan, "On the Nature of Settlement Geography", *Professional Geographer*, Vol. XVIII, 1966, pp. 26-28.
2. R. L. Singh and K.N. Singh (eds.), "Readings in Rural Settlement Geography, Varanasi, *National Geographical Society of India*, 1975, p. VII.
3. C.A. Doxiadis, "The Future of Human Settlement" in Tiselius, A. and Nilsson, S. (ed): *The Place of value in a world of Facts, Stockholm, Almqvist and Wiksell*, 1969, pp. 307-38.
4. C. F. Kohn, "Settlement Geography" in P.E. James: *American Geography: Inventory and Prospects*, University of Syracuse, 1959, pp. 125-139.
5. A.B. Mukherjee, "Spacing of Rural Settlements in Rajasthan", *Geographical Outlook*, Vol. 7, 1970, p. 2.
6. J.M. Houston, *A Social Geography of Europe*, London, 1953, p. 30.
7. C.F. Kohn, *Op. cit.*, p. 125.
8. G.S. Gosal, "Geography of Rural Settlement" in Indian Council of Social Science Research (New Delhi): *A Survey of Research in Geography*, 1972, pp. 188-202.
9. A.B. Mukherjee, *Op.cit.*, pp. 1-19.
10. J. Brunhes, *Human Geography*, New York, Rand McNally, 1952, p. 152.
11. R. L. Singh, "Meaning, Objectives and Scope of Settlement Geography", *National Geographical Journal of India*, Vol. 7, 1961, pp. 11-20.
12. I. Bowman, "Settlement by the Modern Pioneer", in Taylor, Griffith (ed.): *Geography in the Twentieth Century*, Second Edition, 1953, p. 266.
13. *Ibid.*
14. W. Christaller, *Central Places* in Southern Germany, translated by C.W. Baskin, New Jersey, Prentice Hall, 1966.
15. Thapar, Romilla, *History of India*, Pelican, 1970.
16. Studies in Ancient Indian History by K.A. Nikantha Sastri, the Alchins, A.S. Altekar, D.O. Kausambi, amply bring out these aspects.
17. Studies of Moonis Raza and others, *Centre for Studies in Regional Development*, J.N.U., New Delhi.
18. S.P. Chatterjee, (ed.), Fifty Years of Science in India—Progress of Geography, Calcutta, 1968; ICSSR Review, Report on Geography, New Delhi, 1971.
19. *ICSSR Report on Geography*, Chapter on Urban Geography.
20. Studies by Geography Department, Osmania University, Hyderabad; Regional Survey Unit, I.S.I., New Delhi, *Centre for Studies in Regional Development*, J.N.U., New Delhi.
21. R.L. Singh, *Benares*, Varanasi, 1955.,
22. R.P. Mishra, *Regional Development Planning in India*, Delhi, 1974.
23. *Studies by the Geography Department*, B.H.U., Varanasi.
24. Jayakwadi Villages, Thesis, M.E.T.P. Department of Town Planning, *College of Engineering*, Pune.
25. Manzoor Alam, & K.N. Gopi, *Settlement Systems of India*, Oxford and IBH Publishing Co., New Delhi. 1987.

2

APPROACHES AND PRINCIPLES OF RURAL SETTLEMENT GEOGRAPHY

Both ideographic and nomothetic approaches are generally utilized in rural settlement studies. In recent years most of the studies are directed towards quantitative approaches, which are mere tools to explain the complicated problems of spatial analysis in geography. The approaches of settlement geography are mainly concerned with the growth and distribution of settlements, functional classification and hierarchy of settlements, types, patterns, spatial diffusion and development of rural and urban centres; measures of centrality and nodality, settlement planning, problems of settlement growth and model building etc.

Rural Settlement studies generally make use of the following approaches.

(a) Retrogressive approach;
(b) Retrospective approach;
(c) Prospective approach;
(d) Environmental approach;
(e) Case study approach;
(f) Regional approach;
(g) System analysis approach;
(h) Statistical approach;
(i) Interdisciplinary approach; and
(j) Principle approach.

Analysis of the Above

(a) In retrogressive approach the interest centres round the past and it also considered such aspects of the present pattern of rural settlement which throws light on earlier conditions.

(b) The retrospective approach probes the present, and the past is considered for the understanding of the future.

(c) The prospective approach concerns with the future, but the past and the present are considered as relict features of adjustment with future probable needs.

(d) Environmental approach comprises factors like topographic conditions, forest cover, climatic conditions, availability of water, food, employment, technical abilities of people, agricultural prosperity, mineral exploitation and the development of industries. All these factors have profound effect on the types, patterns, growth and dispersal of rural settlement in a particular locality. Only the sum of the conditions as emerged from the association of above mentioned variables can be said to be a particular level of effect in developing a particular character of settlement growth, functions, spatial diffusion, concentration, dispersal and housing conditions at a specific place and time.

(e) In case study approach, settlements are generally selected on random, systematic, clustered or nested sampling basis. The emphasis is given on a particular settlement from all geographical points of view. It also establishes as to when, where, why and how a habitat has evolved and is still continuing on a particular place.

(f) In regional approach, the country may be divided into settlement regions. The regional study approach to settlement is influenced not by political boundaries but by physical factors. In this approach, the repetition of the same study for different units is not possible. For instance, the geographical areas along the equator may constitute separate nations but the regional condition on the equator is the same everywhere and so is the living condition in this region.

(g) The system analysis approach takes stock of the process of feed-back mechanism, open system, closed system and the corollaries of systems and sub-systems studied for different levels of settlements in different time and space.

(h) Statistical approach includes sampling method, model building, cost-benefit analysis, correlation, regression, multivariate analysis, principal component analysis, etc. Settlements are generally chosen on the basis of random, systematic, clustered, multi-stage and purposive sampling. In model building graphical and deterministic models are generally used in settlement geography.

(i) Under interdisciplinary approach, the methods used in other branches of geography or in allied sciences are applied to settlement geography for studying various problems, e.g., the same methods, which are generally used in functional classification of settlements, are applied to crop combination. So far as the principle approach is concerned, the application of the theory of central place can be applied in any region with some positive result.

(j) Applications of paradigms, system analysis and probability theory are currently changing the geographer's attitude towards rural settlement studies. In a system of steady state, it is not necessary to study history of settlements in order to understand its form and the process going on. Such an approach does not fit into the traditional triology of form, function and genesis treated as the approaches to geographical knowledge of rural settlements.

Review of Past Literature

Rural settlement studies on a systematic basis originated with Karl Ritter's work in the early nineteenth century, and the subject has been mostly fully developed in West European countries especially in Germany and France. In these areas most studies examine rural house types, settlement patterns and colonization. On the other hand, K.H. Stone of U.S.A. has offered a more restricted definition of rural settlement geography as 'the description and analysis of the distribution of buildings by which people attach themselves to the land for the purpose of primary production.' Recently a flood of literature has begun to emerge with the establishment of Varanasi school of Settlement Geography in India by R.L. Singh; the Israeli school of Settlement Geography at Tel-Aviv by Moshe Brawer; the Hiroshima School of Settlement Geography in Japan by Zero Yonekura; and the United Nations Centre for Human Settlements at Nairobi by E. Kitonga. But in all these centres only area studies are gaining ground, with lesser attention devoted to the theoretical and planning perspectives of rural settlements in the form of agro-politan development.

The contributions of European scholars to the knowledge of

rural settlement geography are old and original but these could not be synthesized into a specialized branch of geographical knowledge, being much varied in character from country to country and from region to region. The study of urban centres caught the fancy of European geographers as this was a developing subject and also was much more easy to study and analyse. Hence, the advancement of urban geography constitutes the bulk of studies in settlement geography.

In geographical etymology, settlement is a multi-meaning term. It is defined as 'the place, where one person or more dwells regularly, or the act of establishing a permanent residence.'[1] The first meaning has been adopted for the purpose of this study. A full-fledged subject of settlement geography came to be developed around this meaning through the studies of the French and German geographers in the 19th century. The German geographer, Carl Ritter's works during the late 18th and early 19th centuries are considered to be constituting the base of settlement geography. His settlement studies are mainly related to the various phenomena and processes resulting from complex man-land relationship.[2] It is apparent from the bibliography of Freidrich Ratzel that many early contributions on settlements were made by German geographers who examined mainly two aspects of house types and urban centres. In 1895, Meitzen[3] considered the form of European settlements and laid emphasis on the morphology of rural settlements. The same trend was followed by Beresford.[4] Schluter in 1899 who considered things in a wider contest of the location, size and growth of settlements and their relationship with the nature. He was pioneer in identifying the relationship of settlement geography with cultural geography. Wagener has emphasized the importance of dwellings in settlement geography. His studies strengthened the view that the land used by the inhabitants in dwellings, formed part of the settlement.

During the last few decades, settlement in German geography has come to be recognised as temporary and permanent or as rural and urban. According to Schwarz 'rural settlement geography includes the study of man's use of plants and animals to procure food and clothing of an economic area larger than the dwellings and of direct relationship between the economic area and the dwellings.'[5] Paul Vidal de la Blache was an early French settlement geographer, whose voluminous studies enriched the field of human geography. Demangeon made studies of field ownership, cultivation, building materials, house types and the distribution of towns, rural settlements and human dwellings. The credit of spinning up the basic idea of settlement geography goes to the authoritivative work of P.E. James and other.[6] Lefevre of Belgium had made some notable contributions between 1921-1964 to the study of patterns of rural settlements. Aurousseau[7] conceived of settlement as the 'arrangement of dwellings. I.G. Grano undertook pioneer studies in Finish settlement regions and his works are characterised by analyses of the form and location of rural dwellings, hamlets and settlements.

Since the publication of the first report of the Commission on types of Rural Settlements by the International Geographical Union in 1928, considerable work has been done in this area. Matui,[8] a Japanese geographer, did valuable pioneering work on quantitative rural settlement geography in 1932. Yonekura,[9] another Japanese geographer, has made very noteworthy and original contributions comprising about seventy research papers and more than nine books upto 1975. This huge quantum of research is directly or indirectly related to the cultural heritage and the rural settlements of Japan in particular, and Asia and India in general.

C. J. Galpin,[10] the American rural sociologist, published his work on the rural communities of Wisconsin in 1915 and he formulated a new concept of 'rurban community'. The classical concept of central place by Jefferson and Christaller[11] was developed further by Ullman (1941),[12] Dickinson (1947)[13] Brush (1953),[14] Berry and Garrison (1958),[15] and Beavon and Mabin (1975).[16] Beavon and Mabin derived a full set of discrete market areas for any sized region. Their study was based on Losch central place system and also included solutions of mathematical equations as put forward by Losch.

K.H. Stone, another leading American geographer, in his various studies on rural settlements emphazied that the 'settling, stability and abandoning of rural settlements' are important aspects of rural settlement geography.[17] According to him Ritter's approaches to rural settlement geography were confusing and to offset the confusion he gave a more specific definition of rural settlement geography as 'the description and analysis of the distribution of buildings by which people attach themselves to the land for the purposes of primary production.'[18] Jordan found Stone's view narrower and he emphasised that the concept of cultural landscape should be integral to rural settlement study. Cultural landscape is a multitudinous concept comprising settlement morphology, vertical arrangements and dimensions of houses, horizontal arrangements of the houses, distribution of buildings, the floor plans of houses, the pattern of fences and fields, and the material components of houses.[19] Isha Bowman[20] has studied the pioneer fringe of rural settlements. Edgar Kant's study is also very significant as he has represented the density of rural habitations in several ways following the methods of different investigators.[21]

Hillman's[22] work on *Community Organization and Planning* is important but his approach is mainly sociological. The key note of Jacobsen's[23] sociological study is that a scientific way of investigation in rural settlement geography is possible. Chisholm[24] has paid greater attention in showing the relationship between landuse and rural settlements. Doxiadis[25] has endeavoured to develop an independent science to study human settlements to be known as *Ekistics.* Eidt[26] has worked on abandoned settlement analysis. A.T.A. Learmonth[27] has published a number of studies on rural settlements with special reference to the Asian and Indian cultures. F.S. Hudson's[28] work is mainly directed towards the basic ideas of rural and urban settlements.

Attempts have also been made to investigate the mathematical and theoretical aspects of rural settlement geography. J.C. Hudson[29] in his location theory has emphasised the existence of three phases of colonization, spread, and competition in the settling process and the continuity of the settling process is the continuation of the three phases in a cyclic order. According to D. Grossman's[30] theory, African societies have two fundamental characteristics. Firstly, each clan and each cultural unit has its own method of spatial organization, secondly, the communities have control over matters relating to land tenure and land allocation. Through deterministic models, Bylund[31] presented his ideas of settlement diffusion for the Lappland area in Sweden. Morrill[32] has developed probabilistic models taking one from the stochastic processes and random numbers. Curry[33] applied random processes to the making of settlement patterns with varying degrees of industrial specialization. Meining[34] had distinguished three major zones of core, domain and sphere of Mormon influence inside the settlement. Landing[35] has prepared a simulation model in the areal occupance patterning of a group of people. Bjorklund[36] has emphasized the role of religio-cultural decisions in the settlement process of an area.

The Indian geographers have made liberal use of the ideas of the Western geographers. But this trend has resulted into anomalies as the conditions in the Western world are often entirely different from those prevailing in India. It is in recent years only that the study of different aspects of rural settlement geography has acquired some importance in India. Despande[37] has studied *Settlement Types of Bombay Karnataka* with special reference to population size of the villages. S.M. Ali[38] has discussed rural settlement types, patterns, locations, sites and house types of Ghaggar plain in relation to population distribution. Ahmad[39] has discussed rural settlement types of Uttar Pradesh. He has also analysed village patterns in zones of compact and fragmented types of settlements, and their regional distribution.[40] Buschman[41] has examined various aspects of rural settlements. R.L. Singh[42] has elaborated the meaning, objectives and scope of rural settlement geography. He has also traced the evolution of settlements in the Middle Ganga valley from prehistoric to modern times and distinguished compact, semi-compact, fragmented and sprinkled types of settlements.[43] A.B. Mukerjee[44] has discussed the type, size and spacing of rural settlements with special reference to the areas of Punjab, Rajasthan, Andhra Pradesh and Uttar Pradesh.

Lahiri[45] has studied the settlements of Ajoy valley. He has also traced the cycle of growth of settlements through successive stages of youth, maturity and old age. Bhattacharya[46] has examined the effects of caste factor on types of rural settlements in Western Uttar Pradesh, where the inhabitants prefer to live close together in large agglomerated habitations. R.L. Singh[47] in an another study of the typical rural dwellings in the umland of Varanasi found that the rural house was well adapted to the physical and cultural environment of the region.

L.R. Singh[48] has analysed various aspects of rural settlement geography with special reference to Uttar Pradesh. Sinha[49] has discussed houses and house types of Chota Nagpur Plateau in Bihar. R.B. Singh[50] has studied rural settlement types, their distribution and future trends in Varanasi district of Uttar Pradesh. The functional studies have started appearing very recently.[51]

So far as the advancement of existing knowledge and available resources for the study of rural settlements are concerned several symposia have been organized in recent years. The I.G.U. Commission held a symposium in 1971 at Varanasi and its proceedings were published as *Rural Settlements in Monsoon Asia*[52] in 1972. R.L. Singh has also organized other symposia on rural settlements, e.g., at Palmerston North, New Zealand in 1974. Symposium on Rural Settlements in Monsoon Lands in 1975 at Varanasi and Pre-Congress Symposium at Tashkent in 1976. Indian Institute of Technology Kharagpur (India) organised a symposium on 'Rural Community Development' in 1976. The theme of the symposium was multi-disciplinary approach for integrated rural development. The department of Botany at the University of Rajasthan also organized a symposium on the problems of human settlements and multidisciplinary approach for integrated rural and urban development. The 21st International Geographical Congress was held in 1968 in India.

R.K. Mukherjee published his well known, work, *Man and His Habitation* in 1968.[53] R.C. Sharma published his doctoral work entitled *Settlement Geography of Indian Desert*[54] in 1972. Ayodhya Prasad published his post-doctoral work entitled *Chotanagpur: Geography of Rural Settlements* in 1973.[55] V.N.P. Sinha published his Ph.D. Thesis entitled *Settlement Geography of Chotanagpur Plateau*[56] in 1976. National Geographical Society of India, Varanasi has brought out three significant works. They are *Readings in Rural Settlement Geography.*[57] *Spatial Dimensions in Rural Settlement Geography*[58] and *Special Issue*[59] of National Geographical Journal of India, which contains a number of valuable research papers. Rana P.B. Singh completed his doctoral thesis entitled Clan Settlements in the Saran Plain.[60] Thakur[61] published his paper on the types of rural settlements in North Bihar, and this is the only study which has been taken up as the predecessor of this study on this specific region.

Recently 'Commission on Rural Settlements in Monsoon Lands'[62] considered the following approaches of rural settlement study as details of the three approaches discussed above:

(a) Historical development of the methodology of settlement analysis;
(b) Relation to history, anthropology, agriculture, economics and other social sciences;
(c) Field survey and first hand observation and collection of data;
(d) Census records and maps, historical records and documents, toponyms, etc.;
(e) Data analysis, mapping and computer programming;
(f) Conceptual framework, concept of ecumene, position, form,

structure, distribution, growth, hierarchy and continuum, types, patterns, etc.;

(g) Characteristics and elements of rural settlements and inter-relationship among them—theoretical and organic as well as behavioural approach;

(h) Development of paradigms, hypothesis, etc.; and

(i) Methodological approach—empirical, statistical methods, etc.

Principles of Settlement Formation

Geographers have studied rural settlements at different levels. At the lowest level, they have been interested in the characteristics and qualities of structures, such as farmsteads, fences, fields, houses and highways. Considering these aspects Doxiadis[63] has classified settlements into four component parts, i.e., homogenous part (residential houses); central part (courtyard or *chauk);* circulatory part (highways) and special part (tolas besides bigger settlement). At another level geographers have been concerned with the functional interrelationships of these structures that give rise to contrasting and dynamic character in rural settlements. In the beginning, rural settlement geographers were concerned with the 'form, function and genesis like the core concept of 'structure, process and stage' in geomorphology.

In central place study the work done by Walter Christaller (1933) in Southern Germany, development of conceptual framework by Chorley and Haggett (1969) and K.S.O. Beavon (1975) are noteworthy. The Institute of Development studies, University of Mysore has brought out a number of publications viz; *Spatial Organization and Economic Development* (Hermansen, 1971); *Growth Poles and Growth Centres in Urban and Regional Planning in India* (Misra, R.P., 1971); and two volumes (Misra, R.P. 1972) on *Urban Systems and Rural Development and in Spatial Organization,* the author analysed the regional problems of space development with the provision of infrastructure facilities for central places with special reference to Indian problems.

The human settlement evolved with the origin and establishment of a hamlet and the process of change goes on upto the big village. The sustenance and survival of these settlements depend on the flow of labourers and services from the smaller-size settlements towards the bigger size but the flow of goods and money towards the smaller

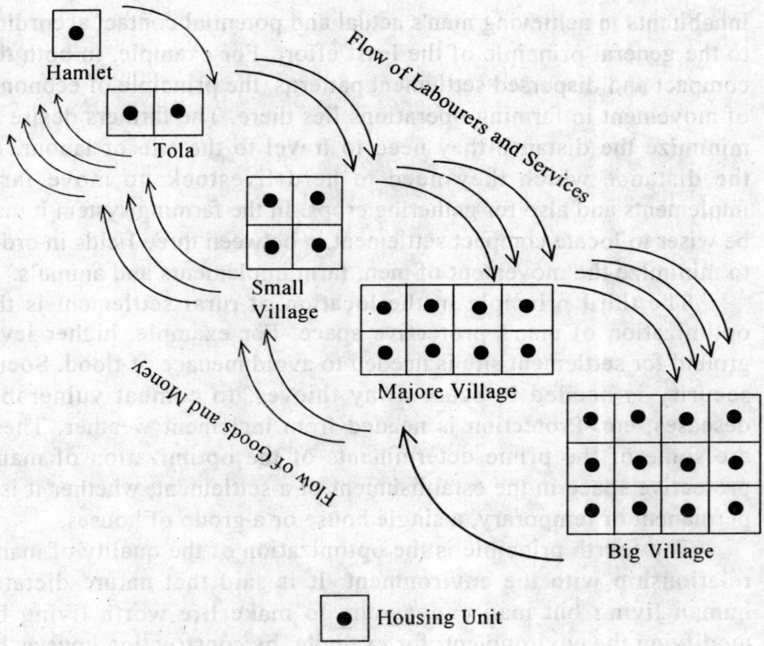

FIG. 2.1: Principal of Rural Settlement Study

size settlements come from bigger villages, or small towns found in the nearby area of a village (Fig. 2.1)

Principle of Rural Settlement Study

The principles of rural settlement formation that emerge out of these two studies are:[64]

(a) Maximization of potential contact:
(b) Minimization of effort;
(c) Optimization of man's protective space;
(d) Optimization of the quality of man's relationship with the environment; and
(e) Optimization of the synthesis of all the above principles.

The first principle is the maximization of man's potential contact with natural elements, cultural elements and the people. The principle of minimization of effort in the location of rural settlement helps inhabitants in achieving man's actual and potential contact according to the general principle of the least effort. For example, in both the compact and dispersed settlement patterns, the principle of economy of movement in farming operations lies there. The farmers desire to minimize the distance they need to travel to the site of labour, or the distance which they need to herd livestock, to move farm implements and also for gathering crops. In the farming system it may be wiser to locate compact settlement in between three fields in order to minimize the movement of men, farm implements and animals.

The third principle in the location of rural settlement is the optimization of man's protective space. For example, higher level ground for settlement site is needed to avoid menace of flood. Social security is needed to scare away thieves, to combat vulnerable deseases, etc. Protection is needed from inclement weather. These are some of the prime determinants of the optimization of man's protective space in the establishment of a settlement, whether it is a permanent or temporary, a single house or a group of houses.

The fourth principle is the optimization of the quality of man's relationship with the environment. It is said that nature dictates human living but man endeavours to make life worth living by modifying the environment, for example, by constructing houses, by harnessing natural resources like water, minerals, food, construction of reservoir, river embankments, transport and communication channels, etc. Even in adverse environmental conditions man tries to optimise the relationship with the environment for his living.

The fifth principle is the optimization of the synthesis of all the above principles. In reality, the rural settlement system may be seen as an adjustment of a mixture of physical, economic, cultural and biological factors in the environment at a particular place and at a particular time. Much also depends on man's abilities to create a synthesis. Besides these, the type of economy and distribution and territorial organization of production also help in determining the character and form of settlement.

Hypothesis is a statement of principles to guide the investigation by finding relationships between variables. The hypothesis can be formulated with various purposes in mind and on the strength and quantum of the available data. The hypothesis will tend to prevent the research from wandering all over a series of closely related phenomena by pin pointing on one or two specific situations of research.

Hypotheses are, generally, used as the statements of the relationships believed to exist between two or more variables. This conceptualization of research process may be descriptive, provisional, vaguely felt, or explanatory in nature. Errors in the hypothesis may be due to side issues or representation of faulty picture of the real world situations.

Hypotheses may also be designed for remedial action that existing research will continue in future or not. Such hypotheses should logically flow from the previous ones. The investigation which stops hypothesis testing from finding relationship between variables would only be superfluous. Thus with the help of personnel ingenuity, hypotheses should be so formulated that they may provide specific direction to the later phases of study. These hypotheses will need to be worked over, revised, combined, and rephrased until they form a hypothetical statement of the relationships, found to exist in real world situations.

The investigation of real world situations and the theoretical ideas suggest that the distribution of population in Bihar Plain should

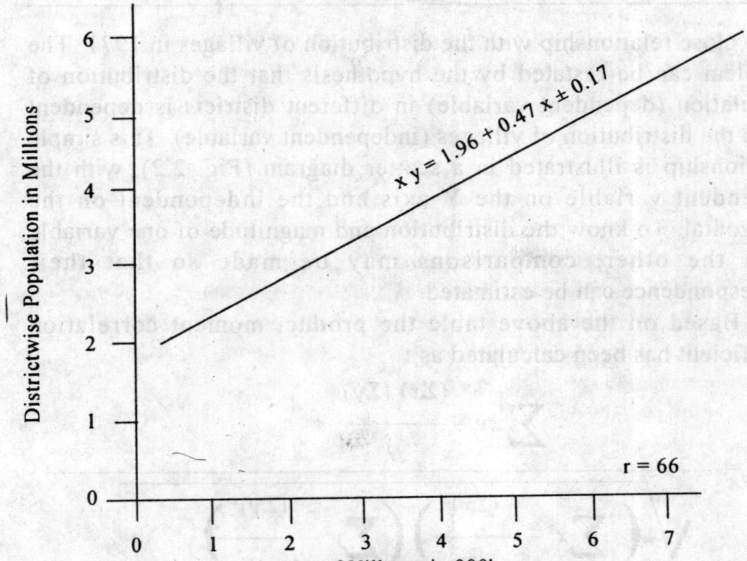

FIG. 2.2: Bihar Plain: Relationship between Rural Settlements and Rural Population (1971)

TABLE 2.1: Relationship Between Population and Village in Bihar Plain

District (1971)	No. of Village in '000's 1971 (X)	Population in millions (1971)	xy	x^2	y^2
Patna	2	3	6	4	9
Gaya	6	4	24	36	16
Shahabad	5	4	20	25	16
Saran	4	4	16	16	16
Champaran	3	3	9	9	9
Muzaffarpur	4	5	20	16	25
Darbhanga	3	5	15	9	25
Monghyr	3	3	9	9	9
Bhagalpur	2	2	4	4	4
Saharsa	1	2	2	1	4
Purnea	4	4	16	16	16
Total	37	39	141	145	149

have close relationship with the distribution of villages in 1971. The problem can be restated by the hypothesis that the distribution of population (dependent variable) in different districts is dependent upon the distribution of villages (independent variable). This simple relationship is illustrated in a scatter diagram (Fig. 2.2), with the dependent variable on the Y axis and the independent on the horizontal. To know the distribution and magnitude of one variable with the other, comparisons may be made so that their correspondence can be estimated.

Based on the above table the product moment correlation coefficient has been calculated as :

$$r = \frac{\sum xy - \dfrac{(\Sigma x)(\Sigma y)}{N}}{\sqrt{\left(\sum x^2 - \dfrac{(\Sigma x)^2}{N}\right)\left(\sum y^2 - \dfrac{(\Sigma y)^2}{N}\right)}}$$

where r = Pearsonian correlation coefficient,

Σx = Sum of all values of independent variables,

Σx^2 = Sum of squares of all independent variables,

Σy = Sum of all values of dependent variables
Σy^2 = Sum of squares of all dependent variables,
Σxy = Sum of products of all x and y values, and
N = Number of units

$$r = \frac{141 - \frac{(37.39)}{11}}{\sqrt{\left(145 - \frac{(37)^2}{11}\right)\left(149 - \frac{(39)^2}{11}\right)}}$$

$$= \frac{10}{\sqrt{231}} = \frac{10}{15} = 0.66\ (r)$$

We get the value of product Moment Correlation Coefficient as r = 0.66. This shows that the relationship is very close. The result has been tested by student 't' test by the formula.

$$t = \sqrt{\frac{r^2\,(n-2)}{1-r^2}} = \sqrt{\frac{.4356(11-2)}{1-.4356}}$$

$$= \sqrt{\frac{39204}{.5644}} = \sqrt{7.00} = 2.64$$

Ho = According to null hypothesis *(Ho)* there is no correlation between the distribution of villages and population in different districts of Bihar Plain in 1971.

Hi = According to alternative hypothesis *(Hi)* there is positive correlation between the distribution of villages and population in different districts of Bihar Plain in 1971.

Table value of 't' at 5 per cent level of significance and *df* 9 is 2,282 where as calculated value of *tc* is = 2.64.

Since the calculated value of 't' is greater than the table value at 5 per cent level of significance and degree of freedom 9. Therefore, null hypothesis is rejected in favour of alternative hypothesis that there is positive correlation between the distribution of villages and population in Bihar Plain in 1971.

REFERENCES

1. K.H. Stone: "The Development of a Focus for the Geography of Settlement", *Economic Geography,* Vol. 41, 1965, p. 348.
2. A.R.H. Baker: "The Geography of Rural Settlement", in Cooke and Johnson (ed.): *Trends in Geography,* Oxford, Pergamon, 1969, p. 123.
3. A. Meitzen: *Siedlung and Agrarwesen der Westgermonn and Ostgermanen, der Kelten,* 3 Vols., Berlin, 1895.
4. M.W. Beresford: *The Lost Villages of England,* London, 1954.
5. K.H. Stone : *op. cit.*
6. P.E. James, C.F. Jones and A.K. Wright: *American Geography Inventory and Prospect,* University of Syracuse, 1959, pp. 125-39.
7. M. Aurousseau: "The Arrangement of Rural Population," *Geographical Review,* Vol. 10, 1920, p. 223.
8. Isamu Matui: "Statistical Study of the Distribution of Scattered villages in Two Regions of the Tonami Plain, Toyama Perfecture," *Japanese Journal of Geology and Geography,* Vol. 9, 1932, pp. 251-66.
9. R.L. Singh (ed.): *Rural Settlements in Monsoon Asia,* Varanasi, National Geographical Society of India, 1972, p. 13.
10. C. J. Galpin: *The Social Anatomy of an Agricultural Community,* University of Wisconsin, Agriculture Experiment Station Bulletin, No. 34, 1915.
11. W. Christaller: *Central Places in Southern Germany,* translated by C.W. Baskin, New Jersey, Prentice Hall, 1966.
12. E.L. Ullman: "A Theory of Location for Cities," *American Journal of Sociology,* Vol. 46, 1941. pp. 853-64.
13. R.E. Dickinson: *City Region and Regionalism,* London, 1956.
14. J.E. Brush: "The Urban Hierarchy in Europe," *Geographical Review,* Vol. 43, 1953, pp. 414-16.
15. B.J.L. Berry and W.L. Garrison: "The Functional Bases of the Central Place Hierarchy," *Economic Geography,* Vol. 34, 1958, p. 145-54.
16. K.S.O. Beavon and A.S. Mabin: "The Losch System of Market Areas Derivation and Extension," *Geographical Analysis,* 1975.
17. K.H. Stone: *op. cit.,* p. 374.
18. *Ibid.,* p. 347.
19. T.G. Jordan: "On the Nature of Settlement Geography," *Professional Geographer,* Vol. XVIII, 1966, p. 27.
20. I. Bowman: *The Pioneer Fringe,* New York, American Geographical Society, Special Publication No. 13, 1931.
21. E. Kant: "Some Notes on the Representation of the Density of Rural Habitations," *Indian Geographical Journal,* Vol. 30, 1955, pp. 1-8.
22. A. Hillman: Community Organisation and Planning, New York, Macmillan, 1950.
23. C. Jacobsen: "Modernity in Traditional Villages," *Rural Sociology,* Vol. 38, 1973, pp. 283-95.
24. M. Chisholm: *Rural Settlement and Landuse,* London, Hutchinson, 1962.
25. C.A. Doxiadis: "Ekistics, the Science of Human Settlements," *Science,* 170, No. 3956, pp. 393-404.
26. R. Eidt and W.I. Woods: *Abandoned Settlement Analysis: Theory and Practice,* Milwaukee, 1974.
27. A.T.A. Learmonth and A.M. Learmonth: "Aspects of Village Life in Indo-Pakistan," *Geography,* Vol. 40, 1955.

28. F.S. Hudson: *A Geography of Settlement,* London, Macdonald and Evans, 1970.
29. J.C. Hudson: "A Location Theory for Rural Settlement," *Annals of the Association of American Geographers,* Vol. 59, 1969, pp. 365-81.
30. D. Grossman: "Do we have a Theory for Settlement Geography—The Case of Iboland," *Professional Geographer,* Vol. 23, 1971, pp. 197-203.
31. E. Bylund: "Theoretical Considerations regarding the Distribution of Settlements in Inner North Sweden," *Geografisca Annaler,* Vol. 42, 1960, pp. 225-31.
32. R. L. Morrill: "The Development and Spatial Distribution of Towns in Sweden, an historical predictive approach", *Annals of the Association of American Geographers,* Vol. 53, 1963, pp. 1-14.
33. L. Curry: "Random Spatial Economy: an exploration in settlement theory" *Annals of the Association of American Geographers,* Vol. 54, 1964, pp. 138-46.
34. D.W. Meining: "The Mormon Culture Region: Strategies and Patterns in the Geography of the American West," *Annals of the Association of American Geographers,* Vol. 55, 1965, pp. 191-200.
35. J.E. Landing: "Geographic Models of Old order Amish Settlement," *Professional Geographer,* Vol. 21, 1969, pp. 238-43.
36. E.M. Bjorklund: "Ideology and Culture Exemplified in South-Western Michigan," *Annals of the Association of American Geographers,* Vol. 54, 1964, pp. 227-41.
37. C.D. Despande: "Settlement Types of Bombay Karnatak," *Indian Geographical Journal,* Vol. XVII, 1942, pp. 115-31.
38. S.M. Ali: "Population and Settlement in the Ghaggar Plain," *Indian Geographical Journal,* Vol. XVII, 1942, pp. 157-82.
39. E. Ahmad: "Rural Settlement Types in Uttar Pradesh," *Annals of the Association of American Geographers,* Vol. XLII, 1952, p. 229.
40. E. Ahmad: "Indian Village Patterns", *Geographical Outlook,* Vol. 3, 1962, pp. 5-15.
41. K.H. Buschman: "Settlements and Habitations in India, Parts I and II," *Geographical Review of India,* Vol. 16, 1954, No. 3, pp. 19-40 and in No. 4, pp. 5-15.
42. R. L. Singh: "Meaning, Objectives and Scope of Settlement Geography," in R.L. Singh and K.N. Singh, (ed.): *Readings in Rural Settlement Geography,* Varanasi, National Geographical Society of India, 1975, pp. 4-11.
43. R. L. Singh: "Evolution of Settlements in the Middle Ganga Valley", *National Geographical Journal of India,* Vol. 1, 1955, pp. 69-115.
44. A.B. Mukherjee: "Spacing of Rural Settlements in Andhra Pradesh," *Geographical Outlook,* Vol. 6, 1969, p. 1.
45. R. Lahiri: "Settlement Types in Ajoy Baraker Basin," *Calcutta Geographical Review,* Vol. 12, No. 4, 1950.
46. A. Bhattacharya: "Effect of Tribal and Caste Factor on Rural Settlement in U.P." *Indian Geographical Journal,* Vol. 31, 1956, pp. 94-102.
47. R.L. Singh: Typical Rural Dwellings in the Umland of Banaras," *National Geographical Journal of India,* Vol. III, 1957, p. 52.
48. L. R. Singh: The Terai Region of U.P.: *A Study in Human Geography,* Allahabad, 1965, p. 37.
49. V.N.P. Sinha: "Houses and House Types of the Chota Nagpur Plateau," *Geographical Knowledge,* Vol. 2, 1969, p. 91.
50. R.B. Singh: "Rural Settlement Types and their Distributions," *National Geographical Journal of India,* Vol. XV, Part 2, 1969.

51. K.N. Singh: "Spatial Pattern of Central Places in the Middle Ganga Valley, India," *National Geographical Journal of India,* Vol. 12, 1966, pp. 218-26.
52. R. L. Singh (ed.): *Rural Settlements in Monsoon Asia,* National Geographical Society of India, Varanasi, 1972.
53. R. K. Mukherjee: *Man and his Habitation: A Study in Social Ecology,* Bombay, Popular Prakashan, 1968.
54. R.C. Sharma: *Settlement Geography of the Indian Desert,* New Delhi, Rajesh Publications, 1972.
55. A. Prasad: *Chota Nagpur: Geography of Rural Settlements,* Ranchi University, 1973.
56. V.N.P. Sinha: *Settlement Geography of Chota Nagpur Plateau,* New Delhi, Rajesh Publication, 1976.
57. R. L. Singh and K.N. Singh, (ed.): *Readings in Rural Settlement Geography,* Varanasi, National Geographical Society of India, 1975.
58. R. L. Singh and K.N. Singh, (eds.): *Spatial Dimensions in Rural Settlement Geography,* Varanasi, National Geographical Society of India, 1976.
59. R. L. Singh (ed.): *National Geographical Journal of India,* Special Issue on Rural Settlements, Vol. XXI, Parts 3 & 4, 1975.
60. R. B. Singh: *Clan Settlements in the Saran Plain,* Varanasi, National Geographical Society of India, 1976.
61. B. Thakur: "Types of Rural Settlements in North Bihar," *Transactions of the Council of Indian Geographers,* Vol. 5, 1968, pp. 157-63.
62. I.C.V. Commission on Rural Settlement in Monsoon Lands (1972-76), *News Letter,* Banaras Hindu University, Department of Geography, 1975, pp. 7-11.
63. C.A. Doxiadis: "The Future of Human Settlements," in Tiselius, A. and Nilsson, S. (ed.): *Place of Value in a World of Facts,* Stockholm, Almquist and Wiksell, 1969, pp. 307-38.
64. *Ibid.*

3

MODELS IN RURAL SETTLEMENT GEOGRAPHY

Model is an abstraction and simplified representation of the real World Geographic situation.[1] It is an analogy, an ideal, a representation, a description, an abstraction, a generalization, a frame of reference, a programme of research, an explanation of how a system works, a theory and a demonstration in the process of simplification of complex situations to a diagrammatic or mathematical form. A model building is understood to be a nomothetic approach in geography which explains the complex perception of any spatial distribution in a logical and the simplest possible systematic manner. The purpose of this chapter is to show the models used in settlement geography and the modes of their formulation. Any consideration of model building in settlement geography should be accountable for the following questions:

(a) What should be the approach of settlement model building?
(b) What should be the methods of settlement model building?
(c) Why the models should be built?
(d) What is the level of model building in settlement geography?
(e) How the models for settlements should be classified?
(f) When and where the model should be used.
(g) How much the model is applicable in the real world.

REGULARITIES IN MODELS OF SETTLEMENTS

Generally most of the models of rural settlement location and structure are measurable in terms of spatial arrangement and human behaviour. This has been established on the following six premises[2] which are implied in most of the models of settlement geography.

1. The Spatial Distribution of Human Activity Reflects an Ordered Adjustment to the Factor of Distance

According to Watson "Geography is a discipline in distance". In case all the space is filled by houses without any areal differentiation, than there would be no geography. At the first glance, the spatial regularities may not be clear enough but "there is more order in the world than appears at first sight is not discovered till order is looked for." As for example in movement models time taken in travel, transport costs and kinds of road surface are more important factors to consider than linear distance. Non-linear models are related with distance decay function e.g. density distance, income-distance and land value distance to reveal regularities in the distribution of these items within settlements.

2. Locational Decisions are Taken to Minimise the Frictional Effects of Distance

This concept is known as the 'Principle of least effort' or the 'Law of minimum effort' which suggests that events reach their goal by the shortest path. In the models of rural settlements, the minimization of movement is fundamental to an understanding of the location of rural settlements.

3. All Locations are Endowed with a Degree of Accessibility but some Locations are more Accessible than Others

Accessibility denotes the 'Ease of getting to a place'. Hence, it is a locational quality of settlements. Relatively one place may be more accessible than others with a particular model transport. On the other hand, it indicates nearness to some functions or locations. In reality, it is a concept of movement minimization in terms of costs involved and overcoming a distance.

4. There is a Tendency for Human Activities to Agglomerate to take Advantage of Scale of Economies

It denotes the savings in operational costs by concentrating various activities in close proximity of central site of the settlement, e.g. the distance of farms and tethering ground, the nearness of tethering ground to grain storage, place of livestock tethering ground and place of water to wash them and allow them to quench thirst. Residential houses in a village may be considered as agglomerations and distance to the place of work farm as scale of economies.

5. The Organisation of Human Activity is Essentially Hierarchical in Character

The places which are more accessible appear to be the sites of larger agglomerations. The sites which are larger in population size are the places of higher order goods and services, whereas in smaller settlements lower order goods and services are found, such as central place hierarchy.

6. Human Occupance is Focal in Character

This concept highlight the functional region or the zone of influence of a place. The bigger service centres have larger zone of influence and smaller centres it is very small. Hence, the least cost effort, accessibility, scale of economies in agglomerations and hierarchical ordering of settlements are linked together to form a systems of settlements in space.

TYPES AND FORMATION OF MODELS

Content-wise the model may be classified into the following types:

(a) An iconic model is a three dimensional representation of a real world situation, and the globe is a very succinct example of this model;
(b) In analog model, one phenomenon is represented by another,
(c) In symbolic model, the situation is represented by mathematical symbols or diagramatic representation; and
(d) Theoretical model deals with concepts only.

Form-wise the model can be classified into the following types:

(a) Descriptive model presents a description of the reality;
(b) Normative model is obtainable under certain defined and controlled conditions. Deterministic and stochastic models are

examples of normative models;

(c) Static model concentrates on equalibrium structural features; and

(d) Dynamic model concentrate on processes and functions through time.

In model building, it is necessary to have complete and thorough information about the real world situation for which the model is going to be constructuted. A cyclic and logical arrangement of important facts is also necessary so that a feedback mechanism naturally emerges from the model.

Model of Central Places

W. Christaller developed diagramatic models for central places in 1933. In the school atlases he observed a typical settlement phenomenon in the fact that smaller towns constitute the surrounding zone of influence of a big city and these smaller towns are located in a circular pattern. As a first step in model building he tried to join the smaller towns by a circle. Thus contiguous circles were formed in the surrounding areas of big towns. In most cases only six towns surrounded the bigger one and a fraction of area was left unserved in between these circles. As a second step he tried to join all the small towns hexagonally according to degree of similarities noticeable in functions. This hexagonal linkage of points also covered the fractional area left unserved in between circles previously, and ultimately a hierarchical hexagonal net of centres from higher to lower level was formed.

For a real world situation, only a distorted shape of the hexagon is obtainable. This is due to the differentiation of environmental factors distributed over space. On account of this, Christaller postulated isotropic landscape feature which is conduceive to a hexagonal arrangement of towns and central places. In this way, the central place model as a theoretical distribution of market centres was formulated.

Models Applied in Settlement Geography

Settlement geography includes both rural and urban settlements. The models in these areas are simplified ones and they are really an abstraction from reality. Conceptual model is a 'web of reality' in image while deterministic model is based on the classic mathematical notion of direct cause and effect relationship, consisting of a set of logical mathematical argument.[3] *Stochastic models* which are based on probability instead of mathematical certainty are obvious of more promise in investigations relating to human geography, rather than to the physical branches of the discipline. With the help of analog natural model Bunge[4] has compared the shift of highways with the shift of rivers and has applied the mathematics of crystallography to central place theory in considering the growth and shrinkage of market areas as similar to the patterns associated with two-dimensional crystals. Garrison has developed an *icecap analogy of city growth*[5] just like law of allometric growth of living beings. In rural settlement geography Bylund has given deterministic models which make certain assumptions about the nature of new colonization through time.[6] In Morril's[7] *probabilistic model* the growth of settlement patterns is simulated by random processes which are in turn restricted by the operation of certain rules based on empirical observations of colonization process. The formulation of deterministic and stochastic models is not different. The deterministic gravity formulation can be related to several existing stochastic models of human interaction which itself can be transformed into a model of that type.[8] Typically, these interaction models consider two sets of probabilities, one set specifying the number of opportunities already reached and accepted by a trip-maker, and the second set specifying the proportion of trip makers going beyond a certain distance to reach an acceptable opportunity.

The probabilities in some *cell-counting models* can be interpreted in essentially the same manner. For example, Medvedkov[9] has employed the entropy concept of information theory as a technique for quantifying the agreement between empirical and theoretical settlement distributions. He has, further, suggested that Christaller's hexagonal central place pattern be regarded as the signal, and the random element be attributed to deviations from the isotropic conditions. Medvedkov viewed the spatial distribution of places as a result of a set of regulated accidents in which randomness has affected the outcome from the otherwise deterministic central place theory. A similar approach has been adopted by Dacey[10] who felt that urban places as points are dislocated by institutional factors from their theoretical position on the hexagonal lattice. A variant of the cell-counting techniques was used to verify that the distribution of places in almost homogeneous areas follows a double poisson distribution, although the locations in inhomogeneous areas are better described by a double negative binomial. These and other distribution functions have recently been discussed by Olsson.[11] Hudson[12] has used them in analysing the rural settlements while Rogers[13] has used them in studying the shops within cities. Subsequently, Harvey[14] analysed the cell count in detail in diffusion studies showing a way in which time and space could also be treated in the same model.

Simulative Structure Model

K.N. Singh[15] presented a *simulative structure model* which shows the evolution of basic rural territorial and settlement pattern in a small region of eastern Uttar Pradesh. His semi-deterministic formulations are based on four sets of valid assumptions. He has schematised the process of spatial diffussion within five time periods. In time period I (generation 1 through 3), the clan centre is established in the occupance territory and grows through generations one through three by natural growth as well as by immigrational accretion. With increase in population and consequent need for more agricultural land new villages are established around the clan centre. In time period II (generations 4 through 6) the clan area is subdivided into tappas and tappa centres are established beyond the core area by the prospective young families of the viable clan centre. In time period III (generations 7 through 9) the existing nuclei of settlements grow into units of different sizes. In time period IV (generations 10 through 12) new population movements take place within the occupance area and a few new tappas are founded by the families of the core area. In time period V (generations 13 through 15), the growth of population continues, remaining patches and narrow strips of forest land are taken under settlement and a few new tappas appear in the clan territory. Thus, within the above five time periods through 15 generations or about 350-400 years, the entire occupance area of the clan is occupied. The pargana and tappa centres as well as many villages and hamlets have also proliferated on the landscape. A new model has been devised by the author to express the unstable character of spatial organisation of central places and this has been developed as 'the Dynamic Theory of Central Place Location.'

Dynamic Central Place Model

R.B. Mandal[16] is of the opinion that the beginning of settlement by the first settler had taken place in ancient times in the forest environment, when there were no transport routes at all. Later on, the beginning of second settlement in the neighbourhood might have given rise to one way connection of transport linkage. This may be denoted as K = 1. Further, in addition to the original point the growth of two centres provided two directional connections of transport routes as K = 2. Similarly three centres gave three directional linkages as K = 3, four directions as K = 4, five directions as K = 5 and six directions in a hexagon as K = 6 for the densest packing of centres of the same order. (Fig. 3.1)

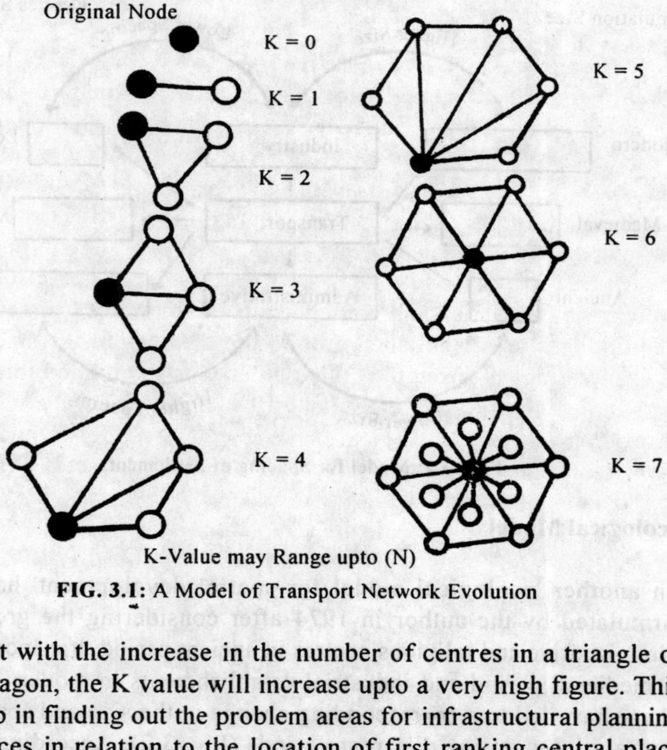

FIG. 3.1: A Model of Transport Network Evolution

But with the increase in the number of centres in a triangle or in a hexagon, the K value will increase upto a very high figure. This will help in finding out the problem areas for infrastructural planning of services in relation to the location of first ranking central place of the region. This model also believes in the hierarchy of central places according to the increasing K value for a particular point in a equilateral triangle. This may be analysed with the number of transport route connections in between the settlements of hinterland and from the original central place. This will automatically give high K value for the centres treated as original point in the centre of the zone of influence of different central places. In this way, the model also satisfies the conditions of hierarchy of central places, keeping in view the consumers of different rural settlements which visit a central place.

In spacing also, transport nodes are in between the higher spacing and lower population size of the ancient period and the lower spacing and higher population size of the present. (Fig. 3.2)

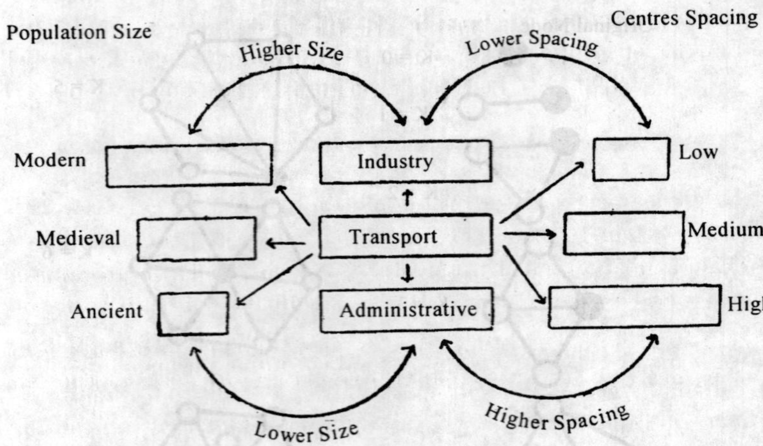

FIG. 3.2: Model for Spacing of Settlements

Ecological Model

An another 'ecological model for spatial development' has been formulated by the author in 1974 after considering the growth of administrative and religious centres in ancient period, transport nodes in medieval period and industrial establishments in modern period. These have led to a corresponding change in the size and spacing of central places during different periods (Fig. 3.2). According to this model the central places in ancient period were few and far between having small population. After the growth of roads and railways and faster modes of travelling, the distance between them has reduced. In between the growth of small administrative centres of ancient period and industrial centres of recent times, are the centres of transport nodes having medium sized population. In spacing also, transport nodes are in between the higher spacing and lower population size of the ancient period and the lower spacing and higher population size of the present. (Fig. 3.2).

Diagrammatic Model

Hiroshi Ishida presented several diagrammatic models[17] while delineating overseas comparison of the location of rural settlements in relation to field pattern in the Middle Ganga Valley (Fig. 3.3). In the village territorial structure of Varanasi district in Uttar Pradesh the zonal arrangement is as follows: (Fig. 3.3)

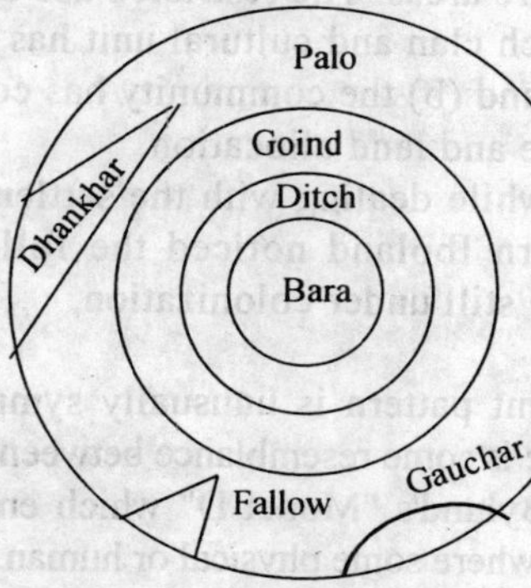

FIG. 3.3 : Field Pattern in Middle Ganga Valley

bara (immediately adjacent to the housing site), *goind* (intermediate land around the village, that is land between the *bara* and the *palo*) and *palo* (outlying unmanured land around the village beyond the inner and intermediate zones and being the least productive). *Gauchar* (village common pasture) and fallow lie generally in the *palo. Bara* means enclosure including male houses (ghar) as opposed to *ghar* (female house). Sex segregation is not so distinct in western U.P. and Haryana as in the Punjab though the male house is in many cases separated from the female house within the enclosure. Apart from this, the outer fringe of settlement is also called *bara.* Around this bara a ditch was dug or a wall was constructed against invaders. An old village is still encircled by the remnants of a ditch or a wall today. Many are encircled by passage ways.[18]

Expansion Model of Settlement

W.B. Morgan[19] while presenting his paper on expansion of

settlements in Iboland, argues briefly, "that the degree of nucleation in northern Ibo settlements is conditioned mainly by the stage of growth that has been attained. The transition is from highly dispersed settlements in the early "colonization stage" to nucleated, well defined "towns" in the later, "continuous settlement" in the eventual "disintegration stage" in which settlements grow towards each other until they fill in all the spaces between them and produce a continuous belt of uninterrupted settlement.[20] However, Morgan made it clear that owing to cultural and ecological differentiation, this model is useful only for describing process in northern and northeastern Ibo culture areas. The restricted use of this model is due to the fact that (a) each clan and cultural unit has its own method of spatial organization, and (b) the community has control over matters relating to land tenure and land allocation.

D. Grossman[21] while dealing with the settlement pattern of the Nike Clan in northern Iboland noticed the following features of settlements which are still under colonization.

A. The settlement pattern is unusually symmetric in its broad outline. There is some resemblance between the Nike settlement pattern and Bylund's "Model D" which emerges according to him, in areas where some physical or human barrier to expansion exists in one side.
B. Under conditions of colonization, we would expect closer areas to be settled earlier than more remote areas. Here, however, frontier areas are settled while more accessible localities are left unused.[22]

According to D. Grossman both these features are intentionally coined rather than random growth and they make sense only if the composition and history of the Nike Clan are understood.

Diffussion Model of Settlement

T. Hagerstrand[23] presented a four stage model for the passage of innovation waves for the dispersal of settlements. In the first stage, origin and evolution of initial agglomeration has been considered. In the second stage, diffusion is marked by centrifugal effect and creation of new centres in distant areas. In the third stage of condensing process, equal relative increase in the size of all locations

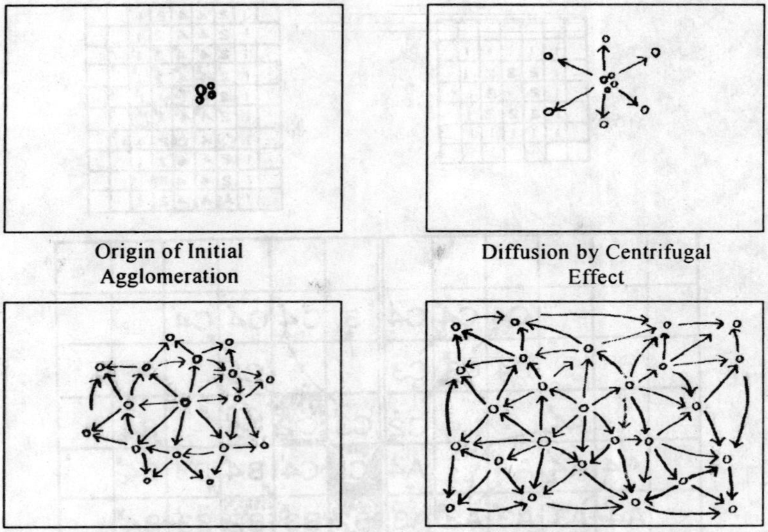

Origin of Initial Agglomeration

Diffusion by Centrifugal Effect

Condensing Process

Maximum Dispersal

FIG. 3.4: Hagerstrand Model of Dispersal of Human Settlements

is contemplated while in the saturation stage asymptotic increase towards maximum dispersal has been analysed.

E. Bylund[24] has presented a four stage diffusion model of settlements in inner North Sweden. This is an important contribution for dispersal process. The only difference among his four stage models is in the number and size of settlements increase and the location of parent settlements. His A and B models assume spread from a coastal location while C and D from inland location (Fig. 3.5) in formulating this model, he assumes that (a) the physical conditions of the land are similar in all directions and (b) further area will not be occupied until those close to the 'Parent settlements' have been occupied.

The processes governing the development of new settlements to create a spatial pattern have been the subject of numerous historical studies. In many cases special factors, such as the land policy in the USA and the homestead acts, the political and religious pressures involved in colonization in Eastern Europe during the late Middle Ages, political decision-making in Russian colonization schemes, make it sum almost impossible to set up theoretical models of settlement development. One interesting study is of E. Bylund (1960) of the settlement process in Lappland. The problem that

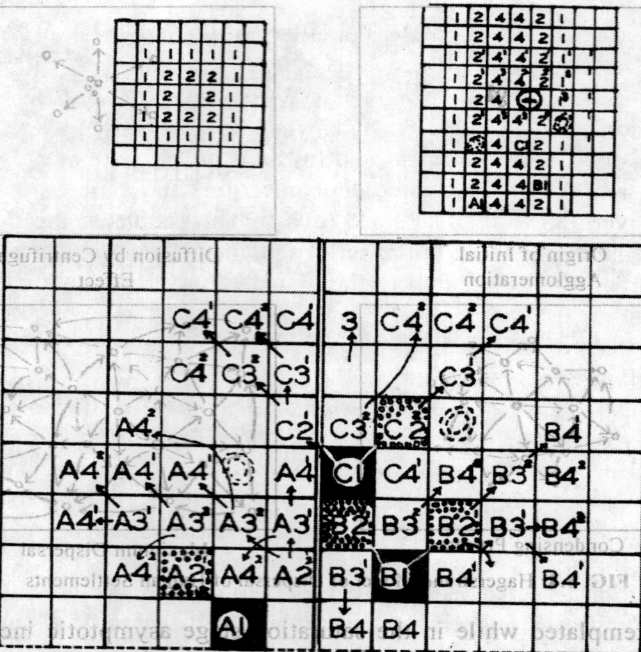

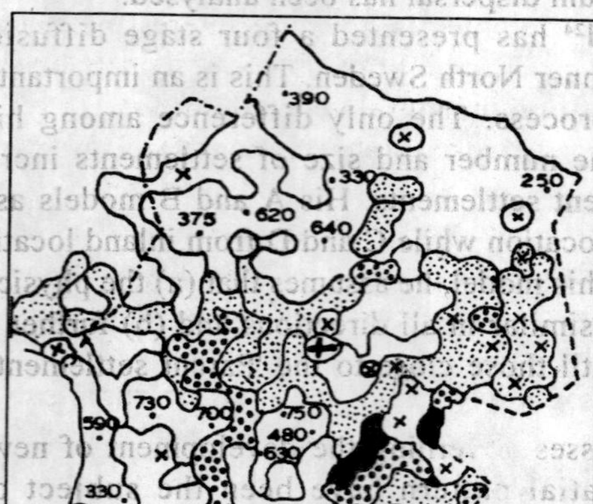

FIG. 3.5: Bylund's Colonization Model

Bylund set out to explain was the failure of the colonizers to locate on the best lands before bringing poorer lands into cultivation. A model was developed which contained three major features (Fig. 3.5). The colonizers, it was assumed, wished to minimized distance between their new settlement and (a) their parent settlement, (b) a church, and (c) an available communication link. Using arbitrary values over a grid of equal sized cells Bylund simulated the spread of settlement around an initial set of settlements and drew attention to the broad similarity between the simulated map and an actual map of dispersion of settlement in the area. This very simple deterministic model indicates how formal models of the colonization process might be developed to some advantage.

J. C. Hudson after adopting principles operative in biological sciences proposed general laws of changes in rural settlement distribution over time. He postulated that the patterns of human mobility are arranged at random, a kin to the random dispersal of plant species. The spatial distribution of rural settlement usually passes through three stages of 'colonization', 'spread', and 'competition' as these patterns are observed in plant growth. Hudson does not subscribe to preplanned settlement distribution excepting that "the existence of highly regular settlement distribution in carefully planned colonies is no more interesting than the regular spacing of plants produced by a mechanical planter. This is the theory of spatial competition in natural vegetation.[25]

Cross-examing Hudson's observations D. Grossman argues that human settlement pattern and expansion even in the underdeveloped economy are more similar to the planting of a mechanical planter than the growth of natural vegetation.[26] Thus, free competition in the spread of settlement rarely occurs and when it does, it is a matter of specific cultural values of the people rather than normal human behaviour. Grossman felt that the laws of rural settlements are meaningless outside the specific cultural and technological context in which the settlement is located.

Structural Model of Doxiadis

A. Doxiadis[27] has developed a four stage model which can be applied to the composite individual settlement of all sizes in a territory as well as in its constituent parts. (Fig. 3.6) Hypothetically any settlement consists of four parts: (a) homogeneous part, (b) central

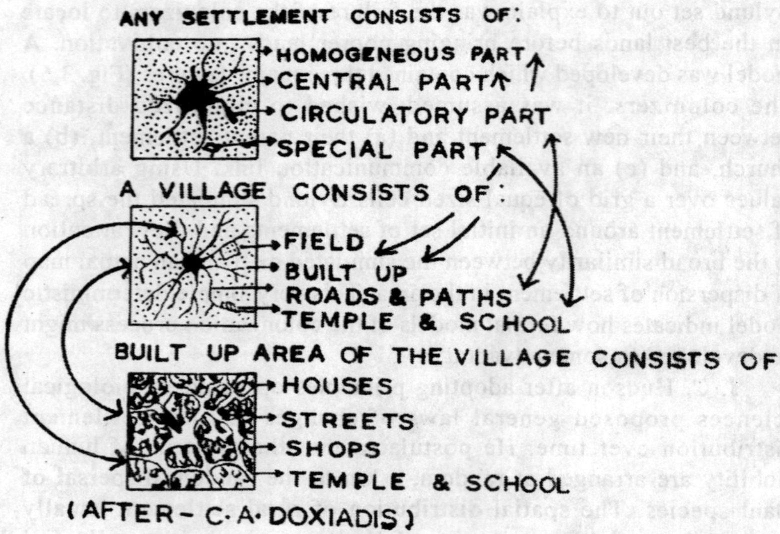

FIG. 3.6: Structural Model of Doxiadis

part, (c) circulatory part, and (d) special part. These parts are subject to change but they are always present in a living settlement or ekistic unit.

Model of Alpha and Beta Technologies in Settlement

Alpha is clearly the organization of the modern state, exemplified by the airline network emanating from the capital city; the Beta is a structure that consists of many smaller units, less related or even unrelated (Fig. 3.7)

By and large the picture given by the table is simply this: strengthen the local basis of the beta unit by reviving traditional techniques and introducing new ones, compatible with the beta structure; weaken the alpha structure above all by recentralizing its periphery and distributing sites of production and consumption more equitably in society-not decentralizing but multi-centralizing society.

Concretely there are at least three ways in which the alpha and beta systems can be integrated: *functionally, in space* and *overtime.*

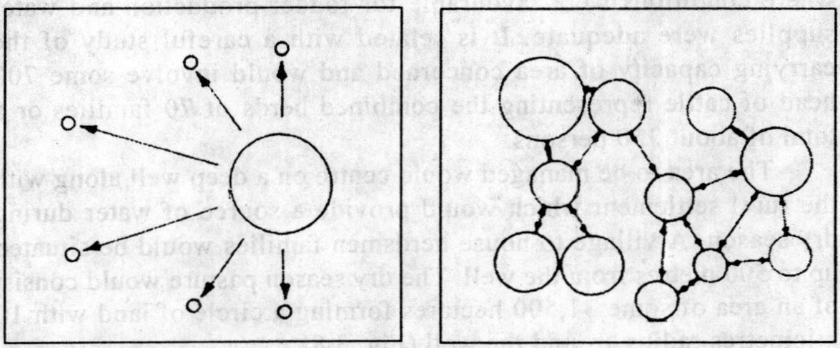

Complex vertical	Alpha (α) Unequal exchange vertical division of labour, penetration/ dependence, fragmen-tation, marginalization, segmentation.	Beta (ß) Unequal exchange horizontal division of labour autonomy, solidarity participation, integ-ration	Simple horizontal

FIG. 3.7: Alpha and Beta Model of Rural Settlement Growth (After-Bugnicourt)

Sector	Alpha Technologies	Beta Technologies
Shelter	Curtail international housing business.	Try to restore local house building patterns of local material
	Make houses and habits less centre-periphery dominated; transfer more work to homes.	Collectivize ground that can be used for housing
Environment	Recycling, cleaning up technology.	Local control and more dependence on smaller economic cycles.

MODEL OF RURAL SETTLEMENTS IN RELATION TO LAND MANAGEMENT

The main problem of the arid zone of Sahel in Africa is the management of grazing lands under marginal and fluctuating climatic conditions in a certain social, economic and cultural context. Considering these points in view Gabriel Boudet,[28] a French scientists in grazingland management has suggested an outline of land management scheme which would involve a change from migratory to sedentary cattle farming. This model would be applicable in areas where conditions were favourable for fodder production and water supplies were adequate. It is related with a careful study of the carrying capacity of area concerned and would involve some 700 head of cattle representing the combined herds of 70 families or a total of about 350 persons.

The area to be managed would centre on a deep well along with the rural settlement which would provide a source of water during dry season. A village to house herdsmen families would be situated up to 500 metres from the well. The dry season pasture would consist of an area of some 31,500 hectares forming a circle of land with 10 kilometres radius around the well (Fig. 3.8)

On outerside of the circumference of this circle would be a ring of land, some three kilometres wide, which would serve a grazing land for the rainy season. Spaced out at regular intervals in this area, would be a series of 10 "guzzlers", or artificial ponds, capable of holding sufficient water between major spells of rain to provide for the needs of 700 head of cattle (1/10th of the total herd) for about 15 days. Around each "guzzlers" would be an 840 hectares grazing area.

In the dry season each herding unit of 700 cattle would be brought inside the 'dry season circle' but would remain towards the outer edge of the circle. Each day the cattle would go to be watered at the central well near settlement, being driven along narrow well defined paths in order to avoid transplanting the pasture land. Later, the herds would move again to within five kilometers of the well, thus reducing the distance to be covered to obtain water during the period of greatest heat. But this scheme needs cooperation of peasants to adopt new habitat and control of herds.

For the rural settlements of west Africa two rural settlement models have been presented by Udo in 1963, and Prothero in 1972.

R. K. Udo's Model

In one of the theoretical statements on rural settlements Udo (1963)[29] claimed that compact settlements characterize the periphery of human land occupation, whereas the dispersed dwellings represent the more developed centre. Udo found the compact settlement to be historically tied to collective agricultural practices, and to a system of defence. Both features are identified as frontier (periphery) phenomena that

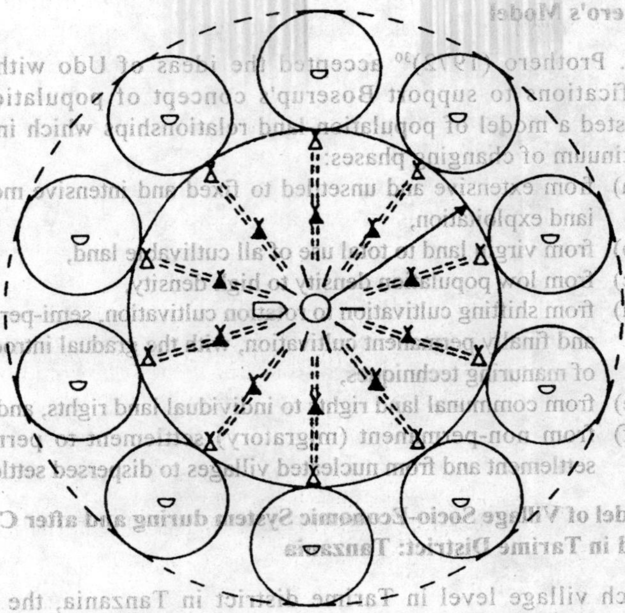

Artificial pond	Encampment-start of dry season
Well	Encampment-end of dry season
Permanent Village	Cattle track

FIG. 3.8: Model for Location of Rural Settlement and Land Management Scheme by Gabriel Boudet in Sahel.

breakdown with peace, population expansion and consolidation of man's control over the land. Changes then take place in the agricultural system where block farming by the entire compound gives way to individual farming on separate plots. Land scarcity arises through population expansion, and places a premium on the occupation of plots: the best proof of one's claim to land is to settle on it. Along with such changes there is a shift from rotation of bush and forest fallow as the entire compound moves to annual cropping in permanent settlements. As the idea claimed by this model near the northern boarder areas of Champaran and Madhubani compact rural settlements are found whereas in the peaceful areas of dense population in Saran, Siwan and Viashali districts semi-sprinkled settlements are found.

Prothero's Model

R. M. Prothero (1972)[30] accepted the ideas of Udo with some qualifications to support Boserup's concept of population. He suggested a model of population-land relationships which involves a continuum of changing phases:

(a) from extensive and unsettled to fixed and intensive modes of iand exploitation,
(b) from virgin land to total use of all cutlivable land,
(c) from low population density to high density,
(d) from shifting cultivation to rotation cultivation, semi-permanent and finally permanent cultivation, with the gradual introduction of manuring techniques,
(e) from communal land rights to individual land rights, and
(f) from non-permanent (migratory) settlement to permanent settlement and from nucleated villages to dispersed settlement.

A Model of Village Socio-Economic System during and after Colonial Period in Tarime District: Tanzania

At each village level in Tarime district in Tanzania, the socio-economic system that had developed two categories of settlements structure, the upper social structures and the lower social structure. (Fig. 3.9).

1. *The Upper Social Structure or Family : A*

The upper social structure consists of rich cattle owners at each village who occupy larger tribal land for cultivation. The rich farmers or pro-Kulaks, are few in number but most of them own more than 200 herd of cattles. Since the dowry to girl party which the boy has to pay, vary from twenty to fifty cows, the rich men were able to get married to more wives and got more children. With a big family, the labour force of the proto Kulak was enough to increase agricultural production. The rich people who can afford to increase agricultural production had ploughs, tractors, bicycles and lorries for transportation.

2. *The Lower Social System or Family: B*

This consists mostly of poor peasants who owns less cattle, (below 100), which come from various rich cattle owners in group A. The

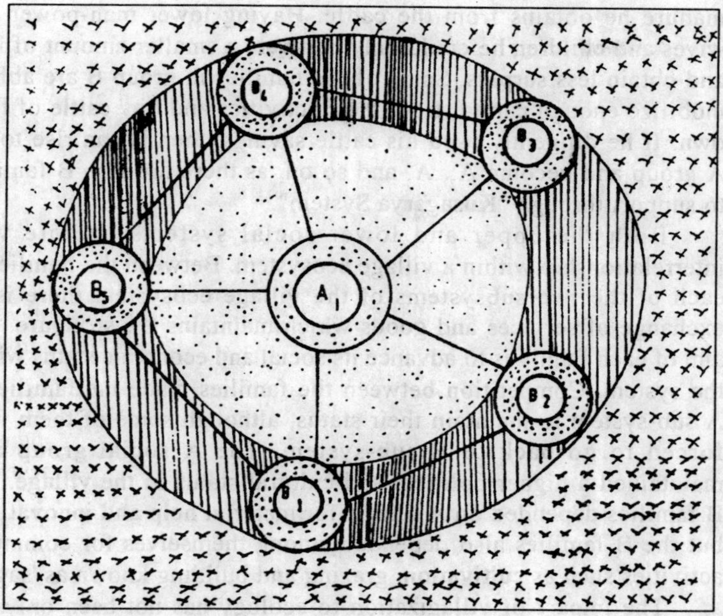

A_1 Rich farmer (Proto-Kulak)
– large homestead many wives and children
– large farm and large herds of cattle

B_1–B_5 Peasant
– small homestead few wives and children
– small farm and few herds of cattle

Cultivation (permanent)

Grass fallow and grazing area

Bush fallow

FIG. 3.9: Socio-Economic Structure, within the villages Ecosystem (Before 1973)

families in group B only take care of these cattle given to them by the proto-Kulaks. The poor farmers are allowed to use the milk and blood from the cows and for ploughing if he has a plough. Whenever the rich farmer, wants his cattle back he is free to take them back. The ofsprings of the cattle also belongs to the owner, the proto-Kulak. If a cattle or its ofspring dies, the meat and skin or the money obtained from the sale of the meat and skin is returned to the owner. The poor peasant in the social systems also profit from the animal manure he obtains from the cattle. Having lower man-power and wives and children he could only cultivate a smaller amount of land and obtain less surplus. Some of the families in group B are able to mobilize enough capital from their activities and buy cattle of their own. If he diligently used his cattle savings, then B can rise to the A group and become A_2, A_3 and so on, as there are also B families to support through "Kusagarya System".

Both the upper and lower social systems operate with interrelationship within a village ecosystem. Between the families of each of the two subsystems of the village ecosystem there is an exchange of services and goods which maintains the structure. The aim of each family is to advance its social and economic status within the system. Competition between the families made the families at A sub-system to maintain their status, although some of them were forced to go back to B sub-system. The A social group also maintained a higher political and cultural status in the village. The B families depended on A family for material help and innovations, but the B families also depended among themselves for communal activities such as cultivation, grazing and building known as 'saga'.

The impact of villagization to ecology has not been only due to the change in settlements but also the change in land use-vegetation system as affected by the increase in mechanisation and communal land tenure. With these changes some private farms have also been put into production. Recently, due to increase in population density in many areas people have disturbed the ecological balance in terms of stoping the regeneration of bush and woodland. (Fig. 3.10).

Model of Zande Settlement Scheme in Sudan

Most of the model of settlements in Africa were formulated without evaluating the efficiency of such a design. They simply stressed the need for cooperation and access to works and services. They were designed as centralized homosteads with small food-production plots in the backside. "One of the earlier models for the clustered village homesteads would front on three roads or paths–the largest of which would be a focus for scheme services (Fig. 3.11).[31] This H-plan is a sort of linear settlement form which does not give a coherent view of village structure because the necessary service facilities which should be given to the village are lacking, and hence the settlement pattern eventually reverted to the sprinkled form.

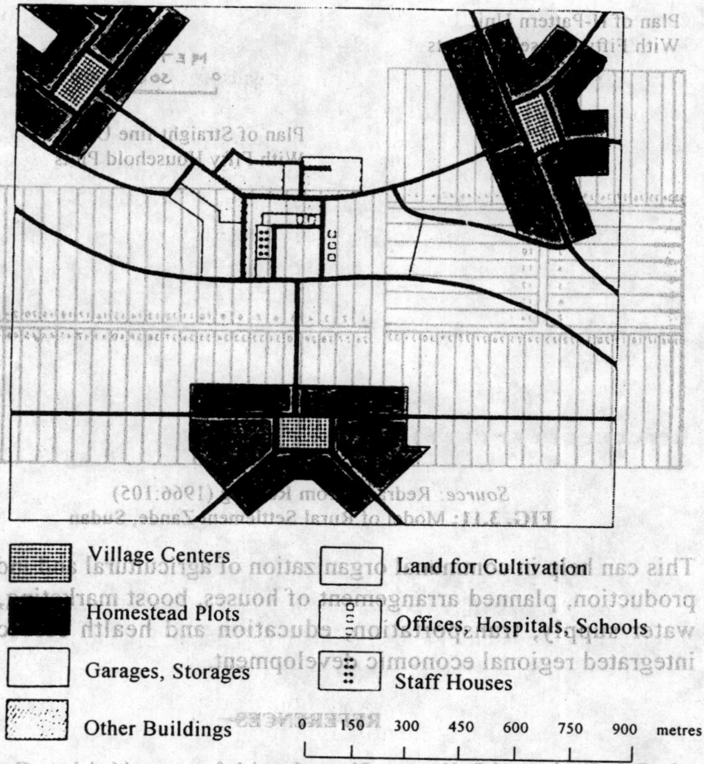

FIG. 3.10: Model for the Establishment of Rural Settlement in Tanzania (After S. Watts, 1966)

Model for Internal Structure of Tanzanian Resettlement Scheme

A model for Tanzanian rural resettlement was designed to provide various services such as school, dispensary, shops and staff quarters in the centre besides three residential sections where settlers built homes and cultivate some crops in one acre of land. Fields for cash crops have been given near the periphery of the settlement and the same may be allocated to individuals or as communal farm according to an overall farm plan. (Fig. 3.10)[32] In Tanzania this type of model cooperative villages has been activated in order to create planned compact rural settlements (Ujamaa villages) which are the resettled homesteads of farmers who were earlier living in scattered dwellings.

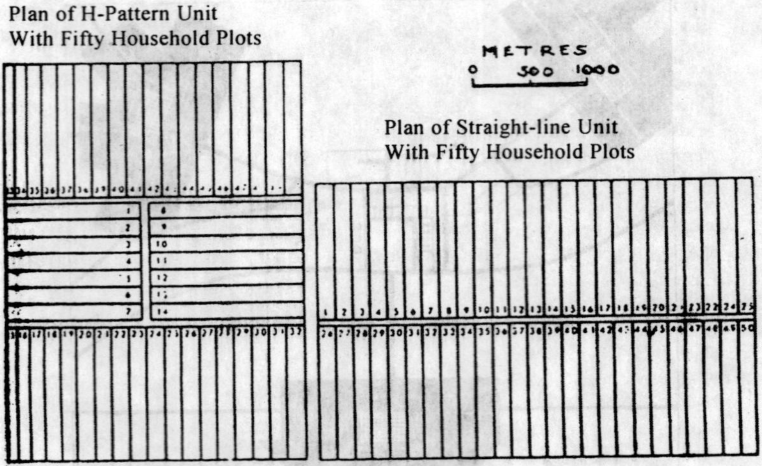

Source: Redrawn from Reining (1966:105)

FIG. 3.11: Model of Rural Settlement Zande, Sudan

This can help in communal organization of agricultural and industrial production, planned arrangement of houses, boost marketing, trade, water supply, transportation, education and health services for integrated regional economic development.

REFERENCES

1. R.J. Chorley and P. Haggett: *Physical and Information Models in Geography;* Methuen, London, 1970, p. 22.
2. B.J. Garner: "Models of Urban Geography and Settlement Location", in R. J. Chorley and P. Haggett (ed.) *Models in Geography;* Methuen & Co. Ltd.; London, 1967, pp. 304-05.
3. C.H. Coombs, H. Raifa and R.N. Thral: "Some Views on Mathematical Models and Measurement Theory", in R. M. Thral, etc., *Decision Process,* New York, John Wiley, 1954, pp. 25-26.
4. W. Bunge: "Theoretical Geography", *Lund Studies in Geography,* Series-C., No. 1, 1962, pp. 7-13.
5. W.L. Garrison: *Lecture delivered at Regional Science Seminar,* University of California, Berkeley, 1962.
6. E. Bylund: "Theoretical Considerations Regarding the Distribution of Settlement in Inner North Sweden", *Geografiska Annaler,* Vol. 42, 1962, pp. 225-31.
7. R. K. Morrill: "Simulation of Central Place Patterns Over Time", *Lund Studies in Geography,* Series B. No. 24, 1962, pp. 109-20.
8. G. Olsson: "Central Place Theory, Spatial Interaction, and Stochastic Process", Papers, *Regional Science Association,* Vol. XVII, 1966, pp. 13-45.
9. Y. Medvedkov: "The Regular Component in Settlement Pattern Shown on a Map", *Soviet Geography,* Vol. 8, 1967, pp. 150-68.

10. M.F. Dacey: "A Probability Model for Central Place Locations," *Annals of the Association of American Geographers,* Vol. 56, 1966, pp. 549-68.
11. W.K.D. Davis: *The Conceptual Revolution in Geography,* University of London Press, 1972, p. 358.
12. J.C. Hudson: *Theoretical Settlement Location,* (Unpublished Doctoral Dissertation) University of Iowa, Department of Geography, 1967.
13. Andrei Rogers: "A Markovian Policy Model of Inter-regional Migration", Papers, *Regional Science Association,* Vol. 17, 1966, pp. 205-24.
14. D. Harvey: "Geographic Processes and the Analysis of Point Patterns: Testing Models of Diffusion by Quadrat Sampling", Transactions and Papers, *Institute of British Geographers,* No. 40, 1966, pp. 81-85.
15. K.N. Singh: "The Territorial Basis of Medieval Town and Village Settlement in Eastern Uttar Pradesh, India", *Annals of the Association of American Geographers,* Vol. 58, 1968, pp. 203-20.
16. R.B. Mandal: *Planned Development of Rural Settlements,* Concept Publishing Company, New Delhi, 1981.
17. H. Ishida: "Village and Field Pattern in the Middle Ganga Plain: A Diagrammatic Model and Some Overseas Comparisons", in R.L. Singh (ed.): *Rural Settlements in Monsoon Asia,* National Geographical Society of India, Varanasi, 1972, pp. 173-74.
18. *Ibid.*
19. W.B. Morgan: "The Grassland Towns of the Eastern Region of Nigeria", Transactions and Papers, *Institute of British Geographers,* No. 23, 1957, pp. 213-24.
20. D. Grossman: "Do we have a Theory for Settlement Geography? The Case of Iboland", *Professional Geographer,* Vol. 23, 1971, pp. 197-203.
21. *Ibid.*
22. *Ibid.*
23. T. Hagerstrand: "The Propagation of Innovation Waves", Lund Studies in Geography, Series B, *Geography,* No. 4, 1952.
24. E. Bylund: "Theoretical Considerations Regarding the Distribution of Settlement in Inner North Sweden", *Geografisca Annaler,* Vol. 42, 1960, pp. 225-31.
25. J.C. Hudson: "A Location Theory for Rural Settlement", *Annals of the Association of American Geographers,* Vol. 59, 1970, pp. 365-81.
26. D. Grossman: *Op. cit.*
27. C.A. Doxiadis: "The Future of Human Settlements", in a Tiselius and S. Nilssa (ed.): *Place of Value in a World of Facts,* Stockholm, Almquist and Wiksell, 1969, pp. 307-38.
28. R.B. Mandal: "Regional Dynamics of the Sahel", in *Patterns of Regional Geography: An International Perspective,* Vol. 3, Concept Pub. Co., New Delhi, 1985.
29. R. K. Udo: "Patterns of Population Distribution and Settlement in Eastern Nigeria", *Nigerian Geographical Journal,* Vol. VI, 1963, pp. 73-88.
30. R.M. Prothero: *People and Land in Africa South of the Sahara,* Oxford University Press, London 1972, p. 332.
31. C.C. Reining: *The Zande Scheme;* North-eastern University Press, Evanston, 1966, p. 105.
32. S. Watts: "The South Busoga Settlement Scheme", Occasional Papers; Syracuse University Program of East African Studies, No. 17, 1966.

4

APPLIED QUANTITATIVE METHODS OF RURAL SETTLEMENT GEOGRAPHY

Shelter is the most important need of man in rural areas, where the irresistible hazards of the climate and the scorching sun rays do impart uninterrupted discomfiture to human life. Rural settlement is the only area in human geography where we may really search and try to locate the genesis of settlement geography. Rural settlement is the outcome of the combination of several physical and cultural factors and these are expressed here with different quantitative methods.[1]

There are two sets of variables which have a bearing on the settlement types in rural areas. These variables may be termed as agglomerating and deglomerating factors. These are both physical and cultural and lead to the formation of compact and dispersed rural settlements according to the relative influence of the centrifugal and the centripetal forces.

In most countries of the world two methods of rural settlement classification have generally been used, (a) personal observation, and (b) quantitative methods for determining the types. The significance of some of these quantitative methods for measuring the indices of agglomeration and dispersion have been discussed in this chapter.

In 1909, Woiekof[2] devised a formula as:

$$K = \frac{P}{H}$$

where K is the index, P is the number of inhabitants and H is the number of inhabited places. This, however, gives merely the average population size of rural settlements, irrespective of settlement dispersion. In the same way in 1924 Kristofferson[3] classified the rural settlements below 50 metres spacing as compact and more than 50 metres as dispersed. In 1926 Lefevre[4] used the number of houses per square kilometre grouped into classes of 1-10, 11-25, 26-50, 51-100, 101-250, 251-500, 500-1000, and 1000+ as the basis of classification of settlement types. But this method only gives the density of houses and not the types of settlements.

In 1931, the French scientist Bernhard[5] devised another formula,

$$K = \frac{S \times M}{N^2}$$

where K is the index of concentration, S is the total number of houses, M is the area and N is the number of settlements. This formula, however, does not distinguish closely between the settlement variations and K can be identical in value with very different patterns.

Another successful formula for measuring dispersion is that of Demongeon[6] who developed this in 1933. He expressed the settlement pattern as,

$$K = \frac{E \times N}{T}$$

where K is the co-efficient required, E is the population of the commune except for that of the chief nucleated settlement, N is the number of isolated settlements, and T is the total population.

In 1934, Zierhoffer[7] devised another formula on the assumption that the degree of dispersion of settlements will increase with the corresponding increase of area per dwelling and the degree of dispersion can be represented as:

$$r = \frac{P \times S}{d} \times K$$

where R is the degree of dispersion, P is the average area per dwelling, S is the number of house groups in commune, d is the total number of inhabitants and the constant K is 0.005. This method, however, does not give sufficient contrast to the value of R in intermediate categories between complete dispersion and absolute nucleation.

In 1938, Pawlowski[8] while studying the concentration of settlements derived the following formulae:

$$C = \frac{A}{AS} \quad \text{and} \quad Mc = \frac{AS}{S},$$

where C is the index of concentration, A is 25 sq. km and represents the area occupied by settlements; Mc is mean index of concentration,

S is number of settlements. Debouverie[9] in 1943 tried to relate regional variations of settlements with the standard concept of concentration. His formula is as follows:

$$K = \frac{X \times L}{H}$$

where *K* is the index of concentration, *X* is the minimum number of dwellings per settlement, *L* is the number of settlement units and *H* is the total number of dwellings in the commune. This formula is useful in distinguishing types of nucleation.

In 1950, Kant[10] presented an ingeneous formula to measure the concentration of settlements more precisely. The formula is as follows:

$$C = \frac{1}{M}\sqrt{\frac{A}{D}}$$

where *C* is the relative interval between two settlements, $\frac{1}{M}$ is map Scale; *A* is the area; *D* is the density of habitations.

Based on Demongeon's formula, Houston[11] devised another method in 1953.

$$K = \frac{S \times N}{T - E}$$

where *K* is the index of dispersion, *S* is the area of commune, *N* is the number of isolated settlements, *T* is the total population and *E* is the population of commune minus its chief place or urban centres.

In 1957, Tanioka[12] devised a new formula to measure the index of dispersion of rural settlements. The formula is as follows:

$$K = \frac{S \times T}{S \times N}$$

where *K* is the index of dispersion, *S* is the area of map sheet (1/50,000 scale), *T* is the per cent of land cultivated, *S* is the average agriculture area worked per family, *N* is the average number of rural houses per village.

In 1962, K. H Stone[13] devised a formula to measure the continuous and discontinuous settlements in any region. The measure developed by him is as follows:

$$R \text{ or } FZ = Nh + Nr,$$

where *R* is the measure of continuous or discontinuous settlement, *FZ* is the fringe zone in discontinuous settlement region, *Nh* is the pattern of permanent residences within 3 miles long 1-6 major directions from any one permanent residence, *Nr* is the number (1-4) of inter-regional and local routes of transport within 10-20 miles of each permanent residence.

In 1964, Inouye[14] devised a measure of dispersion of rural settlements on the basis of 50 metres of spacing. In this measure isolated means less than 3 houses within 50 metres of each other, concentrated means more than half of the houses in a village distributed into one group within 50 metres range and condensed means more than half of the houses in a village centralized into one core.

In 1969, R. B. Singh,[15] expressed the following formula to measure the compactness and dispersal of rural settlements.

$$Hn = Vn \qquad = \text{Compact}$$
$$Hn = Vn + 1 \text{ to } Vn \times 2 \qquad = \text{Semi compact}$$
$$Hn = Vn \times 2 + 1 \text{ to } \frac{OUn \times 2}{3} \qquad = \text{Hamletted}$$
$$Hn = \frac{OUn \times 2+1}{3} \text{ to } OUn = \text{Dispersed}$$

where *Hn* represents the number of hamlets, *Vn* is the number of villages in an administrative unit and *OUn* is the number of occupance units in the same area. In 1972, R.B. Mandal[16] devised the following measure of dispersal of rural settlements.

$$1 = \frac{\text{Average Population Size of Tola}}{\text{Average Spacing Tola}}$$

where 1 is the index of dispersal. Index of dispersal values grouped according to median and quartile values (the highest value shows the agglomeration while the lowest shows the dispersal).

In 1973, A. Prasad[17] while studying the rural settlements of Chhota Nagpur Plateau devised a formula of descriptive nature after considering the *deviation from standard index.* Ten highly compact villages from the adjoining parts of Gaya district have been selected. On the basis of village maps of the concerned settlements, the actual built up area in each case is reduced to the percentage of the total area within the homestead boundary. The average percentage of the ten villages has been taken. This average is expected as the standard index of agglomeration for Chhota Nagpur as a whole. To determine the agglomeration quotient similar percentage value for any other cluster is divided by the standard index and is then multiplied by 100. If it is 100, the cluster has the highest degree of agglomeration and compactness. If it is more than 100, the agglomeration is of exceptionally high order. The quotient under 100 indicates a decrease in agglomeration tendency and a corresponding increase in deglomeration tendency. Fifty is the critical value. As the quotient declines below 50, the settlements are to be classed as dispersed. Dispersal can be easily determined by subtracting the agglomeration quotient from 100. The remainder is dispersal quotient for a cluster.

In 1977, R.B. Mandal,[18] while studying the *Planned Development of Rural Settlements in North Bihar* devised a new measure of dispersal index to determine types of rural settlements. The formula is as follows:

$$\text{Dispersal Index} = \frac{\text{Total Rural Population of an Anchal} \times \text{Number of Tolas in an Anchal}}{(\text{Total Rural Area})^2}$$

To determine the validity of this formula, the relationship between the rural area of anchals in thousand square kilometres (X) and the number of tolas multiplied by rural population (Y) of an anchal were plotted along the x axis and y axis respectively. Both axes were on logarithmic scale and data was plotted for all the 241 anchals of North Bihar. (Fig. 4.1) For this set of data, the product moment coefficient of correlation value comes to $r = 0.56$ and regression value of $y = 10.30 + 0.14X$. On the basis of this idea, and with the help of the dispersal index of each and every anchal, the difference between the logarithm of the highest value of 1,507 and the lowest value of 76 has been taken. The logarithmic difference has been divided by three so as to get three categories of rural settlement types. This is because in North Bihar the population density is so high that nowhere dispersed settlement have actually been found except in a few localities in the Kosi basin as well as some in the forested and rugged terrain of north-west Champaran. Elsewhere all rural settlements are either of compact or of semi-compact type. The geometric progression of the above logarithmic difference comes to 1.688081, 2.31323, 2.74565 and 3.17808; and their anti-logarithmic values 76, 206, 557 and 1507 (index values) respectively.

The density of habitations (d) is the ratio of two quantities—C and A—the number of habitations (C) belonging to a given area (A) :

$$d = C/A$$

For distribution map the density value should be arranged serially either on the basis of Quartile, Octile or Standard deviation. Other methods of grouping can also be used.

Methods for Measuring Spacing of Settlements

Geography is a discipline in distance. Thus the spacing of rural settlement is largely governed by their size. Large rural settlements would be widely spaced, while smaller settlements would be closely spaced.[19] These spatial patterns are constantly changing in time and space which has resulted in an increase in the size of centres and

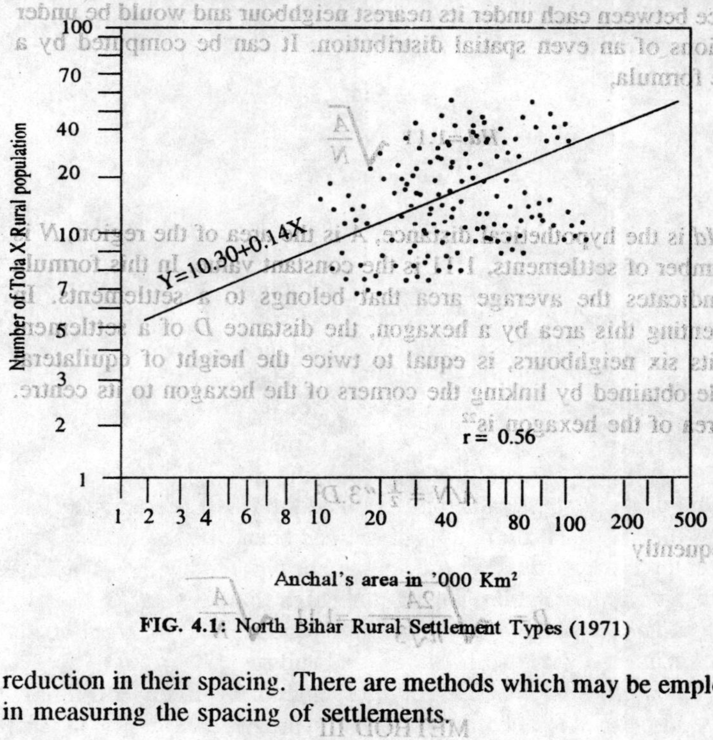

FIG. 4.1: North Bihar Rural Settlement Types (1971)

reduction in their spacing. There are methods which may be employed in measuring the spacing of settlements.

METHOD I

Walenty Winid, a Polish geographer, assumed that settlements are ordinarily placed at the intersection points of a rectangular grid, and the best figure to use for inter-settlement distance is equal to the square route of the area divided by the number of settlements within that area.[20]

$$D = \sqrt{\frac{A}{N}}$$

Here *D* is average distance between settlements, *A* is the total area of the region under study, *N* is the number of settlements.

METHOD II

According to Barnes and Robinson,[21] if the number of settlements and the area of the region are known, we can determine the approximate distance between each under its nearest neighbour and would be under conditions of an even spatial distribution. It can be computed by a simple formula,

$$Hd = 1.11 \sqrt{\frac{A}{N}}$$

here *Hd* is the hypothetical distance, *A* is the area of the region, *N* is the number of settlements, 1.11 is the constant value. In this formula *A/N* indicates the average area that belongs to a settlements. In representing this area by a hexagon, the distance *D* of a settlement from its six neighbours, is equal to twice the height of equilateral triangle obtained by linking the corners of the hexagon to its centre. The area of the hexagon is[22]

$$A/N = \tfrac{1}{2} \text{''}3.D^2$$

Consequently

$$D = \sqrt{\frac{2A}{n\sqrt{3}}} = 1.11 \sqrt{\frac{A}{N}}$$

METHOD III

In 1944, Mather[23] devised a formula to measure the spacing of settlements. The formula is as follows:

$$D = 1.07 \sqrt{\frac{A}{N}}$$

where *D* is average distance of a settlement to its six nearest neighbours, *A* is the total area of study and *N* is the number of settlements.

The verification about the correctness of Barnes-Robinson and Mather methods was presented by Rana R.B. Singh.[24] He endeavoured to solve this disputable method in this way:

If in Figs. 4.2 and 4.3, *A* and *B* are the two points, then *AB* will be their interpoint distance. Take first the $\triangle ADC$ (right angled at *C*)

$$\text{Total area of } \triangle ADC = \left(\frac{AC.\ DC}{2}\right)$$

(MATHER'S METHOD) SPACING- $1.0746\ d^{-\frac{1}{2}}$	(ROBINSON'S METHOD) SPACING $1.11d^{-\frac{1}{2}}$

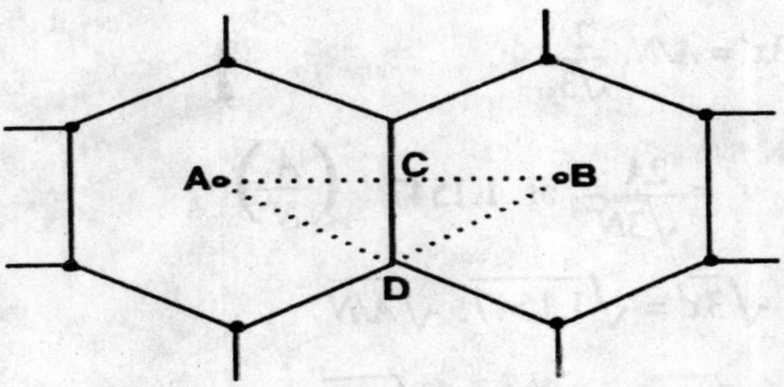

FIG. 4.2: Hexagonal Arrangement of Rural Settlements

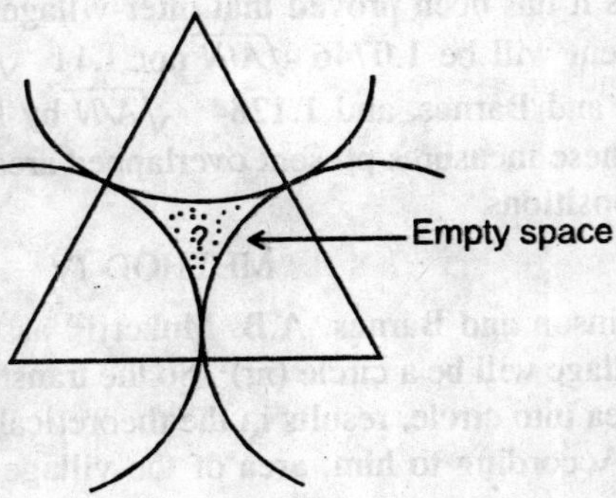

Fig. 4.3 Circular Arrangement of Rural Settlements and Empty as Unserved Area (Mukherji's Method)

Let $AD = X$,

and it is known that $AC = \frac{\sqrt{3}}{2} \times$ and

$DC = \frac{X}{2}$; and AB, the required inter-village

distance $(D) = \sqrt{3X}$

Total area of $\Delta ADC = \frac{\sqrt{3}}{2} \times \frac{x}{2} \cdot \frac{1}{2}$

$$= \sqrt{\frac{3}{8}} x^2$$

The area of the hexagon should correspond to the average area of a village i.e.; A/N;

$$\therefore \frac{3\sqrt{3}}{2} . X^2 = A/N$$

$$\text{or } 3x^2 = A/N. \frac{2}{\sqrt{3}}$$

$$= \frac{2A}{\sqrt{3N}} \text{ or } 1.1547 \left(\frac{A}{N}\right)$$

$$\therefore \sqrt{3x^2} = \sqrt{1.1547}. \sqrt{A/N}$$

$$\sqrt{3x} = 1.0746 \sqrt{A/N}$$

Thus it has been proved that inter-village distance in hexagonal arrangement will be $1.0746 \sqrt{A/N}$ not $1.11 \sqrt{A/N}$ as formulated by Robinson and Barnes, and $1.1284 \sqrt{A/N}$ by Mukerji.

As these measures present overlapped area, so they are wrong in their propositions

METHOD IV

Like Robinson and Barnes, A.B. Mukerji[25] assumes that the average area of village will be a circle $(\pi r)^2$. So the transformation as of average village area into circle, results in the theoretical distance between two villages. According to him, area of the village will be πr^3,

Now, If $\pi r^2 = \frac{A}{N}$; $r^2 = \frac{A}{N \times \pi}$

or $r = 2\sqrt{A/N\pi}$

Thus the inter-village distance $(D) = 2\sqrt{A/N\pi}$

$$= 1.1284\sqrt{A/N\pi}$$

In this method empty space is left in between three circles, so this method is also not suitable for measuring inter-village distance. Thus, it is apparent that the theoretical spacing between settlements will be $1.0746\sqrt{A/N}$, not $1.11\sqrt{A/N}$; nor $1.1282\sqrt{A/N}$.

Finally the formula used by A.B. Mukerji for the computation of spacing in miles of rural settlements in an anchal or taluka is as follows:

$$S = 2x\sqrt{\frac{A}{n \times \sqrt{3}}} = 1.11\sqrt{\frac{A}{N \times \pi}}$$

here S is spacing in miles, A is the rural area of an anchal and N is the number of rural settlements.

METHOD V

In the given co-ordinates of any two points on a plane, the distance between them can be easily computed by using the Pythagoras Theorem. This question can be generalized to measure distance between points in n dimensional space for given coordinates and is as follows[26]:

$$dij = \sqrt{\sum_{z=1}^{n} (Xiz - Xjz)^2}$$

here dij is the distance between points i and j in a space of n dimensions with Xiz and Xjz being measures along the zth co-ordinate. This is the simplest distance measure and has been used by Berry in 1961.

METHOD VI

If (x_1, y_1, z_1) and (x_2, y_2, z_2) be the rectangular coordinates of two points P_1, P_2 respectively and O is the origin point then[27] :

$$\overrightarrow{OP_1} = x_1 i + y_1 j + y_1 j + z_1 K$$

$$OP_2 = x_2 i + y_2 j \div z_2 k$$

$$\therefore \overrightarrow{P_1P_2} = \overrightarrow{OP_2} - \overrightarrow{OP_1} = (x_2 - x_1)\, i + (y_2 - y_1)\, j + (z_2 - z_1)\, K$$

Hence $P_1P_2 \mid P_1P_2 \mid = \sqrt{(x_2 - x_1)^2 + (y_2 - y_1)^2 + (z_2 - z_1)^2}$

This will give the distance between the points P_1, P_2.

In 1981 S. K. Brahamachari while studying the rural settlements of Munger district devised the following formula for calculating the dispersion index of rural settlements:

$$D = \frac{\text{No. of Persons Per House} \times \text{Population Size of Rural Settlements}}{\text{Spacing of Villages}}$$

METHOD VII

As early as in 1901, Bannerman used the following formula for calculating the distance between each village:

$$2\left(\frac{\cos 30^0}{3}\right)^{\frac{1}{2}} \times \left(\frac{\text{Area}}{\text{No. of villages and towns}}\right)^{\frac{1}{2}}$$

$$= \frac{\text{Log } 2}{3} - \frac{\text{Log } 3}{3} - \frac{\text{Log areality}}{3}$$

$$= 0.0312347 + \frac{\text{Log. areality}}{3}$$

Where 0.0312347 is a constant

METHOD VIII

According to Clark and Evans, the nearest neighbours, scale can be referred to as *R* scale, and the individual *R* value can be calculated as follows:[29]

$R = \frac{\bar{r}A}{\bar{r}E}$ Where $\bar{r}A = \frac{\Sigma r}{N}$ or the mean of the series of distances to nearest neighbours $\bar{r}$ being the distance from each point to its nearest neighbour (actual) and

$$\bar{r}E = \frac{1}{2\sqrt{p}} \quad \text{or } \bar{r}E = \frac{1}{2\sqrt{\frac{N}{A}}}$$

where the expected mean distance ($\bar{r}E$) to the nearest neighbour in an infinitely large random distribution of density *P* (*E* meaning expected),

$$\text{and } P = \frac{\text{No. of settlement}}{\text{Total area}}$$

The *R* value should range between 0.21491 meaning maximum dispersal at the end, with unity (1.00) indicating the presence of a random observed distribution, while the values near *O* indicate clustering of settlements. This index of *Rn* value can be correlated with variance (*V*) for further testing which can be calculated with the help of following formula:[30]

$$V = (4 - \pi/4\ dx)$$

In case the $\bar{r}E$ value is larger than the *V*, the distribution is termed regular; when *V* is larger than $\bar{r}E$, it is termed clustered and the term random is applied to the case when *V* and $\bar{r}E$ are equal, i.e., the variance mean ratio is one.

The test of the significance of $\bar{r}E$ was made about the hypothesis of randomness on the basis of standard error ($\sigma\bar{r}E$)[31] which is as follows:

$$\sigma\bar{r}E = \frac{0.26136}{\sqrt{(nd)}}$$

where *n* is number of total villages in the areal unit and *d* represents density of villages per square kilometre.

In the nearest neighbour analysis, the differences between the observed and expected frequencies were analysed by a Chi-square test. Chi-square tests were made because it was assumed that the distances are not normally distributed. Thompson[32] has provided a suitable procedure of Chi-square test and it has been reviewed by King.[33] The values of Chi-square are given by[34] :

$$2\pi d^{\frac{1}{2}} \sum_{i=1}^{n} rij$$

where n is the number of points in the pattern, d is the observed density, rij is the order nearest neighbour distance for i and is distributed as chi-square with n-2 degree of freedom.

The index of standard variate of normal curve (C) can be calculated as:

$$C = (\bar{r}O - \bar{r}E) \,/\, O\bar{r}E$$

where $\bar{r}O$ is observed value and $\bar{r}E$ is expected. The upper and lower ranges of random matching at the 95 per cent probability will be computed with the help of $O\bar{r}E$

$$i.e. = \frac{(2\,\sigma\bar{r}E \pm \bar{r}E)}{\bar{r}E}$$

The application of these tests has been made by Rana P.B. Singh in his paper related to distribution of rural settlements.

METHOD IX

King suggested the formula for calculating the R value in nearest neighbour analysis is as follows[35]:

$$R = 2\bar{D}\sqrt{\left(\frac{A}{N}\right)}$$

where D is average of the observed distances between each point and its nearest neighbour, N is the number of points and A is the area under study.

METHOD X

In 1967, Birch had applied nearest neighbour measures in Midwest of U.S.A.[36] The formula is as follows:

$$R_1 = \frac{\bar{r}A}{(A/N) - \frac{1}{2}}$$

TABLE 4.1 : Results of Nearest Neighbour Measures

Class of Urban Places	No. of urban places	Density per sq. mile	Average observed distance in miles $\bar{r}A$	Average Expected distance in miles $\bar{r}E$	Pattern Statistics R	Chi-square X^2	Degree of freedom	Significant
Hamlets	59	0.0127	4.881	4.442	1.098	194.484	118.0	Yes
Villages	93	0.0200	3.487	3.538	1.126	314.393	186.0	Yes
Towns	37	0.0079	5.931	5.609	1.057	117.363	74.0	Yes
Cities	14	0.0030	10.407	9.119	1.141	47.934	28.0	Yes

Source : B. Thakur, *Indian Geographical Studies*, 1973.

where R_1 is index of randomness of regularity or agglomeration of farmsteads, $\bar{r}A$ is the observed mean distance between each point and its nearest neighbour, A is the area, and N is the number of rural settlements.

METHOD XI

In 1975 a modification in nearest neighbour technique has been presented by Pinder and Witherick.[37] According to him nearest neighbour analysis is generally used in two-dimensional point patterns. No exploration has been done for distribution of points along a line. The method presented by Evans and Dacey is simple but its result is misleading especially when the number of points in the pattern is low.

In the normal analysis of nearest-neighbour by Clark and Evans method, the formula for predicting the average distance between randomly distributed nearest-neighbours ($\bar{r}E$) is as follows:

$$0.5\sqrt{(a/n)}$$

where a is the area studied and n is the number of points. This methods designed to fit in two dimensional patterns.

In order to predict the mean nearest neighbour distances in a unidimensional situation, the average distance between randomly distributed linear nearest neighbours ($L\bar{r}E$) may be derived from the following formula:

$$L\bar{r}E = 0.5 \left(\frac{L}{n-1}\right)$$

where L is the line length and n is the number of points. This is the first stage of this linear nearest neighbour technique. This indicates that the predicted random average is half the mean distance that would separate the points if they were distributed regularity throughout the line.

TABLE 4.2 : Comparison of Predicted and Experimental Values of $L\bar{r}E$

No. of Points per pattern	Predicted mean 0.5 (*L*/*n*–1)	Experimental mean	Predicted Mean Less Experimental Mean
10	55.56	55.89	– 0.33
20	26.32	26.62	– 0.30
30	17.24	17.57	– 0.33
40	12.82	12.74	0.08
50	10.20	10.21	– 0.01
60	8.48	8.34	0.14
70	7.25	7.12	0.13
80	6.33	6.23	0.10
90	5.62	5.59	0.13
100	5.05	5.04	0.01

Source **: After Pinder and Witherick, *Geography*, 1975.**

In this table, for a line of 1000 units comparison of predicted and computer generated experimental values of $L\bar{r}E$ have been given. This provides extremely close correspondence between the two sets of means as given in the second and the third columns, and further emphasis is put forward by the last column, where the discrepancies between the predicted and experimental means are presented.

Further, linear nearest neighbour statistic (*LRn*) can be defined as :

$$\frac{\bar{D}obs}{L\bar{r}E} \text{ or } \frac{\bar{D}obs}{0.5\ (L/(n\text{-}1))}$$

where $\bar{D}obs$ is average observed distance between nearest neighbours, *L* is length of the line studied, *n* is the number of settlements. In case *LRn* value is 1.00 this suggests random situation. Less than 1.00 values are indicative of clustering while more than 1.00 shows the presence of some regularity. In a perfect regular situation *LRn* equals 2.00 and this is half the observed mean distance between settlements.

METHOD XII

Order Nearest Neighbour Analysis

Dacey has given the formal derivation of Poisson Probability law for two dimensional random point process. He assumed that those neighbours whose distance is greater than the parent point-distance from the boundary of the map, the number and distance of such neighbours should be ignored from the study. The formula through which the mean observed distance upto four neighbours can be calculated is as follows:[38]

$$\bar{r}j = \frac{1}{N} \sum_{i=1}^{n} rij$$

where n is the number of points in the area, $\bar{r}j$ is the mean distance from i to any other point, j is any point, and rij is the distance between i and jth nearest point.

Dacey has generalised these concepts of order distances to nearest neighbour to handle the description of pattern in multi-dimensional space. The non-standardized mean value of distance of urban places in Bihar upto four neighbours is given below:

TABLE 4.3: Order Distance Statistics for Urban Places in Bihar, 1971 (Measurement in Miles)

Order j	n	$\sum_{i=1}^{n} rij$	
1	163	1361.00	8.35
2	143	1693.75	11.84
3	133	1894.50	14.24
4	127	1997.75	15.83

The above observed mean distances can be used in comparison with the hypothetical estimated distance for pattern interpretation.

METHOD XIII

Regional Method of Nearest Neighbour Analysis

Dacey and Tung has put forward alternative approach to the description of point patterns is known as regional method. They divided the map around each point into six K equal sectors. The distances from the central point to six neighbours in each sector are measured and 'these observed distances are used to classify the regions in some systematic fashion and a separate mean is obtained for each kind of region.[39] The formula used is as follows:

$$\bar{r}ik = \frac{\sum_{i=1}^{k} \bar{r}ik}{n}$$

where i is the central point, 1 is the set of n points for which the measurements are made, n is the number of point in a region.

He again assumed that those neighbours whose distances is greater than the parent point distance from the boundary of the map than the number and distance of such neighbours can be deleted.

METHOD XIV

Bachi's Standard Distance Statistics

Bachi's standard distance is a measure of the dispersion of a set of points in respect of two right angled axes. It may be expressed as:

$$dij = \{(xi - xj)^2 + (yi - yj)^2\}^{\frac{1}{2}}$$

where x and y are two coordinates, and dij is the standard distance.

The above formula will give us distance between two points in Euclidian space (Fig. 4.4). For the n set of points n^2 of distances can be calculated, so that the distance between the two points is itself included and every standard distance is measured twice, once for i and secondly for j.

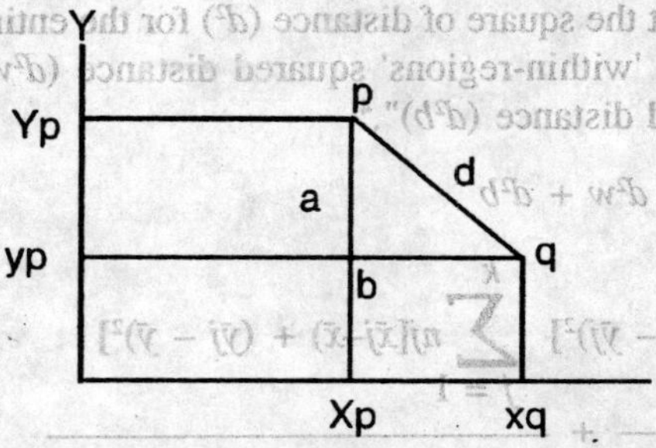

$$d^2pq = d^2 + b^2$$

$$= (YP - yp)^2 + (xq - XP)^2$$

FIG. 4.4: Bachi's Standard Distance Measure between two points

For this set of n^2 distance, Bachi suggested the mean quadratic distance as:

$$D = \left[\left(\frac{\sum_{i=i}^{n}\sum_{j=1}^{n} dij}{n^2}\right)\right]^{\frac{1}{2}}$$

Then, the mean centre of the distribution have the coordination as:

$$\bar{X} = \frac{\left(\sum_{j=1}^{n} \times i\right)}{n}, \text{ and } \bar{y} = \frac{\left(\sum_{i=1}^{n} yi\right)}{n}$$

$$\text{then } D = \frac{\left(\sum_{i=1}^{n} d^2ic\right)^{\frac{1}{2}}}{n}$$

where *dic* is the distance from point *i* to the mean centre

$$C = \{(xi\text{-}\bar{x})\ 2 + (yi - \bar{y})\}\ \tfrac{1}{2}$$

then the standard distance is[40]:

$$d = \left[\frac{\sum_{i=1}^{n} d^2ic}{n}\right]$$

Further "Bachi noted that the square of distance (d^2) for the entire area is equal to the sum of a 'within-regions' squared distance (d^2w) and 'between-regions' squared distance (d^2b)".[41]

$$\text{Then } d^2 = d^2w + d^2b$$

$$= \frac{\sum_{j=1}^{k}\sum_{i=1}^{nj}[(xij - \bar{x}j) + (yij - \bar{y}j)^2]}{n} + \frac{\sum_{j=1}^{k} nj[\bar{x}j - \bar{x}) + (\bar{y}j - \bar{y})^2]}{n}$$

where (xij, yij) are the coordinates of the *i*th point in the *j*th region
$(\bar{x}j, \bar{y}j)$ is the regional mean centre,
$(\bar{x}, \bar{y})$ is the mean centre for the whole distribution.
(d^2b/d^2) is the ratio, provides a crude measure of

significance of the regional divisions. Ratio 1 is the maximum differentiation.

where *O* shows the same mean centre as exists in the total pattern.

METHOD XV

Computer Function to Measure ARC Distances

The calculation of the arc distance comes from spherical trigonometry. It assumes that the earth is a sphere. The necessary formula for determining the arc distance between points *A* and *B* is given by Robinson. The formula is as follows[42];

Cos d = (Sin a Sin b) + (Cos a, Cos b, Cos P)

here d = arc distance between *A* and *B*.

a = latitude of *A*,

b = latitude of *B*,

P = degrees of longitude between *A* and *B*.

Using this formula to calculate distances has proved satisfactory. Accuracy has been good (calculated distances between cities on opposite sides of the pacific have varied only a few kilometres from distances quoted by air lines) and seems to be limited more by point measurement than by computer rounding errors or the off spherical shape of the earth.[43]

If all settlements are equally spaced over a region, a uniform distribution is obtained. This distance (δ) is obtained by the relation,

$$\delta = \sqrt{\frac{A}{N}}$$

where *A* is the total area, and *N* is the number of settlements. The degree of concentration (*DC*) of settlements (*nc*) is given by,

$$DC = \frac{\delta}{N}$$

where *S* is the average separation between settlements. The quality nCS^2 is designated as the derived area (*ac*) of the concentration. We get a level of concentration (*LC*) expressed in the form-

$$LC = \left(\frac{\delta}{S}\right)\frac{nc}{N} = DC^2\frac{nc}{N}$$

It should be noted that any quantity of *LC* in fact represents a set of values with varying δ *nc*; hence its designation as 'level'. A number of concentrations in a region can be grouped together to form agglomerations. If the distance (*As*) between two contiguous concentrations is less than or equal to, the sum of the average separations of settlement, within the concentration, thus the concentration can be grouped to form an agglomeration. Two contiguous concentrations are brought together under an agglomeration if—

$$AS \leqq S_1 + S_2,$$

where S_1 and S_2 refer to the average separations of settlements in concentrations. To demarcate the dispersion group, the distance relevant to dispersion (*s*) is derived as follows:

$$\triangle = \sqrt{\frac{A - \Sigma ac}{N - NC}}$$

where *N* is total number of settlements, *NC* is the number of concentrated settlements, and Σac is the sum of the areas of all concentration. As in the case of concentration, the degree of dispersion,

$$Dd = \frac{C}{\triangle}$$

where *C* is the average separation in a dispersion group. The area of dispersion,

$$ad = nd\ C^2$$

where *nd* represents the number of settlements involved in the dispersion group. The level of dispersion.

$$Ld = \left(\frac{c}{\triangle}\right)^2 \frac{nd}{N} = Dd = \frac{nd}{N}$$

The change in any settlement is generally introduced by transport linkage. Inversely in this formula the rate of transportation is determined by the change in a settlement. The formula is as follows:

$$Rn = \frac{Dn}{Tn}$$

where Rn = rate of transportation
Dn = degree of transportation
Tn = time unit of transition in a settlement

$$\therefore Tn = \frac{Dn \rightarrow \text{Length of phase of development}}{Rn \rightarrow \text{Rate of Transformation in n th phase.}}$$

$$\therefore T = \sum \frac{D}{R}$$

$$\therefore T = \sum_{n-1}^{n} \frac{Dn}{Rn}$$

where *T* is the time required for attaining total development through transformation.

To express the change in number of lower order central places mathematically, the average rate of change can be calculated with the help of the formula[45]:

$$b = \frac{Pn - Po}{n}$$

and the arithmatic approximation to an average rate is given by

$$r^1 = \frac{b}{\frac{1}{2}(Po + Pn)} \times 100$$

where, *Po* is the initial number of centres, *Pn* is the number of centres at the end of the period (*n* year), *n* is the time in years, and *b* is the annual amount of change.

In a geometric series, the frequency distribution increases or decreases at the same rate over each unit of time, e.g. each year. If this constant rate of change is represented by *r* and the initial number is represented by *Po*, then after *n* years the final frequency of central places is given by :

$$Pn = Po\ (1+r)\ n$$

with the observed data that is available, we get

$$1 + r = n\sqrt{\frac{Pn}{Po}}$$

$$\text{or } \log(1 + r) = \frac{\log Pn - \log Po}{n}$$

or

$$\frac{\log\left(\dfrac{Pn}{Po}\right)}{n}$$

$= \frac{1}{2}$ [(log 342 – log 239)] $= \frac{1}{5}$ [(2.53403 – 2.37840)]
= 0.03112 Taking antilog 1 + r = 0.10748
∴ r = .10748 i.e., the rate of change is 10.75 per cent per annum.

Data Matrix* : *D* matrix has been used in network analysis in order to know the accessibility of rural settlements and measure the connectivity of points or efficiency of a particular route.

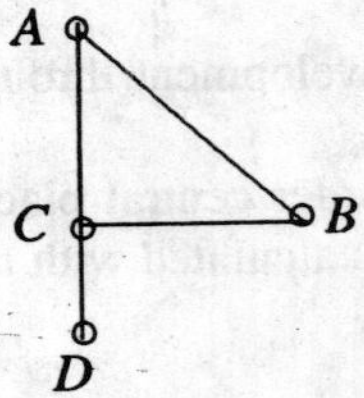

C \ R	A	B	C	D	Total
A	0	1	1	0	2
B	1	0	1	0	2
C	1	1	0	1	3
D	0	0	1	0	1
Total	2	2	3	1	8

Fig. 4.5 Connectivity Matrix

In this way, it is clear that *C* settlement is most accessible point whereas *D* is least accessible point.

Regional Peculiarities in the Dynamics of Rural Settlements

The visual evaluation of the degree of change in setting patterns may be supplemented by an objective measure of the magnitude of change in the form of sum of deviations of the 1970 distribution curve from the 1959 curve. For this purpose use was made of the simple index *Kr* (the coefficient of redistribution of population among size classes during the study period). If the distribution of population by size classes did not change, then *Kr* = *O*; the index will increase with the scale of structural changes in the network of places. The co-efficient can be calculated as follows[46]:

$$Kr = \sqrt{\sum_{P=1}^{n} (P_{70} - P_{59})^2}$$

where *n* is the number of size classes, P_{70} is the percentage of the 1970 rural population living in places of particular size class; P_{59} i.e. the same for the 1959 rural population.

* S. K. Brahmachari, Spatial Variation of Rural Settlements in the District of Munger, Unpublished Ph. D. Thesis, Bhagalpur University, 1981, p. 14.

The formula applied for size of the rural settlements is as follows:

$$S = \frac{P}{N}$$

where S is the average size of population per village, P is the rural population of the anchal, and N is the number of villages in the anchal.

Another possibility is as follows:

$$S = \frac{\text{Number of Houses in an Anchal}}{\text{Number of Settlements in an Anchal}}$$

Information may be collected from Census returns.

Measurement of Shape of Rural Settlements

METHOD I

In order to determine the shape, a circle with its circumference touching the two extreme points of settlement was drawn. Now the pattern seems to be obvious in its geometrical perspective in comparison with the circle. The formula for the measurement of this is:

$$MC = \frac{100 \times Aa}{\pi r^2}$$

where MC is the measure of circularity in shape; Aa is the actual area contained in a settlement and πr^2 is the area of circle of settlement=A

METHOD II

The shape of settlements can also be measured with Simmon's measure. He devised a method based upon area of a settlement and its outer boundary. The measure is defined as the ratio of the sum of distances of all settlements arranged in a regular network within the boundary of the residential area of a settlement to its centre. The formula for measuring shape is as follows[48]:

$$S = \frac{\sum_{i-1}^{n} Ri}{\sum_{i-1}^{n} ri}$$

Where *Ri* is the distance for the settlement area, and *ri* is the area for the circle. Here for a given settlement with given centre and boundary; *S* is a function of *n* type of network of settlements.

METHOD III

According to Boyce and Clark, the formula for measuring the outer boundary of a settlement is as follows[49]:

$$S=\sum_{i-1}^{n}\left|\frac{\frac{Ri}{n}}{\sum_{i-1}^{n}Ri}.100 \quad \frac{100}{n}\right.$$

where *S* is the measure and the *Ri* (*i* = 1,2 . . . . *n*) are the length of radial lines measured from the settlement centre to the boundary along equally spaced radi.

METHOD IV

The shape of rural settlement is theoretically circular at its peripheries for the distance between the central point and the edge of the territory is always shorter and quicker in space and time in comparison with any other geometrical shape of the settlement. But circles either overlap or leave gaps between them. The hexagonal pattern of rural settlements, therefore, is the ideal shape as it approximates the shape of a circle. Settlements in the area are neither equally spaced nor have equal size. The distance that should actually exist among settlements in a particular region with homogeneous character throughout, has been called as 'mean actual distance' (Da). It has derived from the following equation.

$$Da=\frac{\Sigma Ps_1 + Ps_2 + Ps_3 + \ldots Ps_n}{\Sigma N}$$

where *Ps* stands for the distance of possible straight line joining the different villages and '*N*' stands for total number of lines joining *n* villages. In case the same number of settlements are supposed to be arranged on a hexagonal pattern in the same region occupying the same area, their inter-distance, as it is called Hypothetical Distance (*Dh*), is derived from the following equation:[51]

$$Dh = \sqrt{\frac{\Sigma A_1 + A_2 + A_3 + \ldots\ldots + A_n}{\Sigma N}}$$

where '*A*' denotes the area of settlements upto *n* th number in Km^2 and *N* stands for the number of settlements.

In case *DA* equals *Dh*, there is a likelihood of equi-spaced normal settlement pattern. If *Da* is more than *Dh*, there will be a tendency towards dispersed pattern and if *Da* is less than *Dh*, the settlements will adopt a concentrated pattern. Hence, the above mentioned technique will help in determining the spacing, regularity and type of settlements in the study area. Now *Dh* being the ideal distance, is supposed to be 100 per cent and the regularity index (1*r*) is derived from the following equation:

$$1r = 100 - \frac{Da \times 100}{Dh}$$

The indices derived out of this formula will be either positive or negative. The negative indices will suggest concentration while the positive dispersion.

The smaller urban settlements or the larger villages have been described variously as rurban settlements. A rurban centre is essentially a local focus of activities and is marked by commercial, industrial, administrative and cultural institutions. Centres, having at least three out of 9 central functions (viz., education, medical, communication, finance, transport, administrative, trade, recreation and percentage of workers engaged in tertiary occupations) have been considered as rurban centres. Classification of urban centres on this basis from the list of villages is easy, but a problem arises in the selection of rurban centres from the list of towns. Both towns and cities have functions of a higher order as compared to the rural, which creates confusion. In the selection of rurban centres from the list of towns, the following formula may be used.

$$R1 = PC \times \frac{tw \times 100}{TW}$$

where *R*1 = Rurban index

PC = Total Population of the centre

tw = workers engaged in tertiary occupations in that centre, and

TW = Total number of workers in that centre.

After calculating the value of $R1$ by giving proper weight to above mentioned 9 functions for all towns, the mean was determined. On accepting the mean as the line of demarcation, all towns having an $R1$ indices less than mean were classified as rurban centres.

Mean Centres of Rural Settlements

Using the idea of 'mean centres of population' of Hart[53], D.K. Singh and others have wrote a paper on rural settlements of Orissa which deals with the mean centres of rural settlements. Their idea about this method is as follows:

Rural settlement types and patterns give the simplest description of arrangement of settlements according to the physiography, drainage, transport and communication system. But this,

> "would not help in assessing the grouping of settlements around the centrally located important rural settlements which might help in representing the mean centre of settlements for the State as a whole in order to act as the point of diffusion for rural development innovation."

In all, 7724 rural settlements with functional centrality have been considered to find out thier mean centres at various levels dividing the whole state into 20 × 20 mile grid. The co-ordinates to the mean centre (xc, yc) have been calculated using the expression:

$$XC = \frac{\Sigma(xi\ fi)}{n}$$

$$\text{and } \bar{Y}c = \frac{\Sigma(yi\ fi)}{n}$$

where xi and yi are the coordinates of ith point in the area and 'n' is the total number of settlements in the state, while fi represents the frequency of settlements in the individual grid along the 'x' axis and 'y' axis separately. The mean centre for functionally important rural settlements of Orissa is found out to be represented by—

$$\bar{x}c = 236.3$$
$$\bar{y}c = 181.6$$

It is observed that though the coastal area and the north-western area have highest concentrations of functionally important rural settlements, the frequency for xi as well yi clearly indicate a thin representation in the centre and the arrangement of frequency depicts a bimodel concentration.[55]

Chi-Square Test

The hypothesis, that the environmental factors are also responsible for the pattern variation of settlements, is tested by Chi-square analysis[56] (Table 4.4). The calculated value (13.07) of Chi-square is greater than the tabulated value (11.07) for 5 degree of freedom but significant only at 5 per cent level and poses a weak challenge to our hypothesis. It may be inferred that the physical factors are not so strong, though important, as to influence the pattern of settlements to a great extent in the study area, but nearness to urban centre has exerted a stronger influence to the pattern of sttlement distribution. The formula for Chi-square test is as follows:

$$\text{Chi-square} = \frac{(D-E)^2}{E}$$

where *E* stands for expected number of settlements, *D* stands for number of settlements.

The degree of freedom: $n - 1 = 6 - 1 = 5$

The Table 4.4 as given will clarify the calculation of Chi-square test.

TABLE 4.4: Chi-Square Test

Sl. No.	Factors affecting Rural settlements	Observed number of settlements (*D*)	Expected number of settlements (*E*) 278/6 = 46.33	$(D-E)^2$	$\frac{(D-E)^2}{E}$
1.	Plains	48	46	4	0.80
2.	Hills	56	46	100	2.10
3.	Ravines	38	46	64	1.40
4.	Swampy Forests	58	46	144	3.10
5.	Reserved Forests	49	46	9	0.19
6.	Around Urban Centres	29	46	289	6.20
	Total Observations	278	276	610	13.07

Thus, it can be said that most of the statistics used in rural settlement geography are concerned with the formulation of types of rural settlements, spacing of settlements along with the density, size and functional hierarchy. Only some of the methods which are simpler in relation to others are presented here for the students of geography, sociology, anthropology, economics and statistics and this is not exhaustive in real sense of the term.

REFERENCES

1. J. Brunhes: *Human Geography*, New York, Rand McNally, 1952, p. 152.
2. A. Woiekof: "Le groupement de la population rurale en Russie", Annales de *Geographie*, Vol. 18, 1909 pp. 1323.
3. A. Kristofferson: *Landskapsleildens foṛan dringar i norra och ostra delen av Fars Harad*, Lund, 1924, p. 141.
4. M.A. Lefevre: *L-Habitat Rural en Belgique*, Liege, 1926, p. 114.
5. J. Bernhard: "Une Formule Pour la Cartographie de l'Habitat rural avec Application au Department de youne", *Comptes Rendu*, 1931, Vol. III, pp. 108-117.
6. A. Demongeon: "Une Carte de l'Habitat," *Annales de Geographie*. Vol. 42, 1933, pp. 225-232.
7. A. Zierhoffer: "Sur Une Formule Servant a Exprimer la Dispersion et la concentration Absolve de l'Habitat Rural", *Comptes Rendu*, 1934, Vol. III, pp. 410-41
8. S. Pawlowski: 'Encore Une Methode de Representation Cartographique Generale de l'Habitat Rural", *Comptes Rendu*, 1938, Vol. 2, pp. 129-30.
9. A.H. Debouverie: "Pour la Cartographie de l'Habitat Belgique," *Bulletin, Societe Belge de Etudes Geographeques*, Vol. 13, 1943, pp. 146-196.
10. E. Kant: *Quelque Problems Concernaut la Representation de la Densite des Habitations Rurales*, Lund Studies in Geography, Series B. No. 2, 1950, pp. 1-9.
11. J.M. Houston: *A Social Geography of Europe*. London 1961, p. 83.
12. T. Tanioka: "Differenciation Regional des Types de l'Habitat au Japan," in *Proceedings of the International Geographical Union Conference*, Tokyo, 1957, pp. 503-512.
13. K.H. Stone: "Swedish Fringes of Settlement," *Annals of the Association of American Geographers*, Vol. 52, 1962, p. 374.
14. S. Inouye: "Settlement Measurement in Japan," in *Abstracts of Papers, XX International Geographical Congress*, London, 1964, p. 308.
15. R.B. Singh: "Rural Settlement Types and their Distribution", *The National Geographical Journal of India*, Vol. XV, 1969, p. 100.
16. R. B. Mandal: *Geography of Rural Settlements in Bihar Plain*, (Unpublished Ph.D. Thesis) Patna University, Department of Geography, 1972, p. 148.
17. A. Prasad: *Chota Nagpur: Geography of Rural Settlements*, Ranchi University, 1973, pp. 314-315.
18. R. B. Mandal: *Planned Development of Rural Settlements, in North Bihar* (Unpublished Doctor of Literature Thesis) Patna University, Department of Geography, 1977, pp. 117-18.
19. P. Haggett: *Locational Analysis in Human Geography*, London, Edward Arnold, 1966, pp. 107-13.
20. G.T. Trewartha: "The Unincorporated Hamlet: One Element of the American Settlement Fabric," *Annals of the Association of American Geographers*, Vol. 33, 1943, pp. 32-81.
21. J.A. Barnes and A.H. Robinson: "A New Method for the Representation of

Dispersed Rural Population," *Geographical Review*, Vol. 30, 1940, pp. 134-137.

22. Edgar Kant: "Some Notes on the Representation of the Density of Rural habitations," *The Indian Geographical Journal*, Vol. 30, 1955, pp. 1-8.
23. E. C. Mather: "A Linear-Distance Map of Farm Population in the US.," *Annals of the Association of American Geographers*, Vol. 34, 1944, pp. 173-80.
24. R. B. Singh: "Pattern Analysis of Rural Settlement Distribution and Their types in Saran Plain: A Quantitative Approach," *National Geographical Journal of India*, Vol. 20, 1974, p. 126.
25. A.B. Mukerjee: "Spacing of Rural Settlements in Andhra Pradesh: A Spatial Interpretation," *Geographical Outlook*, Vol. VI, 1969, p. 3.
26. C. Board *et al.*, (Ed.): *Progress in Geography*, London, Edward Arnold, Vol. 2, 1970, p. 14.
27. R.S. Lall and A.N. Mehra: *A Text Book of Vector Analysis*, Lucknow, Prakashan Kendra, 1965, p. 14.
28. A.D. Bannerman: *Census of India*, 1901, part 1, Lucknow Government Press, 1902, Quoted by R.C. Sharma: *Settlement Geography of Indian Desert*, New Delhi, Kumar Brothers, 1972, p. 107.
29. P.J. Clark and F.C. Evans: "Distance to Nearest Neighbour as a Measure of Spatial Relationships on Population," *Ecology*, Vol. 35, 1954, pp. 445-453.
30. M.F. Dacey: "Order Distance in an inhomogeneous random point pattern," *Canadian Geographer*, Vol. 9, 1965, pp. 141-153.
31. P.J. Clark and F.C. Evans: *Op.cit.,*
32. H.R. Tompson: "Distribution of Distance to nth Neighbour in a Population of Randomly Distributed Individuals," *Ecology*, Vol. 37, 1956, pp. 391-94.
33. L.J. King: *Statistical Analysis in Geography*, New Jersey, Prentice Hall, 1969.
34. B. Thakur: "Nearest Neighbour Analysis as a Measure of Urban Place Patterns," *Indian Geographical Studies*, No. 1, 1973, p. 66.
35. Peter Ambrose: *Analytical Human Geography*, London, Longmans, 1969, p. 119.
36. B.P. Birch: "The Measurement of Dispersed Patterns of Settlements," *Tijdschrift voor Economische en Sociale Geographie*, Vol. 58, 1967, pp. 68-75.
37. D.A. Pinder and M.E. Witherick: "A Modification of Nearest Neighbour Analysis for use in Linear Situation," *Geography*, Vol. 60, No. 266, 1975, pp. 16-23.
38. L.J. King: *Op.cit*, p. 89.
39. M.F. Decey and T. Tung: "The Identification of Randomness in Point Patterns," *Journal of Regional Science Association*, Vol. 4, 1962, p. 85.
40. R. Bachi: "Standard Distance Measures and Related Methods for Spatial Analysis," *Papers, Regional Science Association*, Vol. 10, pp. 83-102.
41. L.J. King: *Op.cit.*, pp. 92-93.
42. A.H. Robinson: *Elements of Cartography*, (Ed. 2) New York, John, Wiley, 1964, pp. 16-23.
43. W.J. Craig: "A useful Computer Function to Measure Distance," *Professional Geographer*, Vol. XXIII, 1931, pp. 157-58.
44. K.K. Khatu: "Significance of the study of Rural Settlements in their Transitional Stages," *Indian Geographical Journal*, Vol. XLIV, No. 3-4, 1969, pp. 52-63(61).

45. R.B. Mandal: *Planned Development of Rural Settlements in North Bihar* (Unpublished Doctor of Literature Thesis) Patna University, Department of Geography, 1977, p. 204.

46. S.A. Kovalav: "Regional Peculiarities in the Dynamics of Rural Settlement in the USSR (1959-70)," *Soviet Geography*, Vol. XV, 1974, p. 5.

47. Jack P. Gibbs: *Urban Research Method*, New Delhi, 1966, p. 101.

48. J.W. Simmons: Relationships Between the Population: Density Pattern and Site of Cities, (Unpublished M.A. Thesis) University of Chicago, 1962, Quoted by B.J.L. Berry, etc.: "Urban Population Densities: Structure and Change," *Geographical Review*, Vol. 53, 1963, pp. 389-405.

49. R.R. Boyce and W.A.V. Clark: "The Concept of Shape in Geography," *Geographical Review*, Vol. 54, 1954, pp. 561-62.

50. I. Singh and V.K. Asthana: "Spatial Distribution of Rural Settlements in the Foot Hill Zone of Haryana," *Paper presented at Varanasi Symposium*, December, 1975, pp. 3-4.

51. L.J. King: *Op.cit.*, p. 103.

52. R.B. Mandal: "Rurban Centres in Bihar Plain," *Indian Geographical Studies*, No. 1, 1973, p. 16.

53. J.F. Hart: "Central Tendency in Areal Distribution," *Economic Geography*, Vol. 30, 1954, pp. 48-49.

54. W.H. Theakstona and C. Harrison: *The Analysis of Geographical Data*, London, Heinemann, 1971, p. 59.

55. D.K. Singh, B. Routary and S. Jena: "Spatial Analysis of Rural Settlement Pattern in Orissa," *Paper presented at Varanasi Symposium*, December, 1975, pp. 5-6.

56. C.R. Pathak and R. K. Dhabai: "Rural Settlement Structure of Mewar Rajasthan," I.I.T. Kharagpur, *Silver Jubilee Symposium on Rural Community Development*, April, 1976.

5

ECOLOGY OF PLANNED RURAL SETTLEMENTS

The term 'Ecology' was applied to the physical sciences of botany and zoology in their study of the relationships of plants and animals and micro organisms with their physical environment. The application of certain principles and processes of biological ecology to the field of social science gave rise to human or social ecology, a field which was first developed in America, associated with work done at Chicago. It was the use of biological analogies in the study of human populations which provided the initial impetus to the theory of human ecology. In case plant ecology, animal ecology and human ecology provide three fields, and a fourth field is general ecology. General ecology is considered as holistic, as according to W.P. Taylor," it is the study of all relations of all organisms to all their environment".[1]

There are several concepts which are derived from the ecological analogy in terms of the logical spatial expression of the ecological principles e.g. central dominance, segregation, invasion and succession.[2]

1. *The Process of Central Dominance :* It is known as the concept of gradient. The ecologists noted that analogously within the city there was a gradient of land values which declined outward from the central core and that many other social phenomena assumed this gradient form influenced by the shifting and sorting effects of land values. Income groups can be graded outward from the centre.

2. *The Process of Segregation:* It is known as the concept of natural areas. Natural areas are generally dominated by patterns of land utilization, which are moulded by transportation, industrial

organization, topography and like which are "the unplanned, natural product of settlements growth.[3] On the other hand, McKenzie viewed segregation as cultural features rather than cultural which are considered to be composed of homogeneous area of race, language, income and occupation. (Fig. 5.1) In the real senses the natural areas should be seen as small areas of homogeneity produced through the operation of competition and the segregating effects of land values. The high degree of internal homogeneity within them generally make them act as sub-systems within the larger community.

FIG. 5.1: Five Aspected Ecology of Rural Settlements

3. *The Processes of Invasion and Succession :* In the concentric zone model of Chicago by Burgess the development of land use patterns from central part of the city to outwards has been found to be accompanied by the differentiation of the successive rings of new urban growth and the invasion by different elements of the older inner rings of the city. The second zone of transition has been considered as the area of invasion of new encoming ethnic groups who found in it cheap accommodation and a lack of strict enforcement of social controls. The third zone, the zone of workingmen's homes, contained the small inexpensive farm houses of the working class. Burgess considered this a zone of second-generation settlement, which illustrates the process of successive invasion.

Ecological Relations with Economy and Rural Settlements

Recently, it has been widely realized that economic activities and human settlements are exerting, increased pressure on the life giving ecosystem. The linkage between economy, settlements and ecologic environments can be seen out of the economy through settlements (households) and back into the ecosystem. This shows the increasing pressure of economic growth and settlements on ecosystem in two ways: (a) the increasing flow of E.F. depletes the natural resource base and feeds the flows of FE and HE, (b) these two pollute the ecosystem with their waste and often toxic substances. It is now widely felt that the ability of the ecosystem to withstand these two pronged attack is limited.

The demands made upon the ecosystem by the settlements and economy are increasing for two main reasons. First, the continuing growth of world population creates new demand for shelter and productive capabilities of economies and is responsible for the environmental pollution, and widespread use of ecologically dangerous technology in order to increase agricultural production. Thus the interaction of the economy with its higher order society and ecosystem illustrates the problem posed by the environment of rural settlement system.[4]

Planned Communities

The latter stages of settlement in the U.S.A. reminds that not all patterns evolve naturally, but that some are planned before the land is settled, and their distinctive form may be derived from a pure abstract design based on a square or a circle. In Britain this is particularly true of new villages which arose during the 17th and 18th centuries, when the age of reason left its imprint on all parts of life, and the truths of a new scientific age were reflected in the symmetry of a village layout. Estate villages of this period are no longer haphazard or even orderly clusters, but a regular balanced exercise which has been more marked in Scotland and Ireland where the village was virtually absent before, rather than in England, the land of villages. In Wales the planned village is almost non-existent. But in Scotland, the settled period following the 45 rebellion saw the growth of over 150 planned villages. They were not closely related to agriculture. Many were estate villages, some tiny mill villages, some coastal villages: but all absorbed a surplus population which the land could not hold. Their pattern varies from those with a green, resembling some English villages, to some of which are very loosely knit, and which by now have all but lost their plan.

Planned communities in Ireland, particularly in the north where Scotish and English influence was so great, are more like market towns than villages: but they arose in a country where the market towns was non-existent. In a sense all new, i.e. English, settlement was planned, and its main contribution to the landscape, apart from the large country house, was the planned towns of the 17th and 18th centuries. The centre was often a square market place, sometimes out of proportion to the size of the town, or a wide street, nowhere more disproportionate than in Cookstown (Co. Tyrone), where it was based on Dublin's O'Connell Street. (But unfortunately Cookstown never grew beyond its one street). Sometimes the plan became very elaborate as in Castlewellan (Co.Down), where one 'square' is an octagon and one a circle, connected by a very broad, tree-lined street. These are impressive in spite of their small size because they are still so foreign to the landscape.

The planned community everywhere indicates new elements, the pushing forward of frontiers, whether in 18th century Ireland, 19th century Idaho or 20th century Hokkaido. It is most striking when it contrasts so markedly with indigenous village patterns. Nothing could be more different from the loose cluster of houses in a native Arab village than the Israeli village. In the earlier Jewish settlements defence was a primary consideration, and many began as desert, forts, walled and with a watch tower, in which a strongly united community worked and slept. Two basic types have emerged. The first is the co-operative village. Some of these are arranged linearly, though this is disadvantageous with growth away from the centre: and some are built on a circular pattern, the fields rediating outwards like the sun's rays, the houses, their back courtyard walls still combining to make a protective wall, facing inwards to the community centre, to the school, and to the place of worship.

The second type is the collective village or kibbuz. This is more directly related to the early fort settlements, because although they are now planned freely, with no conscious defence element, the social organisation is clearly reflected in the functions of the different parts—the living quarters, the common dining and kitchen quarters, the separate farm units, and so on. This is taken to the extreme in the children's kibbuz, which is a replica of the larger unit. So plainly may social structure be revealed in settlement form and function.[5]

Planned Development of Rural Settlements in U.S.A.

Beyond the Appalachians, and particularly beyond the Ohio, the varieties of patterns disappear settlement was no longer haphazard. But controlled by a federal government. Land was accurately surveyed before it was settled, and this produced the familiar grid pattern of the unified settlements. The basic unit was a square of 10 km., divided into 36 townships. They don't want to perpetuate its nucleated villages in westward expansion and in the south wanted dispersal. Dispersal became the general rule further west, but the pattern is often broken by the village of market towns: and even community foci like schools which have no nucleating effect. The landscape of innense fields, is broken by solitary farms with tiny clumps of shelter trees. The market towns are collecting points. In the wheat belt, for instance, they follow the railway line, are quite frequents, and monotonously alike-each with its storage silos, water tower station and single main street. On the whole the impression is of a planned rural settlements and until one sense a Hope Pueblo or a Navajo encampment in the south-west, it is easy to foreget that this landscape was peopled long before its present scene.[6]

Ideal Village

An ideal village will be so constructed as to bud itself to perfect sanitation. It will have cottages with sufficient light and ventilators built of a material readily obtainable within a radius of five kilometres of it. The cottages will have courtyards enabling householders to plant vegetables for domestic use and house their cattle. The village lanes and streets, will be free of all avoidable dust. It will have wells according to its needs and accessible to all. It will have houses of worship for all, also a common meeting place, a village, common for grazing its cattle, a co-operative dairy, primary and secondary schools in which industrial education will be the central fact and it will have panchayats for settling disputes. It will produce its own grains, vegetable and fruits and its own cotton.

The cottages in the present day village would remain what they are with slight improvements to ensure ventilation and sanitation and healthy living. Given co-operation among the people, almost the whole of the programme can be worked out at an expenditure within the means of the villages. With Government assistance, there was no limit to the possibility of village reconstruction.

Villages then would be places worth visiting and enjoying. Villages in England are models of cleanliness and stay therein for how so ever a short duration its analysis, would give an idea of return to nature, as its were.

Its mutual co-operation is assured and contribution on voluntary basis for the common good would be available. The village people under intelligent guidance can double the village income, as distinguished from individual income. There are in our villages resources for local purposes in every case, though they may not be for commercial purposes. But as matters stand, there is hopeless unmillingness on the part of the villagers to better their lot. This will have to be taken into account in any scheme drawn up for their reconstruction.[7]

Owen's Idea of Planning

Owen was the pioneer of modern 'planning'. His 'plan' for curing underemployment aimed at settling the unemployed in self-sufficient communities of about 500-1,000 people and he described in detail the buildings and services which each of these colonies would need.

This idea of small, self-sufficient colonies, which he grew used at New Lanark, because the most persistent be in Own's leonnet. He believed that people would be better off if they all worked for the common good. Owen took a great deal of trouble to get his ideas accepted. He reported to parliament, gave lectures, and spoke at meetings so crowded that several ladies fainted.

At last in 1824 he had the opportunity to found his own colony which held its property in common and worked for the common good—a kind of "communism". He brought land and property in America and took over a party of settlers who founded the colony called New Harmony. Here about nine hundred people lived according to Owen's ideas, working according to their ability, and receiving food, clothing and shelter according to their needs. New Harmony lasted as a colony for four years. It cost own forty thousand pounds. It was a failure. The odd collection of people who went there could not live together contentedly. They quarrelled and argued and refused to carry out Owen's principles. Owen failed to allow for the fact that most people prefer living dependent lives to living in a place where everything has been arranged for them. People called Owen's plan a "nursery" and a "barnacks". One newspaper advised him to "let the poor alone. The working be can always find alive".

This time people had forgotten the great things which "Mad" Robert Owen had done at New Ganark.

In Soviet Russia today, and in parts of China, we can see more advanced "Owenism" at work in the communal factories and collective farms. Some one claimed Owen as "the first intelligent capitalist"

Robert Owen was "so dazzled by the splendour of his aims" That he fathered some of the most adventurous experiments in the social history of mankind.[8]

Importance of the Village: As Administrative Unit

India is essentially a rural country. Throughout the greater part of India the village constitutes the primary territorial unit of Government and it is from the villages that the larger administrative units like tehsils, sub-divisions and districts are built up. Apart from this, the importance of the village in Indian administration has consisted in the fact that a vast majority of the Indian population—85 to 90 per cent, still lives in the villages. Since very ancient times villages have played a very prominent role in our nation's history. Until a little more than a century ago village was the only real unit of local self government in the country. Every village had a Panchayat of its own to supply the villager with all community services and to organise the village defence against any external danger. The villagers rarely expected any help from central or provincial governments. The Indian village community continued to exist in some form or other in nearly every part of India despite the world shaking and catastrophic political movements to which the Indian culture was frequently exposed, and ever since it has always served as the bed-rock and sheet anchor of India's social and economic system. It was so deep rooted that even the vississitudes in India's fortunes caused by the numerous political and religious upheavals to which this country was subjected from time to time left its not only undisturbed but full of municipal ciyour. Sir Charles Metcalfe commenting has the superim tenacity of ancient Indian village communition remarked.

"They seem to last where nothing also lasts. Dynasty after dynasty tumbles down, revolution succeeds revolution.... but the village community remains the same. The union of village communities each forming a separate state in itself which has to conceive, contributed more than any other cause to the preservation of peoples of India, through all the revolutions and changes which they have suffered and is in a high degree condueive to their happiness and to the enjoyment of a great position of freedom and independence".[9]

The fundamental characteristic of the village of the past was its self-sufficiency. All its economic needs were supplied by the efforts to its own cultivators and artisans. The village council or Panchayat was the most characteristic features of the government of a village community. Originally the number of those who formed the council were five but the number was not necessarily adhered with any regularity. The Panchayats commanded a traditional sanctity and they were entrusted with administrative and judicial work. To promote the comfort and conveniences of the people they organised all the collective effort, provided watch and ward, constructed and maintained irrigation works, arranged for the celebration of local festivals, maintained peace and order and looked after the essential needs of the local community. The principal functionaries of the village were the head man, the Patwari, the Watchman or Chowkidar, the school master and a number of artisans and traders like astrologer, smith, carpenter, potter, barbar, washerman, vaidya and its band of musicians and other artists to satisfy the higher wants of life. All these village functionaries were public servants and they served each and every member of the village community. They have customary monopoly of hereditary duties and were not remunerated in cash but were given a grant of land free of rent or shares out of common heap of grain. Later on, the establishment of the British rule gave the final death blow to the ancient village autonomy.

Conclusion

Rural settlement planning must be realistic and operational in nature following the situation and data analysis of a particular area in question, and must be oriented towards the needs of that area. Also planners require to create an atmosphere which allows people's participation, and must make sure that all organs and government parasitals who are supposed to implement must be coordinated in all sections of the plan.

Hence planning alaways involves conflict of values, clash of organized pressure groups, defence of vested interests, and the confusions may arise the interrelationship of complex decisions, at different levels at different scales and in different point of time. The use of cybernetics is a great help to the planners in coming to particular decision, but it's decisions may not always be a rational one for the villagers. Because the village is a place of face to face relationships and self-expression, and the planner should maintain this character in rural settlement planning for development.

REFERENCES

1. W.P. Taylor: *What is ecology and whât good is it?*
2. E.W. Burgess: "The Growth of the City: An Introduction to a Research Project", *American Sociological Society,* Vol. XVIII; 1924, pp. 85-97.
3. H.W. Zorbaugh: "The Natural Areas of the City" in E.W. Burgess (ed.): *The Urban Community,* Chicago, 1925, p. 222.
4. B.W. Hodder & Roger Lee: *Economic Geography;* Methuen & Co. Ltd.; London, 1974, p. 9.
5. Emrys Jones: *Human Geography,* Chatto & Windus, London; 1967.
6. Emrys Jones: *Human-Geography,* Chatto & Eindus, London.
7. Raghubir Sahai: *Panchayati Raj in India—A Study;* Kitab Mahal, Allahabad, 1968; pp. 109-10.
8. E.H. Carter: *Pioneers of the Modern World.* Arnold & Sons; London, pp. 31-33.
9. R.P. Dholakia: *Village Panchayats in Uttar Pradesh:* Friends Book Depot Allahabad, 1951; pp. 1-3.

6

THE UNITED NATIONS AND HUMAN SETTLEMENTS

The United Nations has since its inception been involved in the field of human settlements. In fact, the first post-World War II international programme in the field of human settlements had been formulated by the United Nations Reconstruction and Rehabilitation Agency (UNRRA) in 1944. When the United Nations Organization itself was established in 1945, responsibility for this sector was vested in the Economic and Social Council (ECOSOC). In 1962 a specialized ECOSOC Committee on Housing, Building and Planning was established. The Committee met annually from 1963 to 1966; since then it met every second year. Its secretariat was converted into the erstwhile UN centre for Housing, Building and Planning in 1964.

A new chapter started when the 1972 Environment Conference recommended that a United Nations Conference on Human Settlements be convened. The 1976 United Nations Conference on Human Settlements which brought together representatives of 132 nations, was one of the largest ever held by the United Nations.

Commission and Centre

In December 1977 the United Nations General Assembly decided on new institutional arrangements for international co-operation in the field of human settlements. It created a 58 member inter-governmental Commission on Human Settlements. It also established the United Nations Centre for Human Settlements (Habitat) which absorbed the former Centre for Housing, Building and Planning, the Habitat and Human Settlements Foundation and some other relevant resources.

Among the function of UNCHS (Habitat) is to serve the

Commission on Human Settlements and focal point for action, co-ordination and evaluation of human settlements activities in the United Nations system. It also assists the Commission on Human settlements in co-ordinating human settlements activities in the UN system, to keep them under review and to assess their effectiveness.

The first Executive Director of the Centre, Dr. Arcot Ramchandran –a noted Aministrator, scholar and scientist–has joined the post in October, 1978.

The Centre carries out an integrated research, technical co-operation and information programme structured into the following eight sub-programmes; (i) settlement policies and strategies; (ii) settlement planning; (iii) shelter and community services; (iv) development of the indigenous construction sector; (v) low-cost infrastructure for human settlements; (vi) land use; (vii) mobilization of finance for human settlements development; and (viii) institutions and management.

The staff of the centre comprises 103 professionals in Nairobi and in the field-among them engineers, architects, urban planners, economists, and administrators and 128 general service staff. In 1983 there were, in addition, 410 short-term consultants and technical co-operation experts serving in the field.

The Commission has met once in a year since 1978. The agenda of each session contains one or more substantive themes, in addition to such items as budgets, work programmes and other diverse subjects. The next (eighth) session of the Commission will be held in Kingston, Jamaica from 29 April to 10 May 1985. The theme selected for that session is "planning and management of human settlements, with emphasis on small and intermediate towns and local growth points."[1]

The question could be posed: why is it necessary in 1984 to draw attention to an International Year which is still three years ahead? The answer is: The programme for IYSH is different from that of other International Years. Its purpose is not only to focus world attention on human settlements problems in the Third World; it is hoped that the year will also advance practical solutions to some of these problems.

Governments are urged to establish new "demonstration projects" between now and 1987 or to select existing ones with a view to testing and showing new approaches to basic problems in urban and rural areas. Projects must be affordable and replicable–so that the new approaches can be put into practice on a large scale. The aim is to evaluate the results of these projects at the end of 1986 so that in 1987, on the basis of these experiments, new policies and strategies can be adopted for improving the shelter and neighbourhoods of the poor.

Work in Progress

The United Nations Centre for Human Settlements (UNCHS/Habitat), the United Nations body serving as lead agency for the organization of International Year of Shelter for the Homeless (IYSH), has asked all Governments to designate a national focal point to stimulate and co-ordinate a national programme for the year. Many Governments have already done so. A number of demonstration projects have also been identified, and in some countries national commissions consisting of representatives of governmental and/or non-governmental bodies have been established to prepare and execute national programmes. Plans are being made for the printing and distribution of information material; for the organization of conferences, seminars and exhibitions; for the drawing of attention to human settlements problems through radio, television and the press; for the issuing of special postage stamps and for a host of other activities to mark the occasion.

Demonstration Projects

A major element of the programme of the International Year of Shelter for the Homeless consists of demonstration projects. What are these projects about and what should they demonstrate? UNCHS/Habitat, stated that project for the International Year should test and demonstrate new approaches to basic problems in urban and rural areas, such as providing or improving shelter; providing an improved drinking water supply, sanitation and waste disposal; generating jobs in the formal and informal construction sector; improving environmental and health conditions and services; upgrading infrastructure and services for the poor including roads, public transportation, energy, and medical, social, educational and recreational facilities, and improving low-cost building techniques and materials, especially through more widespread use of indigenous methods, skills and construction materials.

In addition to projects of a physical character, the national programme and project for the International Year of Shelter for the Homeless (IYSH) should include the review and strengthening of policy, legislative, organizational and financial measures to assist the poor in improving their shelter and neighbourhoods. Areas of special concern might be legislation on land and tenure; building codes and regulations; financing-including credit and loans for shelter for the poor; and institutional arrangements within and between national and local authorities.

In order to meet the objectives for the International Year of Shelter for the Homeless, countries should take the following guidelines into account in the design, selection, implementation and monitoring of demonstration projects for the year:

(a) Projects must explore, test and demonstrate existing or new ways and means of improving the shelter and neighbourhoods of the poor and disadvantaged, particularly those below the poverty line in urban and rural settlements;

(b) Projects must contribute to or result in a clear and visible improvement in the shelter or neighbourhoods of at least some of the poor and disadvantaged before 1987;

(c) Projects must be replicable, in order to reach many more of the poor and disadvantaged, leading to affordable improvements for many rather than major improvements for a few; and

(d) Projects must seek a practical balance between what is desirable (in terms, for example, of basic health requirements and structural safety), attainable (technically and administratively, and using local skills, methods and materials), and affordable by the poor themselves and the nation as a whole.

Global Strategy for Shelter

The United Nations centre for Human settlements formed Commission on Human settlements".[2] In its Twelfth session held at Cartagena in Columbia in 1989 discussed on "Global strategy for Shelter". The achievement of the session was acceptance by the governments of the various elements of Global strategy for shelter to the year 2000 as the appropriate framework for formulating national shelter policies and actions. The strategy's emphasize of a most suitable and effective framework for promoting the provision of shelter, infrastructure and services as a contribution towards achieving social and economic development in an environmentally sound and sustainable manner. In this approach, the governments, rather than directly becoming providers of shelter, will provide a legal, institutional and regulatory environment to encourage people themselves to build and improve their homes. Each contributor's in the human settlements sector should be mobilized central and local governments, the private sector—both formal and informal, community groups non-governmental organizations, families and individually seeking to improve their settlement conditions.

The World Habitat Day 1988 has been dedicated to millions of urban and rural poor living in slums, shanty towns and scattered rural settlements of the developing world who inspite of their limited means and odds are building and improving their homes, neighbourhoods and communities through their collective efforts so as to provide the basic sustenance of life and a roof for themselves and their children.

In this context the theme chosen for the occasion of the world Habitat Day is "Shelter and community". The attention of the international community, national governments, aid agencies, non-governmental organizations, builders, planners and policy-makers, and all those concerned with shelter and the amelioration of human settlements is focused on the urgency of supporting with all the means at their disposal along with collective self help efforts of the poor's around the world.

Such an effort is essential due to gravity of the shelter situation in the world. In International Year of Shelter for the Homeless (1987) has provided proof of the concern of the world community for the millions of human beings who have no shelter nor they have an environment suitable for nourishing and sustaining family life.

In constructing a semblance, the poors have shown their creativity and ingenuity, their willingness to engage in all forms of self-help and mutual assistance according to their capacity and skills. Now the government should help people especially the low income communities to construct their homes and to work with government in the planning and improvement of their neighbourhoods.

Access to Land

For poors the lack of access to land and the absence of security of land tenure are the most fundamental obstacles to community building in developing countries. It has been demonstrated time and again that nothing stimulates community shelter construction and improvement and the community cannot be evicted from the sites they are occupying especially the squatter settlements of developing countries. It requires flexibility of national authorities as well as innovation in the types of approaches to be used for the squatter settlements which vary from location to location. In case there is good will the needs of the squatters may be reconciled with the land they occupy, the obligation of the government to ensure peace and the land sharing problems.

Accelerated Pace of Community Construction

It covers the provision of community construction, greater access to building materials and at cost affordable to low income groups. The poors may be given seed capital and technical assistance to stimulate the production of low cost indigenous building materials by the rural poor themselves organized in the form of cooperatives and associations for the purpose. Such an approach would not only serve to promote the building and construction of shelter and basic infrastructure facilities in the slums, shanty towns and rural settlement but it would generate employment and income and contribute to the economic viability and social cohesiveness of these communities. In order to facilitate such efforts the governments should also revise building codes and standards to allow for the use of indigenous building materials and activities of the poor fall within acceptable norms.[3]

Provision of Finance

For the construction of shelter the assistance from the government should percolate to the poorest sections of the community. To ensure finance the poors should be given loans, employment and subsidy to construct houses. The government should promote community based financial institutions which can capture the small scale savings of low income groups. The purpose of such a policy is to make these institutions viable and self-sustaining so that they can constantly support the construction of shelter and community improvement activities of small builders. These may be self-help groups or individual family. Now there is a need to turn these financial projects into national programmes and policies for the improvement of rural settlements.

Shelter Construction and Neighbourhood Improvement

For the rural communities the construction of shelter requires an institutional framework capable of supporting and sustaining the process. The attitude and responses of the government are not satisfactory for the present due to indifference and incompetence. The poor should redress and contribute substantially in the construction of better village communities. There is a need for training programmes to assist physical conditions of life and planning the village community as a whole.

Starting with the Ideal and Aiming for the Impossible

For over three decades, central governments in developing countries have been aware of growing shortages of adequate shelter particularly in rural areas. The increasing urbanism is the most powerful social and economic trend in the developing world which curtail the flow of rural poor to cities by large-scale rural development programmes to reduce the "push factors". In most developing countries of the world the governments ignored the housing needs of the society and hence illegal construction of shelter developed in the form of slums and squatter settlements. In some pockets the governments have started low income group housing in terms of not loosing the standards of houses in comparison with developed countries of the world. In most countries of the world, these projects are extremely limited in scale and proved incapable of making any significant impact on the long ques of people waiting for better housing opportunities e.g. low income, middle income and sometimes even higher income groups. In reality the beneficiaries are not taken into account following by the corruption, panefficiency of the project staff along with the massive expenditure did not made any significant impact in terms of providing shelter to the poor. Hence, the cost recovery goals and national debts have nullified the ambitious housing schemes and this has stem the tide of homelessness thereby increasing slums and squatter settlements in villages and towns which are striving for modernity.[4]

Habitat International Council

Habitat International Council (HIC) is the successor of the committee which organized the non-governmental Habitat forum on the occasion of the United Nations conference on Human Settlements in Vancouver, 1975. Its present board consists of the representatives of the following organizations:

1. Afro-Asian Housing Organization;
2. Austrialian Institute of Urban Studies;
3. Commonwelath Human Ecology Council;

4. Housing Research and Development Unit, University of Nairobi;
5. International Council of Building Research and Documentation;
6. International Cooperative Alliance;
7. International Institute for Environment and Development;
8. International New Towns Association;
9. International Real Estate Federation;
10. International Rural Housing Association;
11. International Union of Architects;
12. International Union of Local Authorities;
13. Mazingira Institute;
14. Postgraduate Centre for Human Settlement, Katholieke Universitiet Leuven;
15. Town and Country Planning Association; and
16. United Towns Organization.

The activities of the Habitat International Council are as follows:

It promotes and exchanges the ideas on housing, land and other human settlement problems, policies, and activities among non-governmental organizations and United Nations bodies. It also stimulates public awareness for increased support regarding human settlement programmes through contribution of research papers, holding international conferences and by publishing NGO News.

SINA Newsletter

Settlement Information Network in Africa, (SINA) Mazingira Institute, Kenya publishes bi-annual newsletter about the activities of scientists and the government of Africa regarding their actions and reactions concerning human settlements. Under its auspices various seminars, symposiums and training camps have been organized on self-help basis for the better arrangement of settlements, alleviate housing shortage, improvement in sanitation besides site and service schemes, and community participation. In 1982 "Shelter-Afrique" has been established in Nairobi by 23 African countries with the hope to assist member governments through financial and technical support, to formulate and implement housing policies to beneift appropriate target groups.

SINA links together people working on community based self-help projects in the Africa region to consolidate and disseminate the experience gained in the region.

Newsletter No. 7, January 1985, was the first to carry the description which is still on the masthead: "This network is for people working on self-help settlements projects in Africa. This doesn't just mean self-help building, but also the other kinds of community and individual self-help, including education, health, nutrition, skillful training, employment projects, community organizing and so on."

Members define themselves into the group and there is no screening. SINA has no elected officials or formal structures. It does not act politically because it has no mandate although it promotes the role of communities, NGOs and women. It has also disseminated information on global compaigns for housing rights, and the struggles for justice in Namibia and South Africa.

International Year of Shelter for the Homeless (1987)

The General Assembly of the United Nations proclaimed 1987 as the International Year of Shelter for the Homeless (IYSH) with the help of governments and non-governmental organizations (NGO's) to achieve this objective. It is essential as the problem of shelter is increasing for the world Community and it affects the daily lives of hundreds of millions of people who suffer from inhuman housing and living conditions.

The problem of providing low income group with adequate shelter and basic services has been easily solved in industrialized countries. But in the Third World it is of such intensity and dimensions that it deserves a much higher priority on the international agenda. The magnitude of the problem can be illustrated by the fact that in most large cities in the Third World 40 per cent or more population live in slums or squatter settlements. Due to the lack of safe drinking water, sanitation and other facilities, living conditions in the rural areas are usually not so congenial for human living. Altogether it is estimated that more than one billion (1,000,000,000) people in the Third World are deprived of the basic right to adequate shelter.

REFERENCES

1. Arcot Ramchandran; *Habitat News,* United Nations Centre for Human Settlements, Vol. 14, No. 2, August, 1992.
2. *Habitat News,* United Nations Centre for Human Settlements, Vol. 11, No. 2, 1989, pp. 10-11.
3. SINA *News Letter,* No. 28, October, 1992.
4. *NGO News on Human Settlements,* No. 2, 1984, p. 2.

7

GEOGRAPHICAL INFORMATION SYSTEM (GIS) AND RURAL SETTLEMENTS

Recently, it has been studied that the combined use of geographical information system with digital image processing and simulation models can provide a new tool for better environmental monitoring in rural settlements besides the management of rural development within shortest possible time. The use of GIS in temporal perspective could develop forecasting model and provide an optimization model in order to achieve effective rural settlement policy in years to come.

Geographical Information System is an integrated data base which contains spatial information about different levels of observations.[1] GIS is emerging as a powerful tool for integrating each land-based data of diverse types in the field of rural settlement studies, environmental situations and natural resource management. The use of GIS is to harmonise the available information from various sources i.e. field work, aerial photographs and satellite imageries with existing data sets along with maps so that the resultant synthesis becomes compatible with the National/Global Data Base Management system. GIS has the capacity to integrate and analyse all these techniques and information available from geo-sciences. There is a need to give emphasis on spatio-temporal data which should clearly specify the three aspects of rural ecosystem modelling:

1. Where each feature of rural settlement is located in the geographic space?
2. What are the characteristics of each feature of rural settlements? and
3. What are the features of rural settlements and their spatial relationship to other features on the map?

Review of Literature

Donald C. Dahmann (1992) in his paper on Geographic Entities to Represent the US Settlement system suggests that the quantity and quality of information available to represent the geographic dimension of human settlement in increasing dramatically. New data sources and advances in computer technology have conveyed us from a period of data non-availability to one characterized by over-abundance. Requirements for handling and analyzing the current quantities of place-specific geographic information have led to the development of increasingly sophisticated geographic and land information systems (GISs and LISs) to meet user needs.

Changes in the ability to effectively handle the mushrooming quantity to geographic information on human settlements have been accompanied by change in the orientation of social science towards in corporating the settlement context into research. Changes in effectively handling and analyzing geographic information have resulted from inquiries into the inherent properties and structures of geographic information, the modifiable areal unit problem, effect of scale on spatial units, aggregation of spatial units, effects of spatial autocorrelation, and similar issues. Changes in what is variously termed multi-level, contextual, or structural research within the social sciences have led to a renewed emphasis on understanding the roles of geographic setting which performs as mediating contexts between individuals and social-economic-cultural systems.

Several methodological issues of importance for the effective analysis of the geographic dimension of settlement are still little investigated. These include the selection and delineation of geographic entities to represent aspects of settlement, which is related to an even more basic question. This geographic units of analysis be constructed independently of specific research contexts, as is done when geographic data are arrayed in grids, or should they depend upon, and indeed to derived from, the substantive research context?

The selection and delineation of appropriate substantive geographic entities to depict human settlement is crucial for the success of empirical investigations. It also obviates the need for solutions to many of the geographic methodological issues related to the handling and selection of data from GISs.

D.C. Dahmann (1992) develops a general set of empirically or substantively—based (as opposed to place or grid based) geographic entities for depicting the US settlement system. It discusses the empirical under-pinnings of a set of entities derived from contemporary geographic research, and then reviews the availability of statistical areas to represent them as units of analysis. The set of geographic entities choses to represent components of the national settlement system which are residence or home based, and range in scale from the dwelling unit to macro-scaled supra-national regions.

Units of analysis available to represent settlement areas such as metropolitan and non-metropolitan settlements are explored more fully. Categorizations of counties representing nucleated and dispersed forms of settlement areas are reviewed, and a set of attributes for the categorization of settlement areas is presented. Dahmann (1992) concludes by discussing the ability of existing statistical units to represent the geographic entities of human settlements in the United States, and by raising the question of the appropriateness of this set to represent the settlement dimension of other countries as well.

Operational Methods of Geographical Information System

The GIS may be of Raster type or vector type. Raster scanning provides a review of some important recent developments on mass automatic digitizing efforts and the dual process of converting between raster and vector format. The coverage of area depends upon computer compatible tape. The methods of study could be of four types such as[2]:

1. *Over Lay*

The arrangement of one map over the other landscape feature map is known as overlay which follows the path of ceive method.

2. *Matrix*

In matrix the relationship of one data with the other is shown in a Tabular form;

Land cover	Forest	No Forest
Forest	Forested	Partly Forested
No-forest	Party Forested	Afforestation Needed

3. *Index*

The Index may be of two types: (a) the Main index and (b) An Auxiliary index. In the main index a regular title structure base map will be equivalent to the smallest map size that is frequently used as the basis for data collection and data upgrading.

An auxiliary index is one or more indexing which will be prepared as per need with the tiles defined by the boundaries of the 'Land Units' which represent the user's spatial view of the data.

4. *Buffer Zone Creator*

In this method we keep data and the map of different items separately in computer and the investigator may recall them as per his requirements.

This could be possible with the computer software such as : DOS, IDRISI, ERDAS, ARCINFO and the Map.

With the help of these software one has to open file in the computer for :

1. Administrative Division
2. Soil Types
3. Rainfall
4. Slope category
5. Skyline of the houses
6. Areal extent of the village and others as desired.

In the form of matrix one can show this for settlement and non-settlement as :

1991-2001	Settlement	Non-Settlement
Settlement	Settlement Area	Establishment of Settlement
Non-Settlement	Decline of Settlement	No. Settlement

In order to show in the form of Map we have to divide the whole study area into squares as small segments and then we have to put figures in each squares for each parameters to be considered for analysis. In this way, we can prepare maps for different variables separately or taken together of different variables. (Fig. 7.1) This is the benefit of Geographical information system, generally which we could not do in thematic mapping.

FIG. 7.1: An example of Line Printer Map Output

On the basis of GIS the rural settlement regions found in India are tentatively as follows:

Major Geosystems of Differentiated Rural Settlements in India

1. Himalayan Mountain
2. Thar Desert
3. Indo-Gangetic Belt
4. Deccan Plateau
5. Malabar Coastal Tract

6. Coromandel Coastal Tract
7. North-Eastern Rainfed Tract
8. Laccadive Islands
9. Andaman and Nicobar Islands
10. Delta Areas.

These rural settlement regions have been chalked out on the basis of parameters of rural settlements e.g. landscape feature, climatic conditions, size of settlement and functional linkages of rural settlements.

Application of GIS in Rural Settlement

Geocoding of information about rural settlement is the digital representation as geographical information. Here two methods of GIS mapping has been introduced which underlie many of the Geographic Information Systems (GIS) available for microcomputers spatial data processing and computer mapping.

Human settlements planning requires spatial information, especially for land-use and physical planning exercises. The use of maps to display and analyse spatial information which will certainly change with the use of intensive way of micro-computer

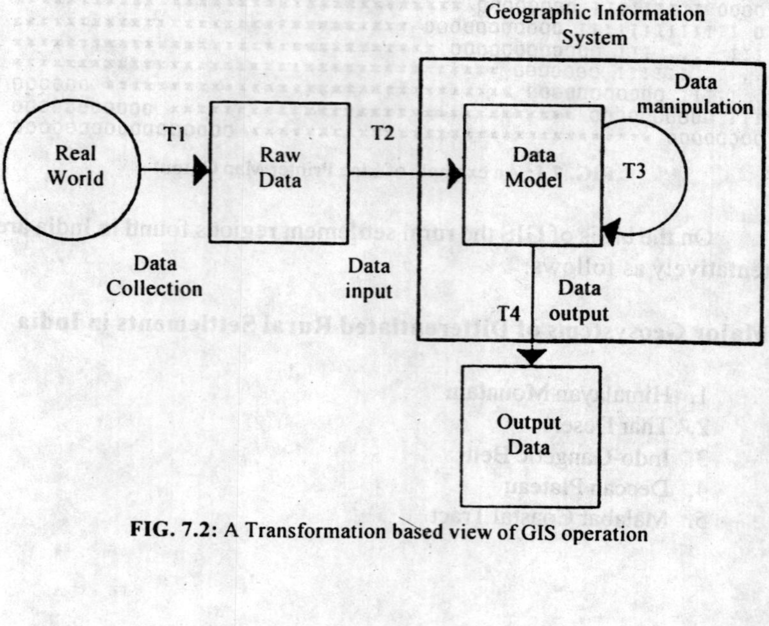

FIG. 7.2: A Transformation based view of GIS operation

cartographically hand drawn maps are less important with the growing importance of availability of low-cost computers with powerful graphic capabilities. Indeed, many land-use plans, land suitability, studies, and the resulting presentation drawings can be prepared using standard lowcost micro-computer software equipment and programme. (Fig. 7.2)

Although the impact of micro-computers on traditional mapping methods is uncertain, their use for storing, analysing and displaying spatial information is growing. This edition of macro/micro discusses two basic GIS methods: VECTOR systems, and GRID systems.[4]

Vector systems usually store information based on Cartesian . . . co-ordinates. Because the data are recorded in numeric form, vector systems rely heavily on matrix algebra and geometry: the location of each map element is recalculated every time the map is used. (Fig. 7.3)

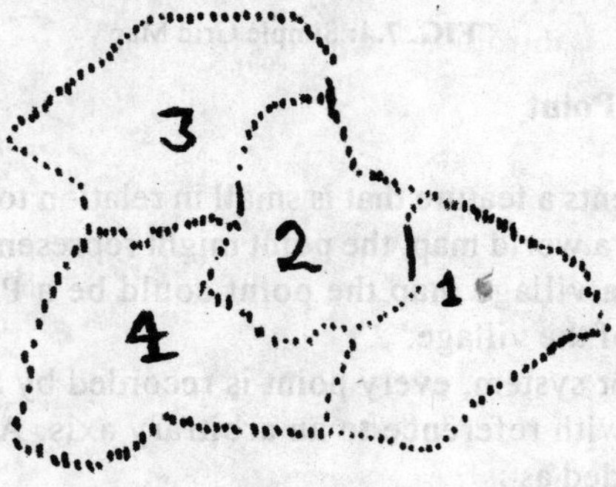

FIG. 7.3: Sample Vector Map

Grid systems often store information as a list of 'string' of characters, in which each character represents a real location. The locations are defined by a regular grid overlaid on the mapped area. Each feature to be mapped is assigned a unique character or symbol. (Fig. 7.4)

Most Spatial features can be divided into three classes:

(i) Point locations,
(ii) Linear entities, and
(iii) Areas of polygons

```
      3333333333
    333333333333
  333333333333332222
3333333333333222222
    33333333222222
    333333332222222222111
    44 344444222222222111111
   44444444222222222211111111
  444444444222222222111111111
4444444444444444111111111111
4444444444444444111111111
444444444444444111111 1
444444          1111
```

FIG. 7.4: Simple Grid Map

How to Map a Point

A point represents a feature that is small in relation to the overall scale of the map. On a world map, the point might represent a capital city or an island. On a village map the point could be a Panchayat hall or Central Point of the village.

In a vector system, every point is recorded by a pair of *X* and *Y* co-ordinates, with reference to an arbitrary axis. A series of points might be recorded as :

Point Number	*(X)* Co-ordinate	*(Y)* Co-ordinate
1	5.2	2.0
2	3.0	4.0
3	2.0	1.3

The co-ordinates can be stored electronically, manipulated by a computer program, and mapped to a printer, plotter, or video display.

In a grid system, a point-feature is recorded by changing the symbol representing the cell in which the feature is found.

How to Record a Line

Roads, pipelines and political boundaries are examples of linear

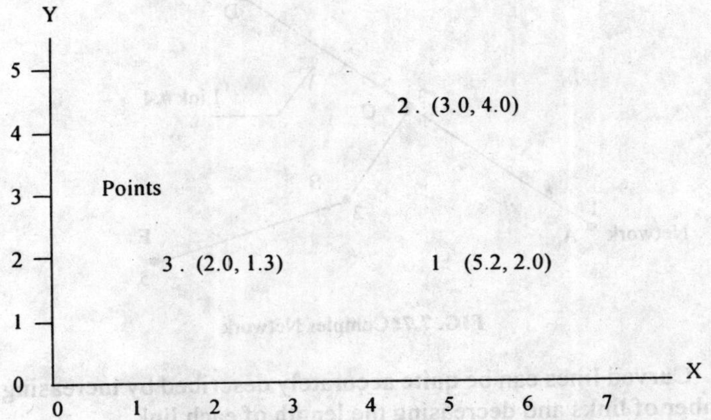

FIG. 7.5: Scatter Diagram Showing Location of Points

```
0 0 0 0 0 0 0 0 0 0 0 0 0 0 0
0 0 0 0 0 0 0 0 0 0 0 0 0 0 0
0 0 0 0 0 0 * 0 0 0 0 0 0 0 0
0 0 0 0 0 0 0 0 0 0 0 0 0 0 0
0 0 0 0 0 0 0 0 0 0 0 0 0 0 0
0 0 0 0 * 0 0 0 0 0 0 0 0 0 0
0 0 0 0 0 0 0 0 0 0 0 * 0 0 0
0 0 0 0 0 0 0 0 0 0 0 0 0 0 0
```

FIG. 7.6: Schools are shown by the* symbol. The map can be stored in the same way as text created on a word processor.

features. In a vector system each line segment or 'link' is recorded as the straight line connecting two points. Thus each link is defined by two end-points, which are recorded as discussed above. A complex network (Fig. 7.7) is composed of many such links. For example:

Link Number	Start Point	End Point
1	1	3
2	2	3
3	2	5
4	3	4

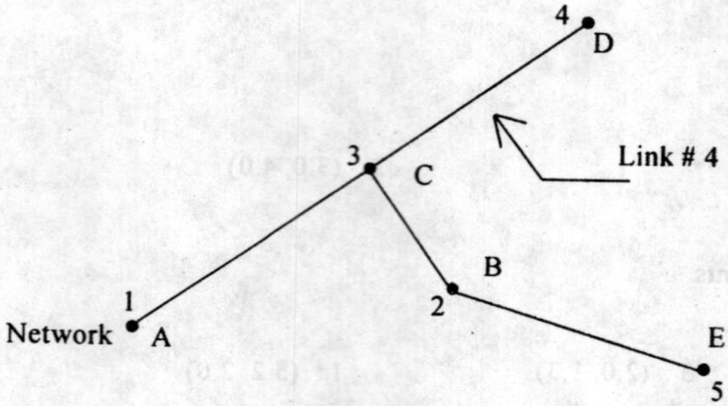

FIG. 7.7: Comples Network

Curved lines can be quite accurately described by increasing the number of links and decreasing the length of each link.

In a grid system, the character in each cell indicates the presence or absence of a linear feature. A road network could be shown as : (Fig. 7.8)

How to Geocode an Area

Most GIS use the word "polygon" to refer to any area or region. For example, political subdivisions, soil classes, or vegetation zones are mapped as polygons.

In the simplest vector systems, a polygon is a set of links (as described above) forming a closed figure. A polygon with seven sides could be defined:

```
0000+0000000000
00000+000000000
000000+++000000
000000000+00000
0000000000++---
0000*0000+00000
0000000++000000
000000+00000000
```

FIG. 7.8 : Where + indicates the presence of a paved road; and — shows the presence of an unpaved road.

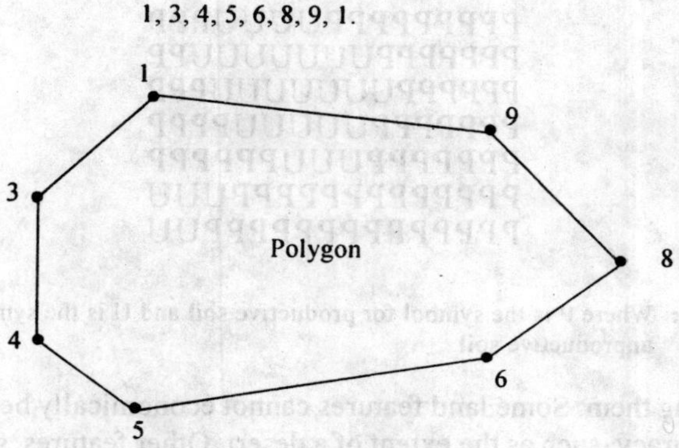

FIG. 7.9: Closed System of Polygon

In a grid system, the cells describe each polygon by carrying an appropriate symbol. For example, a simple soil map:

Comparison

Grid-based geographic information systems are usually simpler to understand, an advantage when the computer programs are written or modified.

Though they require a better understanding of algebra and co-ordinate geometry, vector-based systems are more efficient when highly accurate maps or measurements are required.

Because the grid itself is a consistent framework for all maps in the GIS, grid systems are better suited to operations involving the comparison of land areas. Grid systems can easily simulate traditional overlay mapping techniques, since logical operations (e.g. finding where two areas or features intersect or cross-tabulating many land characteristics) are easily carried out. Furthermore, analyses which depend on recognizing spatial patterns may be easier using a grid system.

Efficiency and precision in calculating links are strengths of vector-based GIS, giving them the advantage for network analyses such as finding the shortest paths through networks such as roads or pipelines.

Finally, although neither method of geocoding is inherently more accurate, the quantity and resolution of data must be considered when

```
PPPPPPPPPUUUUPPP
PPPPPPPUUUUUUUPP
PPPPPPUUUUUUUPPP
PPPPPPPUUUUUPPPP
PPPPPPPUUUPPPPPP
PPPPPPPPPPPPPUUU
PPPPPPPPPPPPPPUU
```

FIG. 7.10 : Where P is the symbol for productive soil and U is the symbol for unproductive soil.

comparing them. Some land features cannot economically be measured with accuracy, such as the extent of a desert. Other features, such as the border between two vegetation zones, which are difficult to define, and there is no advantage to using very precise tools, such as vector-based GIS, to map them. However, some features must be precisely located and require an accurate map; property boundaries and rights-off-way.

Under the auspices of UNCHS in August 1986, 22 human settlements planning professionals met at the Asian Institute of Technology near Bangkok to attend a workshop entitled "Microcomputer Applications to Human Settlements Planning and Management". The two week workshop was convened jointly the AIT and UNCHS (Habitat), Nairobi, Kenya.

Of the 15 observers, five from the ESCAP/UNCHS Joint Unit on Human Settlements (Bangkok) took part on rotational basis in the workshop hosted by Asian Institute.

The purpose of the Workshop was to expose planners and managers from various human settlements agencies throughout the Southeast Asia to the potentials of microcomputer applications. They were to receive an introduction to, and preliminary training in the use of, micro-computers and their applications to human settlements planning–so that on their return, they could apply their newly acquired knowledge to their jobs and help formulate plans for their agencies to make more effective use of computer technology.

The six workshop leaders included two experts from UNCHS (Habitat), three from the Human settlements division of AIT, and one from the ESCAP/UNCHS Joint Unit on Human Settlements.

The workshop covered eight aspects of microcomputers and their applications to human settlements planning and management, including:

(i) Introduction to microcomputers in planning.
(ii) Spread sheets
(iii) Database management
(iv) Mapping and computer-aided design,
(v) Computer programming,
(vi) Geographic information systems,
(vii) Planning models, and
(viii) Implementation guidelines.

The workshop made use of eight IBN PCs and four sharp PC 7000 micro-computers, each of which was used a team of two participants. The majority of working sessions emphasized hands-on, practical experimentation with the micro-computers and software packages, additional resources available to the trainees included a daily video presentation, a workshop manual containing original and reprinted articles, and a library of appropriate reference materials.

In their concluding assessment of the Workshop, participants concurred that they would be able to transfer knowledge gained to their fellow planners who were unable to attend, and to apply new techniques in the workplace. They also noted, however, that the increasing use of microcomputers in human settlements planning agencies will foster the demand for additional workshops and institutional training programmes to assure that planners are equipped to take advantage of rapid advances in microcomputing.

Finally, it was widely agreed that planning professionals in Southeast Asia would benefit from the formation of a 'Microcomputer Users Group' through which they might share new techniques and insights on the application of microcomputer technology in human settlements planning and management institutions. The Users Group would serve as a forum for co-operation and communication amongst micro-computer users and would thus raise the base of theoretical and practical knowledge underlying the exciting changes which micro-computers are bringing to human settlements planning and management.

Microcomputer Software for Planning Rural Settlements and Public Services

The benefit of microcomputers compared to minicomputers and mainframes is the availability of ready-made software. There are thousands of programmes already written which runs of standard microcomputers in comparison with the dozens which are available for the bigger machines.

Microcomputer software is relevant to human settlements analysis is typically of two types. It is either a generic package (such as a word processor or a spreadsheet) that can be applied to human settlements, or it is a more specialized program meant specifically for human settlements planning and management.

Microcomputer software is still relatively rare. UNCHS (Habitat) Nairobi Kenya has accordingly acted to encourage its development. One result of this policy is the development of Urban Data Management Software (UDMS), now available in Version 5.2.

The purpose of GIS is to help planners, decide where best to locate public facilities such as schools, hospitals, mosques or markets. This public-facilities location program integrates two widely known analytical techniques: the Guttman Scalogram and the Accessibility/ Centrality Index developed by Prof. Dennis Rondineli.

The results of the analysis are then "mapped" using contour lines (isopleths) or shading (choropleths) to provide a graphic picture of the spatial distribution of different levels of access to public facilities. These maps can also be overlaid with information on population centres (villages, towns, neighbourhoods, etc.) and transportation or communication links (roads, bus services, etc.) to provide a complete picture of access to those facilities.

The development of such a programme represents a marriage of some of the more sophisticated techniques of geography and regional economics to the increasing capabilities of microcomputers. Owing to the practical limitations of manual computation, complex decision-making techniques have been difficult to apply beyond research and educational contexts. Thanks to microcomputers, however, the techniques of central place theory can be put into the hands of planners and policy-makers at local and national levels.

Preliminary versions of the package have already been fieldtested in Indonesia (1985) and the Philippines (1986), where it was found useful in several different applications. The package has a throughly "user friendly" interface so that it can be used by ordinary professional people without specialised computer training or support.

More specifically, the programme allows planners and policy-makers to identify and evaluate a wide range of investment options on a "what if" basis. For example, the programme can provide answers to such questions as:

1. Given the present distribution of facilities and infrastructure, which locations are served best and which are least well served?
2. What would be the effect on public access of investment in new facilities (such as a school or hospital) compared to investment in infrastructure (such as improved roads or better public transport)? In order to maximize these effects, how should this investment be distributed spatially?
3. What would be the relative effect of investment in new facilities versus the same investment in better infrastructure in terms of making services more accessible to people living in certain target settlement areas?
4. How sensitive is public access to increased investment? In other words, will anticipated levels of investment (whether in facilities or infrastructure) have any significant effect on access to services?

Microcomputers can provide precise answers to questions like these–subject of course, to the techniques and the data being used. As one of the program's authors has explained.

Taking the case of central facilities such as markets, secondary schools or health centres, an assessment of existing conditions requires a planning tool which would clearly show the respective catchment areas and the underserviced areas. A well founded planning response to such a situation would be expected to point out locations for viable new markets, schools or health centres, or alternatively it may show how the transport and road network can be improved in such a way that the existing facilities can be better utilized by wider catchment areas.

The programme works by analyzing the physical location of facilities in relation to three factors.

(1) The spatial distribution of population,
(2) The relative influence or attraction that population centres exert over their surrounding populations, and
(3) The nature and capacity of transportation and communication systems.

By providing a sound and consistent framework for relating the location of public facilities to their accessibility, the program allows planners and policy-makers to assess current service levels, to simulate the impact of alternative investment plans, and to display the results graphically.

The sample printout shows how access to a particular service is distributed spatially in relation to the location of different population centres. The small squares indicate the location of individual human settlements and the various intensities of shading reflect different levels of access to the service. Thus the attached map shows how accessibility in a relatively well-serviced area (shown in white) gradually declines for settlements located further to the east or west. A tool such as the program described here gives planners and decision-makers compelling evidence of how to improve access to public facilities in the most effective way–and to make sure that maximum benefit is derived from spending public funds.

Conclusions

Digital geocoding or GIS introduces some interesting new elements to map-making and to human settlements planning. Once a map on paper is drawn, the relative arrangement of features is fixed, and the map is not redrawn. Permanence is thus an important physical property of traditional maps. In contrast, a digital map is redrawn over and over again: Whenever needed, the map must be recreated from its electronic description. In fact, the location of the data on the storage device bears no relationship to the location of features on the map.

Moreover, the data is quite likely to be stored in different places and different sequences every time and it could be reproduced anytime without any hindrance with ample quantity and proficiency as well.

Although the growing power of microcomputers make possible GIS that combine vector and grid methodologies, many landuse and physical-planning exercises can be performed using simple tools. There are several GIS software packages in the public domain (e.g. UDMS from UNCHS (habitat), allowing microcomputer users to experiment with different GIS methodologies at low cost geographical mapping.

The 'best' GIS is one which does the job, through experience with other kinds of software which shows that every user approaches the job differently. Thus there are literally hundreds of commercial software packages all designed for the same jobs.

Every geocoding method has strenths and weaknesses, and there are many methods in addition to the two presented here. Facing such a wide choice, how can the user choose a suitable geographic information system? Start with the basics, it is not difficult one should try over it.

Rural settlements environmental monitoring and forecasting for diverse geographical areas have now become information intensive geographical research field. Besides analysis of the existing regional status, data bases help in formulating strategies to cope with problems and formulation of action plans for utilizing development potentials. This type of data base would enable geographers to make prediction for the future.

The GIS has opened new possibilities of data coverage, storage and treatment. Now, even the geographers are interested to integrate GIS for national, regional and microlevel rural settlement planning and management. Micro-level integrated rural settlement planning establishes close linkages between resource potentialities of the rural settlements with the environmental situations for forecasting disasters. GIS is a computer based system which allows the capture, retrieval, editing, output and analysis of information regarding environmental situations of rural settlements for which the country may be divided into different administrative units which may be geographic in perspective and tabular in form:

> The GIS could be considered useful to qualify the sensibility of land to degrade and implement land and rural settlement management strategy. The GIS provides detailed information on specific locations and quantification of critical trouble spots. It will also help rural settlement planners, resource managers and environmental management experts to assign priority to future land and rural settlement development efforts. At the end, this will provide ground for appropriate rural settlement planning in order to achieve sustainable regional development.

QUESTIONNAIRE

Microcomputer Applications to Human Settlements Planning and Development

Answer Questions (1) Through (7) Using the Table below. Each column corresponds to one question and numbered. Please mark answers with an X.

1. In column (1) mark the tasks which were first implemented at the time the microcomputer system was installed.
2. In column (2) mark the tasks for which microcomputers are being used in your agency or office.
3. In column (3) mark the additional new tasks for which your agency or office intends to use microcomputers during the next two years.
4. In column (4) mark the tasks for which commercially available software packages have been purchased by your agency or office.
5. In column (5) mark the tasks for which your agency or office has developed or plans to develop software.
6. In column (6) mark the aspects of human settlements development work in which you believe current microcomputer technology is most useful (whether or not you are at present applying this technology).
7. In Column (7) mark the tasks for which you feel there is a lack of useful microcomputer software available.

	(1)	(2)	(3)	(4)	(5)	(6)	(7)
(a) Database Management							
(b) Electronic Spreadsheet							
(c) Word Processing							
(d) Statistics/Trend Analysis							
(e) Computer Graphics							
(f) Mapping							
(g) Telecommunications							
(h) Remote Sensing Analysis							
(i) Land-use Planning							
(j) Computer-Aided Design							
(k) Project Planning							
(l) Project Monitoring							
(m) Other (specify)							

8. How long have microcomputers been in operation in your agency or office? ------------ years --------- months.
9. In your agency or office are Microcomputers:

   ( ) Decentralized ( ) Accessible to all Staff as users

   ( ) Centralized ( ) Operated by specialized staff only.

   ( ) Both of above ( ) Both of above
10. Please indicate the specifications of the microcomputer system.

Fill in below how many of each type of equipment are in operation.

RAM Memory in System	*Storage Devices*	*Communications*
( ) 64 K or less	( ) 5-1/4-inch floppy	( ) Network with in office or agency
( ) 128 K	( ) 8-inch floppy	( ) Network outside office or agency
( ) 256 K	( ) Hard Disk	( ) Modem
( ) 512 K or more	( ) Other:–	

Operating System	*Printer*	*Input*
( ) CP/M-80	( ) Dot-Matrix	( ) Card Reader
( ) CP/M-86	( ) Daisy-Wheel	( ) Tape Reader
( ) MS or PC-DOS	( ) Ink-Jet	( ) Digitizer
( ) Unix or Similar	( ) Plotter	( ) Light Pen
( ) Other:–	( ) Other:–	( ) Other:–

11. Describe the Agency or office in which these microcomputers are being used (check as many boxes as needed to provide a full description).

(a) Field of work of the agency or office:

( ) Urban/Regional Planning	( ) Economic Planning/ Development
( ) Housing	( ) Social Planning/ Development
( ) Building/Public Works	( ) Environment
( ) Transportation	( ) Other:–

(b) Type/Authority of the Agency or Office:

( ) Government/Public	( ) Private
( ) Parastatal	( ) University/Training
( ) Non-Governmental Organization	( ) Research organization
( ) Inter-government	( ) Other:–

(c) Jurisdiction of the Agency or Office:

( ) Global	( ) Regional (Sub-national)
( ) Regional (Multi-national)	( ) Local
( ) National	( ) Others :–

12. Any comments or information you may wish to supply in addition to this questionnaire will be greatly appreciated.

Your Name: -------------------------------- Job Title: -------------------------
Address : ---
Initial here ------------------------ if you wish your name and address to be included in a directory of human settlements planners and managers who use microcomputers. The directory will be circulated only to other users on the list.

REFERENCES

1. David Martin, *Geographic Information Systems and Their Socio-Economic Applications;* Routledge, London, 1990.
2. I. Backen and C. Webster, Towards a Typology of Geographical Information on System; *International Journal of GIS,* Vol. 3, No. 2, 1989, pp. 137-152.
3. G.P. Crossman; An Operational Objective Analysis System, *Monthly Weather Review;* 87, 10, 1959 pp. 367-74.
4. Habitat News, *United Nations Centre for Human Settlements,* Vol. 8, No. 3, 1986.

8

EMINENT CONTRIBUTORS IN THE FIELD OF RURAL SETTLEMENT

Many Europeans and other scholars have contributed substantially to the knowledge of rural settlement study Karl Ritter (1779-1859) is the pioneer of rural settlement study. But the history of systematic study of rural settlement goes back to the 1920's when scholars like Paul Vidal de la Blache, Aurosseau, Ahlmann, Demangeon[1], Brunhes[2] and others started laying foundations of the branches of settlement geography. In India the substantial contributions done in the field of rural settlements are by Ayodhya Prasad,[3] R.L. Singh,[4] A.B. Mukherjee,[5] V.N.P. Sinha,[6] B. Thakur,[7] and Rana P.B. Singh.[8] The real interest aroused with the establishment of the commission on types of rural habitation[9] under the Auspices of the International Geographical Union. This is a landmark in making definite beginning in the study of rural settlement geography.

Contributions by A. Demangeon (1872-1940)

Demangeon was the third French scientist of human geography. In 1911 he joined in the university of Sorrebore as professor of human geography. He wanted to write a book on human geography which should be more philosophical in comparison with Brunhes on the other hand he wanted to write a book on economic geography of France.[10]

His book entitled *Problems of Human Geography* published after his death in 1942. From 1947 to 1948 in Geographic universalle his concepts of Economic Geography has been published. Demangeon's one of the interesting subject matter of study was rural settlements. He published several research papers on rural settlements in *Annals of the Association of American Geographers.* Demangeon's several book on rural settlements published in between 1920 and 1936. In the establishment of a residential houses he considered agricultural operations and internal structure of houses as basic elements. His studies are mainly of rural settlements. His investigations were mostly on rural hamlets, agricultural systems and methods whose results could be seen in Atlas of France and Problems of Human Geography. He has much interest in urban studies which could be seen in *Journal of Urban Geography*.

Contributions by Jiro Yonekura

Jiro Yonekura born in 1909 A.D. in Hachimai village which lies 12 kilometres east of Saga city in Japan. He grew up in rural settlement and his contributions in the field of rural settlements in Monsoon Asia is really outstanding.[11]

Fig. 8.1: Jiro Yonekura

Education

Yonekura studied human geography in the university of Kyoto. His teacher was Professor Takuji Ogawa one of the eminent pioneers in the field of human geography. He travelled widely in different parts of the world in order to study about various problems of rural settlements. He served as professor in the University of Hiroshima, Japan upto 1975. He also taught in wakayama commercial college as lecturer, of economic geography.

Contributions

Yonekura conducted geographical investigations under difficult conditions, covering different parts of Monsoon Asia. The greater part of his study is covered with morphogenetic study of rural settlements but after 1970 he paid attention to functional aspects particularly those of urban settlements.

Contributions in the Field of Historico-Geographical Study

Yonekura conducted historico-geographical study in the field of Japanese settlements in between 1931 to 1937. During this period he worked as one of the staff member in the university of Kyoto. In this university the study of jori system was initiated by Prof. Takuji Ogawa and the continuation of this study by J. Yonekura have been rewarded with meaningful researches. Yonekura proposed the Jori settlement system as the land plan (A-2) for numbering system of the land. He proposed that the allotment was combined with the ditches and the lands from the point of view of agricultural planning. Yonekura discussed the concept of rural settlement plan with Jori (A-3). His hypothesis was one ri (planned village) and is composed of 30 Ko (large family). Although in the beginning this hypothesis was highly criticised but nowadays it has been approved by the historians as he has been indicated the ideal type of village with the furtherance of research in Jori system. He reconstructed allotments and identified provincial sheets (A7, 10 & 11). By alloting jori system he identified the manor map of Toda-no-sho (1338 AD). He also used diagrammatic model to clarify the understanding of the development of the village during Medieval period.

Contributions About East Asia

Yonekura's interest was to study the rural settlements of China, Korea, Formosa and Japan besides highlighting the regional and economic geography of Monsoon Asia. As a visiting lecturer in the University of Kyoto his interest was mainly focused on the historical study of human settlements in Japan. In most of his studies Yonekura made comparative analysis of Japanese villages with the chinese. He expanded his work on settlements of Greater East Asia co-prosperity to South-East Asia. These investigations have been done in 1944 and 1945 especially for Singapore, the Philippines, Vietnam, Cambodia and Laos. Later he expelled from his job even then he continues to serve rural settlement geography from his village, and he visited several counting of South-East Asia.

Historical Geography of Settlements in Japan

He joined as professor of Geography at the University of Hiroshima in 1952. He started the study of Jori system of Japan which published in various journals. On Jori system Yonekura under taken research projects in collaboration with several professor's of Japan.

In his book entitled *Historico Geographical Study of Settlements in China and Japan* covers history of geography, the tradition of Geography in South East Asia, development of settlement geography, settlements in East Asia, Ancient and Medieval settlements in Japan, villages in Ancient Japan, Towns in Ancient Japan, settlements in Medieval Japan, settlements in China and towns in China.

Yonekura, also undertaken research project entitled "Recent changes in settlements in India" financed by the Ministry of Education, Japan in 1968. He was awarded Jawahar Lal Nehru Medal for his remarkable contribution to the geographical studies in India. He was a pioneer historical geographer who took interest in excavation of historical sites besides establishing the Meitzens idea of rural settlement geography in South-East Asia specially in finding types of villages. His last project was on rural settlements in Monsoon Asia.

On the basis of above contributions of Prof. Yonekura in the field of rural settlement geography we can say that he has done a lot and left a lot of task for future generations to do.

Contribution of R. L. Singh in Rural Settlement Studies

Ram Lochan Singh born on 20 March, 1917 is a giant personality in the field of rural settlement geography. He has contributed a lot to this field through tour, organising seminars and symposia, editing books and writing research papers. His fields of specialization were human geography, settlement geography and applied geography all based towards rural development. R. L. Singh obtained M.A. degree from Calcutta University in 1945, Ph.D. from London University in 1953, joined as Lecturer in Banaras Hindu University in 1946, appointed Professor of Geography in 1955 and retired from Job on 31st March, 1977.[12]

FIG. 8.2: Prof. R. L. Singh

Administrative Experiences

He was associated and served the cause of rural settlements through various administrative capacities e.g. Head of the Department of Geography, Banaras Hindu University, Varanasi (1955-1977), Honorary Secretary, National Geographical Society of India since 1945, Chairman of International Commission on Rural Settlements in Monsoon Lands since 1968 and Chairman International Working Group on "Transformation of Rural Habitat" 1976-80.

Prof. R. L. Singh served the cause of rural settlement studies by visiting several countries of the world and participating in the seminars and symposia. He visited 34 countries of the world including U.K., U.S.A., U.S.S.R., France, Spain, Italy, Switzerland, Middle Eastern countries, South East Asian countries, North Africa, Japan, Newzealand, Australia, Brazil and central American countries. R.L. Singh participated in symposia aborad as Brazil (1955), Malaya (1962), London (1964), Ghana (1970), Japan (1971), Montreal (1972), Newzealand (1974), Singapore (1975) and Moscow (1976).

Organised Seminars and Conferences

1. International Symposium on Rural Settlements in South Asia, B.H.U.; January, 1971.
2. International Symposium on Rural Settlements in Monsoon Asia, Tokyo, April 1971.
3. International Group Meeting of Geographers Working on Rural Settlements in Monsoon Lands, Newzealands, 1974.
4. International Symposium on Rural Settlements in Monsoon Lands, BHU, December 1975.
5. International Symposium on Rural Settlements in Developing Countries, Tashkent in July, 1976.

Doctoral Works on Rural Settlements Guided

1. K.N. Singh–Rural Markets and Rurban Centres in Eastern U.P. 1963.
2. M.S. Vishwanath–Rural Market and small service centres in Mysore State, 1966.
3. R.Y. Singh–Malwa Plateau: A Study in Rural Settlement Geography, 1974.

4. Daksha C. Barai–Central places in Tamilnadu, 1975.
5. Rana P.B. Singh--Clan Settlements in the Saran Plain, 1977.
6. Ram Bali Singh–Rajput Clan Settlements in Varanasi District, 1975.
7. Kumkum Majumdar–Eastern Gujarat Plain, A Study in Rural settlement Geography, 1977.
8. S. B. Singh–Landforms and Settlements in Simla and its Environs, 1977.

Papers Published on Rural Settlements

1. Evolution of Settlements in Middle Ganga Valley, *National Geographical Journal of India,* Vol. 1, Sept. 1955.
2. Typical Rural Dwellings in the Umland of Banaras, *NGJI,* Vol. III, Part 2, June, 1957.
3. Mungara–Badshahpur: A Rural Settlement in the Ganga-Ghaghara Doab West, *N.G.J.I,* Vol. III, Part 4, Dec. 1960.
4. Meaning, Objectives and Scope of Settlement Geography, *N.G.J.I,* Vol. III, Part 1, March, 1961.
5. The Evolution of study in Rural Settlements; Read in Geography Post-Graduate Research Unit, BHU, 1962.
6. Bases of small Rural Service Centres in Middle Ganga Valley, Pub. 20th IGU, London, 1964.
7. Morphology of villages in the Middle Ganga Valley, special Lecture, Magadh University, Gaya, 1965.
8. Rural-Urban Fringe: A Review, Read in the Seminar held at Nainital, 1965.
9. Histogenesis of Settlements in the Middle Ganga Valley, Lecture at the 55th Indian Science Congress, Jan. 1968.
10. The role of Geographers in Town and Country Planning, Presidential Address at Kanpur, 1968.
11. Spatial diffusion of Rajput Clan Settlements in a part of Middle Ganga Valley, BHU, 1971 and N.G.S.I., No. 14, 1975.
12. Spatial Organization and Integrated Area Development: Case of the Mirzapur Region (A.C. Seri, AVARD, New Delhi, 1975).
13. Shape Analysis in Rural Settlement Geography; N.G.S.I., Publication No. 14, 1975.
14. Some Approaches to the Morphogenesis of Indian Village; NGSI Research Publication No. 14; 1975.
15. Evolution of clan Territorial Unit Through Land Occupance in

the Middle Ganga Valley; NGSI Publication No. 14, 1975.
16. Mechanism of the Diffusion of a Rural Settlement in an Indian Environment; *International Geography,* Vol. 7, 1976.

Research, Monographs Published on Rural Settlements

1. Ed. Rural Settlements in Monsoon Asia, N.G.S.I., Varanasi, No. 10, 1972.
2. Ed. Readings in Rural Settlement Geography, N.G.S.I., No. 14, 1975.
3. Ed. Geographic Dimensions of Rural Settlements, N.G.S.I., No. 16, 1976.
4. Approach to Rural Settlement Geography, Conceptual Framework and Bibliography, N.G.S.I., No. 27, 1977.

Details of Contributions

In 1955 R.L. Singh traced the evolution of rural settlements in the Middle Ganga Valley through various periods of Indian history. In 1968 he examined the territorial basis of medieval town and village settlements in Eastern Uttar Pradesh. Both these studies emphasize the role of clan territories in influencing the human settlements of the area.

In his paper on shape analysis of rural settlements R.L. Singh adopted traditional view of shape of rural settlements as well as geometrical form of shapes. Saran Plain has been taken as a sample study. This may also be considered as a tool for the comparative studies of at least two dimensions i.e. area and shape, and the third dimensions may be time or connectivity. Through these indices the organisational set up of villages may also be analysed in terms of controlling spill-over effects, i.e. internalizing positive spillover effects and externalizing negative spillover effects.

Prof. R.L. Singh's (1961) presents a comprehensive account of the meaning, scope and nature of settlement geography. He has defined settlement as "Comparative unit representing an organized colony of human beings, starting from simple and sedentary camp of a hunter or herder and culminating into metropolis which exhibits highly complex features and spatial patterns.

R.L. Singh (1972) discussed the spatial diffusion of Rajput clan settlements in four phases corresponding to four phase sequence of the models of spatial diffusion origin, first stage before A.D. 160, second phase A.D. 1600 to 1800 A.D. and third phase A.D. 1800 onwards. The stage sequence derived from the theoretical nodels of settlement diffusion and empirical evidence of diffusion of settlements. R.L. Singh (1974) in his paper on evolution of clan territorial units in the Middle Ganga valley discussed the process of land occupance and actual settling, emotional and historical ties tend to emerge, intensity and binding people, firstly the corporate groups and later other settlers of the territory.

Contributions of Arcot Ramchandran

As executive director of UNCHS (Habitat) since 1977 A. Ramchandran contributed a lot to the cause of settlement study. Although he contributed through organising seminars, participating in discussions and it could be said that he is the sole force in ameliorating the situations of human settlements for the better throughout the world. His view on evolution of settlements, settlement dynamics, global strategy and urbanization could be seen as follows.[13]

Fig. 8.3: Arcot Ramchandran

Evolution of Human Settlements

The evolution of human settlements conditions in the past ten years has to be traced following two parallel tracks: first, the physical dynamics of settlement and the evolution of settlement demand; and secondly, the response from international organizations, individual governments, and all the actors who have been the protagonists of these dynamics in each country, whether inside or outside the recognized mainstream of development.

Settlement Dynamics

The broad dynamics of settlement have confirmed the sustained growth forecaste formulated in the mid-1970s-although in absolute terms, population growth rates have abated in all regions of the world. If one takes a look at the most comprehensive publication available on human settlements, the Global Report on Human Settlements, one can see that both urban and rural population growth rates are on the downswing worldwide and also in the developing countries taken as a whole. However, closer observation of available statistics, no matter what indicators may be chosen, reveal very disturbing trends. For example, the world's urban population growth is now overwhelmingly a third world phenomenon. Around the year 2000, approximately 9 out of 10 new urban dwellers will be in the developing countries. In addition, the majority of them will be in the poorest of the developing countries, those which have the least resources to cope with settlement demand in the urban areas.

Another indicator is the scale of individual settlements in the developing countries. By the year 2000, 4 out of 10 urban dewellers in the developing countries will live in cities of one million or more, and 2 of 10 in so-called "megacities" (cities of more than 4 million). And up to 50 per cent of these urban populations will be living in shanty towns, favelas, tugurios, miserias, bidonvilles and other informal settlements sharing similar characteristics: precarious tenure, make shift construction, a lack or total absence of basic infrastructure and services.

Urban figures are, of course, the most vivid aspect of the whole phenomenon. The straggering reality is that in the last decade of this century alone shelter, infrastructure and services will have to be provided for an additional half billion people in the cities of the developing world.

How have governments and countries cope with a demand of such vast scale: The answer is in front of us. Lack of resources and skilled personnel, coupled with legislative and administrative systems often inherited from previous colonial administrations, are only two of the enormous obstacles developing-country governments have had to face in meeting the human settlements challenge. Generally speaking, one can say that the gap has widened because of the dynamics of demand and the slowness of national and international institutional systems to address it in an adequate manner.

Strategy of Settlement of 21st Century

At the same time, UNCHS (Habitat) has always maintained that settlement demand in the developing countries is not a "bottomless pit". And the solution to this apparent paradox rests in the second aspect of human settlements evolution as mentioned before: national and international policy and the evolution of a strategic approach to human settlements development. This is where the Global Strategy for Shelter to the year 2000 comes in.

The Strategy does not come out of the blue. Its "launching platform", of course, was the International Year of Shelter for the Homeless in 1987. But the Strategy has its foundation in the practical experience. The Centre has accumulated in these past ten years in conjunction with practically all governments and multilateral programmes and financing institutions (the United Nations Development Programme (UNDP), the World Bank, the regional development banks), bilateral donors such as the Finnish International Development Agency (FINNIDA), the Danish International Development Agency (DANIDA), the United States Agency for International Development (USAID), and non-governmental organizations grouped around the Habitat International Coalition. This experience can be synthesized at two levels—conceptual and strategic. At the conceptual level, we have been very active in promoting the notion that human settlements are not solely a key aspect of the 'Basic needs' approach; they are a fundamental component of development.

What is needed is an understanding of the importance of human settlements at the highest level of government, and a resource mobilization and co-ordination strategy involving all sectors of society: central and local government, financial institutions, universities, the private sector and the community sector. This approach is known as an "enabling strategy." It is only in such a context, incidentally, that innovative and exciting but also fairly esoteric concepts like "sustainable development" can be understood and put into practice. The Global Strategy for Shelter to the Year 2000 is an effort to apply these new concepts and strategic approaches to the most visible and immediate among human settlements needs.

The response to the Strategy and its plan of Action, which were adopted unanimously by the General Assembly, in December 1988, has been very positive. But the real test will be the support of the global community, donors and recipients alike.

Urbanization

The staggering urbanization is indeed a challenge, at world level. But it is a challenge we must face with realism and a sense of participation. The issue here is how to diffuse urbanization, not how to defuse it. We must continue to pursue vigorously national policies aimed at "optimizing urban demand" and at formulating and implementing nation-wide urban development strategies, as we are doing in Indonesia, for example, and as we hope to do elsewhere—particularly in Africa, which presents the lowest level of urbanization and the highest rate of urbanization. We must also expand and deepen our knowledge of urbanization processes and of the way the impact on national economies and individual well-being, particularly the urban and rural poor. This is why we hope to expand our global human settlements database, HSDB. To cover many urban situations all over the world in a much more detailed fashion, and also why we are seeking the financial assistance of all those potential funding partners who share our view that a policy is only as good as the information it is based on.

We must also expand our capacity to assist governments and municipalities on key aspects of urban planning and management such as land, infrastructure, and municipal finance–and this is why we are one of the partners of the UNDP/World Bank/UNCHS (Habitat) and global programme on urban management. We must also multiply our knowledge and technical assistance capacity on another crucial issue: mass urban transport.

However, the basic, immediate question is how to produce shelter and infrastructure for the people who migrate to the cities of the developing world, as estimated 40 million people per year. This demand is so massive and so urgent that individual municipalities, particularly the smaller ones, cannot cope with it. This is why national shelter strategies are needed. However, I think that the strategy offers a great opportunity for generating mechanisms for an internal response to shelter demand. The shelter sector is also suited for import-substitution strategies–for reducing expensive and unnecessary imports, promoting indigenous industry, and developing technology, building materials and construction techniques suited to local conditions. This is not only true in theory, but also in practice. The Colombian 1982-1986 national development plan, which focused on a massive housing investment programme was based on this concept.

Contributions by Otto Koenigsberger

Koenigsberger is a renowned teacher. He has devoted his professional life to planning, design and management of human settlements. He introduced the concept of "Action Planning" for the rapidly growing cities of the south 25 years ago. His theory urges governments to see their role as promoters and enablers of private sector and community organizations and to encourage a partnership in the planning, management and development of human settlements. He received the award of "Habitat scroll of Honour in 1989". It is an International award introduced to recognise outstanding contributions by individual to the improvement of human settlement.

Contributions by Hassan Fathy

He received the "Habitat Scroll of Honour" of United Nations (Habitat) in 1989. Hassan Fathy received this prestigious award as he was architect, artist and poet, and contributed substantially in the improvement of human settlements. He also received other impressive awards among which the International Union of Architects Gold Medal of 1985 is important. The United Nations Centre for Human Settlements has honoured him for his innovative proposals for adopting traditional building materials and techniques for their use in modern low income housing.

Contributions by John Norton

John Norton is Associated with Development Workshop (DW) in

Canada. His woodless construction programme has won the UNCHS Habitat scroll of Honour Award for 1992.

His contributions in the field of settlement geography could be seen through his paper given below originally reported to SINA, Africa.

Woodless Construction in Niger and Mali: Meeting Shelter Needs and Environmental Concerns

The introduction by Development Workshop (DW) of Nubian vaults and domes to Niger came as a result of the recognition by several international organizations that over-consumption of wood for building was leading to depletion of timber reserves and thus enhancing desertification. Scarcity of wood, branches and even grasses has in turn made domestic building increasingly difficult and costly for the people, who in some instances can no longer find the materials they need. In other cases they have been obliged to use species of wood with very poor durability, which have to be replaced more frequently, thus speeding up the rate of overall timber consumption.

Building and Training

Development Workshop was invited in 1980 by a small Canadian NGO, USAID, to demonstrate the vault and dome techniques in Chikal, Niger, Following this, DW's associate Peter Tunley continued to build with the same techniques, initially for USAID and other organizations, in the area of Filingue, north east of Niamey, and they subsequently in the Air Tenere area in northern Niger on behalf of the IUCN/WWF programme for the conservation and management of natural resources.

Progress started with the construction of their project offices, and continued over the next five years with the construction of a large number of houses and public facilities. Using the basic techniques of vaults and domes built with unstabilized earth blocks, a very diverse range of building types evolved through a collaboration with local masons and through an imperative need to find building solutions which could really meet local needs and affordability. The construction provided excellent opportunities for training on building sites, and strengthened the development of builders skills. Training Programmes for masons were started in 1988, bringing masons from as far as field as Chad and Mali, as well as from other parts of Niger. The techniques began to spread throughout the region, and some masons now face a greater demand than they can meet.

With on-going technical assistance being provided by DW, training has now become a key activitiy, with a number of masons now working as trainers, and instances of the techniques already being passed on to a younger generation in masons' families in both the Agadez and Filingue regions.

Using Local Resources and Building Skills

The Woodless Construction Programme is based on building with unstabilized earth blocks. No presses, cement or line are used, and where possible the bonding patterns of block laying are now adapted to suit the local traditional block sizes to make production easier. The basic elements are vault and dome roofs built without shuttering, and masonry arches. But in practice there are numerous variations in these elements, permitting a wide variety of built forms, and importantly allowing masons to develop their own distinctive styles.

In the 12 years the techniques have been used in Niger, there has been considerable refinement in the methods of building, to increase both strength and safety, and to ensure better protection from water. The building process has also become easier to learn and use.

Spontaneous Construction

By 1990 several hundred buildings were complete, of which 25 per cent had been built for private clients, including villas and several government buildings. But more significantly, over 20 per cent were already the spontaneous construction by local masons using these techniques to meet their own building needs and those of their families and neighbours–including mosques as well as houses, kitchens and stores.

The amount of spontaneous construction is constantly increasing. Where the techniques are now known, village builders are convinced of their usefulness of redressing what they see as a problem of obtaining good durable wood, and so too are the organizations concerned with the conservation and management of natural resources. In Mali and Niger, the ministries concerned with the environment are beginning to give their active support. Each building saves about 0.5 cubic metres of wood per square metre of construction, and of this, for a building of 30m 2, on average 14 tree trunks are saved: all of which adds up to increased chances of trees being saved and regenerated.

From the user's point of view, the vault and dome roofs are proving durable, and eliminate the need to replace timber in the roofs. Costs are either the same or lower than those for building with good timber roofs. The woodless construction techniques almost completely eliminate the need to bring in non-local materials for the basic structure of a building. It is in effect the ease of access to materials and the use of increasingly locally understood techniques which contribute to the techniques' growing popularity and sustainability. Indeed, in the Sahel, for many families there are few other options than to use those resources available locally, and in some case the woodless construction techniques have enabled families to build houses with almost no financial cost at all.

Adapting to Local Needs

Any project should go through changes during its life–and in the case of the Woodless Construction Programme, time has been in its favour and a factor in its emerging success. Twelve years of constant technical assistance in the field along side local masons has allowed the techniques to be improved and changed to suit varying local conditions, and has encouraged the masons to take pride in their work and maintain a high standard in their buildings.

Time has also enabled small structures to be built in new regions which can then be observed during one or more rainy seasons to monitor their response and to identify improvements that need to be made, and to give time for the population to develop confidence in the techniques. The result has been that, whilst there are parts of the Sahel where these techniques are not suited, the performance of buildings over several years show that woodless construction is possible and durable in much of the region, and that it is a viable contribution to meet building needs and conserving resources in a sustainable manner.

Contributions of Baker

In the beginning of 1970's for the construction of public houses the idea of Baker's helped. Larry Baker is known as the "architect of

FIG. 8.4: Larry Baker

poor". He was born in England and studied as student of Birmingham school of Architect. Later on he took the citizenship of India. As influenced by Gandhiji Baker's concept of construction of houses took the shape of movement in 1970's when he settled in Tiruanantpuram and started advertising the technique of construction of low input houses.[14]

Baker was of the view that the shortage of houses for village folk and urban poor could be solved by the search of new method to reduce construction costs. Too much of designs, costly construction materials, lack of consciousness of labourers and the owner, besides the cost could be reduced in unscientific construction. He cautioned that too much use of cement and steel should be avoided because such houses are not so confortable.

Baker's method of house construction is based on local building materials available from the surrounding environment. The houses should be so designed which can suit the occupation and life style of people. In order to have less and less use of steel and cement Baker suggested Filler Slab in which tile has been used on both sides of the brick while in making.

Baker has proved that local bricks and mud could be an important materials of house construction. The houses so constructed are also strong defensive and stable. According to a rule plaster has not been used in the houses. The use of wood has been made less and less. The inner part of the wall kept vacant to control heat and it will reduce 25 per cent lesser number of bricks. Filler tiles also used in the roof and floor in order to allow proper ventilation. Eavesline in the roof should be so constructed which could protect the wall from rainfall and other weather hazards. Baker has been given Padamshri Award by the Government of India for his constribution to the settlement sector. In 1987 he has also been awarded by the Ministry of Urban Developement and the University Grants Commission, New Delhi. The government of Holland has also accepted his contributions in the field of housing designs and construction.

REFERENCES

1. A. Demangeon, "L, habitation Rural in France," *Annals de Geographic,* Vol. 23, 1920.
2. J. Brunhes, *Human Geography,* Harap, 1952.
3. Ayodhya Prasad, Chhotanagpur: *Geography of Rural Settlements,* Ranchi University, Ranchi, 1973.
4. R.L. Singh, "Meaning, Objectives and Scope of Settlements Geography," *The National Geographical Journal of India,* Vol. 7, 1961, pp. 11-20.
5. A.B. Mukherjee, "Spacing of Rural Settlements in Rajasthan" *Geographical Outlook,* Vol. 7, 1970, p. 2.
6. V.N.P. Sinha, *Chhotanagpur: A Study in Settlement Geography,* K.B. Publications, New Delhi, 1976.
7. B. Thakur, *Urban Settlements in Eastern India,* Concept Publishing Company, New Delhi, 1980.
8. Rana P.B. Singh, "Pattern Analysis of Rural Settlement Distribution and Their Types in Saran Plain: A Quantitative Approach," *National Geographical Journal of India,* Vol. 20, 1974, pp. 109-27.
9. Mark Jerozynske, *The National Settlement System,* International Geographical Union, Warsaw, 1983.
10. A. Demangeon, *Op. cit.*
11. R. L. Singh, (Ed.): *Rural Settlement in Monsoon Asia,* NGSI; Varanasi, No. 10., 1972.
12. R. L. Singh," Evolution of Settlements in Middle Ganga Valley; *The National Geographical Journal of India,* Vol. 1, September, 1955.
13. Arcot, Ramchandran, *Developing A National Shelter Strategy: Lessons From Four Countries,* United Nations Centre for Human Settlements, Nairobi, 1990.
14. B.K. Damodaran: "The Ideals of Building Construction", *Manorama Year Book* (in Hindi), Kottayam, 1992.

9

ENVIRONMENTAL RELATIONS WITH HUMAN SETTLEMENTS

Human being obtains food, clothing and settlements with the help of their technological know how from the nature. The work under natural environment and use of natural resources to get a certain type of food, shelter and clothing. Hence, shelter has a dominant impact on the built environment, while at the same time its characteristics are influenced by the natural environment. Human settlements can influence the environment by consumption of natural resources, adding cultural elements to the environment and act as an intermediary between human being and nature.

The form of human settlements is generally determined by social requirements and the physical environment. The origin of settlement

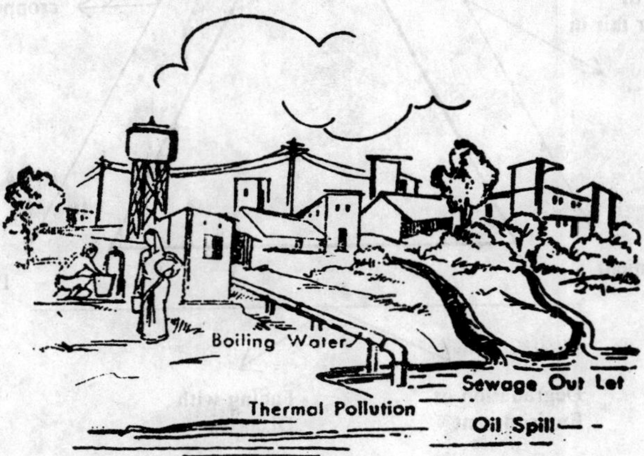

FIG. 9.1: Types of Pollution in Rural Settlement

starts depleting natural resources and its metabolic processes pollute the land, air and water at the same time because all these are related with the process of feed-back mechanism.[1] Hence, the productivity of land, labour and metabolic processes of settlements determine the environmental conditions for human comfort. This chapter will highlight some of these points through macro, meso and micro level analysis.

Organization of Rural Space and People

India is a land of villages where people live in the huts and cottages of olden days. The environment is still dominated by physical elements, because the pace of urbanization is slow 34 per cent in 1991 and the level of industrialisation is also slow because due to the lack of capital and appropriate skill of man power found in the area. A high sounding words of integrated rural development is still present but the lack of resources, immorality of people,

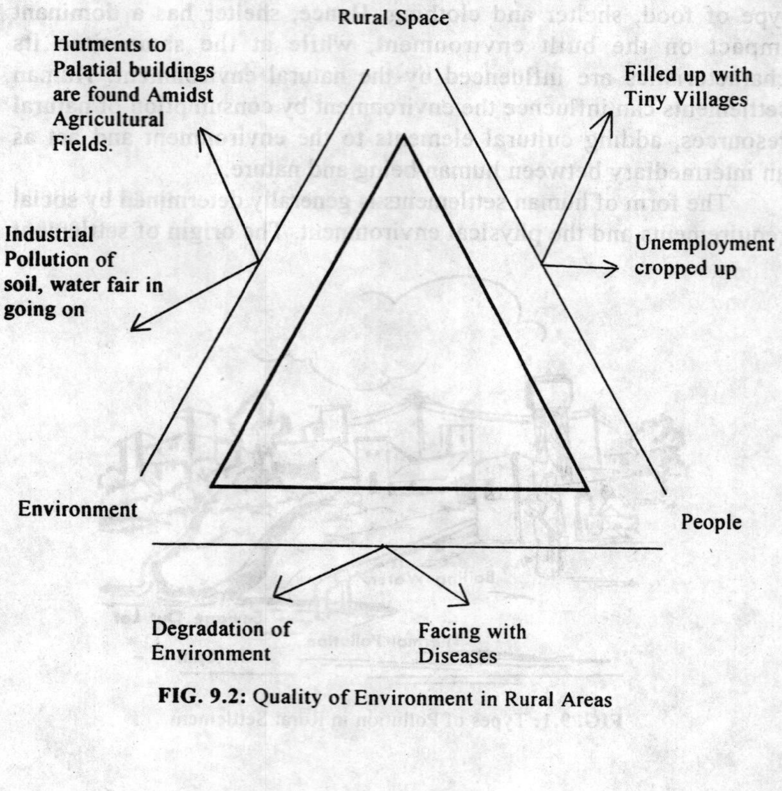

FIG. 9.2: Quality of Environment in Rural Areas

criminalisation of politics and sence of irresponsibility of public servants have really degraded the healthy environment in the area into drudgery, misery and squalore where the cutting of forest is going on unabated, rural poors are either getting killed or they are being deprived of their wealth and social rights by the rich people of the area.[2]

The above model shows the quality of environment in the rural areas of India. The people live in hutments where the occupancy rate is very high, the unemployment situation has forced them to adopt even criminal activities and the pollution of land, air and water are going on as the people are still ignorant about their misdeeds. Recently, a very poor show of environmental modification has been considered in its programme by the Forest Department Government of India; who wants to plant trees on road sides, railways siding, fallow lands and wastelands present in the area under the programme of social forestry. The rate of achievement of the target is just 40 per cent.

The purpose of this chapter is to analyse and correlate the rural space, people and their environment properly so that the problems may be sorted out and the planning measures may be suggested in order to create a beautiful environment for human living in rural areas of India.

Rural Settlements and Slum Improvement

Human settlement is a total concept which is applicable to a city, town, village and even a small hamlet in a farflung areas. Each one of them has got a basic organisation with its own social, economic and cultural aspects. At some places it may have a spiritual content. Among other aspects, it has some basic requirements like housing, water and sanitation, transport and communication, food, energy, education and health, protection and welfare, facilities for culture, art, recreation and leisure, and an economic management.[3] In the final analysis all these aspects are looked after by the government. Often it is difficult to implement all these things in their entirety due to negligence of large human settlements (like metropolitan cities). The system breaks due to over congestion of houses and people in the residential space. Housing in general is indeed one of the much felt needs which is perhaps next only to food. Therefore, shelter is one of the very important minimum needs which enables to give the people a minimum quality of life that they are entitled to implicit with shelter. It needs the provision of site with secured land tenure and facilities like potable water, sanitation, etc. Perhaps it is for this fact that historically settlements developed wherever there was abundant water supply and some basic facilities including fuel wood available.[4]

Future expansion and growth of settlements will depend on several socio-economic, ethnic, cultural and other considerations, including agricultural productivity in relation to availability of goods and services from the ecosystem. This picture is not likely to change because the disparities between urban and rural areas as also the influx of rural poor into urban areas for livelihood will continue for the foreseeable future.

There is an urgent need for shelter for the disadvantaged houseless pavement and slum dwellers and squatters. This segment of our population is deprived of a decent living, sanitation, health and education because of the total lack of socio-economic opportunities. They have no shelter to live and thus must sleep on pavements, or do not own land because they are so poor that they cannot afford anything. They work as unskilled, semi-skilled or sometimes even as skilled labour. Squatters settle on land and build houses without any legal right or without taking permission from any one.

India is facing a shortage of at least 21 million houses, out of which 76 per cent (16 million) are needed in rural areas, while 24 per cent (5 million) in urban areas. Maximum shortage is in Bihar (3.7 million).

To provide housing of this magnitude and in fiscal terms, the negative impact of the absence of housing are indeed the cause of a lot of human misery with consequent degradation in physical health, economic and socio-cultural environment.

Slum settlements arise as part of a village or city, particularly metropolitan ones, and are essentially the result of acute shortage of housing in towns and villages. Due to influx or rural poor into urban situations, in search of some means of livelihood, they are not able to find a dwelling. Thus people tend to occupy vacant land outside the city, where they build a dwelling with any available material, however, flimsy it may be. This is done in a haphazard manner with no civic facilities of water supply, drainage, road, transport and other amenities which also leads to all types of social evils. The decision makers are oblivious to these aspects when they decide on developmental plans, industrial belts, etc., in a particular city. In fact, no serious thought is given to low-income housing. It is reported that China is the only developing country which has totally eradicated slums within 25 years.

The slums are in a chaotic and unhygienic state and being not serviced, overcrowded and dilapidated, need improvement in both physical and socio-economic environment. Slum becomes a dirty spot not as much due to poor quality of structures lent on account of the environment of insanitation that breeds social complications and health and economic problems.

In a survey conducted by the National Building Organisation in India there are nearly 25 million people in slum settlements of which 40 per cent live in metropolitan cities of Ahmedabad, Pune, Bombay, Nagpur, Bangalore, Chennai, Calcutta, Lucknow, Kanpur, Delhi and Jaipur. About 67 per cent of population in Calcutta and over 45 per cent in Bombay are slum dwellers.

Although slums face environmental, social, economic, health, educational and cultural problems, even then, slum dwellers make their contribution to the development of urban economy, as small traders, contractors, workers, hawkers, drivers, carpenters, etc., who attend to several types of utility services. They have skills, creativity and energy. Even so, to get excluded from legitimate access to land and housing because policy-makers and planners feel that slum dwellers have no place in a city. The most ill-fated and vulnerable section is that of children in the slum areas who on account of poverty, malnutrition, poor drinking water and insanitary environment together with sickness and disease and lack of education are deprived of the facilities available. The country is talking of brain drain, but no one is bothered about the genetic drain in slum areas; who knows how many geniuses of the country has lost just because the children in these areas could not be provided some basic minimum facilities. They are people who should not be despised but sympathized. Pt. Jawaharlal Nehru once remarked that "if you cannot provide buildings for those dwelling in slums, give them open space to live and give them at least some social services like good sanitation and water supply for proper living.

There is need to accelerate the provision of houses to homeless and this should be stressed time and again. The UN had declared 1987 as the International Year of Shelter for the Homeless (IYSH).

It was not only a means of providing shelter but also an instrument of social policy and ensuring social justice for the economically weaker sections of the society.

A scheme for Environmental Improvement of Rural and Urban Slums (EIRUS) was launched in 1972 which envisaged one tap per 150 persons, one lavatory seat for 20 to 50 persons, one community bath for 20 to 50 persons, and one street lighting 30 metres apart. The cost estimated for this was Rs. 150 per person, which had gone up to Rs. 500 in 1993. This would also include sewer drains, storm water drains including widening and paving of lanes. The targets set for Sixth plan are reported to have been achieved and 10 million slum dwellers have been covered at an expenditure of Rs. 185 crores.

Side by side improvement in health services needs to be made under the plan "Health for all by 2000 A.D." Proper facilities for imparting minimum literacy, and should have basic understanding of the world events and functional skills relevant to the daily life and to the local environmental need. Such education is indeed an investment in human resource which concerns all groups of people.

Another aspect is the improvement in access through road system and pavement and transport facilities. This is very essential on account of the job opportunities being in towns and cities and the influx from rural to urban areas. Transport has considerable negative impacts on environment. India's transport needs range from pedestrian, bicycle to public transport system. In fact, this is an area which merits a close study in order to evolve a transport policy for urban and rural areas. Animal power is still relevant and will remain so, for many years to come. If transport facilities are good and well within the reach of the poor, then, there is a possibility that pressure on cities and towns will be very low particularly areas in where poor lives. The rural influx to urban situation can also decrease with better agricultural, forestry and animal husbandry facilities in rural settlements.

The picture in the next two decades would be such that India would become increasing industrial and there would be 70 per cent people live in urban areas. Thus housing cannot be treated as an isolated issue but it has intimate relationship with several related aspects. The unchecked growth of big cities needs to be drastically cut down if not checked altogether. Side by side, small and medium towns and rural centres need to be upgraded. These have a better growth potential and can attract influx of small urban population and also serve as service-cum-marketing and employment generation centres. This is only possible if small and medium towns are developed in an integrated manner. These can act as a counter-magnet to metrocities and halt the rural influx into urban areas.

Further, architecture has to be location-specific and taken into account climates, soil type, geology, local building materials, socio-economic, asthetics and linkages with past, present and future. There is also need for compulsory afforestation as green areas are the heart of a settlement. A policy is also needed to be enunciated regarding location of industrial areas and their future spread. Due emphasis has to be given to water supply, sewage and sewerage because all these are linked with each other.

The rural planning has to be based on the needs of the poor and low income group because poverty will remain with us for some time to come.

Time has come to make good deal of funding to improve the environment in the settlement areas. In case this has not been done then a time will come when most of the human settlements will turn into slums as the growth of population is very high both in urban and rural areas.

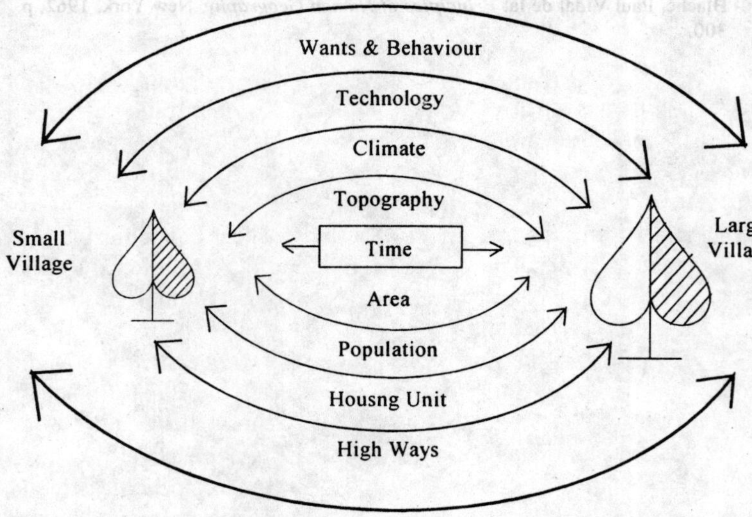

FIG. 9.3: Changing Dimensions of Rural Settlements and the Process of Feedback Mechanism

Changing Environment of Rural Habitat

It has been found that the environment of small village is quite different than that of large villagers. These variations may be due to variations in the areal extent, climatic conditions, age of rural settlement, concentration of population, wants and behaviour of local resident, farmers technological know-how besides the number of houses and highways. The size, spacing and functions of rural settlements also vary considerably. All these factors are associated, with each other through the process of feedback mechanism in which one function give boost to the other to be present in a settlement. The lack of one factor religates other so far as their presence is concerned.

REFERENCES

1. R.L. Singh, "Meaning, Objectives and Scope of Settlement Geography" *National Geographical Journal of India,* Vol. VII, Part-1, March, 1961, pp. 12-13.
2. M. Aurousseau, "The Arrangement of Rural Population," *Geographical Review,* Vol. 10, 1920, p. 223.
3. A.V. Perpillion, *Human Geography,* Longmans, Edinburgh, 1966, pp. 406-14.
4. Blache, Paul Vidal de la: *Principles of Human Geography,* New York, 1962, p. 300.

10

REMOTE SENSING AND RURAL SETTLEMENTS

The viewing of rural settlements from a distance by the space satellite or aeroplane is known as remote sensing. Hence, in the field of rural settlement space technology is a modern and revolutionary system of collection of information and the development of cartographic method for mapping rural settlements and their resources as forests, soil, wastelands, wetlands besides agricultural fields and crop pattern. It includes both satellite imageries, aerial photographs and oblique photographs taken from the ground.

Remote sensing is the process of obtaining synoptic mountain view picture of the earth's surface by means of cameras or other devices which can look down on the ground from above either through aeroplane or satellites. Hence, the outcome of remote sensing in the form of aerial photographs and satellite imageries are the well established tools for geographers and the spatial analysis of regional data obtained from photographs.

There is a saying that "you cannot see the forest for the trees".[1] Similarly, if you are standing in the centre of the village as an investigator you cannot get the idea of the whole village for two-three houses of the nearby areas. But if you observe the whole village through aeroplane then you can see the shape, size, street pattern, skyline, arrangement of houses in space at a glance, and hence it is useful for the geographers to get up above the village or forest to obtain the "mountain view" of the whole landscape environment.

Development of the Subject

The beginning of aero-space was made by Montgolfier voyage of balloon near Paris on 21st November 1783.[2] This provided a powerful tool to the geographers for the study of landforms and terrain conditions of all sorts including rural settlements.

So far as the hyper-altitude photographs are concerned they are available from 1946 onwards beginning with Atlas Sounding Rockets (V-2, Viking, Aerobec), and thereafter from suborbital and orbital flights in the framework of the space programmes of the USA (TIROS, NIMBUS, ESSA, ATS, Mercury, Gemini, Appollo, Landsat, Skylab, etc.) and others by ESA (The European Space Agency) and Indian Space Research Organisation (ISRO), Ahmedabad. According to an estimate in January 1985 about 360 satellites were found moving in the sky. Some satellites have a power to scan the same settlement on the ground on every 9th day after moving the entire world, whereas others on the 12th and 18th day. Since orbital photographs are usually taken from high altitude it has a hundred times more power than the most surveys aircraft. It is quite clear that they opened new vistas especially for small scale reconnaissance of terrain, resources, and settlement systems of areas in which we cannot do fieldwork. As for example— "Philip porter's air-photo and field study told the government of Liberia for the first time how many citizens it governed and just where they lived and what land they used."[3]

The word remote sensing was first of all used by Evelyn Pruitt in 1960. Virtually it is the product of willow Run Lab of Michigan University. Most of the aerial photographs are Electro-Magnetic Records of terrestrial mapping or ground viewing by the satellite which needs processing and analysis of rural settlement location, siting and patterns of rural landuse.

Characteristics of Aerial Photographs and Their Utility

Photogrammetry has been defined as the art, science and technology of obtaining reliable information about physical objects and the environment through process of reading, measuring and interpreting photographic images and patterns. It is highly useful for geographers because:

1. It gives instant recording of required information.
2. It gives very detailed information,
3. The method gives almost objective results,
4. The information is readily reproducible, and
5. Photographs are the most acceptable substitute for maps.

Types of Sensor

Photographic instruments are known as sensor which records electro-magnetic view of ground on infra-red panchromatic or other films. They are photographic sensors, videocon Television camera, optical scanner, and Return Boam videocon.

Selection and Analysis of Satellite Data

For the analysis of digital information available from satellite figures the following methods are adopted:

1. Manual interpretation by inexpensive instruments.
2. Manual interpretation employing more costly optical equipments.
3. Special digitally enhanced data
4. Computer compatible tapes
5. Interpretation of vertical photographs and satellite imageries are done with the help of stereoscope either it is pocket type or large one.

By using stereoscope an object which is found on both photographs is brought into coincidence by optical means and is seen as a three dimensional plastic image.

Definition of Characteristics

1. **Aerial Photograph:** Aerial Photograph is perspective image that is geometrically related to the type of camera with which it is taken from the air or parts of the terrain.
2. **Types of Photographs**
   (a) *Vertical Photographs:* A photograph taken with the optical axis of the camera coinciding with the direction of gravity.
   (b) *Oblique Photograph:* A photograph taken with the aoptical axis of the camera intentionally titled from the vertical. High oblique contain horizon at the upper end where as low oblique do not (Fig. 101.

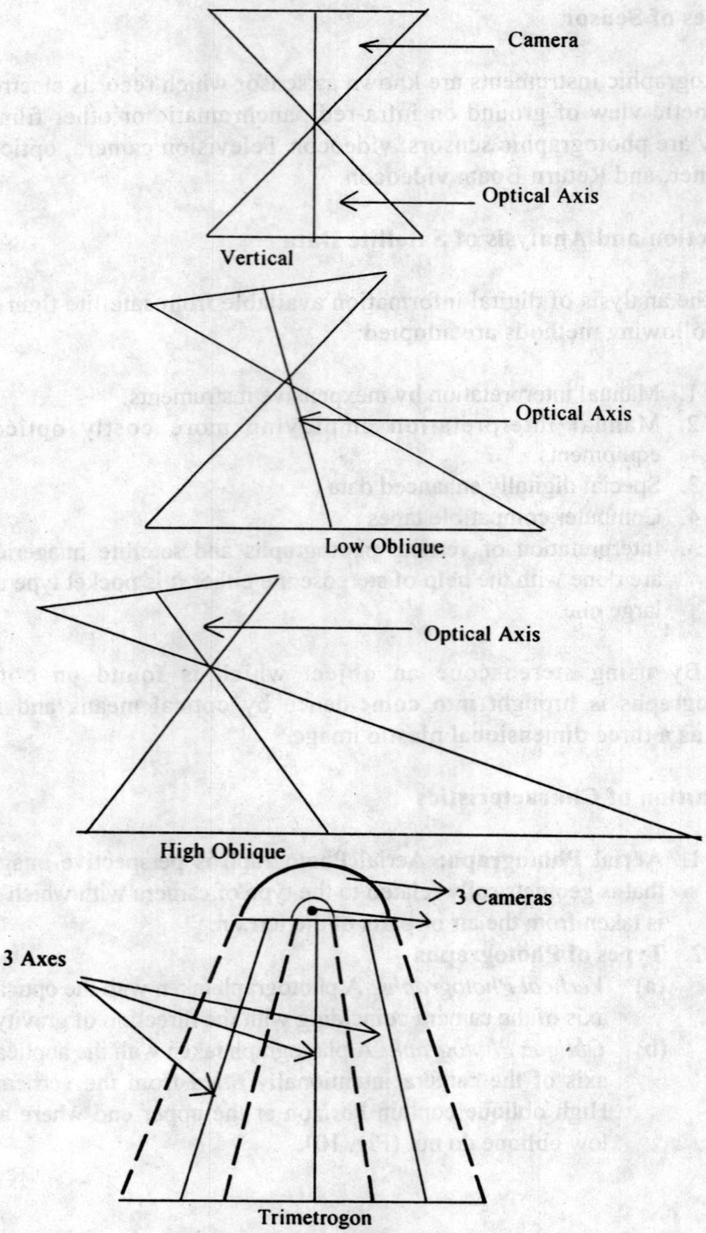

FIG. 10.1: Types of Aerial Photographs

3. Scale of a Photograph

$$\frac{\text{Focal Length of the Camera} = f}{\text{Flying Height above datum} = H}$$

$$\frac{6''}{24000'} = \frac{1''}{4000'} \times 12'' = \text{R.F.} : 1: 48000$$

$$RF\ \frac{1}{H} = \frac{0.5''}{50000''} = \frac{0.1''}{1000} = 1:10000$$

4. *Image displacement:* Due to differing altitutde of the ground horizontal displacement of the objects on the photographs are found which is known as image displacement or parallactic displacement on a truly vertical photographs. This displacement is directly proportional to the relief of the terrain and to the distance from the principal point, and is inversely proportional to the camera altitude. Displacement may also because due to (a) photographic deficiencies (b) tilting of the camera lens axis at the instant of exposure, and (c) variations in local relief.
5. *Overlap and Sidelap:* Along a given flight line, photographs are taken at such frequency as to cause successie photographs to overlap each other by about 55 to 65 per cent. This percentage is referred to as forward overlap. Overlap between the photographs of adjacent flight line is called sidelap. It usually amounts to 15 to 30 per cent.
6. *Vertical Exaggeration:* It is exaggeration of vertical distances with respect to horizontal distances. This exaggeration makes slopes to appear steeper than they are and objects seem taller than they are.
7. *Photo Interpretation:* It is an act of examining photographic image of objects for the purpose of identifying the objects and deducing their significance by reading, analysing and interpreting the photo for relevant results of landforms, drainage, settlements, erosional features, etc.
8. *Mosaics:* A mosaic is a series of overlapping vertical photographs assembled in sequence on mounting board to form one single picture of the terrain.

Types of Mosaics

1. An assembly of photographs laid in a sequence as to allow the

photo number and flight number of each photograph to appear on the finished assembly is called index mosaic or a photo index.

2. A mosaic which is assembled from a single strip of photography is called a strip mosaic.
3. A mosaic which is assembled without considering any plotted control is called an uncontrolled mosaic.
4. A mosaic assembled to fit control which has been plotted on the mounting board is called a controlled mosaic.

Advantages of Mosaics

1. It can be compiled more rapidly and economically than conventional maps.
2. It has vast amount of detail in which terrain features can be easily recognised and interpreted.
3. No detail is omitted, and
4. To the layman, mosaic may be more intelligible because terrain images can be seen as they would actually appear from above.

Application in Settlement Studies

Air Photographs provide the means of bringing settlement patterns study upto date, and they are of basic value where Cadastral survey is lacking altogether such as in many African countries. The ordnance survey use 1:2,500 scale aerial photographs for revision. They are providing detailed supplementary information about settlements which does not appear on maps, for example, relationship with 'ridge and furrow' to settlement form, relationship of settlement of land-use and land-forms and evidence of the relict feature of ancient settlements.

The use of aerial photographs and remote sensing to archaelogical investigation has been well established in many parts of the world, but their utility for the analysis of rural and urban settlements as modern investigation has also been established.[4] Such as Kohn (1951) used both field observation and photo interpretation techniques in the study of rural settlements in Wisconsin dairy area, North-Dakota spring area and Washington irrigated area.[5] Tator (1951) studied about Indian village sites in Mississippi delta areas[6] and remarked "the flatness of the delta terrain, along with the factor of subsidence, make difficult the location of old sites, particularly on the ground. Careful study of large-scale aerial photographs, with detailed analysis of contrasts of tone and shape of soil and vegetation pattern in required."

In this way, remote sensing of the rural environment and rural settlements is an effective tool for the study of human occupance features of the Earth's surface. The method, character and arrangment of facilities men build in the process of occuping an area are easily subjected to study from above.

Mostly the settlement patterns are composed of visible and spatially arranged facilities, more can be learnt of them from remote sensing than any other single source. Kohn (1951) recognised distinct ways in which aerial photographs facilities the study of rural settlement geography:

1. They provide information concerning the character and aerial distribution of the contemporary elements and types of settlement.
2. They reveal the detailed physical conditions and accurate areal patterns involved in the process of original settlement and the subsequent occupance, thus relating the distribution and spatial orientation of the settlement features to their physical environment.
3. They indicate the inter-relations between settlement features and their surrounding areas.

Rescoe (1960)[7] reported on Kohn's work that the first step in rural settlement photography is a spatially arranged inventory of the various structures and cultural conditions. Items to be interpreted, in general order of the ease which they can recognize, include road nets, villages, hamlets, field patterns, farmsteads, the spacing of farmsteads, road and lane turning, farm lanes, farm boundaries, farm size, individual farm buildings, minor farm facilities, and rural non-farm facilities (e.g. churches, temples, ponds, school, fire service stations). After the completion of inventories, these features can be analysed in terms of their origin, function and the associated elements which could be grouped into recognisable settlement types and regional patterns. The identification of regional settlement pattern in its sequent occupance provides the geographer with information required to demarcate geographical regions. It also helps geographer to advise the regional planner on matterns concerning redevelopment of the area or the pioneering development of similar but unoccupied areas.[8]

Principles of Object Recognition in Rural Settlements

It is easy to recognize features on oblique photographs but in vertical photographs of the objects besides examining the 1. shape, 2. size, 3. photographic tone, 4. pattern, 5. shadow, 6. topographic location and identification, and 7. texture of the photograph.

A checklist for typicalfeatures of settlements is as follows:

TABLE 10.1: Coding of the Features of Rural Settlements for Air Photo Interpretation

Code	Colour	Features
2.00	Black	Houses
2.01	Dar Green	Metalled Road
2.02	Brokenline (black)	Footpaths
2.03	Hollow circle (black)	Well
2.04	White	Wall
2.05	Broken pink	Roof
2.06	Broken green	Courtyards
2.07	Black Dots	Fallowland
2.08	CF (black)	Cultivable Fallow
2.09	Wa (black)	Wasteland
3.00	W (blue)	Water bodies
3.01	Broken line and stroke (black)	Fence
3.02	Double brokenline (black)	Unmetalled road
3.03	Black Mound	Graveyard
3.04	T (Red)	Temples
3.05	M (Red)	Mosque
3.06	C (Red)	Church
3.07	IN (Brown)	Industries
3.08	Sch (Green)	Schools
3.09	Ad (Green Flag)	Administrative
4.00	PO (Brown)	Post Office
4.01	HOS (Green)	Hospital
4.02	SU (Blue)	Surface Well
4.03	Ta (Blue)	Tank

Aerial Photo Interpretation

It requires photo reading, scientific analysis and interpretation. The aerial photo should be supported with topographical sheet of the area R.F. 1:63,360 or 1:50,000 and census figures if possible, although in settlement analysis the aerial photographs and satellite imageries are not in much use upto now due to smaller areal extent of building and even settlement as a whole.

Results from Aerial Photograph of Kipande Village

Location: Kipande village is located in Kipande ward of Sumbawanga district in Rukwa region of South-Western Tanzania. One metalled road is running through central part of the village from Mpanda in the north to Sumbawanga in the south. It is an Ujamaa village with 1800 persons (1978) situated along both sides of the road in a planned way. Piped water is available in the village (5 points) but ditch in the surrounding area is also serving the purpose. Due to crystalline basal rock and poor amount of rainfall there are many limitations in agricultural development, but according to the 1975 call of Chama Cha Mapinduzi (CCM) party, people have collected and constructed their huts on planned settlement site in order to achieve more collective advantage than dispersed living. The surrounding area of the village seems to be an erosional plain surface with patchy undulations and cultivated land. On northeastern part of the village rainfall stream is following the fracture line in Gondwana rocks, and the similar situation is found in southern part of the village. But in spite of some favourable and some negative points Kipande village is well placed along the main highway of the area. (Fig. 10.2)

Features of Kipande Settlement

Kepande is a linear rural settlement along the metalled road. Its northern end is narrow due to lowlying area on both the eastern and western parts of the road. The total number of houses is 250. About 25 footpaths are radiating from the centre of the village to different directions like roots of a tree. These footpaths are connecting the various groups of households with the surrounding villages, agricultural plots and grazing land. The material of wall of the

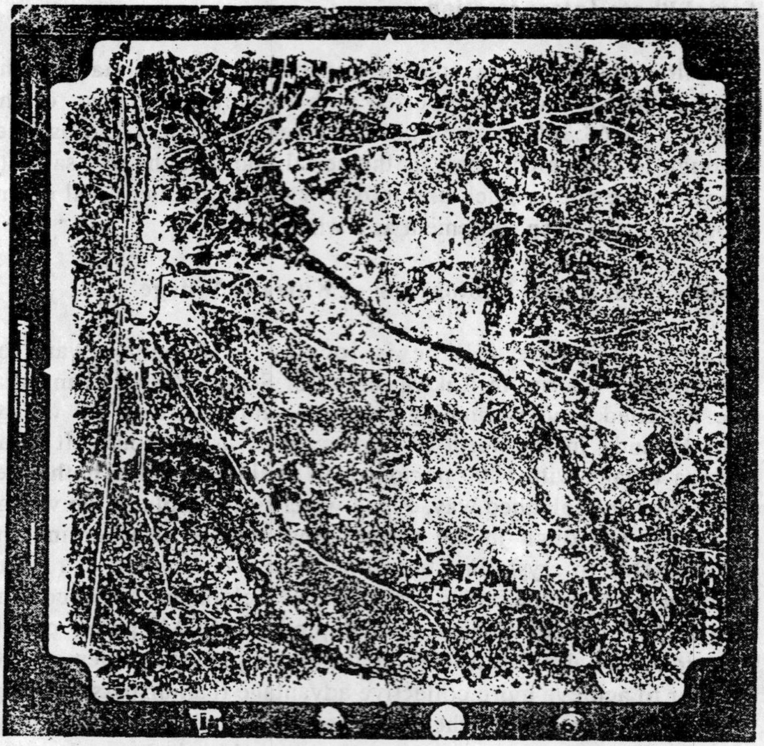

FIG. 10.2: Aerial Photograph of Kipande Village, Rukwa Region, Tanzania

house is either stick plastered with mud or cement bricks. The material of roof is either dried grass or corrugated iron sheets. The average number of windows are four in one Kiswahili house with having four wooden doors. In each house either the kitchen room is found separate or the central corridor is used as kitchen. Kipande village has one post office and one administrative office of village chairman.

Land System of the Kipande Ward in General

Area	652 km^2
Latitude and Longitude	7°52'S31°32'E
Mean annual rainfall	828-950 mm
General Relief	Coarse textured very gently undulating plain (moderately dissected-ruggedness value (0.08)
Rock	Very limited metabasite. Very extensive Ufipa schists, gneisses and granitegneisses
Local relief	40-50 m from MSL
Altitude	1760-2049 m
Gemorphic process	Peneplanation and valley incision
Dominant land facets	Very gentle convex interfluve, very gentle concave valley, gentle to low moderate convex valley, gentle piedmont.
Model Slope class	Very gentle
Drainage density class	Low (0.25)
Drainage pattern	Angulate
Geomorphic history	Youthful dissection of Post-Gondwana and African plantation surface.
Agriculture	
Suitability for maize	Marginal (moisture and nutrient availability limitations) except for soil physiographic unit 3.1 which is moderate
Suitability for cotton	Not suitable (high soil temperature limitation)
Suitability for fluecured tobacco	Not suitable (high soil temperature cured tobacco limitation)
Suitability for rice	Not suitable (high soil temperature limitation).
Suitability for irrigation	Marginal on soil-physiographic unit 3.2 on slopes less than 8 per cent (moisture holding capacity limitation) and on soil-physio-graphic unit 3.1 on slopes between 5 and 8 per cent. Not suitable on soil physiographic unit 3.5 (soil depth limitation) and on slopes greater than 8 per cent suitable on soil-physiographic unit 3.1 on interfluves and in very gentle valleys.
Soils	
Soil -physiographic units	Very extensive 3.2 on upper interfluves 3.5 on lower interfluves and in very gentle valleys. Limited 3.2 and very limited 3.1 in gentle to low moderate

	valleys. 3.1, 3.2 and 3.5 on piedmonts
Soil Map of the World	Very extensive Orthic Ferralsoils and very limited ferric Luvisols on upper interfluves. Ferralic Arenosols on lower interfluves and in very gentle valleys. Extensive Lithosols, limited Orthic Ferralsoils and very limited Ferric Luvisols in gentle to low moderate valleys. Ferric Luvisols, Orthic Ferralsols and Cambic Arenosols on piedmonts.
Soil Taxonomy System	Very extensive Typic Eutrustox and very limited Typic Haplustalfs on upper interfluves. Ustoxic Quartizipsamments on lower interfluves and in very gentle valleys. Extensive Typic Ustorthents, limited Typic Eutrustox and very limited Typic Haplustalfs in gentle to low moderate valleys. Typic Haplustalfs, Typic Eutrustox and Typic Ustipsamments on Piedmonts.
Vegetation	Very extensive grassland and bushed grassland very limited woodland savana in the east.

This chapter has been organized to highlight the principles of remote sensing employed in settlement studies. Although most of the rural settlement studies based either on aerial photographs or satellite imageries are quite different from each other due to the nature of terrain, spatial organization of rural settlements and the purposes involved of the investigator.

Even after all these interpretations the ground checks are essential components of any remote sensing programme. Hence, remote sensing is the application of photogrammetry to the operation of finding and delineating about rural settlements, their types, patterns and position etc. on the surface of the earth.

REFERENCES

1. Robert H. Alexander: "Man's New Views of the Earth: The potential of Remote Sensing," *Problems and Trends in American Geography* (Edt. S.B. Cohen: Basic Book Inc. Publishers, New York, 1967, pp. 239-50
2. H.T. Verstappen: *Remote Sensing in Geomorphology:* Elsevier Scientific Publishing Company, New York, 1977, p. 1.
3. Philp W. Porter: *Population Distribution and Landuse in Liberia:* Ph.D. dissertation, University of London, 1957.

4. G.A. Strokes, "The Aerial Photograph: A key to the cultural Landscape", *Journal of Geography,* Vol. 49, 1950, pp. 32-40.
5. C.F. Kohn: "The use of Aerial Photographs in the Geographical Analysis of Rural Settlements", *Photogrammetric Engineering,* Vol. 17, 1951, pp. 716-25.
6. B.A. Tator: "Some Applications of Aerial Photographs to Geographic studies in the Coastal Gulf Region", *Photogrammetric Engineering,* Vol. 17, 1951 pp. 716-25.
7. Robert G. Reeves et. al (Edt.): Mannual of Remote Sensing: American Society of Photgrammetry, *Falls Church,* Virginia, 1974, p. 2044.
8. *Ibid.*

11

TYPES OF RURAL SETTLEMENTS

Rural settlements show the reciprocal relationship of human occupance features and environment.[1] Aurousseau has used the expression 'arrangement of rural settlements as geographical entities to express the grouping of dwellings and their inter-relationship.[2] Essentially, a rural settlement is mainly an agriculture workshop and, as such, it cannot be separated from the land whose use it ensures. Its shape and arrangement are often in strict accord with the kind of work, the agricultural technique and the way the soil is used.[3]

Factors Affecting Settlement Types

There are two sets of factors which affect settlement types in rural area. The factors may be called the agglomerating factors and the deglomerating factors. These factors are both physical and cultural and lead to compact and dispersed settlements according to the relative influence of centripetal and centrifugal forces as given in Fig. 11.1.

The old settlements are necessarily compact where as the newer one's are sprinkled type. In India the Muslims want to reside in struggling houses due to conservative view whereas the Christians live in detached hamlets due to openness of mid. The compact settlements are found near nodal point or cross roads whereas footpath favours sprinkled settlements. In area of bigger land holdings the settlements are found farther apart but in areas of extreme division of fields the nucleated settlements are found. In private land the peasants want to reside in detached hamlets but on the public land they reside in a tightly nucleated hamlets. Fertile land attracts compact but smaller hutments whereas unfertile land repels population concentration and

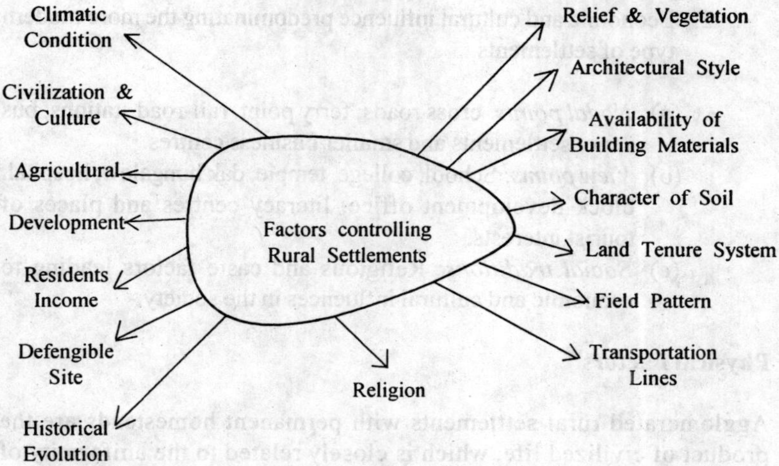

FIG. 11.1: Centripetal and Centrifugal forces

attract only fewer hutments. In areas of RCC roofs the vertical and compact houses are found whereas grass-leaves houses are located farther apart. The houses having modern architectural styles are compact whereas the rudimentary huts are generally constructed in a dispersed manner as the demand of such a society is very limited. The areas of hot and cold deserts do not favour compact settlements whereas temperate and sub-tropical areas have compact settlements type found in different parts of the world. Agricultural development favours more and more nucleation but the areas of floods and extreme drought can attract only dispersed settlements. In areas of high income of the farmers the settlements are huddled together but poor and backward economy favours sprinkled settlements.

1. Physical influence predominating older type settlements.

   (a) *Water seeking:* forest village, valley village, contact point village, scarp belt or spring line settlements in South Bihar Plain.

   (b) *Water shunning :* contact line village in marshy and flooded areas of Saharsa and Purnea.

   (c) *All settlement seeking:* Level land, fertile soil, favourable climate, elevated site and physically good land for settlement.

2. Economic and cultural influence predominating the more modern type of settlements.

   (a) *Nodal points:* cross roads, ferry point, rail-road stations, bus depot settlements and smaller business centres.
   (b) *View points:* School, college, temple, dak bungalow, hospital, block development office, literacy centres and places of tourist interests.
   (c) *Social traditions:* Religious and caste factors leading to economic and cultural influences in the society.

Physical Factors

Agglomerated rural settlements with permanent homesteads are the product of civilized life, which is closely related to the uniformity of relief, fertility of soil and moderate rainfall. Paul vidal De La Blache has aptly observed that the clustered village is indigenous in districts where the arable area is continuous, admitting of uniform and extensive exploitation.[4] In Bihar Plain the fertility of land is coupled with a rapidly growing population, leading to intensive cultivation which is also conducive to the concentration of settlements.[5] Compact settlements are relatively common in the more fertile central and western parts of the study area. Another factor leading to compactness is occasional floods in several areas of the almost flat land of the Bihar Plain. In these areas, elevated sites are few and far between. These are built up into compact settlements. In low-lying areas libale to be inundated, large elevated sites are absent and, hence, settlements are necessarily hamletted. The same is the case in marshy areas and near meandering rivers which change their courses frequently.

The rainfall affects settlement types in two ways. Areas of heavy rainfall are marked by the deglomerating factors of floods and marshy lands. But in areas of moderate rainfall such as Saran, and Gaya districts surface water accumulates in lakes and ponds. Compact settlements are built around these water-bodies. In areas where the ponds are infrequent, deep masonary wells are constructed for the purpose. These wells are costly to construct. Therefore, they are found rarely. But the settlements around these wells are compact. Such settlements are common in Champaran, Muzaffarpur, Darbhanga, Saran and in parts of Patna district where the water table is low as compared to areas farther east "the collective building of dams and irrigation channels for the storage and distribution of rain water and the construction of tanks for artificial irrigation have promoted the evolution of compact village.[6] Physical factors which act as a hindrance to easy living lead to fragmentation of settlements. About this phenomenon Paul vidal De La Blache observes that "the scattered manner of grouping suits localities whereas a result of the dissection of relief, soil and hydrography, the arable land is itself divided up."[7] Sprinkled settlements are found on account of adverse physical conditions like the relatively rugged lands near the southern margin of the study area, the Siwalik hill region in the north, and the Kosi flood plain in the east. There are only a few small sites in the Kosi flood plain which remains above the water during the monsoon. These sites are small in size and can, therefore, accommodate only a small hamlet. Thus large compact settlements are relatively absent here. In the scarp lands and hilly areas, the land is too poor to support large compact settlements, and mixed cropping and pastoral farming leads to fragmented settlements.

Settlements are generally built near water-bodies. If they have to depend upon deep wells or rivers, they are generally compact. However, in areas where the water table is high and wells can be dug easily or where the drainage texture is dense, that is where surface streams and rivulets are numerous, settlements can be built practically all over the region. In such case, therefore, hamlets, semi-sprinkled or semi-compact settlements are more common than compact settlements. Such areas are found in the Kosi basin and the Panar-Mahananda valley in Purnea and Katihar districts.

Compact settlement are well adapted to the economic conditions of paddy cultivation.[8] This type of agriculture periodically requires a large labour force for transplantation, irrigation and harvesting. Hence, both the farmers and the associated agricultural labourers tend to reside in the same nucleated settlement. Moreover, the village community tends to be self-contained, hence, other non-agricultural activities and cottage industries are also located in the same settlement. These include the village backsmith, carpenter, potter, weaver, tailor, etc. Due to the lack of transport facilities till very recently, this economic self reliance was a major factor leading to compact settlements.

During the historical times, the need of defence from external lawless elements was of paramount importance. This requirement could be met only if the settlement was compact. Quite often this led to the establishment of walled villages. Settlements having a fort in the middle or those inhabited by the same clan or tribe also belong to this category. Social relationships and cooperation amongst the villagers have also been important for the generation of centripetal forces. A pond, temple, well, community hall, panchayat house or even a mango orchard in the central part of the village could be utilized by the entire village community on cooperative basis. It, therefore, attracted houses which clustered around it. Social relationships or customs guided and controlled by the village elders have always been important in village life. The Panchayat (Village Council) is one form of this control. Although less important during the British period[9] it is again becoming extremely important.

Superstitions, though less significant than other factors, also have played its role in causing agglomeration. The *dih* (ancestral site) is considered auspicious and people do not like to shift their buildings from it. Also a settlement does not tend to expand towards the south and the west because these two directions are considered inauspicious.[10] Thus even when the houses have to be rebuilt in course of time due to increase in population or division of the family, they continue to cluster in the same locality. This increases compactness of the settlement.

On the other hand, the same social customs and traditions involving the caste system, particularly in relation to the untouchables has led to the fragmentation of rural community. The lower castes, particularly *Harijans,* are forced to build their houses a little away from the main settlement, often towards its south. These hamlets or tolas drive their name after the caste inhabiting them, for example, Chamartoli, Mushartoli, Domtoli, etc. In the past, the landlords preferred to settle tenents of different castes in separate hamlets, allotting to them poor lands. The best land was reserved for the families belonging to the upper castes or their own relatives.

In areas where the physical factors did not prevent dispersal and the land was relatively free from invadors or robbers, small hamlets rather than large clusters came into existence. This factor has been important in the Bihar Plain which has remained relatively more peaceful than other parts of India during the last few centuries. Sometimes, the emergence of a market site around a railway junction or a railway station, a little away from the main settlement, attracts a few residential buildings also. This in turn results in the creation of a separate hamlet. It is possible that during the course of years this hamlet may outgrow the older cluster on account of better economic advantages.

Major Rural Settlement Types

A cursory glance at the rural landscape or the toposheets reveals a variety of rural settlement types. Broadly speaking, the accumulation of agrarian houses and highways in the countryside, where people lead their life by ranching of cattle and agriculture with a few secondary or tertiary occupations, is known as a rural settlement. Primarily rural settlements may be classified into two broad groups of compact and sprinkled types. Compact or agglomerated settlements have narrow lanes and tortuous streets separating the houses. Sprinkled or dispersed settlements exhibit privacy marked by scattered dwellings and raised by farmers in their respective farms and fields. In between these two extremes, semi-compact and semi-sprinkled types are more numerous and these 'result from physical, social and economic history of the community.'[11] The ratio between compact and sprinkled settlements may vary from place to place and from time to time because human habitations are something dynamic as innate social centrifugal and centripetal forces are constantly at work within them.[12]

The typology of rural settlement has been discussed here on the basis of size and spacing of rural settlements. The settlements, having lower spacing and greater population size, have been declared to be compact settlements. The hamlets, having a higher spacing and lower population size have been classified as dispersed settlements. But the nature of their compactness or dispersion can only be judged after a detailed spatial analysis of the physical and cultural characteristics of the settlement patterns.

In other words, a settlement of one hamlet only without any sub-hamlet may be known as a compact settlement while a settlement having one large hamlet and one or two smaller sub-hamlets falls in the category of semi-compact settlements. Similarly, a settlement having a number of hamlets and, therefore, no recognisable central site is classified as a semi-sprinkled settlement. A settlement built in a secluded place where the hamlet is small and the houses are also comparatively far apart, is called sprinkled or dispersed.

The phenomenon of dispersion under Indian environment is quite different from that of the American prairie where the settlements are raised by individual farmers on their respective farms, as the agriculture is highly mechanised and the size of the farms is also enormous. These factors compel the inhabitants to settle separately from one another because it facilitates agricultural operations. But under Indian conditions, a large peasant family has only one to five hectares of land to support it. This makes people settle close to each other as far as possible because they have to cultivate their fields with manual help from their neighbours and the agricultural operation can be successful with this cooperation alone. The isolation, thus, is not inherited but is due to certain compelling physical and cultural conditions.

The first report of the Commission on Types of Rural Settlements published by the International Geographical Union in 1928 recognized only two types of settlements, compact and dispersed. This classification has been recognised universally by now. Several generalised classifications have been attempted by different authors, but no general laws, covering all these generalisations, have been formulated as yet.

Two methods of classification personal observation and statistical analysis, have been predominantly used in determining the types of rural settlements. The most successful methods have been based on personal study of settlement types from topographic maps and a detailed knowledge of their variations. Such maps of settlement types have been constructed for Belgium[13], Netherlands[14], Germany[15], Switzerland[16], Italy[17], the Balkans[18], Rumania[19] and Poland[20]. The diverse definitions and the subjective view of the authors, however, make it difficult to use such maps for comparative study either of the whole or Europe or of the region under consideration here.

A new and simple technique has been devised for the study of this region. It takes all settlement units into consideration and is based on the ratio between the population size of settlement units and their dispersal. This method can be applied for determining the index of dispersal of rural settlement on the basis of population size of settlements units (hamlets or tolas) of an anchal divided by the spacing between them in the same unit area. The settlements are products of socio-economic and physical factors which sometimes harmonise with the clustering of settlements and population but sometimes are at variance with them. The different values of the index of dispersal of settlements, can be grouped according to quartile values. This will give the settlement classes at different levels, such as compact, semi-compact, semi-sprinkled and sprinkled forms.

$$\text{1. Index of Dispersal Values} = \frac{\text{Average Population size of the Tola}}{\text{Average spacing of the tola}}$$

2. Settlement form = Index of dispersal values grouped according to median and quartile values

The average population size of the *tola* (hamlet or settlement unit) was calculated by dividing the rural population of the *anchal* (administrative unit) by the number of tolas contained in it. Similarly the average spacing between tolas was calculated by dividing the rural area of the anchal by the number of tolas and then by working out the square root of the figures to arrive at the distance in kilometres between tolas. The index of dispersal value is the ratio between the two values and ranges between 2 and 12 for the Bihar Plain.

Types of Rural Settlements

This could be decided on the basis of relative distance from one house to another, external form of the houses taken together and the dimension of extent of the human habitation.

Rural Settlement may be divided into four types:

1. Compact 2. Semi-Compact 3. Semi-Sprinkled and 4. Dispersed

1: *Compact Rural Settlements*

It is known as nucleated, clustered or compact rural settlement. In this type the houses are closely located and the streets are very narrow. The narrow lanes function like nervous system in a human body. The streets connect centre of the village with the periphery and *vice versa.* Tank, temple, Baniyan tree, fort and landlords house are centre of attractions in a village around which the houses are located. (Fig. 11.2)

In India the compact rural settlements are found in northern plains besides the coastal plains of Peninsular India. In these are the amount of rainfall is sufficient for agricultural practices, the soil is fertile, and due to transport development the concentration of population is relatively high. Especially in those areas where the water table is low nucleated settlement is a characteristic features in East

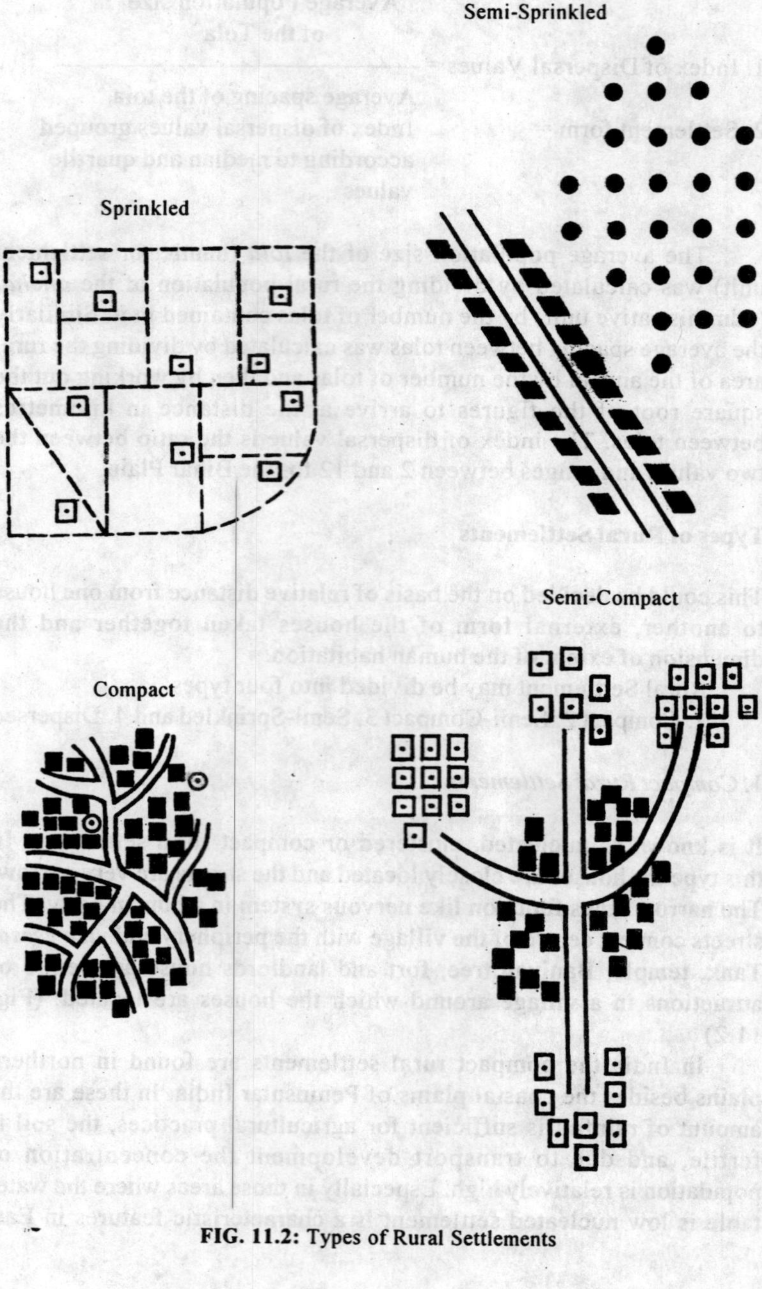

FIG. 11.2: Types of Rural Settlements

Champaran and Sitamarhi districts of Bihar, Malabar coast in Kerala and Pondicherry of Tamilnadu. The position is more or less same on the East coast of China, Japan, Australia and the United States of America. Hence, it could be said that compact rural settlement is found mainly in areas of fertile land of low relief, river valleys where one village coalesces with the other and the subdivision of holdings and the concentration of population are intense. In compact settlement the satellite settlements are absent and the main village expands in different directions in a star or rectangular shape. (Fig. 11.3)

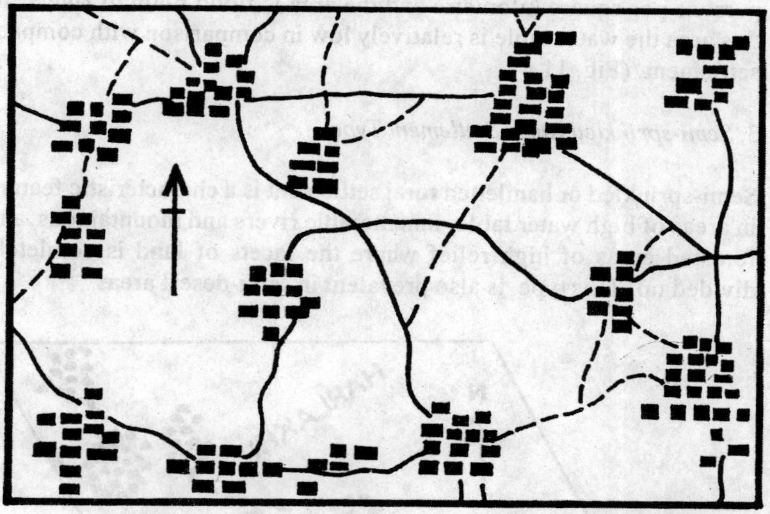

FIG. 11.3: Compact of Rural Settlements

In compact rural settlement people may enjoy sillow feeling at the time of harvest, they can enjoy the facilities of bank, school, college, hospitals and club which may not be possible in sprinkled settlement type but in compact settlements due to high population density and congestion of houses the environmental pollution is very high.

2. *Semi-Compact Rural Settlements*

It may be called quasi-compact rural settlement. In this type besides the main human settlement one or more satellite settlements are found which are linked with the foot path or metalled or unmetalled road.

The characteristic feature of semi-compact area is liable to occasional flood, the transport development is relatively poor and the one habitation is closely associated with the neighbouring tola of low income group people i.e. Mushahar, Chamar, Washerman, Dome and Fisherman who wants to maintain a bit distance from the upper caste people besides they live in secluded manner in order to hide their poverty. Such a settlement are the labour reserve for the landlords because mostly agricultural labourers reside in a satellite settlement. In semi-compact settlement are the population density is 250 to 500 persons per square kilometre and the area is flood plain of rivers. In this area the water table is relatively low in comparison with compact settlement. (Fig. 11.4)

3. *Semi-sprinkled Rural Settlement Type*

Semi-sprinkled or hamletted rural settlement is a characteristic feature in areas of high water table, innumerable rivers and mountainous and forested areas of high relief where the facets of land is comletely divided up. This type is also prevalent in semi-desert areas.

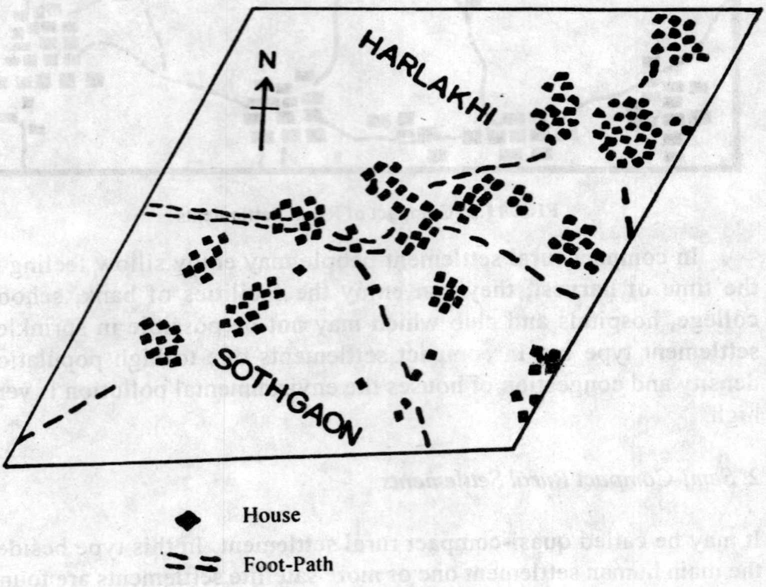

FIG. 11.4: Semi-Sprinkled Rural Settlements

Semi Sprinkled

- High Water Table
- Areas full of rivers
- Semi-Desert Areas
- Semi Mountainous Areas.

In the state of Bihar the area east of Sarai station of Vaishali has high water table where the farmers houses are located respectively in their fields where the digging of a raw water well is a characteristic feature due to high water table. In Saharsa and Madhepura districts the rivers have divided the facets of land and hence linear settlements developed along embankments giving rise to semi-sprinkled type. The situation is more or less same in the scarp belt of Chhotanagpur Plateau, Himalayan foothills and the semi-desert aeras of Karnataka, Maharashtra, Madhya Pradesh and parts of Rajasthan and Gujarat. In semi-sprinkled type areas of the world the environmental pollution is relatively low.

4. *Dispersed Rural settlement Type*

Whereever and whenever the houses are found quite apart from each other due to low sustainable capacity of the land than it is known as dispersed or sprinkled rural settlement. Thus dispersed rural settlement is a characteristic feature of rough terrain, intense flooding areas, desert lands and the land which are waterlogged for a long duration in a year. In India this type of human settlement is found in northern Kosi tract, Moribund Ganga delta, Thar desert of Rajasthan and the mountainous tracts of Himalaya, Nilgiri and Vindhyachal. Here the facets of land is completely divided up due to undulating topography, extremes of climate and poor productivity of soil. In dispersed settlements of Iowa state of USA and the Sahelian deserts of Africa people feel that life is monotonous and lack of sillow feeling is harrasing. In dispersed rural settlement due to location of few hutments and low population density the environmental pollution is on its lowest ebb, but the problem remains in polar areas of the habitat of Eskimo, Smenoid and Finni people where the night soil does not decompose for a long time due to lack of sun rays and slow fermentation in the cold climate. (Fig. 11.5)

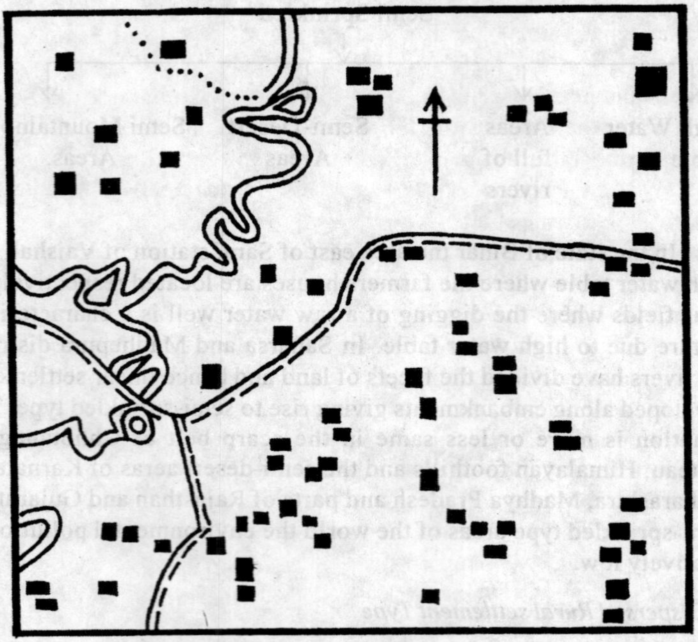

FIG. 11.5: Sprinkled Rural Settlements

Hence, we can say that compact rural settlement is the product of permanent agriculture, productive land and favourable climatic conditions whereas dispersed rural settlement is found in areas of rugged topography where the landscape is itself divided up in various facets leading to the dispersed rural settlements.

The Pattern of Rural Settlement

Varied sizes and densities of settlement can be found in rural areas too. This has important implications for planning. The way the rural population is dispersed through the countryside can be crucial to the success of rural development policies. Road networks are likely to remain sparse where there are many small settlements widely scattered, for roads can only be maintained economically when they connect substantial villages or towns. Schools, hospitals, co-operatives, electricity and other factors of development are also easier to provide where the population is relatively concentrated. It is particularly important that there should be a good scatter of small market towns to bring services and professional help and advice within the reach of villagers and peasants. But villages which depend on farming can grow too large for their accessible farmland.

In some industrialised countries the difference in standard of living between urban and rural areas is disappearing, but in developing countries the distinction between the two remains clearly marked, with important consequences for planners and administrators. There are, however, problems of definition. While it is generally accepted that a rural area is one in which agriculture, forestry or fishing predominates and in which population densities are low, there is no consensus on what constitutes a rural settlement. Population criteria vary between as low as two hundred and as high as five thousand or more. Moreover, in many countries the rural population is enumerated without any break-down by type or size of settlement. It is simply what is left when the urban population is subtracted from the total. There are nevertheless several criteria which may serve as a framework for discussing rural settlements in developing countries. In general there is a greater preponderance of 'natural' elements in the environment than in urban areas. The population is mainly engaged in agriculture, using land extensively and without the benefit of modern technologies. People are isolated, conservative in their attitudes and have fewer contacts with others. The buildings are predominantly traditional in design, materials and construction and utilities and community services are scarce or lacking.

Rural settlement patterns may be characterised as 'dispersed' or 'clustered', but here again there is no general agreement as to how each category should be defined. The United Nations Seminar on Rural Housing and Community Facilities[21] considered the 'dispersed rural population' referred to families living in social and spatial isolation and defined the upper limit of a dispersed settlement as twenty people. By this criterion it was estimated that in Latin America about 35 per cent of the rural population live in dispersed settlements. There are indications that in Africa the percentage may be much higher. But while 'dispersed' is generally associated with 'isolated' it has been observed in parts of Brazil, Colombia, Chile and other countries that dispersed settlements are linked by complex social and economic networks. The term 'dispersed' is also applied to the transitory settlements of nomadic people, which are found in many parts of the world, and not only in remote areas. In many countries temporary

TABLE 11.1: Rural Population of the World, more developed and less developed Regions, and Major World Areas, 1950-200

(in millions)

Area	1950	1960	1970	1980	1990	2000	2000 per 100 in 1970
World total	1782	1997	2283	2614	2939	3186	140
More. dev. regions	418	394	374	347	316	280	75
Less dev. regions	1363	1603	1910	2267	2623	2906	152
Europe	185	179	170	158	145	131	77
Soviet Union	109	108	104	97	89	77	74
North America	60	60	59	56	54	50	85
Oceania	5	5	6	7	9	10	167
South Asia	587	711	888	1116	1355	1561	176
East Asia	552	601	664	708	725	703	106
Africa	187	221	268	332	413	498	186
Latin America	97	110	125	139	150	157	126

settlements for migratory workers are common place in agricultural areas at harvest time. Motorised nomadic groups gathering in camps form another variation. In the U.S.A., for example, mobile homes constitute 10 per cent of the housing stock.

'Clustered' settlements may be defined by the number of people or the distance between houses or by a combination of both factors. In form these larger settlements may be nucleated (arranged around some central feature such as a market place) or linear (strung out along a road or water-way). The physical structure of villages and the type of housing in them usually depends on cultural traits, the kind of agriculture practised, the climate and other factors. In India the village structure is often influenced by the caste system. In central and southern Africa it is influenced by the extended-family and tribal system. In Latin America the patterns introduced by spanish colonists are still being followed wherever spontaneous settlement takes place, and are often adopted by professional planners.

Village houses in many tropical countries are flimsy and primitive. Often nothing more substantial is needed since most of the work and a great deal of family and social life takes place in the open. Where temperature is comfortable, people often sleep outside on the ground or on rooftops. In colder climates the high Andes of Peru and Bolivia for instance-the family may share their house with their livestock for warmth and safety.

In developing countries, generally speaking, there has been little change in the centuries-old tradition of village designs and construction. Such improvement as taken place has been mostly in the provision of public utilities. Even in western Europe, where settlement planning and rural housing standards have improved rapidly, there are still areas where housing and village facilities have advanced very little. In eastern Europe there have been great efforts to rationalise settlement patterns in order to increase agricultural production and facilitate the provision of community services.[22]

Generally, the main problem is that rural planning and village designs have been neglected fields. Rural settlements, therefore, tend to develop in an uncontrolled fashion, exposed to many environmental hazards, natural and man made, and themselves sometimes cause environmental damage. Both of these tendencies could be avoided by proper planning. In particular the haphazard location of rural settlements lays them open to natural disasters and makes them liable to damage the natural environment. In many parts of the world rural settlements are located near rivers or creeks that periodically overflow and flood the surrounding areas. In tropical countries the retreating flood waters breed mosquitoes and other disease carriers. Where the best land is owned by wealthy farmers, as frequently occurs in the Andes, poorer peasants are forced to settle on steep slopes exposed to the danger of landslides. In other circumstances villages are located without regard to the risk of avalanches, hurricanes or tidal waves.

There always in some sort of rationale behind the location of settlements: commercial convenience, ease of access, security against attack or some other good reason. But no one reason, however valid, can ensure that the location is suitable for all aspects of human welfare. Comprehensive planning would take into account the whole range of factors essential to a rewarding and healthy environment.

In addition to the hazards of location most rural settlements in developing countries suffer environmental deficiencies of their own-notably poor housing, a lack of uncontaminated water and inadequate facilities for disposing of human, animal and household wastes. These problems are interrelated and often aggravated by acute poverty and rapid population growth. Absence of decent drinking water is perhaps the most common and crucial problem. Lacking centralised water supply systems, most villages depend upon wells, tanks, ponds, rivers and lakes as sources of drinking water. In rural India about 99 per cent of households depend on a water source of doubtful wholesomeness which is usually more than one hundred yards from the house. Similar conditions prevail in several countries of Africa and Asia. Traditional building materials add to the health hazards by harbouring disease-bearing insects and rodents. In the Philippines, for instance, the typical rural dwelling has walls and roof of nipa or cogood grass and a slatted bamboo floor raised five feet or more above the ground on bamboo or wooden posts, the underfloor space being used to store agricultural products or to shelter animals. In Kenya most rural dwellings are built of mud and wattle with grass thatch. Generally, throughout the developing world, the use of organic building materials brings the dangers of fire, decomposition and water damage.

In the rural regions of the tropics, in spite of a great deal of progress in public health, epidemic and endemic diseases remain a constant threat to millions of people. Although malaria has been eradicated in some areas, it remains man's most common disease, followed by snail fever *(schistosomiasis)*. Intestinal infections are the most common cause of infant mortality. Onchocereiasis blinds enormous numbers of people. Yaws and guinea-worm strike down villagers at the beginning of the rainy season when they need good health to plant food crops.

In many rural areas man destroys the ability of the land to support him. Cutting down forests or burning scrub and grassland for farming impoverishes the soil and may lead to the drying up of water courses and to soil erosion. More 'advanced' techniques can be equally damaging. Large irrigation reservoirs breed insects and change established life cycles, thereby threatening crops. Pesticides, while increasing agricultural output, may poison water courses. Large-scale mining, quarying and logging and the introduction of mechanised industries have modified the environment by destroying natural features and generating pollutants. Some governments and entrepreneurs consider that environmental hazards are the price that has to be paid for industrialisation and development but many of these detrimental effects can be avoided by proper physical planning and regard for environmental consequences.

REFERENCES

1. R.L. Singh, 'Meaning, Objectives and Scope of Settlement Geography", *National Geographical Journal of India,* Vol. VII, 1961, pp. 12-13.
2. M. Aurousseau, "The Arrangement of Rural Population", *Geographical Review,* Vol. 10, 1920, p. 223.
3. A.V. Perpillou, *Human Geography,* Edinburgh, Longmans, 1966, pp. 406-414.
4. Paul Vidal de la Blache: *Principles of Human Geography,* New York, 1962, p. 316.
5. E. Ahmad, "Rural Settlement Types in U.P.", *Annals of the Association of American Geographers,* Vol. XLII, 1952, p. 230.
6. R.K. Mukerjee, *Man and His Habitation,* London, 1940, pp. 63-64.
7. Paul Vidal de la Blache: Op.cit. p. 316.
8. R. B. Hall, "Some Rural Settlement form in Japan", *Geographical Review,* Vol. XXI, 1931, p. 98.
9. O.H. K. Spate: "The Indian Village", *Geography,* Vol. 37, 1952, p. 148.
10. R. L. Singh, "Evolution of Settlement in the Middle Ganga Valley", *National Geographical Journal of India,* Vol. 1, 1955, p. 104.
11. R.E. Dickinson, "Rural Settlements in German Lands", *Annals of the Association of American Geographers,* Vol. XXXIX, 1949, p. 240.
12. M. Anass, "The Pattern of Rural Settlement in the Sub-Himalayan Region (East)", *Geographer,* Vol. VI, 1954, pp. 24-25.
13. M.A. Lefevre, *'L' Habitat Rural in Belgique Liege,* 1924.
14. H.J. Kauming, 'L' Habitat Rural aux Pays-bas', *Tudsch, Kon, Ned. Aardrs. Gen.* Vol. 55, pp. 644-45.
15. R. Martiny, 'Grudrissgestaltung der dentschen Siedlungen' *Petermans Milt,* 1928, p. 197.
16. Ch. L.Biermann, Habitat Rural in Suisse Comptess Rendu, *Union Geographique Internationale, de Paris,* Section IV, pp. 17-32.
17. R. Biassuti, 'Richarche suit tifi degli insediamenti rurali in Italia, Comptess Rendu, *Union Geographique Internationale,* de Paris, Section III, pp. 7-16.
18. Crijic, *La Geographie Humaine des Balkaniques.*
19. V. Mihaelescu, Une Carte de l'Habitat Rural en Roumania Comptess Rendu, *Union Geographique Internationale de Paris,* Section III, pp. 33-35.
20. B. Zaborski, "Surele Forme des villages en Ploguet Laur repartition. *Boletin, Societe Geographique de Owlac,* Vol. 22, 1928, pp. 65-76.
21. Paul Vidal de la Blache, *Op. cit.,* p. 300.
22. R. L. Singh, *Op. cit.,* p. 102.

12

DISTRIBUTION OF RURAL SETTLEMENTS

The distribution of rural settlements is quite uneven in the world. The factors which affect the distribution of rural settlements are physical, cultural and economic. This chapter mainly concerns with the distribution of rural settlements in different parts of the world.

TABLE 12.1: Distribution of Rural Settlements in the World

Continent	Number of Villages	Settlement Types	Patterns
Asia	15,00,000	Compact	Rectangular
North America	3,00,000	Dispersed	Farmstead
South America	5,00,000	Semi-sprinkled	Amorphous
Europe	9,00,000	Semi-compact	Square/ Rectangular
Africa	10,00,000	Semi-sprinkled	Lineors
Australia	1,00,000	Semi-sprinkled	Amorphous

Source: Compiled by R.B. Mandal, 1993.

Rural Settlements in Europe

In European countries the rural settlements are found from dispersed to nucleated type and sometimes they are mixed in nature. Dispersed human settlements are found in mountainous plateau and rough terrain. Hamlets are quite commonly found. According to Houston in Europe dispersed rural settlements are found in North Belgium, lower valley of Rhine, Neitherland, Mid German Plateau to Karpethian mountains, Alps mountain, Perenese mountains,

Cantabrian mountain chain, Apenine Mountain ranges and Balkan Peninsula. About the rural settlements of Mediterranean lands Blache opined that the rural settlements found on the southern slope of sieraneweda are very close to the olive cultivated area. In Sciesly Island dispersed rural settlement is found above the height of 300 to 800 metres. Beyond this dispersed rural settlements are also found in areas of chestnut cultivation on the slope of Alps mountain. Semi-sprinkled rural settlement is also found in medium densely settled area's. In lower river valley's of grapes cultivation nucleated rural settlement is found.[1]

In Northern Europe where glacial soil is mainly distributed such areas are also favourable spot for dispersed rural settlement. On the karst plateau of Yugoslavia compact rural settlements are found where as the plateau lands of Scotland, Ireland and Wales dispersed rural settlements are found. In the Peninsula of Iberian and Bulgaria due to rough terrain hamletted rural settlements are found. In the Eastern part of France Strassendorf settlements are found in which outside the house plough, bullockcart and other agricultural implements are kept, which shows the lack of space in rasidential area. In Narmondy fishing area hamletted rural settlements are found. Similar is the case in terraced farming areas of perenese mountains.

In the frontier areas of France and Spain on hill tops Bosque villages are found which have a characteristic of fencing wall from all sides. In many parts of Spain the roof of the houses are covered with palm leaves. In the inner parts of Spain where the rainfall is relatively low shephered resides in these areas of pasturelands where seasonal migration could be witnessed. In the central part of France and Spain several villagers are located in the valleys of plateaus. Due to difficult geographical conditions the human life is very problematic, where in one house men and beasts live together.

On the southern slope of Alps several villages are located in order to get sufficient sunrays, whereas on the northern slope of Alps very few rural settlements are found. On the sea coasts small but beautiful rural settlements are found here and there.[2]

In the agricultural tracts of Italy compact rural settlements are found since long. Similar is the case in plainlands of Belgium, Neitherlands and Luxemberg where redroofed rural settlements are found.

Rural Settlements of Mediterranean Lands

In Europe large rural settlements are mainly located in Mediterranean lands. Such large settlements are distributed in industrial tracts, Ligurian in the Rhone valley, Scisly and Turkey. In Greece large villages are found in the southern part where fruit cultivation prevails.

1. *Discontinuous Nucleated Settlements or Eschdorf*

In this type the rural settlements are not continuous. These settlements originated during medieval period after the cleaning of forests especially in valley plains. The settlements are considered in between compact and dispersed type which is known as hamlet. In this type, the people of several occupations and castes reside. This type of rural settlements are found in Scandinavia, Poland, Central Germany, Belgiüm, Neitherland, Luxemburg and Denmark.

2. *Einzclhorf or Isolated Village*

This type of rural settlement developed in the beginning of colonisation which have a very low expansion. This type is found mainly in Kent, Iceland and celtic settlement area of wales.

3. *Haufendorf or Clustered Villages*

This is also a type of discontinuous human settlements which is found in western part of U.S.S.R. to Northern France. Germany, Southern Poland to Hungàry and Ukrain.

4. *Strassendorf or Street Settlements*

In North Central Europe, Poland, Germany and Czekoslovakia street settlement Pattern is found. It has got prominency in Bulgaria and in Slavic villages street is a dominant feature.

5. *Rundplatzdorf or Round Village*

This type of rural settlement is found from the south-eastern part of Denmark to western part of Poland and in the plains of Bohemia. In these area the houses are constructed inside fencing wall where a big gate is also constructed in order to get out of the house. Even today in many areas such round villages are found.

6. *Ciflik or Square Villages*

Square villages are found in Turky which developed during Ottomon empire. The settlements are found around fencing wall which is known as ciflik. This type of settlement is still found in Black sea area and Balkan peninsula. Most of the ciflik settlements are one storey building and the centre of the house has a courtyard.

7. *Hamletted but Clustered Settlements*

This type of rural settlement is especially found in Rumania and Transcaucasia to Mid-eastern part of Europe. It is a settlement of clustered fashion.

8. *Marschufendorfer or Marsh Settlement*

In wetlands of Europe houses have been constructed on pillars. In some areas large human settlements have been made on wetlands but the main difficulty is that such settlements are getting submerged inside the water whose examples are found in Hamberg and Rotterdam besides the surrounding areas of Baltic sea and Finland.[3]

Rural Settlements of U.S.S.R.

In agriculturally dominant areas of U.S.S.R. old and compact rural settlements are found especially west of Ural. Nowadays this type of rural settlement spreads each in Eastern part of Siberia where community house and kulaks are found in case of Kolkhoz farms. The allotment of houses are done by the government and the houses have been constructed by the proposed housing committee. In kolkhoz settlements besides peasant family, government godowns of foodgrains, agricultural implements, motor garrage, cold storage, poultry farm, hospital and technical centres of schools are found. In Eastern Europe where the urban influence is widely observed they are the areas of compact rural settlements.

In the forest tract of Taiga backward people reside which includes, Yukagir, Chukchi, Yakut, Tungu, Osteyak, Samoyed, Koryak etc. In Taiga area these people reside in community homes. Their houses are quite temporary made of the bark of reindeer in the form of tent. These people also transport their goods from one place to another on reindeer. They lead a life of transhumance in search of pasture land, food and water. Near Arctic ocean Eskimose reside on Kamchatka Peninsula. Their houses are made of snow pieces known as "Igloo". It has a length of 12 to 19 metres covered with the bark of whale and reindeer. Such houses are completely adjusted with the local environment.

Rural Settlements of China

In China temporary houses are known as yurt. Such house is completely supported by string and look like tent. This type of house is found in Northern China and Mongolia and it is known as "ridge Pole tents". Several Yurt help in making the village. In mountainous, plateau and cold climate areas hamletted settlements are found, whereas in plain lands of river basins and agricultural tracts nucleated rural settlements are found. In mountainous *Hsien* (Janpad) of China due to low density of population dispersed rural settlement is found but in Hwangho basin compact rural settlement is found. In China head of the house is known as *Yuzbashi* whereas head of the several houses is known as *onbashi.* The person who look after nine families is known as "Mingbashi". In Shanshi province the person who look after a family is known as 'Tutung' in the plateau of Tibet. In the desert of Gobi temporary settlement is found in Tarim basin areas but permanent settlement is found in the market centres of khotan yarkkand and kasgar. In the loess area of China fragmented settlements are found here and there. In Fukin province of China dispersed rural settlement is known as 'sentak' which belongs to aboriginal tribes of the area. 'Sentak' is completely made of bamboo structure.[4]

Rural Settlements of Japan

In Japan the majority of population resides in rural settlements but due to increased influence of industrialisation they may be called urbanised villages because shop is located in one corner of the house. In the plains of Kwanto and Ishikari nucleated rural settlement is found but on the slope of mountains settlements are found in a terraced fashion. On the western mountains of Honshu and Hakaido dispersed rural settlement is found.

Rural Settlements in South East Asia

South-East Asia covers the areas of Myanmar, Thailand, Cambodia, Laos, Vietnam and East Indies. All these are areas which comes under Monsoon climate but Indonesia and Malaysia come under equatorial climate. In these areas compact settlements are found in plain areas but fragmented settlements is the rule of mountainous tract. In agriculturally prosperous areas double storey houses are found but in areas of poor land capability mud wall and tiled roof single storey houses are found. In mountainous and plateau area of forest cover wooden structure is also found in Meghalaya of India, Shan Plateau of Myanmar and Vietnam. In the river valleys of Irawady, Chindwin, Minam, Miping, Miyom and Mekong nucleated rural settlement is the rule. In the Eastern coastal tract of Malaysia ridge type dispersed villages are found which are made of local raw material of forest wood. In the riverine plains of Pahang and Kelantan nucleated rural settlements are widely distributed.[4]

In Cheribon, Rimbag, Bogor Priyaggan and Madura Plantation area of Java nucleated rural settlements are distributed. Villages are widely distributed and they are densely settled. On the rural houses of Java the effect of European architecture is quite evident.

In some of the marshy areas of South-East Asia hutments of grass and leaves are found especially in the delta area of Ganges, Godavari and Krishna rivers. Such settlements are also belong to Sakai and Semang tribes who made it out of bamboo, reeds besides wattle and daub available locally.

American Rural Settlements

Before colonization Red Indians resides in North America. At present their population is about 52,00,000 who resides in different states of USA. In USA first of all human settlements established in 1607 A.D. in James Town, in 1609 in Point comfort and 1610 in Kigngtan, Henric and cocksindel. All these rural settlements were established near Chesapik bay along James river. Rural settlements were established in 1680 in Norfolk and 1752 in Portsmouth. Later on these rural settlements transformed into urban settlements. In 1624 A.D. crown coloney had been declared in Virginia state. In 17th century with the help of Negro migrants from Africa agricultural farmstead established in Iowa, Wyoming, Kentucky, Nebraska,

Dakota and Texas states of U.S.A. The farmers house is located in one corner of the agricultural plot. They are connected with good metalled roads so that childrens could be sent to school, grain bins could be established in the nearby areas for easy handling of export and import. Each farmstead has the facility of car Garrage, tethering ground of cattle, separate residence for servants besides tractor repairing station and poultry farm. Such farmstead has the facility of telephone connections, tractor repairing station and electricity supply.

REFERENCES

1. World Habitat Day, 1986, *Report on Global Observations,* pp. 4-5.
2. Marc Jerczynski, The National Settlement System, *Various Reports IV*, Warsaw, 1963.
3. R.B. Mandal, *Systems of Rural Settlements in Developing Countries,* Concept Publishing Company, New Delhi, 1989.
4. B.S. Negi, *Rural Geography,* Kedarnath Ramnath, Meeruth, 1989.

13

SIZE AND SPACING OF RURAL SETTLEMENTS

J.W. Watson has identified, geography as a discipline in distance.[1] Unfortunately uptil now it has attracted little attention of the geographers especially the size and spacing of rural settlements.

The variation in size and spacing of rural settlements is a physically established fact on the earth surface due to variations in environmental conditions. According to Mukerjee,[2] the covariance of spacing of rural settlements depends on such fundamental factors as fertility of land, productivity of agriculture, nature of crops grown, agronomic characteristics, distribution and availability of water, density of rural population, population size and types of rural settlements, mode of living, history and stages of land occupancy, relative strengths of tribal population and several other factors. But according to Donglass[3] the spacing of rural settlements depends on three factors e.g.:

(a) The agricultural prosperity,
(b) Surface relief of the land, and
(c) Historical perspectives of the area.

Donglass was of the opinion that rural settlements are rural luxury and they are densest where greatest agricultural prosperity is found.

The objective of this study is to identify the regional patterns of spacing of rural settlements in India and to valuate the characteristics of determinants which command the spatial character of settlements in different areas. Spacing is also another expression of density, but it does not imply a geometrical pattern in the arrangement of settlements.

The formula for determining the spacing of rural settlements is based on their density in the rural area. Walenty Wineed, the polish geographer, derived a formula[4] to determine the frequency of towns in any area. As the settlements are ordinarily placed at the inter-section points of a rectangular grid, he assumes that the best figure to use for inter-settlement distance is equal to the square-root of the area divided by the number of settlements within that area. The formula is as follows:

$$D = \sqrt{\frac{A}{N}}$$

where D is considered as the average distance between settlements. A is the total area under consideration, and N is the number of settlements within that area. The method applied for size of the rural settlements is as follows:

$$S = \frac{P}{N}$$

where S is the average size of population per village, P is the rural population of the anchal and N is the number of villages in the anchal. The data was calculated for all the states and grouped into four classes of hierarchy on the basis of quartile value. A distribution map was prepared by drawing isopleths which gave a good regional pattern for the analysis of the population size of rural settlements.

In India, the size and spacing of rural settlements are mainly dependent upon three factors:

(a) Effects of floods,
(b) Natural fertility of soil, and
(c) Surface configuration.

North Indian Plain is a region of destructive floods. Numerous rivers and rivulets draining the Himalayan foothills in the north and Peninsular plateau in the south flow towards each other and ultimately discharge their water into the Ganges in the middle. The effects of recurrent floods in these rivers seem to be most potent on the landscape of the region and guide the size and spacing of rural settlements in their respective commands.

The flood affected areas increases the size of village population, their spacing also increases. This dual relationship of size and spacing in the flood affected areas suggests that it is the most significant controlling factor for both higher size and greater spacing of rural settlements in the region.

In areas prone to floods, the lands are fertile, because of annual inundation by the rivers that bring new alluvial deposits in the fields. There is, however, medium density of population in these areas. The relatively higher sites fit for human settlements are somewhat rare in such areas because of the lack of slope. Thus, these areas turn into a vast lake as far as our eyes can see during the rainy season. During this period one has to travel by boat from one settlement to another. Settlements are therefore, large in size but at greater distances from each other. In flood affected areas, the spacing of rural settlement is over 2.40 kilometres from each other and the size of population of the village ranges from 900 to over 3000 persons.

The areas which are not affected by floods have smaller villages and their spacing is also closer. The fertile plains of U.P., Bihar and Himachal Pradesh have very little effects of floods. Here the settlements are closely spaced within 2 kilometres distance from each other and their size also decreases roughly from 300 to 1000 persons per village. This shows that as the fertility of the soil increases, the size and spacing of the settlement also register a decline to a certain limit.

It may be noted that in spacing of settlements there comes a stage when the land reaches the limit of its capability to support the population. Under such conditions, if the settlements grow larger in size, their spacing may not increase in all cases to maintain the balance of the man-land ratio.

In South India the states of Maharashtra, Kerala, Tamilnadu and Andhra Pradesh have assured irrigation facilities from canals, pynes and ahars, and with greater use of fertilizers in the field they produce larger quantities of food grains. Thus they are also aided by the natural fertility of the soil and an adequate amount of rainfall. Thus these areas can support larger villages with closer spacing. In Northern India the plain of Bihar, West Bengal, U.P., Himachal Pradesh and Rajasthan also have good fertile soils coupled with sufficient rainfall and relative freedom from floods. They are thus able to support large sized villages with less than two kilometres spacing. (Table 13.1)

Human habitations are often found in rugged terrains, forest clad mountain slopes and non-cultivable waste lands. Such lands never support a dense population, because the fertility of the soil is low. The few inhabitants in such areas depend upon cattle rearing, hunting and also forest products like timber, lumber or herbs, etc. for their livelihood. The whole of Dun and Sumeshwar hills in north-west Champaran district and the Chotanagpur Scarp Belt in South Bihar Plain are devoid of population concentration, except for a few tribal and scheduled caste people. Here the factors like the fear of wild animals, the lack of transport facilities and building materials and above all the poverty of people are the important as they retard the size and increase the spacing of rural settlements. The conditons are not favourable for human settlement above 150 metres contour line, because such lands have a high slope coupled with over 150 cms of rainfall, which leaches the soil and reduces the fertility to a great extent. These areas are also rugged and covered with dense forests, with the settlements few and far between.

In this regard, it is also noticeable that where the density of road is high, population tends to live in small villages as in Gujarat and the Punjab and conversely, where the road density is low, there is greater concentration in large and medium sized villages, as in the states of Bihar, West Bengal and Assam.

Spatial Pattern of Rural Settlements

Four types of spacing of settlement areas have been identified with the help of Median and quartile values of data on spacing of rural settlements. The discussion of these spatial groups are as follows:

(a) Areas of Very High Spacing (more than 3.46 kilometres)
(b) Areas of Medium High Spacing (3.45 to 2.57 kilometres)
(c) Areas of Low Spacing (2.56 to 1.95 kilometres)
(d) Areas of very low spacing (less than 1.94 kilometres).

(a) *Areas of Very High Spacing*

In plain lands of India the spacing of rural settlements are found to be high and size of villages are also very high e.g. Assam and Kerala. In areas of rough terrain also the spacing of settlements is high but due to low agricultural productivity of the land their relative population size is small. For example, in Arunachal Pradesh the spacing between rural settlement is 5.68 kilometres and the average population size is just 289 persons only.

TABLE 13.1 Size and Spacing of Rural Settlements in India, 1991.

States	Population Size Average	Distance between Settlements Average (in Km)
Andhra Pradesh	2436	3.41
Assam	1003	2.01
Bihar	1278	1.71
Gujarat	2253	3.50
Haryana	2424	2.73
Himachal Pradesh	302	1.94
Jammu & Kashmir	1187	6.25
Kerala	22879	5.93
Madhya Pradesh	937	2.67
Maharashtra	2199	3.13
Manipur	934	3.59
Meghalaya	384	2.34
Karnataka	1671	2.86
Nagaland	1266	4.50
Orissa	671	1.95
Punjab	1656	2.16
Rajasthan	1317	3.43
Tamilnadu	3535	0.97
Tripura	581	1.55
U.P.	1233	1.73
West Bengal	1786	1.62
Andaman and Nicobar	713	4.84
Arunachal Pradesh	289	5.68
Chandigarh	24643	2.09
Delhi	38561	2.17
Dadra and Nagar Haveli	1924	2.82
Goa	2878	3.39
Laccadweep	5168	1.85
Pondicherry	2371	0.41
Total/Average	1466	2.56

Source: Calculated from census of India, 1991.

In flood affected areas the higher sites are relatively infrequent and the need of cooperation in paddy cultivation and crop storage makes compact settlements imperative.

(b) *Areas of Medium High Spacing*

In this category the spacing of rural settlements varies from 3.43 for Rajasthan to 2.67 for Madhya Pradesh. The other states fall within this category are Andhra Pradesh, Goa, Maharashtra, Karnataka, Dadra and Nagar Haveli and Haryana. In all these areas the relatively high distance between rural settlements is caused due to lesser amount of rainfall and rough terrain which do not permit closer spacing of settlements.

(c) *Areas of Low Spacing*

In this category the relative distance between rural settlements vary from 2.66 to 1.95 kilometres. It comprises the states of Meghalaya, Delhi, Punjab, Chandigarh and Assam. These areas are relatively dry which force people to settle closely due to high depth of masonry wells in order to fetch potable water. But Assam is a state where flood and rough terrain both dominate the scene. The flood has an effect of closer settlements where as undulating landscape disfavours closeness.

(d) *Areas of Very Low Spacing*

In this category the spacing of rural settlements vary between 1.94 to 0.41 kilometres which is the lowest. The States which come in this category are Pondicherry (0.41), Laccadweep (1.85), West Bengal (1.62), Tripura (1.55), Himachal Pradesh (1.94) and Bihar (1.71) kilometres. In all these states tightly nucleated rural settlements are found. The spacing of rural settlements and population size of the villages decrease drastically in areas free from floods even though the density of population per square kilometre is high. This means that the availability of water is the main consideration for the development of settlements in such areas. Wherever a well is constructed, some houses are built and a settlement unit is established. In the fertile plains of Pondicherry and Bihar, rural settlements are very closely spaced because the land capability is high. For example, all the well irrigated tracts of North Indian Plains have a closer spacing of rural settlements coupled with relatively lower population size and high density of population.

The coefficient of correlation for the population size of rural settlements and spacing in India comes to $r = 0.34$, which is a clearcut sign of low correlation value as the relationship is not directly related but they are variable in character.

Rank-Size Relationship of Rural Settlements

Under the rank-size rule, the number of settlements should continue to increase as their size decreases so that we should expect not only villages with higher population size, but more smaller sized settlements than villages and more isolated farmsteads than smaller settlements. Haggett[5] has noted that this relationship may not hold true universally, because isolated farmsteads are not everywhere more numerous than hamlets.[6] The existence of a straight line rank size curve for settlements in many countries and regions of the world[7] e.g. in Darbhanga, Saharsa, Purnea, Bhagalpur and Munger are found. These are the lands of rivers, Chaurs, lakes, tals and marshes and all of them present a similar character in the size and spacing of rural settlements. For example in Bhagalpur district the riverine anchals of Bihpur, Naugachhia and Gopalpur have a population size of 2246, 2545 and 2934 persons per villages and a spacing of 2.57, 2.64 and 3.49 kilometres respectively.

In the Chotanagpur Scarp Belt of South Bihar Plain villages are situated at relatively greater distances. Siting is selective and related to forest clearings, slope, extent of alluvium, water supply, etc. The distance between villages may be abnormally large if wide patches of forest or difficult terrain such as steep ridges intervene. Except small residual hills and rocky exposures, the soil is uniform in thickness and fertility and the land is level in the plains so that the villages are fairly evenly distributed. All the marginal anchals of flood affected area with assured natural irrigation and good fertile soil come under this category. Here the inter village distance is reduced to some extent and their population size also gets decreased.

Under this category, the rural settlements with a population of 933 and above, and a spacing of 1.31 to 1.81 kilometres are fairly widely distributed over the entire flood plains of the Ganges, the Kosi, the Kamla, the Balan and the Bhuthi rivers, except in the marshy areas of Saharsa and Purnea districts in the north-eastern sector of the plain. The marginal flood plains of the Gandak, the Burhi-Gandak and the Adhwara group of rivers are typical example of this class of settlements in the west.

In South Bihar Plain, due to relatively more recent development of settlements and an inferior quality of soil, villages have a lower population size coupled with higher spacing. Only agriculturally prosperous anchals such as Paliganj, Bikram, Arwal, Karpi, Daudnagar and others come under this category of spacing.

The areas which are fertile and free from floods are included in this category. Here the spacing of rural settlements ranges from 0.88 to 1.30 kilometres. The spacing of rural settlements and the population size of the villages decrease drastically in areas free from floods even though this suggests that it is a 'normal' condition[8] even though the reasons of its existence are far from clear.

An examination suggests that the villages 1800 and 3410 population size deviate considerably from the trend established by these centres with a population of less than 1800. The same type of deviation is also noticeable in the lower reaches of the graph which shows villages with a population of less than 300. Both these categories of villages are significantly smaller in number than one would expect. The value for anchals in the flood affeted zone lies well above the projected general trend of the rank-size rule on the upper north-eastern part of the graph. Table 13.1 shows that the number of rural settlements decreases towards the higher population group but it increases rapidly towards the lower population size.

An attempt has been made to statistically analyse the relationship between the rank order of anchals according to the number of settlements they contain, and the average 1961 population of settlements in each anchal. The rank order of anchals has been taken as the independent variable since the number of revenue mauza was fixed by revenue authorities long ago, while the population size changes every year.

It is interesting to note that the value of product moment coefficient of correlation comes to 0.92, showing that the relationship between the two is positive and extremely close. Correlation coefficient has been calculated according to the following formula:

$$r = \frac{\Sigma xy - \dfrac{(\Sigma x.\ \Sigma y)}{N}}{\sqrt{\left(\Sigma x^2 \dfrac{(\Sigma x)^2}{N}\right)\left(\Sigma y - \dfrac{(\Sigma y)^2}{N}\right)}} = r = 0.34$$

where r is the pearsonian correlation coefficient, x is rank and y is population size. The number of observations N is 350.

TABLE 13.2: Population Size of Rural Settlements in India, 1991

States	Below 200	200 to 500	500 to 1000	1000 to 2000	2,000 to 5,000	5,000 to 10,000	Above 10,000	Total
Arunachal Pradesh	4,790	4,068	5,227	6,464	5,609	1,058	163	27,379
Andhra Pradesh	2,498	532	146	63	16	2	—	3,257
Assam	—	—	—	—	—	—	—	—
Bihar	14,785	19,040	15,792	10,841	5,842	1,054	192	67,546
Goa	47	78	60	102	90	34	1	412
Gujarat	1,386	3,472	4,956	5,108	2,725	418	49	18,114
Haryana	465	1,034	1,776	1,883	1,346	221	20	6,745
Himachal Pradesh	10,544	4,561	1,243	364	92	3	—	16,807
Jammu & Kashmir	1,275	2,027	1,715	1,046	393	20	1	6,477
Karnataka	4,112	7,177	7,342	5,239	2,722	401	35	27,028
Kerala	3	2	2	13	72	222	905	1,219
Madhya Pradesh	15,806	25,941	19,282	8,118	2,046	155	4	71,352
Maharashtra	4,523	9,248	12,330	8,954	3,604	579	116	39,354
Manipur	938	556	264	174	90	12	1	2,035
Meghalaya	3,199	1,290	304	85	24	—	—	4,902
Mizoram	235	267	127	62	30	—	—	721
Nagaland	297	383	241	143	47	1	—	1,112
Orissa	15,924	14,981	9,805	4,561	1,234	47	1	46,553

(Contd.)

TABLE 13.2: *(Contd.)*

States	Below 200	200 to 500	500 to 1,000	1,000 to 2,000	2,000 to 5,000	5,000 to 10,000	Above 10,000	Total
Punjab	1,571	2,863	3,712	2,819	1,256	120	1	12,342
Rajasthan	7,861	10,425	8,537	5,468	2,335	47	21	34,968
Sikkim	58	177	137	60	8	—	—	440
Tamilnadu	794	1,732	3,172	4,570	4,381	1,000	182	15,831
Tripura	34	91	40	253	274	56	8	856
Uttar Pradesh	22,391	30,817	30,027	20,380	8,148	751	52	1,12,566
West Bengal	6,168	9,755	9,396	7,538	4,383	702	82	38,024
Andaman and Nicobar	306	100	54	23	8	—	—	491
Chandigarh	4	2	6	5	7	—	—	24
Dadra and Nagar Haveli	1	16	16	27	7	3	—	70
Daman-Diu	—	—	—	—	—	—	—	—
Delhi	9	9	36	74	71	15	1	214
Laccadweep	1	—	—	1	4	1	—	7
Pondichery	48	78	83	48	28	6	—	291
Total	12,0973	1,00,722	1,35,928	94,486	46,892	7,202	1,834	5,57,137

Source: Statistical Handbook on India, T.T. Maps, 1991, pp. 10-11.

On n–2 degree of freedom the correlation would be significant if 't' is greater than 1.96 with a probability of 95 per cent and 2.23 with a probability of 98 per cent. The calculated value of 't' in our case is 43.45, showing that the correlation is highly significant.

The regression of y on x has been calculated by the method of least squares according to the formula:

$$Y = a + bx$$

where Y is the dependent variable, x is the independent variable and a and b are given by the following formula:

$$b = \frac{N\Sigma xy - (\Sigma x)(\Sigma y)}{(N\Sigma x^2) - (\Sigma x)^2}, \text{ and}$$

$$a = \frac{(\Sigma y - b\Sigma x)}{N}$$

where all other values are same as given above for the coefficient of correlation.

The regression of y upon x has been determined as 200.75 + 4.83x, that is the average population size of villages in an anchal would be 200.75 + 4.83 times the rank of that anchal. The standard error of estimate, Sey was not calculated as the rank order is entirely an independent factor but is affected by the change in population size of a place and, therefore, there is no point in carrying the estimate to a definite mathematical conclusion. The main purpose of this study, was only to demonstrate the close relationship that exists between average population size of villages in a state and the rank of state in India according to population.

REFERENCES

1. J.W. Watson, "Geography: A Discipline in Distance", *Scottish Geographical Magazine,* Vol. 71, 1955 pp. 1-13.
2. A.B. Mukerjee, "Spacing of Rural Settlements in Andhra Pradesh", *Geographical Outlook,* Vol. VI, 1969, p. 1.
3. G.T. Trewartha, "The Unincorporated Hamlet: The Element of the American Settlement Fabric". *Annals of the Association of American Geographers,* Vol. 33, 1943, pp. 32-81.
4. *Ibid.*
5. R.H. Alan Baker, "Reversal of the Rank-size Rule", *The Professional Geographer,* Vol. XXI, 1969, p. 386.
6. P. Hagget, *Locational Analysis in Human Geography,* London, Edward Arnold, 1965, p. 106.
7. F.W. Boal and D.B. Johnson, "The Rank Size Rule", *Professional Geographer,* Vol. XVII, 1965, p. 21.
8. B.J.L. Berry and W.L. Garrison, "Alternative Explanation of Urban Rank Size Relationships", *Annals of the Association of American Geographers,* Vol. 48, 1958, p. 83.

14

RURAL DWELLINGS AND HOUSE TYPES

A house is one of the three basic needs of the mankind. It is being used by man as a safeguard of the body from various natural elements since times immemorial. Though its importance varies in various climatic conditions yet the basic need remains more or less the same, as it provides shelter and protection from the rigours of climate.[1] Therefore, it is essential to consider the location, architectural style, shape and size, building materials, house plan, cost, classification and occupancy rate of houses.

The agglomeration of houses marks the origin of settlements and reflects the nature of a region since their character is related to the environment and the cultural heritage of the people.[2] This is because the rural houses are simple structure designed to provide facility of residence for the family of peasants and for storing of grains and implements. Types of granary of Upper Volta could be seen below (Fig. 14.1)

In prehistoric times, people lived in caves and bushes in the north western Terai region of Champaran district and on the edge of the Chotanagpur Scarp Belt.

Evidences have been found in Lomas Rishi cave and Nigope cave,[3] 26 kilometres north of Gaya in Barabar hills and some caves of Rajgir hills regarding these settlements. Thus the earliest shelters used by man were caves. Rocks rolled against the entrances, kept wild beasts away and gave safety to their occupants. Where there were no caves, man took to erecting piles, on which they placed platforms. On the platforms they built huts of grass, reeds (wattle) and wooden stakes. (Fig. 14.2) Sometimes they laced their buildings with the tendous of animals they had killed, sometimes using rope woven from grasses. Always in these early forms of buildings, the idea of

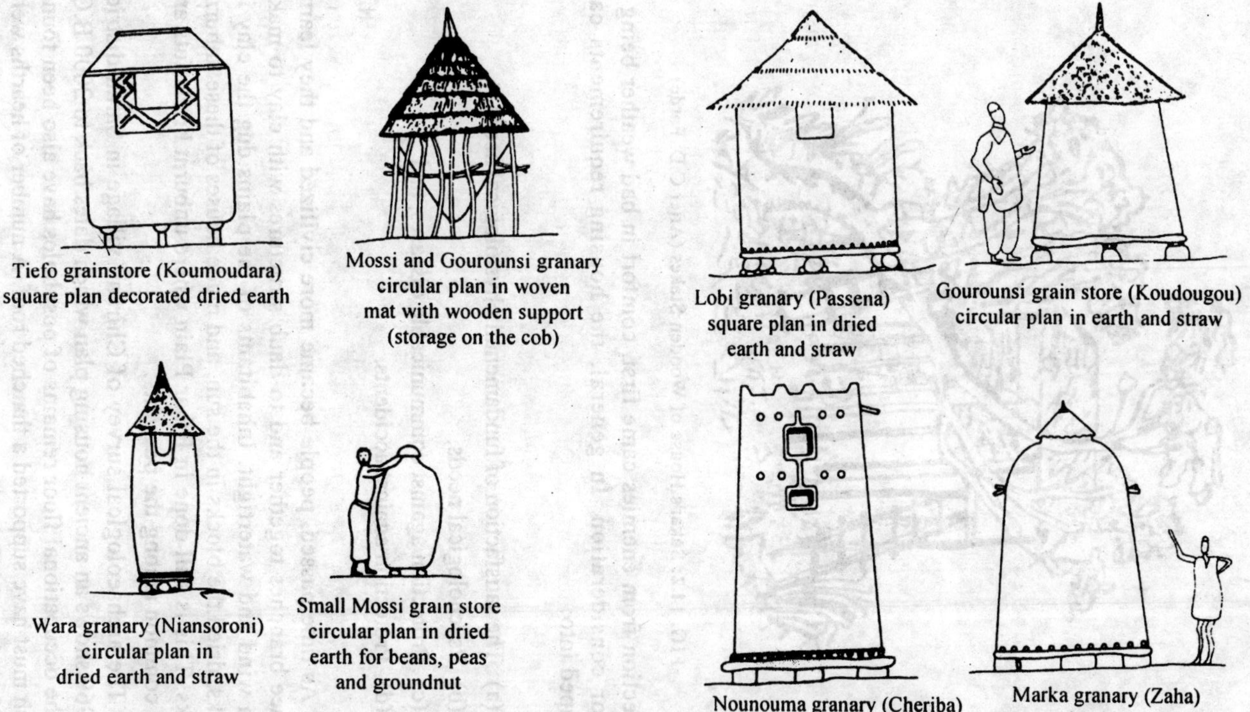

FIG. 14.1: Types of Grainary in Upper Volta (After Da Silva)

FIG. 14.2: Sakai's House of Wooden Stakes (After C.D. Forde)

protection from enemies came first, comfort in bad weather being a minor consideration. In general, the housing requirements can grouped into:

(a) The satisfaction of fundamental physiological needs,
(b) Psychological needs,
(c) Protection against communicable diseases, and
(d) Protection against accidents.

As time passed, people became more civilized and they learnt to lace branches together and to daub structures with clay to make them wind and watertight. Inhabitants of the plains dug the clay in blocks, dried the blocks in the sun, and made houses of these unburnt bricks. This is still done in Bihar Plain where unburnt brick huts are very common among the peasants.

The archaeological survey of Chirand village in Saran district in 1969 shows an ancient housing plan which dates back to 2000 B.C. On the occupational floor remains of post holes have also been found which must have supported a thatched roof. A number of hearths were also found on the floor.[4]

The early houses of this period were, generally, simple circular structures of reeds or thatch with a sloping thatch roof supported by bamboo or wooden poles. Gradually, the huts took in oval, rectangular or square floor plan with a symmetrical roof sloping on two sides (Fig. 14.3). The supply of building materials depends upon locally available trees, reeds, bamboos or similar vegetation.

The development of two or more buildings in a house surrounding an inner courtyard is a much later development. This was necessitated by an increase in the size of the family coupled with greater skill in construction and increase in the affluence of the society. This naturally resulted in the evolution of mud walls and tile roofs which are relatively more permanent materials for house construction.

The monasteries and stupas built with burnt bricks or stones were predominant features during the Buddhist period. Temples were common in the Hindu period but during the Muslim period most of the tombs and mosques were built by demolishing or converting the Hindu temples as is evidenced by their characteristic features even today. The British period was marked by the construction of kothis, dak bungalows, churches and buildings for government offices of that time. These are built of burnt bricks cemented with lime or mortar, and are with tile roofs. In recent years, the construction of government offices in rural development blocks, hospitals and educational institutions shows pucca flat roofs and brick built walls reinforced with cement and concrete.

In the rural areas, however, the mud built house continues to be, by and large, the most common dwelling of an average person. Thatch, reeds or wattle are common building materials for the poorer people particularly in the eastern parts of the Bihar Plain where rainfall is heavy. Economically better off people prefer to have mud-built or brick-built houses with tiled roof, as in the central part of the study region. The more affluent people, are gradually resorting to burnt brick walls with pucca (masonry) roofs.

The outer shape of a house varies considerably in different parts of the Globe. In this variation the guiding factor is use of building materials, the variations in climate and third the purpose for which the house is built. For example, a mosque must be different from a temple or church due to variations in religion.

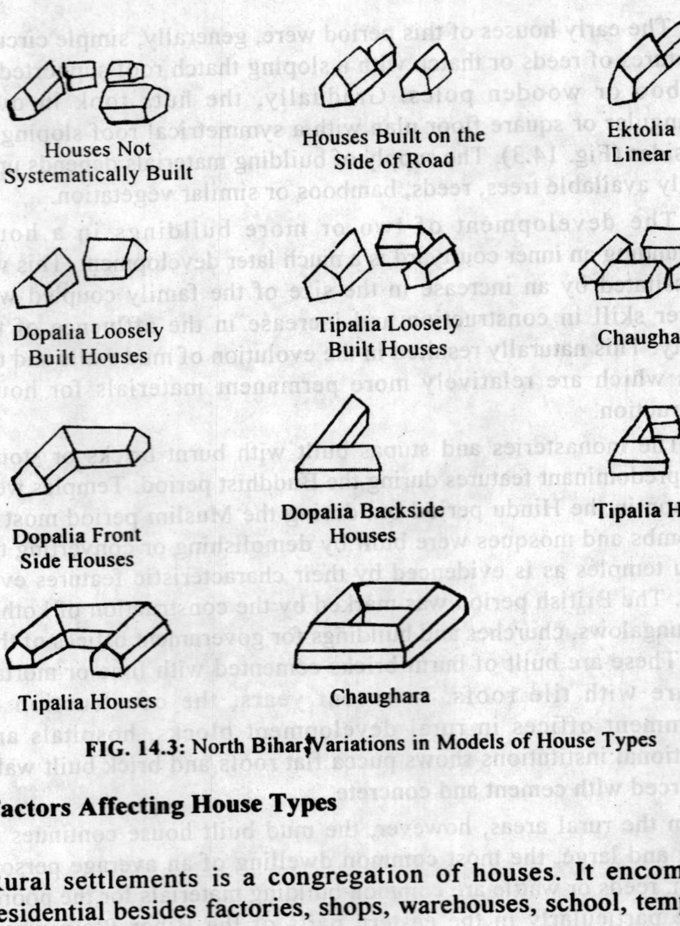

FIG. 14.3: North Bihar: Variations in Models of House Types

Factors Affecting House Types

Rural settlements is a congregation of houses. It encompasses residential besides factories, shops, warehouses, school, temple and

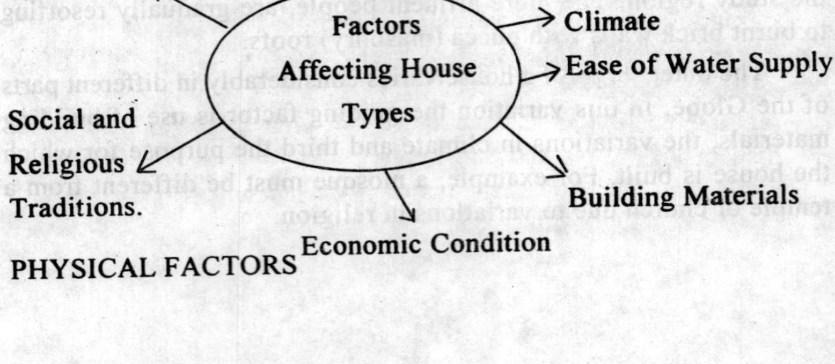

PHYSICAL FACTORS

mosque etc. House is one of the most important need of mankind where people sleep take rest and carry on their occupational activities.

The landform and locational environment are responsible for the variations of house types in different parts of the world. Among, these factors some of the important ones are as follows:

Relief of the Land and Slope

The higher site in plain land are generally get selected for the construction of houses. On hill slopes all the buildings of a village could not be placed on the same height, therefore, they are generally placed at different heights on contour level. In such a house the wall on the mountain side is made smaller whereas it is taller in the front. On the loess Plateau of China the cave shapped houses are made in the hard sandstone of the area.

In the same way, cave dwellers are found in Romania, Bulgaria, Italy and France.

Climate

There is a marked impact of climate on the house types. Such as in equatorial belt people live in hutments, in dry areas people live in mudwall houses, in steppes tent is the main items of shelter followed by snow house of 'Igloo' in the polar region. The impact of climate could also be seen separately.

Temperature: Most of the houses are made east facing just in order to get the first ray of the sun. In the desert people lives in cave in order to save themselves from the scorching sunrays. In temperate region the thicker mud wall is a bit cool than thin walls. Due to these variations the houses are different in different climatic conditions.

Man taps resources and builds houses out of local materials.[5] Physiography, drainage, climate and vegetation have profound effect on the rural house types. Due to the difference in these physical factors, particularly, because of the high intensity of rainfall, the districts of Purnea and Saharsa have thatch or *wattle* (bamboo, reeds, straw, grass or leaves) as the dominant building materials used in the construction of houses. On the other hand, the dwellers of Kaimur plateau in Rohtas people live in houses built of stone pilings. The people of Southern upland plains in South Bihar use mud for the walls and tiles on a bamboo frame as the roofing material in their houses. Mixed type of houses predominate in the North Bihar plains. This distribution attests to the profound influence of physiography and climate. Thus the inhabitants of Saharsa and Purnea districts do not build mud walls because of their destruction by waterlogging during the rainy season as it is a lowlying area and is further subject to a heavy rainfall. Similarly, the inhabitants of Gaya and Rohtas districts cannot use bamboo in their houses simply because bamboos are not cheaply available there, as compared to North Bihar where they are in plenty of supply. North Bihar in general has a heavy rainfall of over 150 cms in comparison with 125 cms of rains in South Bihar plain.

Climate has a pronounced effect upon various architectural designs and the climatic factors like the amount of rainfall, snowfall, directions of wind and storms, aspects of slopes of sunrays, are important. 'The rural interiors are much more stingy of air and light than those of the towns.[6] The amount of rainfall determines the variation in the construction of roof and the walls. The intensity of slope of the roof depends upon the intensity of storms in summer season, level of temperature and amount of rainfall. Climate is also the main reason why most of the inhabitants of the region build their houses facing east instead of west. East facing houses are better ventilated, and the sun rays of the early morning are able to enter it while the west facing house is subject to the scorching after-noon sun, as well as westerly dust storms in the summer season. The slope of the roof ranges between 40° and 60° so that rain water may be quickly drained. An open courtyard is an essential part of the rural house because it provides the family with sunshine in winter days and cool and safe sleeping space during the warm summer nights. It is also used for drying grains, tethering cattle and for various household chores.

Cultural Factors

The socio-economic structure of the region determines the regional variation in dwellings. The cultural factors include the economic condition of the inhabitants, traditions and social conditions, religious superstitions, administrative laws and the materials used in the construction of houses. There are marked differences between houses of the upper and the lower classes of people. The economically advanced areas of the region such as Patna district and parts of Gaya district have good rural houses, but economically backward areas such as Saharsa and Purnea districts have relatively poor materials used in the construction of houses. These houses also represent the cultural attainment of the past and the survival of the tradition may be seen in their simple architectural features.[7]

In the region under study, the cultural environment becomes more effective in determining rural-house types because of the great diversity in castes and classes, and a wide gap between the rich and the poor. In certain localities there are some socially backward and untouchable castes such as Mushars, Doms, etc. People of these castes practically live away from the main village and have only small thatched hovels indicative of their proverty and backwardness. Inhabitants, belonging to the richer classes have better residential buildings built with burnt brick walls and concrete or lime mortar roofs and are located in the best part of the village.

The hamlets of the poor or the backward *Harijan* (untouchable) classes are generally built with thatch or wattle walls and thatch roofs. Even amongst them, the extremely poor may use discarded tin sheets, wood scarp and other waste materials in the construction of houses. Such houses are low, generally less than two metres in height and the doorways rarely more than one metre high. The houses are also single roomed structures, less than 30 sq. metres in area, and are no better than beggar shacks.

In contrast, the upper caste Hindus or the well-to-do peasants prefer to build their houses with mud walls and tile roofs. The more affluent amongst them may construct flat pucca (masonry) roofs supported by brick built walls. These houses face towards the east or the west, and may contain a number of rooms, a courtyard, and verandah with separate cattle sheds according to Hindu principles. Their height is also 4 metres or more. Double storied houses, however, are comparatively rare except in urban areas. The less fortunate have to be satisfied with mudwall houses with thatch roofs, or partly tiled and partly thatched roofs. In the eastern parts of the study area, the thatch roof is preferred as it is cheaper and easily renewed every year. Here the heavy rainfall and waterlogging forbid the construction of mud walls and tile roofs.

Houses are representative of brief periods of time only, as they last but a comparatively few years of time in the history of the people. They are pulled down or they fall into ruins when new ones are built in their place, so that the types of houses indicate to an extent the stage of civilization and arts which attained by a region at a particular age. But wherever the form is preserved through the ages, the cause may be traced to both tradition and utlity in the type of houses.[8] Man has the peculiar tendency to respect tradition and keep on to time honoured customs not only when they do not cost anything or interfere with progress, but even when the observance of such traditions and customs is economically unsound, and impedes progress. The traditional house in the Bihar plain can be divided into two categories: (i) the mud wall and tile roofed structures, and (ii) the thatch walled and thatch roofed structure. The other house types are a variation or hybrid form of these two basic types. The former belongs to the west and the south, and the later to the east and the north within the study region.

Religion and castes also play an important role in determining the plan and architecture of houses. The Muslim houses are generally marked by a closed inner courtyard and lack of windows and are so placed in relation to each other that the *purdah* of their women folk is fully preserved. Hindus prefer to build their houses facing in any direction, except the south which is considered inauspicious. The untouchables are forced to build their houses a little away from the main settlement usually towards the south. Such sites are usually low lying, dirty and devoid of lanes and drains. These factors continue to be there even today in spite of the laws calling for equality amongst all the citizens.

Finally, we can say that the character of the rural dwellings is normally determined by the nature of building materials available, their abundance and the ease of handling. In relatively developed areas such as Patna district, where transportation is more developed, the effect of urbanisation has spread over larger areas. Here the inhabitants may bring building materials, such as wood, brick or stone from distant place for construction purposes. In less advanced area like the Chotanagpur Scarp Belt and Parts of Purnea and Saharsa districts, however, building materials can be brought from outside only at a heavy cost due to poor transport facilities. Here it is inevitable that local materials will be mainly utilised[9] in the construction of dwellings.

World Housing Condition

After food and clothing, housing is the most important necessity of human life. It is, however, extremely difficult to make international comparisons of the availability of housing facilities since the relevant data on types of houses, accommodation available in terms of area etc. are not available. For the purpose of international comparison, only data on the average size of dwellings and average density per room are available.

Among the countries selected in this study, only Pakistan has a smaller value (1.7 rooms per dwelling) for the average size of dwellings than India (2.0 rooms per dwelling). In the average size of dwellings, the U.K. (5.5) tops the list. It is closely followed by Canada (5.3), Australia (5.2) and the Neitherlands (5.1). In west European countries, including the USSR, it ranges from 2.5 to 3.5.[10]

In average density, the top position is occupied by Pakistan which is followed by India. In Pakistan, on an average, 3.1 persons share a room, whereas in India 2.6 persons share one room. Compared to Pakistan and India, in the countries of West Europe, North America and Oceania the number of occupants per room varies from 0.6 to 1.1 persons and in East European countries it varies from 1.2 to 1.7 persons. Thus in most of the countries of west Europe, North America and Oceania, the per capita availability is more than one room whereas in the East European countries, it is less than one room. (Table 14.1)

Variations in Building Material

The physical factors have their definite impact in the construction of houses. The areas having dense forest use wood as predominant building material. The river basic clay and black soils are found predominantly and hence they are the cheap building materials found in the area. Burnt brick is the chief material of wall especially in plain lands of the world. The carved brick with beautiful designs have started appearing during ancient period in Iran, Iraq and other Muslim areas of the Middle East. In drier areas flat roof is predominant. In rainfed areas gabled roof is significantly used but in areas of 150 to 250 cms of rainfall burnt brick with tiles or grass leaves roofs are found. In West Bengal of India bamboo is considered as the chief

TABLE 14.1: Average size of Dwellings and average Density in Different Countries.

	Countries	Reference Years	Average size of dwellings (No. of rooms per dwellings)	Average density (no. of persons per rooms)
1.	Argentina	1960	3.1	1.4
2.	Australia	1966	5.2	0.7
3.	Belgium	1961	4.6	0.6
4.	Brazil	1960	4.1	1.3
5.	Canada	1961	5.3	0.7
6.	Czechoslovakia	1961	2.7	1.3
7.	France	1962	3.1	1.0
8.	East Germany	1961	2.6	1.2
9.	West Germany	1960	4.1	0.9
10.	Hungary	1963	2.3	1.5
11.	India	1960	2.0	2.6
12.	Ireland	1966	4.5	0.9
13.	Italy	1961	3.3	1.1
14.	Japan	1963	3.8	1.2
15.	Neitherlands	1956	5.1	0.8
16.	Pakistan	1960	1.7	3.1
17.	Poland	1960	N.A.	N.A.
18.	Portugal	1960	2.5	1.7
19.	South Africa	1960	3.7	1.3
20.	Spain	1950	4.0	1.1
21.	Sweden	1965	3.6	0.8
22.	Switzerland	1960	4.8	0.7
23.	U.K.	1966	5.5	0.6
24.	U.S.A.	1960	4.9	0.7
25.	USSR	1956	3.3	1.5
26.	Yugoslavia	1961	2.8	1.6

Source: And Miles to Go; Economic & Scientific Research Foundation, New Delhi, pp. 51-52.

building material due to the availability of higher amount of rainfall and problems of flood. Bamboo has the capacity to withstand the wrath of flood due to its light character and cheap availability. The digging of soil in the vicinity of houses is a common issues to make a higher base or plinth area of the houses especially in the flood affected areas as the land is liable to be flooded each and every year.[12]

In the northern plains of China loess soil is found. This soil contains a very high amount of cementing materials. Even raw brick is very strong and it stands for years without any stones are rarely used for the construction of houses. Rural areas are closely connected with grass leaves; bamboo and wood and hence, these are the chief building materials not only in the temperate regions but in tropics also. This situation is more or less found in eastern part of India, Malaysia, Myanmar, Thailand, Laos and Cambodia. In these areas the high amount of rainfall favour gabled roof.

In countries like Canada, Sweden, Norway, Finland, Japan, Siberia and New Zealand soft wood forest is found abundantly and hence, this wood is abundantly used in the construction of houses. Nowadays, the science, has developed so much and the ease of transport has revolutionised the construction of houses in rural areas. People freely use cement, grit, iron rod and lime in the construction of houses in any countries of the world without any climatic or other considerations.[13]

In the construction of house the purpose should be well defined in order to give a particular design of the house. The societal needs should also be considered. In areas of high population density the vertical expansion should be favoured in comparison with horizontal expansion.

House Type in India

The traditional house of India is not the house but its courtyard *(angan).* Courtyard is the centre of attraction in family's. The house is where property is secured and shelter sought from the rigours of climate by the resident. The courtyard is for living and the houses is meant for storage and retiring. The centre of a family's life is not the roofed enclosures but the roofless courtyard where the sun pours into dry and disinfect the food grains, the rain pours in to wash, drain and fill the water vessels and the wind blows to cool the meal.[14]

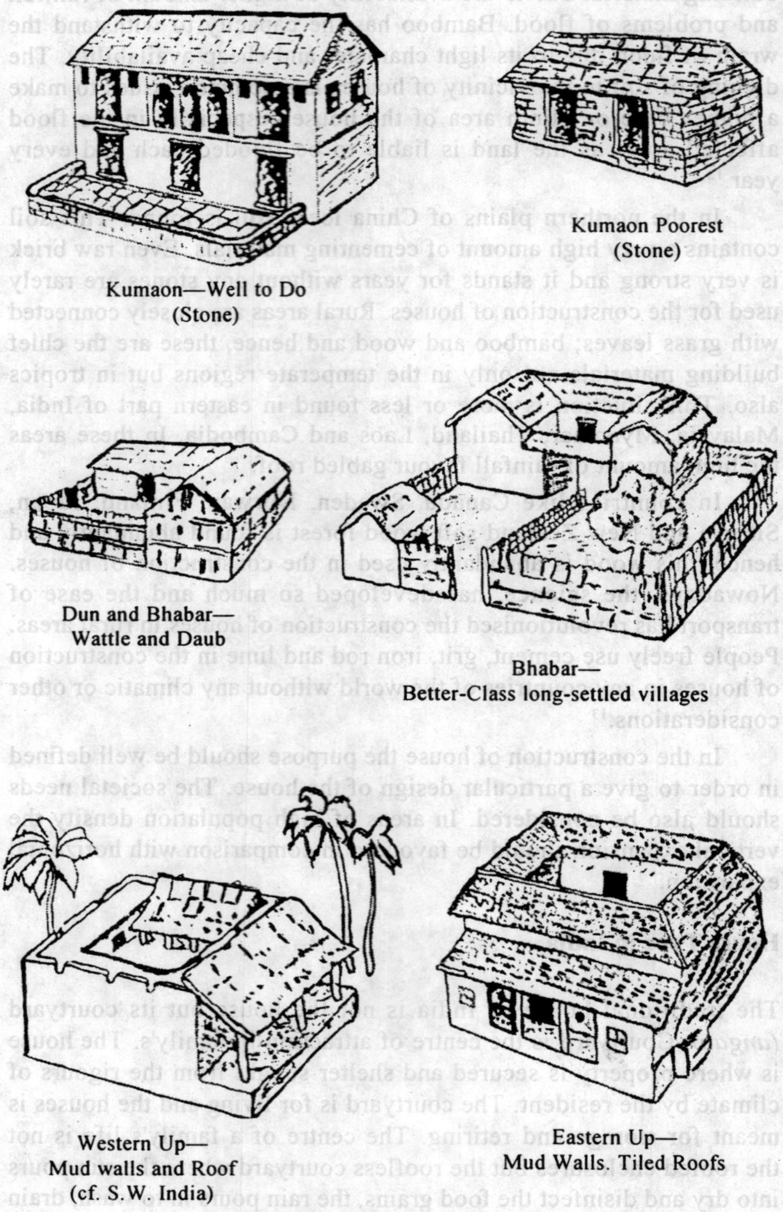

FIG. 14.4: House Types in India

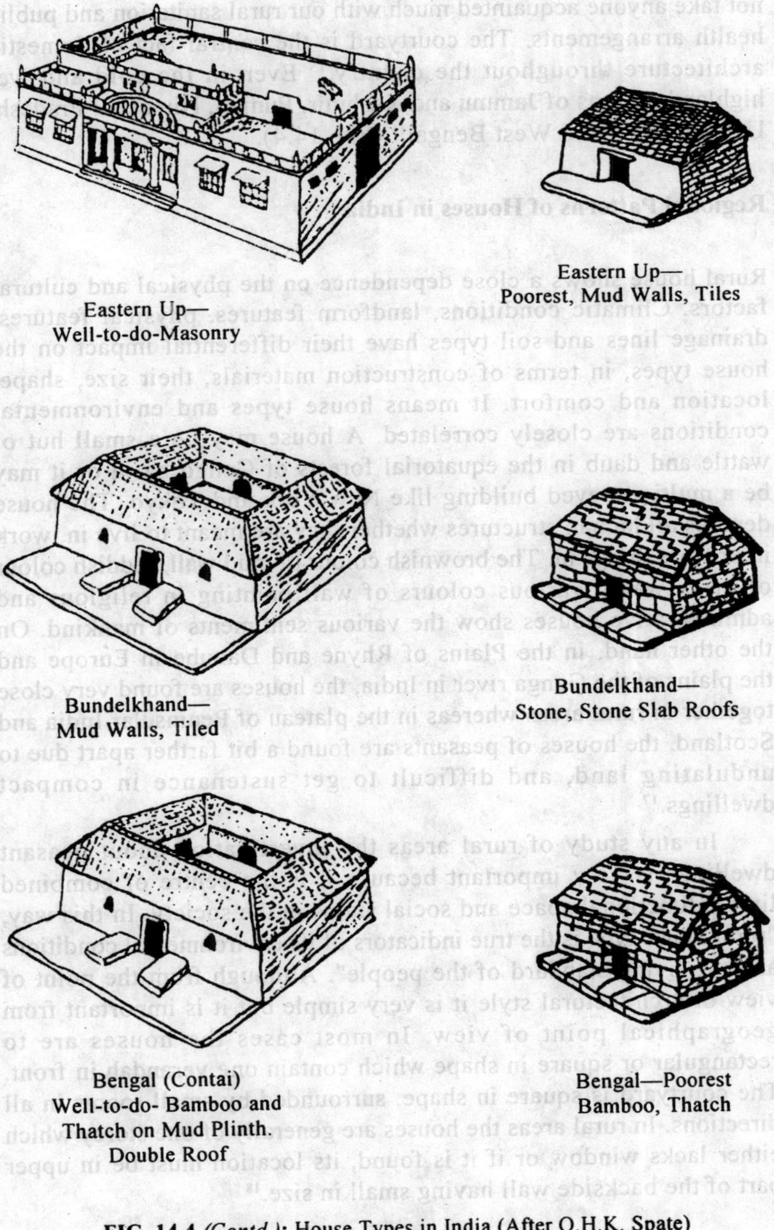

FIG. 14.4 *(Contd.)*: House Types in India (After O.H.K. Spate)

The housing structure in rural areas are so simple that it does not take anyone acquainted much with our rural sanitation and public health arrangements. The courtyard is the central fact of domestic architecture throughout the country.[15] Even in the cold and wet highland regions of Jammu and Kashmir, Punjab, Himachal Pradesh, Uttar Pradesh and West Bengal[16] (Fig. 14.4).

Regional Patterns of Houses in India

Rural house shows a close dependence on the physical and cultural factors. Climatic conditions, landform features, physical features, drainage lines and soil types have their differential impact on the house types, in terms of construction materials, their size, shape, location and comfort. It means house types and environmental conditions are closely correlated. A house may be a small hut of wattle and daub in the equatorial forests of Congo basin or it may be a multi-storeyed building like New York and Tokyo. The house denotes all human structures whether they are meant to live in, work in or store things in. The brownish colour of mud wall, reddish colour of brick walls, various colours of wall painting in religious and administrative houses show the various sentiments of mankind. On the other hand, in the Plains of Rhyne and Danube in Europe and the plains of the Ganga river in India, the houses are found very close together in rural areas whereas in the plateau of Peninsular India and Scotland, the houses of peasants are found a bit farther apart due to undulating land, and difficult to get sustenance in compact dwellings.[17]

In any study of rural areas the investigation about peasant dwellings is very important because it is the centre of combined living, functional space and social status in the society. In this way, "rural house type is the true indicators of its environmental conditions and the living standard of the people". Although from the point of view of architectural style it is very simple but it is important from geographical point of view. In most cases the houses are to rectangular or square in shape which contain one verandah in front. The courtyard is square in shape, surrounded by small rooms in all directions. In rural areas the houses are generally of one storey which either lacks window or if it is found, its location must be in upper part of the backside wall having small in size.[18]

Among the physical factors house type is mostly affected by the insolation, direction of prevailing wind and the amount of rainfall. In areas of extreme climatic conditions, the houses are constructed in such a way so that they keep the interior cool during the summer and warm during the winter. In such a situation thick mud wall is needed but window is not at all considered essential for cross ventilation. In rainfed areas the roof is generally constructed gable shape but with the decreasing amount of rainfall the roof also tends towards flat. In different regions of India the impact of geographical conditions can clearly be observed on house types which are as follows:

In Karnataka the walls of the houses are constructed very thick of mud and the roof is covered either thatch made of grass leaves or tile. In northern Karnataka single roomed circular house with domal roof is more prominent. The main gate of the house has a length of one metre and breadth half metre. The house are constructed very close together in a beehive shape. In southern side of the Pennar river hut looks like egg in shape with conical roof tops.[19]

In Malabar and Konkan coasts of Western India, mud wall and roof tops covered with coconut leaves are the most prominent features found in rural houses. In areas of Travancore and Cochin the lower part of the roof is very artistically made to curved towards up. In Periyar region the house of Urali people is found as semi-circular hut constructed out of bamboo splits. Mala Arya people of Kottayam division make their huts on tree branches with the help of bamboo and grass. On the slopes of Cardamom hills Mulawan people live in square shaped huts.

In Tamilnadu the houses are generally made of brick walls and tile roofs. On Nilgiri mountain–Toda people live in semi-circular houses. The height of such house is 6 metres and ground with 3 metres. For sleeping, Toda people make one rectangular earthern platform inside the house. For houses lying in one row–the roof is constructed jointly. In areas of Deccan Lava Plateau–the houses having flat roofs are very common due to semi-arid climatic condition. On Malwa plateau stone houses are commonly found.

In Rajasthan, Punjab, Haryana and Uttar Pradesh houses having flat roof are very common due to dry climatic conditions. In such houses protection is the prime motto in order to save the property from thieves. On the interfluve areas of the Ganga and the Yamuna rivers houses of the landlords are generally made of cement and

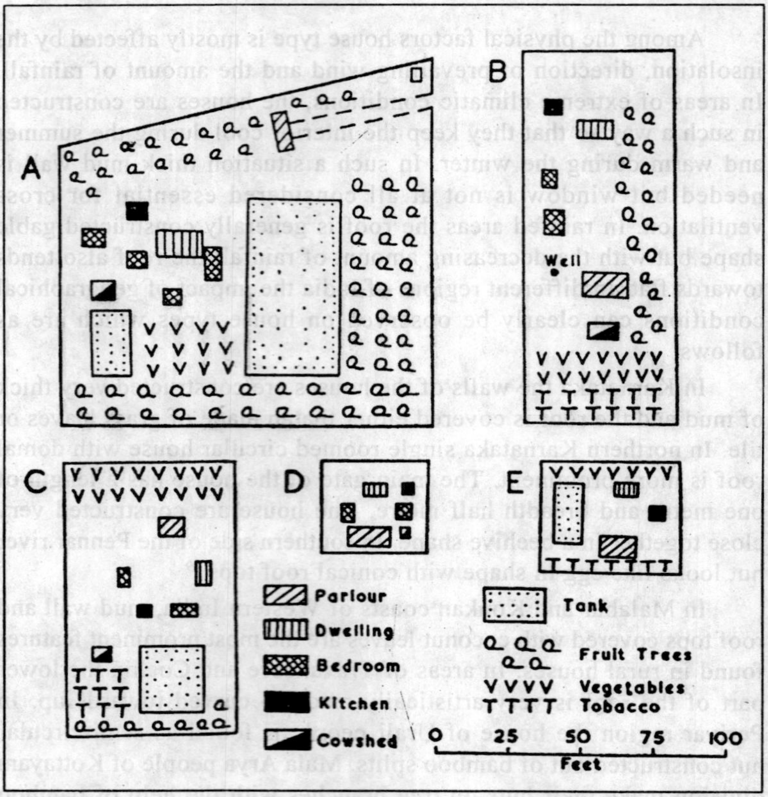

FIG. 14.5: Some East Bengal Homesteads Types

A. Well-to-do Muslim non-cultivator in drier N;
B. Muslim, and **C.** Hindu, Cultivators 'in comfort';
D. Poor Muslim, and **E.** Poor Hindu, Cultivators,
C and **E** are on platforms above marsh. Adopted from J.C. Jacks, *The Economic Life of a Bengal District* (Faridpur) (1916);
Courtesy: Oxford University Press.

concrete, whereas houses of poor peasants are made of mud wall and tile roof.

In Orissa thatch and tile roof houses are more prominent. Here double storey mud wall houses are also found. Bhuiya people live along the roads in double-row houses. In the coastal plains of Andhra Pradesh the poor man's house is generally circular in shape but its variant is rectangular or square shape in the west. In Madhya Pradesh, Gond People are making parallel linear houses on both sides of the road. In most cases kitchen garden is found in backside of the house.

In West Bengal for the construction of houses, the soil is dug out of the tank lying very close to the house. It is essential in order to make the plinth of the house a bit higher from the level of flood plain. Due to higher amount of rainfall the roof is generally made gable except cement and concrete houses.

In West Bengal, "the homestead never consists of a single hut even the poorest families always have a separate kitchen (Fig. 14.5). A prosperous family build larger huts and most of them",[20] up to a dozen grouped near the tank for bathing and domestic water supply. Generally sleeping, living, cooking, and reception houses are under separate roofs, although any of them may be used as a store or sleeping place, and mostly the peasants family lead their life in open space or verandah. In the house storage bins for grains, cots, fishing nets and gear are prominently found.

In the Chakrata area, on southern slope of Himalaya, the houses are found on different terraced contour interval in cluster and linear in shape. The material of wall is either stone or wood, and the roof is either concrete, tile or grasses available locally. Most of the houses are made of double storey, whose lower portion is meant for livestock, the middle portion for kitchen and sleeping, and the third top one for the store of food grains and fuel wood. In the valley of Kangra the houses are found very far apart. The wall may be of wood or stone but the roof is generally made of flat slate. The same type of house is found in the valley of Kashmir but due to lack of space houses are also found on boats in the lakes of Dal, Ulur and others.

Thus in India, "the geography of the house often reflects age-old religious and magical traditions: the round huts of some lower castes in Telangana, with bold vertical strips of white and rusty red are clearly culturally rather than geographically influenced. At the other extreme from the rude massive huts of Bundelkhand, the elaborate courtyard house of the richer Uttar Pradesh farmer, and the carved timber of Kumaon" are important.

The Conditions of Housing in India

In India the housing conditions of the poor and the less privileged, continue to cause grave concern. The task of providing a roof over every head is therefore formidable and would require sustained effort over a long period. In rural area, the problem is of access to even the most rudimentary level of huts.

Housing shortage in India has been estimated to be about 20.7 million, 16.1 in rural and 4.6 million in urban areas. This is only a rough estimate and does not take into account semi-permanent and temporary structures which serve the needs of a large section of our population. However, the figures do give us a broad idea of the extent of housing shortage in our country. The shortage is more marked amongst the economically weaker sections of the society and the low income groups, but the gap is quite substantial in case of the middle income group. The Economically Weaker Sections (EWS) are those who have a total family income of upto Rs. 330 per month; LIG are those with a family income of upto Rs. 600 per month. The corresponding amount for the MIG is upto Rs. 1500 per month and for MIG above Rs. 1500 per month. In the formulation and implementation of housing development schemes in the public sector, the target groups are mainly the EWS and LIG and to some extent the MIG which are the weakest sections of the society. (LIG-low income group, MIG-middle income group, and HIG-high income group).

Housing in Sixth Plan

The sixth plan has indentified, that the public sector has a 'marginal though promotion' role to play in respect of housing and has mentioned that the emphasis of the public sector will be on the 'absolutely shelterless'. In rural housing the primary target group is the landless families and the plan objective is to provide developed house sites to cover each one of the rural landless families. The total number of eligible families has been estimated to be 14.5 million by 1985. The scheme for provision of house sites to the rural landless which was in operation since 1970 had provided house sites to 7.7 million families before the commencement of the sixth plan. The Plan target is to provide house sites to the remaining 6.8 million. The programme component is such that it adopts a low cost solution using locally available building materials as far as possible and the beneficiaries are expected to play a positive role by providing their own labour as a major input. The total provision in the State Plans for house sites and construction assistance is about Rs. 3540 millions. (1985-86).[21]

In case of slums the stress is on providing a package of essential services like potable water supply, paved pathways for access, street lighting facilities and sanitary latrines in place of manually cleaned privately. The components of the programme will show that the major thrust of the scheme is to concentrate on general improvement of the environment and public health and hygiene. The approach is in preference to the less cost effective programme of slum relocation and rehousing of slum dwellers. There is no doubt that the quality of housing in slum is very poor but they do serve the basic need of shelter and in the context of overall shortage, more practical and pragmatic approach is to make the existing houses in the slum areas more liveable by eliminating squalor, filth, improving the environment and providing the basic sanitary facilities and water supply, rather than going for a large scale rehabilitation programme.

Further on international scale the attention given to the subject of providing appropriate shelter has been inadequate. Two significant events marked the growing interest of the international community to the deficiencies of shelter and infrastructure services. One was the Vancouver Habitat Conference of 1976 and the other was the Mar-Del Plata Water Conference of 1977. The Vancouver Resolution for the first time identified the problem of housing on international level. Human settlements as a separate subject area as distinct from other activities and for the first time recognized the need for considering human settlement development programmes not merely in welfare terms but as positive instruments for national development. The Mar-Del Plata resolution decided to launch an international water supply decade from 1981 to 1990 where the global programme of safe drinking water to cover the entire world population was drawn up. Both these are momentous decisions and call for comprehensive action programmes.

So far as human settlement is concerned the historic Vancouver declaration was also followed by the important 'Manila Communique of 1981 which expresses grave concern about the deteriorating conditions of the shelter for the poor and urged the countries to draw up positive action programmes for meeting the challenge. An important development in respect of human settlement improvement programme is the resolution passed in the 36th Session of the U.N.

General Assembly proclaiming 1987 as "the International Year of Shelter for the Homeless". The recently concluded 5th session of the U.N. Commission on Human Settlement in Nairobi has decided to proclaim 1987 as "the International Year of Shelter for the Homeless". Indeed it has an ambitious goal. It is to provide shelter and neighbourhood to all the poor by the year 2000.

Happily India is one of the very few countries which in its internal planning has been acting on these principles for some years. India's National Plan Strategy is based on the principle of direct attack on poverty. It has a well articulated national action programme to improve the physical quality of life of the people. The multipoint Minimum Needs Programme most of which is incorporated in the new 20-Point Economic Programme includes rural house sites, rural health, rural education, rural electrification, rural roads, rural water supply and slum improvement in urban areas which show the awareness and commitment of our country to the programmes involving the improvement of living conditions. Our objective is to provide by the end of the Sixth Plan period, house sites to all the rural landless and at least one source of potable water supply to each of the 2.31 lakh problem villages and cover 10 million slum dwellers through the slum improvement programmes.

Considering the magnitude and complexities of the problem in a country of the size of India it will be idle to presume that the task is a simple one. While one can say confidently that the progress of different schemes is quite encouraging and there can be no room for complacency and long and sustained efforts will be necessary to reach our goal. The International Declaration will only help us to rededicate ourselves to our task.

TABLE 14.2 : Performance of Housing Schemes During Sixth and Seventh Five-year Plan in India

Schemes	Sixth Plan (1980-85) in Lakh		Seventh Plan (1985-90) in Lakh	
	Target	Achievement	Target	Achievement
House sites Families	68.00	54.38	28.99	43.20
Construction (Assistance to Families)	36.00	19.13	22.88	22.55
Financial outlay	35,350.00	46,422.57	57,878.00	—

Rural Housing Schemes in India

The scheme of allotment of house-sites cum construction Assistance is a state sector scheme. It is a part of point No 14 of the 20-point Programme of 1986 and is included in the Minimum Needs Programme (MNP). This scheme is monitored by the Ministry of Urban Development and has been in operation since 1971.

Indira Awas Yojana (IAY)—a central sector scheme for the benefit of Scheduled Castes/Scheduled Tribes and freed bonded labourers implemented by the Department of Rural Development and monitored by the Ministry of Urban Development was initiated in 1985.

The Rural Housing Schemes are also financed by the Housing and Urban Development Corporation (HUDCO), an apex level housing finance corporation under the Ministry of Urban Development. HUDCO provides loans upto 50 per cent of the project cost with unit costs not exceeding Rs. 6,000 and Rs. 10,000 HUDCO's rural housing schemes have been in operation since 1977.[22]

Indira Awas Yojana

Central Government Introduced the scheme of Indira Awas Yojana in 1985-86 in the Central Sector exclusively for SCs/ST's and the freed bonded labourers in the rural areas who generally have substandard housing facilities. The scheme's thrust is on employment generation. It is being implemented with the financial assistance released by the Department of Rural Development under the Rural Employment Programme. Under this programme, Rs. 10,200 per unit

TABLE 14.3: The Overall performance under Indira Awas Yojana in India

	1985-86	1986-87	1987-88	1988-89
Indira Awas (I)	1.58	2.14	1.33	1.35
Dwelling Unit (A)	0.51	1.52	1.63	1.26
Financial outlay Rs.	9,900	12,400	12,400	12,397

Note: All figures are in lakh.

for construction of dwelling unit, low-cost sanitation and infrastructure of dwelling unit, low-cost sanitation and infrastructure development was being provided which is now being revised to 12,700 per unit. It is a 100 per cent subsidised scheme.[23]

HUDCO and Rural Housing

HUDCO has been a pioneer in financing rural housing programmes. HUDCO has sanctioned rural housing projects costing nearly Rs. 1,012 crore with HUDCO loans of over Rs. 538 crore which will enable the construction of nearly 19 lakh or 1.9 million dwelling units in the rural areas.

HUDCO has also launched following schemes for development of rural settlements.

1. Village Abadi Environmental Improvement Scheme;
2. Housing Scheme for Small and Marginal Farmers;
3. Setting up of a National Network of Building Centres and,
4. Housing Schemes for different income groups both for construction and renovation.

State Governments Housing Projects

Besides the above mentioned schemes, the state Governments/UT Administrations are implementing other housing schemes in the rural area. They are as follows:

(a) Village Housing Projects (Punjab & Orissa);
(b) People's Housing Scheme (Karnataka);
(c) Semi-Permanent Rural Houses (Andhra Pradesh);
(d) Rural Permanent Houses (Andhra Pradesh);
(e) Weavers Housing cum Worksheds (A.P.);
(f) Village Housing cum construction Assistance (Goa);
(g) Cooperative Housing Scheme (T.N.);
(h) Village Panchayat (T.N.);
(i) Thadco's Adi Dravida Housing Scheme in Tamil Nadu (T.N.).

LIC-GIC Rural Housing Schemes

In India, the LIC and the GIC have also entered into the rural housing sector and particularly Group Insurance Loans are only available for the social Housing Schemes in the rural areas. The LIC/GIC Loans form part of the Plan funds and are allocated to various states of India on the recommendations of the Planning Commission. In the year 1990-91 the total provision in this sector was Rs. 179 crores.

REFERENCES

1. V.N.P. Sinha, "Houses and House Types of the Chotanagpur Plateau", *Geographical Knowledge,* Vol. 2, 1969, p. 91.
2. S.N. Dickens and F.R. Pitts, *Introduction to Human Geography,* New York, 1963, p. 199.
3. G. Cunningham, *Archaeological Report,* London, 1861-62, p. 47.
4. *Indian Nation,* 15, June, 169, p. 3.
5. L.R. Singh, *The Terai Region of U.P.: A Study in Human Geography,* Allahabad, 1965, p. 37.
6. Victor Olgyay, *Design with Climate,* Princeton Press, 1963, p. 3.
7. R.L. Singh, "Typical Rural Dwellings in the Umland of Banaras", *The National Geographical Journal of India,* Vol. III, 1957, p. 52.
8. K.M. Subrahmanyam, "Four Main House Types in South India", *Journal of Madras Geographical Association,* Vol. XIII, 1938, p. 168.
9. M.L. Fuller and F.G. Clapp, "Rural Dwellings of Shensi, China", *Geographical Review,* Vol. 14, 1924, p. 215.
10. W.A. Noble, "Approaches Towards an Understanding of Traditional South Asian Peasant Dwelling, *Professional Geographer,* Vol. 21, 1969.
11. R.C. Sharma, "Western Rajasthan: A Study of House Types", *National Geographer,* Vol. III, 1964, p. 48.
12. G.A. Grierson, "The Native House" in *Bihar, Peasant Life,* Patna, 1926, pp. 333-44.
13. *Ibid.*
14. Sohan Lal Duggal and Kripashankar Gaur: "Rural House Types", in *Human Geography,* Meerut, 1958, p. 259.
15. V.N.P. Sinha: *Op.cit.,* p. 93.
16. R.L. Singh: *Op.cit.,* p. 40.
17. Shiv Narain Mishra: "Human Dwellings in Sonpur Region (U.P.)", *The National Geographical Journal of India,* Vol. XV, 1969, p. 22.

18. Paul Vidal de la Blache: *Principles of Human Geography,* New York, 1962, p. 238.

19. J. Bruhnhes: "Human Geography", New York, p. 76.

20. E. Ahmad: "Rural House Types", Bihar, *Physical Economic and Regional Geography,* Ranchi University, 1965, p. 278.

21. K.H. Buschman: "Settlements and Habitations in India", *Geographical Review of India,* Vol. XVI, 1954, p. 19.

22. S.D. Prasad: *Report on Housing and Establishments in Gazeetter of India,* Bihar, Vol. IV, Part IVA, 1961, p. 498.

23. Asok Mitra: "House Types in India", *Illustrated Weekly of India,* November, 1968, p. 26.

15

SOCIAL MORPHOLOGY AND SPATIO-FUNCTIONAL ORGANIZATION OF RURAL SPACE

Location shows the significance of settlements where as morphology is guided by its site. Hence, the study of siting conditions of rural settlements is an essential aspect of social and physical morphology. In order to plan our rural settlements the study of their morphology and physical setting is prerequisite as it indicates the level and need of planning, regrouping and relocation of villages, wherever it is necessary. The morphological character is governed by physical and cultural parameters and it affects the internal process of growth of settlements, layout of streets and other structures including spacing of building and material growth of rural settlements. The layout means external and internal (Ahmad, 1962) form of settlements which depend upon the physical and cultural conditions (Singh, 1955) of the landscape and society (Prasad, 1973). In case of unplanned community the morphological growth is haphazard and the placing of houses is irregular. On the other hand, planned communities have well developed houses, material growth is perfect, lanes are wider and houses are always arranged in a row or based on some planning principles. The morphological character and the main thoroughfares of rural settlements are the indicators of development and the functions of a place.

The shape of village is the product of its site and the allied internal morphological pattern which is governed by its thoroughfares leading to principal central place of the region and the nearby linear water bodies. In case of shifting courses of the river the villages are built away from the water bodies but in case of permanent channels they are built just on the side of the river, so as to fetch water easily for ordinary household purposes.

So far as the social morphology and functional organization of rural settlements are concerned, the spatial change of residential activity inside the village continues to be dominated by the concentration of the largest residential establishments in the Chauk Area (CA). Throughout the rest part of the village there seems to be a rather haphazard arrangement of residential areas grouped together in tolas of different castes. Thus the village community as an integrated living whole "consists of a collection of units, all arranged to form a social structure, i.e., a set of social relations" (Singh, 1972).

The village morphology includes grouped plan, general build of settlements and social morphology. These features vary in space on local, regional and national level in close connection with their cultural advancement and functional space. The ground plan denotes the layout including length and breadth of streets, the arrangement of house inside the compound of a household and the location of main cultural features as temple, mosque, fort, headmans residence, walls, moats, market place, gardens, etc. The build of the village encompasses architectural style, length-breadth, height, general conditions of street front of houses, eavesline or any other monumental styles of the past. In these aspects, ground plan and built up area are the permanent feature of the land-scape. The third component, social morphology includes functional and social space articulation of the village communities of soical life is the guiding factor of the former two characteristics of rural settlement morphology.

In the built up area of a settlement, land is intensively used. This becomes the nodal point for a serving community which covers the surrounding space. Morphology of settlement is the expression of those two norms of the system, which can be divided into four basic parts: (a) homogeneous part (field/houses), (b) the central part (built up area/shop) (c) the circulatory part (roads/lanes) and (d) the special part (any unit of distinction) (Doxiadis, 1968: 27-28). These constituent parts of a settlement are closely associated with three dimensions of settlement morphology, i.e., height, length and width, and since settlement cannot exist without their function and people, that cannot be separated by temporal dimension.

The Purpose of Study and Tools of Analysis

This study aims to investigate the existing morphological

characteristics of rural settlements in the region including the analysis of various patterns of unconsciously planned settlements, orientation of main throughfares of settlements and hinterland organization of a service centre, measurement of circularity or shape index in various patterns of settlements and ultimately a detailed discussion of Jajmani system and spatial organization of rural settlements. Thus the present study resolves to highlight the basic structure of rural settlement morphology of the present while inheriting the effect of past cultural and physical processes. These processes are continuously moulding and transforming the morphological patterns of rural settlements in different time and space.

So far as the technique of analysis is concerned one French writer M. Sorre has taken social groupings as "techniques of social life" and its impact is quite visible in rural settlement morphology. In analysing the impact of function and social space in the growth and development of rural settlement morphology it has been said that "Functions is an analogy between social life and organic life" (Singh, 1972). The rural settlement morphology can be best analysed with the help of rural communities as "it consists of a collection of units, all arranged to form a social structure and their interrelations in terms of social contiguity." Social morphology discusses the prevailing social structures in terms of their similarities and variations. The other point is the process of functioning such a structure and the third is its role in evolving the present village morphology in temporal dimensions.

The concept of social space is closely related with the behavioural relations of man in a particular territorial space and its repurcussions are highly felt on residential patterns, streets, siting and location of public buildings and other dominant cultural landscape of rural settlements, etc. The territorial space in rural settlements is comprised of family living, socio-economic life and caste grouping. Hence, in the following section three aspects have been analysed under three sub-heads.

Review of Literature

Regarding social morphology of rural settlements two papers appeared dealing with the settlement patterns of the Malers of the Rajmahal Hills and the habitations of Maitais in 'Man in India' an old Anthropological Journal of Bihar, but the authors (Sarkar, 1933: 156-158 and Singh, 1933: 165-188) have almost neglected the societal aspects of the internal arrangement of households of the village. Their study is limited only to the nature and physical structure of houses. A brief discussion about tribal settlement patterns are also available in tribal monographs of India, but even they do not seem to be significant. Among sociologists while studying about Tanjore village in South India, Beteille (1966:44) said that the people belonging to the same caste live together, no matter they are rich or poor or low in other sense. In analysing the social aspect of settlement pattern, Chatterjee and Das (1964) observed that the linear settlement and close housing are basically related with the clan solidarity. In an study of the settlements of the Middle Gangetic valley Singh (1955) reports that the existing settlement is influenced by caste prejudice. Karan (1967) finds that compact settlement in Bhutan is determined by social and cultural factors and the superstitious beliefs among the Hindu Nepali settlers, but he deals with the locational aspects only, not the internal arrangement of rural dwellings. It has also been found that religion, clan ties and the caste system (Sharma, 1967, 104) play a very significant role in the internal morphology of rural settlements. Mandelbaum (1972: 339) also observes that "the layout of a village generally reflects something of its social structure". Mukherjee (1968:20) maintains that village morphology "bear the impression of caste distance". Similarly, about the rural settlements of West Bengal, Sharma (1960) asserts that the housing pattern is not affected by cultural values or the ideas of social pollution. Thus it can be said that "Social segregation is almost a social reality, especially in the case of agrarian society. The untouchables have to live at a respectable distance from their more fortunate brethren who, because of their higher social status, have been enjoying certain special privileges through the ages. The notion of impurity and pollution has segregated the village community into several social pockets or tolas on the basis of caste at spatial level (Singh, J.P., 1977).

Family Distance Model

A view of the morphology of the entire rural society gives an idea of settlement as a living whole, consisting of various tolas separated by wider lanes. Each tola consists of housing units of various families and castes. There is a respectable distance in between two households and families. It is, thus, apparent that family living is prevalent in almost all parts of North Bihar besides community and clan solidarity living. The structure and process of family formation—one unit separate from the other invites the formation of a settlement in configuration together. Not even a single person in a village lives outside the family which is almost impossible in most cases. Hence, the prevalence of family living with considerable distance from one family to other helps in the formation of village streets. The prevalence of this system helps in maintaining the social and family distance at least in terms of territorial distance of even the people of same caste, clan, income group and other forms of cultural affiliations.

So far as the distance from one family to another is concerned in between the houses of the same caste the interdwelling distance is lesser in comparison with the house of other castes. As for example, in Rahuaman Village of Saharsa district inter-family average distance is 14 metres in case of Rajput, 10 metres among Yadava's and only 7 metres among Brahmin's. Similarly, in Akbarpur Pitaujhia of Warisnagar anchal average inter-family distance is just five metres. In Kharsam village the average distance between Chamar's house is one metre, Dhobi's house is one metre, Kurmi's house is 3 metres.

Socio-Economic Behavioural Model

It is quite often said that social and economic conditions are highly correlated. Generally people of backward community and low social strata give rise to poor economic situation whereas higher social order as rich persons. In such a situation the poor families have low roofed and *phus* house constructed on the side of narrow lanes where as the rich persons have high roofed burnt brick and tile house constructed on the side of wider lanes well above the reach of flood water.

In North Bihar it has been found that various socio-economic status of the inhabitants of rural settlements have differential mode of settlement morphology both in its outer shape and internal pattern. Fig. 15.1 highlights the social behaviour for economic reasons, morphological pattern and spatial organization of rural settlements of North Bihar as a conceptual model. In social and economic behaviour generally the flow of income and food are directed towards backward people from the higher castes. On the other hand, the flow of labour force and nearness is shown from backward and menials to the so-called upper castes people of the hierarchy of castes and width of road have significant relationship as dominant castes people of the village live on spacious roads or footpaths, while narrow lanes have close relationship with backwards and untouchables. The spatial organization of rural settlements gives a clearcut view that with the increasing gap between the rich and the poor, Brahmins and Domes, the segregation of habitation site set apart with considerable distance and this helps in the formation of particular morphological pattern.

It has been found that compact settlements have complex morphological pattern but dispersed and smaller villages have simple morphology with houses arranged in one line on the side of simple structure settlements are represented by single lane hamlets while complex structures are represented by multiple lanes or wider thoroughfares. The characteristic features of roads show the areas of functional specialization of a settlement (Table 15.1)

An analytical view is presented below (Table 15.2) which shows the relationship of village morphology with types and patterns of growth, population size and caste structure of rural settlements as generalised conceptual view of North Bihar.

TABLE 15.1 : Morphological Pattern and Functional Specialization of Rural Settlements in North Bihar

Morphological Pattern and Mode	Functional Specialization
Chauk	Water Place, Meoting grounds, Panchayat Place under baniyan trees or shopping centre in case of central places.
Brick Paved or Wider Metalled Road	Main thoroughfare of the large village or commercial areas of the market
Narrow Unpaved Road	Main thoroughfare of smaller village or residential areas of central places
Footpath	General bye-lanes of the village and areas of slum and economically poor in a central place

Caste Segregation Model

In search of social space of a rural settlement in North Bihar it is quite evident that caste segregation is an important factor in the social morphology of a rural settlement. Generally different caste people try to settle separately according to the traditional beliefs and from the point of view of certain variations in sanitation, location of male and female apartments, *purdah* system among women and

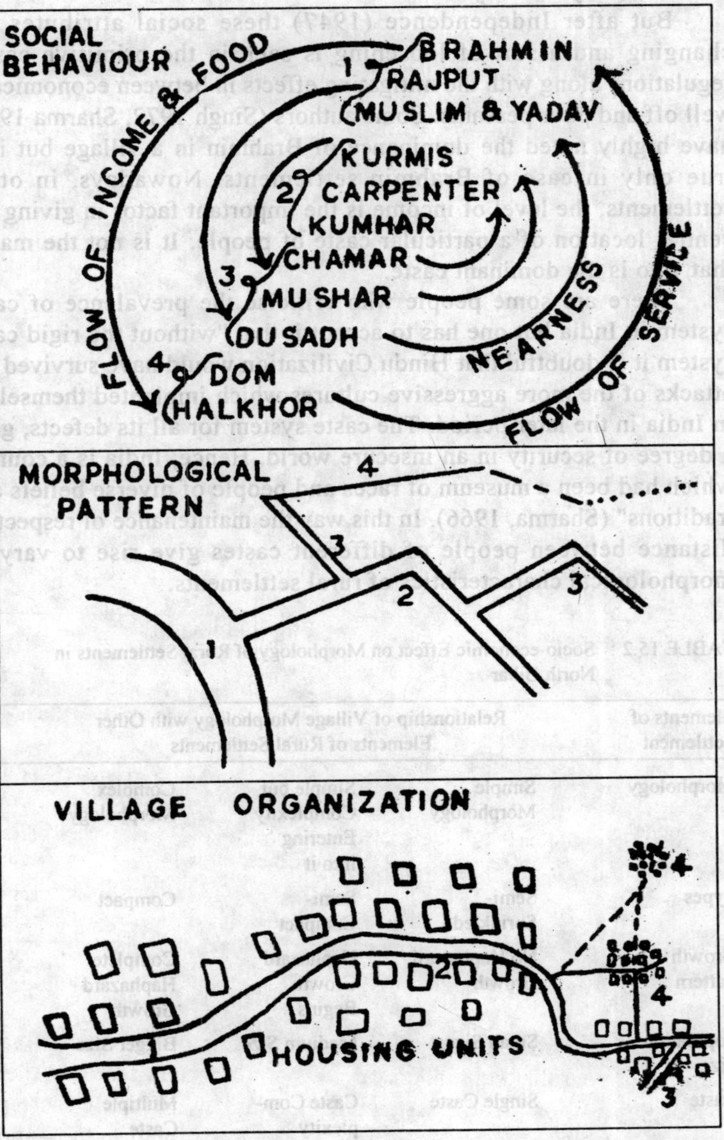

FIG. 15.1: Impact of Social Behaviour on Village Morphology

untouchability to Harijans.

But after Independence (1947) these social attributes are changing and a sort of loosening is seen in the primitive castes regulations along with the mitigating effects in between economically well off and poor peasants. Some authors (Singh 1972, Sharma 1966) have highly noted the dominance of Brahmin in a village but it is true only in case of Brahmin settlements. Nowadays, in other settlements, the level of income is the important factor in giving the central location of a particular caste of people. It is not the matter that who is the dominant caste.

There are some people who criticise the prevalence of caste system in India but one has to accept it that "without the rigid caste system it is doubtful that Hindu Civilization would have survived the attacks of the more aggressive cultures which implanted themselves in India in the later period. The caste system for all its defects, gave a degree of security in an insecure world. Hence, India is a country which had been a museum of races and people of diverse beliefs and traditions" (Sharma, 1966). In this way the maintenance of respective distance between people of different castes give rise to varying morphological characteristics of rural settlements.

TABLE 15.2 : Socio-economic Effect on Morphology of Rural Settlements in North Bihar

Elements of Settlement	Relationship of Village Morphology with Other Elements of Rural Settlements		
Morphology	Simple Morphology	Simple but Complexity Entering into it	Complex Morphology
Types	Semi-Sprinkled	Semi-Compact	Compact
Growth Pattern	No Haphazard Growth	Haphazard Growth Begins	Complete Haphazard Growth
Population Size	Small Size	Medium Size	Bigger Size
Caste	Single Caste	Caste Complexity Entering	Multiple Caste Village
Age	Modern	Medieval	Ancient
Poverty	N^3	N^2	N^1

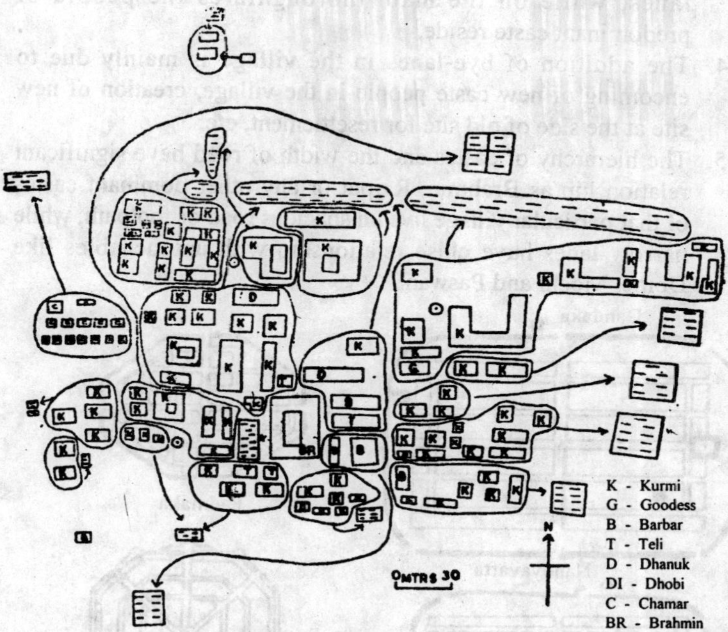

FIG. 15.2: Kharsam: Spatial Organization of Extraction of Mud for the Material of Wall and Caste Segregation 1991

Figure 15.2 shows that in Kharsam village kurmi, barbar, brahmin, teli, dhanuk, dhobi and chamar are living in separate units. Although kurmi is a dominant caste of the village still functionally the same is divided into so many smaller units.

In Table 15.3 the residential location and morphological character is given for certain rural settlements of North Bihar.

On the basis of above studies the following generalizations have been drawn:

1. The multiple caste village gives a complex morphological growth, while simple morphology is the product of semi-sprinkled type rural settlements or of smaller hamlets.
2. The newer settlements with multiple castes give scattered pattern of settlements of different sub-lanes where grouping of houses develops on the basis of castes.
3. The complexity of village morphology gives an idea that the village is old and the minor caste people reside on different bye-

lanes, while on the main thoroughfares the people of predominant caste reside.

4. The addition of bye-lanes in the village is mainly due to encoming of new caste people in the village, creation of new site at the side of old site for resettlement, etc.
5. The hierarchy of castes and the width of road have significant relationship as Brahmin, Rajput or any other dominant castes of that particular village live on spacious road or footpath, while narrow lanes have close relationship with untouchables like Dome, Mochi and Paswan.

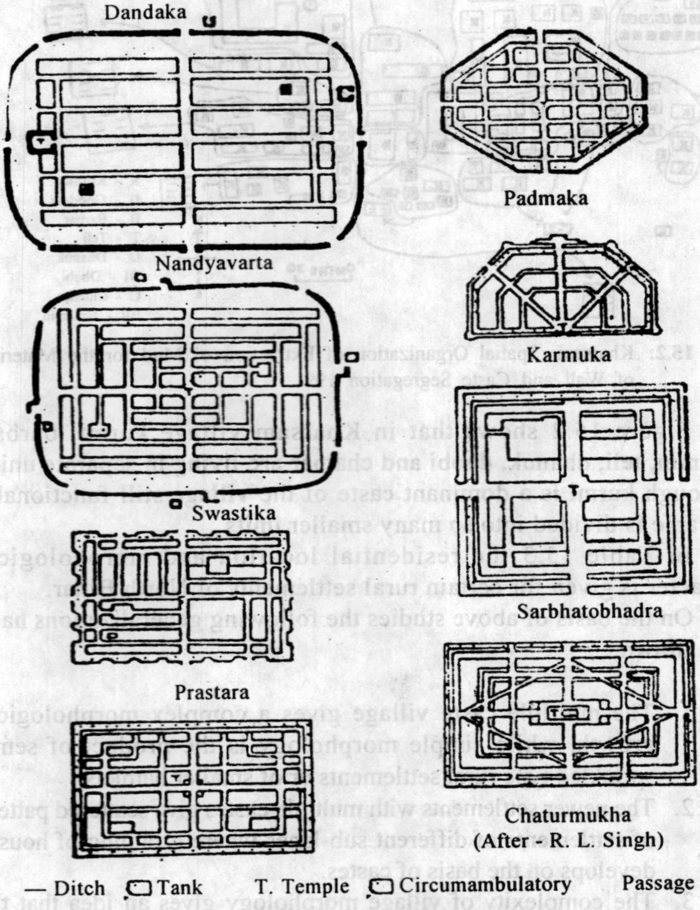

FIG. 15.3: Aryan Settlements

TABLE 15.3: Caste Segregation and Morphological Attributes of Rural Settlements

Kharsam (Rosera Block)

Name of the Caste	Residential Location in the Village	Condition of Lanes	Alignment of Habitation	Nature of Skyline of House	Sanitation of Lanes
Brahmin	Central Part	Wide	East-West	High-High	Dirty
Kurmis	Most Parts	Wide	East-West	Medium	Clean
Teli	Central Part	Wide Narrow	East-West	Medium-Low	
Hazam	South-Central Part	Wide	North-South	Medium	Clean
Dhobi	North Western Part	Narrow	Square	Low	Dirty
Dhanuk	Central and North Western Part	Wide	East-West	Medium	Clean
Chamar	North Western Part	Narrow	East-West	Low	Dirty
Hanshi (Biraul Block)					
Brahmin	**Most Parts**	**Wide**	**North-South**	**High**	**Dirty**
Dhanuk	**Northern Part**	**Narrow**	**Square**	**Low**	**Dirty**
Hazam	**Northern Part**	**Narrow**	**Square**	**Low**	**Dirty**
Tatma	**Eastern and Western Margin**	**Narrow**	**Square**	**Low**	**Dirty**
Teli	**Eastern and Western Margin**	**Narrow**	**Square**	**Medium**	**Dirty**
Badhai	**Eastern and Western Margin**	**Narrow**	**Square**	**Medium**	**Dirty**
Malah	**Eastern Part**	**Narrow**	**Square**	**Low**	**Dirty**

Contd.

Brahmin	Most Parts	Wide	North-South	High	Dirty
Yadav	Western Part	Narrow	Square	Medium	Dirty
Kumhar	Northern Part	Narrow	Square	Medium	Dirty
Chamar	Northern	Narrow	Haphazard Settlement	Low	Dirty
		Rahuaman (Kahara Block)			
Rajput	Southern Part	Wide	Circular	High	Very Clean
Brahmin	North-Western Part	Wide	Aligned on the side of Lane	High Medium	Clean Clean
Yadav	Eastern	Wide	East-West Along Road	Medium	Clean
Dusadh	North Central Part	Narrow	East-West	Low	Clean
Chamar	Western Part Along Road	Wide	North-South East-South	Low	Dirty
		Khanpur (Rosera Block)			
Muslim	Eastern	Wide	East-West	Medium	Clean
Kurmi	Middle Eastern	Narrow	East-West	Medium	Clean
Malah	Central	Wide	North-South	Medium	Clean
Chamar	North-West	Narrow	East-West	Medium	Dirty
Dome	South-Western	Wide	Haphazard	Very Low	Very Dirty
Musher	South West	Wide	East-West	Very Low	Very Dirty
Halwai	Middle Part	Narrow	North South	Medium	Clean

The author had an opportunity to observe thousands of rural settlements in North Bihar and did not find even a single where the people of different castes do not maintain spatial distance. This segregative tendency is quite apparent in almost all rural settlements of the region.

Environmental Control

The physical factors affecting form of the rural settlements are the configuration of site, rivers, ponds, wells, slope and elevation of land such as plains, uplands, valleys, watertable and waterlogged areas, etc. All these variables are of paramount importance in the growth of village under certain physical environment. Among cultural factors historical events, patterns of roads and lanes, field patterns, religious institutions, i.e., mosque, temples, place of Goddess and village deities, etc., are intimately related to the structure of the village. Insecurity in the past and the present social make-up of the village are other significant factors in the development of village patterns and their internal morphology. Morphologically, the condition of villages in North Bihar is haphazard with narrow turning-twisting lanes and irregular pile of buildings so that only a rough estimate about the village pattern can be made.

The village pathways and cart-tracks are skeleton of the internal layout of the village. The buildings represent the flesh of the body, and determine the form and shape. The nucleus of the village develops at the most accessible place from where, if possible, the surrounding agricultural land can be easily observed (Duggal, S.L.: 1961). The study of morphology of villages refers chiefly to the clustered settlements, as only the congregation of a number of dwellings and arrangement of associated lanes can give rise to different village patterns. Villages with semi-sprinkled and sprinkled settlements can only be analysed roughly.

Layout of Ancient Communities

The region having a long history since Prehistoric times and varied physical and cultural conditions, is marked by several patterns of villages. In each physiographic region the physical elements have differently affected the village forms and so is the case with cultural and social elements also.

The recent archaeological investigations of few ancient sites in the region have made valuable contribution towards this branch of settlement geography. It has been found that the villages of the early times were guided by the ancestral plan as suggested by excavations of Chirand (Singh, 1977) in Saran District, Vaishali in Vaishali District, Naulagarh in Begusarai District and Balirajgarh in Madhubani District. For the first time at Chirand and Balirajgarh definite evidence of Kushan period settlement plan was discovered. On occupational floor were found remains of postholes which must have supported thatch roofs and on the floor a number of hearths and remains of charcoal were found (Singh, 1977). The village which Kautilaya defines as "a group of Sudras and cultivators" numbering from a hundred to five hundred families, distant from one or two krosa from the next village "appears to have a very outstanding characteristic". During Aryan period the Mansara (Acharya, 1925) describes eight types and the Kami-Kagama as many as fifteen types of settlements in the past (Fig. 15.3). A passage in the Mahabharata (V. 47) speaks of villages of straw huts, which burnt easily—village fortification seems to have been mentioned in ancient texts (Yajnavalkya Smiriti ii. 167). The Buddhist literature such as Jatakas (Mukerji, 1969) has thrown light on the size of villages, such as Gamaka (Vinaya Pitaka 1:208: Jataka 119,253,107) small village, gama (Ibid., 1:109,110,111,46; Jataka 163,366) (an ordinary village), Nigama Gama (Ibid., 1:110,188, Jataka, 330) (a large village), Duaragama (Jataka; 361) (sub-urban village) and Pachchanta gama (Jataka: 78:302) (a frontier village) as exemplified by Sursand and Bel in Sitamarhi district.

Early history shows that the villages were arranged on eitherside of the road (Malley, 1907). One of such ancient highways was the "Emperial Road of Buddha" which runs from Rajgir-Palibothra-Hajipur-Vaishali-Areraj-Lawriya to Kushinagar of Uttar Pradesh. In this way, the villages were connected with one another on the one hand and with administrative centres on the other. These centres have been described as a fortress in the centre of 800 villages, a Dronamukha commanding 400 villages, a Kharvata controlling 200 villages and a Sangrahna in the midst of a group of ten villages (Mukherji, 1967). In ancient times, the inhabited area of the village was fenced on all sides by wall or wooden palisades. The village wall was at a distance of 22 yards from the border houses, so that people coming by the village gate would be seen by the inhabitants from their houses. Even areas inhabited temporarily were fenced with bamboos. The village wall had four large gates facing the main road. At the main gate of the village there was planted a sacred *pipal* or banyan tree where the presiding deity of the village was supposed to dwell (Louis, Renou: *op.cit.).* The historical records also show that in ancient times the hierarchy of village pattern was well-planned, while at present it is the result of natural growth.

In North Bihar different types of settlement patterns are apt to develop under different environmental conditions which are discussed here (Fig. 15.4).

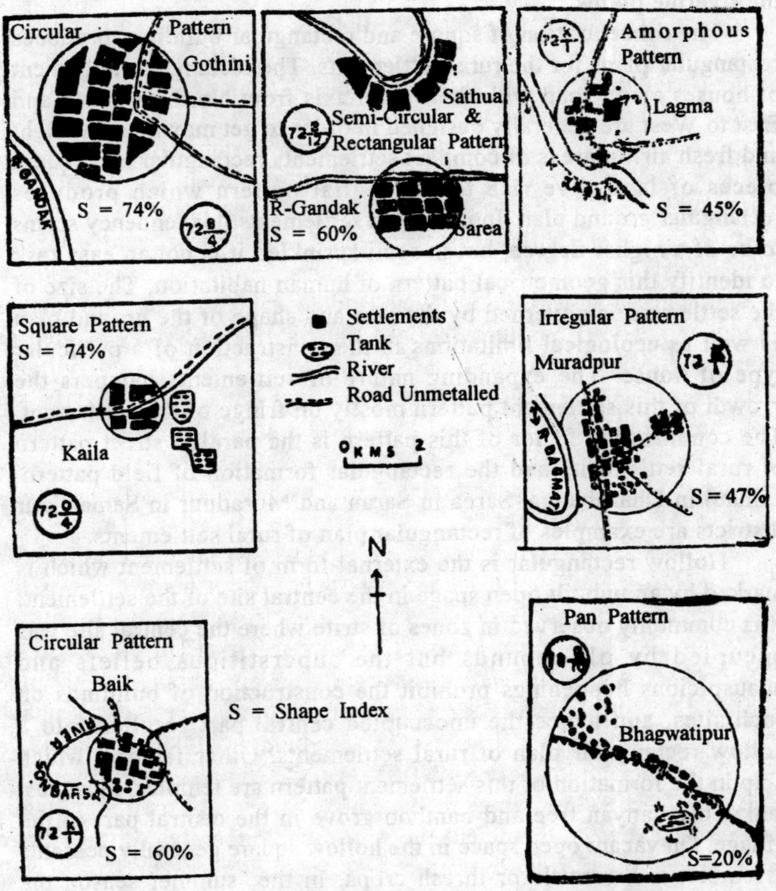

FIG. 15.4: North-Bihar: Patterns of Rural Settlement

Rectangular Pattern

In most parts of North Bihar rectangular layout is the common morphological pattern of rural settlements. Such plans are also found in China, Japan, Italy, Egypt and Argentine pampa where agricultural practice along river embankments is largely responsible for the growth of such a pattern. Rectangular village plan also become a common feature in ancient period which is quite evident from the settlement plans of Mansara Shilpashastra (Havel, 1959). The cause of such village plan is the rectangular form of cultivated fields in the riverine plains.

The concentration of square and rectangular buildings produces rectangular plans for the rural settlements. The rectangular alignment of houses along road with their main axis from North to South and East to West are generally designed in order to get maximum sunlight and fresh air. In areas of compact settlements rectangular and square pieces of land give rise to residential pattern which produces rectangular ground plan. In nucleated settlements this tendency seems to be of a higher degree, but in semi-sprinkled it is not an easy task to identify this geometrical pattern of human habitation. The size of the settlement is governed by the size and shape of the ground plan as well as ecological limitations in the construction of a particular type of house. The expanding nature of settlements hampers the growth of this settlement pattern mostly on fringe of the settlement. The commanding factor of this pattern is the parallel street pattern of rural settlements and the rectangular formation of field pattern. Lilhaul in Dharbhanga, Sarea in Saran and Muradpur in Samastipur districts are examples of rectangular plan of rural settlements.

Hollow rectangular is the external form of settlement which is marked by an unbuilt open space in the central site of the settlement. It is commonly observed in zones of strife where the central site was occupied by old mounds but the superstitious beliefs and unauspicious happenings prohibit the construction of buildings on such sites, and hence the unoccupied central part resulted into a hollow rectangular plan of rural settlements. Other features which help in the formation of this settlement pattern are temples, mosques, tanks, big banyan tree and bamboo grove in the central part of the village. On vacant open space in the hollow square generally peasants assemble, tether cattle or thresh crops. In the summer season the shady trees help in the get-to-gether of farmers with their odd functions of string making, cot weaving, etc. Whereas the winter evening is marked by the gathering of people around a fire burning place *(Ghura)* where the village folk exchange talks of agricultural situation, prevailing weather conditions and short stories. In most of the rurban communities weekly or bi-weekly markets are held. Matter in Samastipur, Sonar in Sitamarhi and Pokharbhinda in Madhubani districts are examples of hollow rectangular settlements.

The Square Pattern

The square and rectangular patterns of rural settlements are in most cases complementary to each other. This is the product of restrictive and attractive forces of the environment. This pattern is associated with the crossings of cart tracks of roads. At present the location of orchard, tank and road around the village forced the village to develop in square form. The four square unit at the junction of cross roads are occupied by people of four castes. The best examples of square pattern are village Santhi in Saran and Gulma in Saharsa districts.

The hollow square pattern is associated with a hollow space amidst the centre of the village. This unbuilt space is caused by the presence of a square tank, a temple, mosque, garden or pasture land. One of the best examples of hollow square is Ranjodha village in Bhagalpur district.

Hollow Square Village

The hollow square pattern is again similar to the square pattern, with a hollow space in the centre of the village. Similar to hollow rectangular settlements, the unbuilt space is caused by the presence of a square tank, a temple, mosque, garden or pasture. One of the best examples of hollow square pattern in Ranjodha village in Bhagalpur district. Here the villagers have dug-out the earth from the middle of the village to build the plinth of their houses. This has resulted in a ditch full of water located in the centre of the village.

Linear Village Pattern

The linear pattern is recognized by the arrangement of house along a line or a series of lines. The settlement is prolonged in one direction and restricted in another due to certain physical features. The occurrence of this pattern is associated with the flood affected areas and the proximity of a river. Whenever, the site is a narrow strip in between two streams flowing very close together the village becomes elongated. Clusters situated on a bank marking the edge of an alluvial terrace also show a similar influence. So far as the cultural features are concerned roads either metalled or unmetalled, have greater importance in the elongation of a village. In case the road is recently built and the village has no marketing centre the settlement pattern might be different. But if there is a market it is invariably situated along the road, and the settlement is necessarily elongated. Such villages are known as strassendorf (Street village). For example, Phulwaria in Raghopur Diara of Vaishali district is an elongated village along the river Ganga and only one cart tract passes through the village. Village Laukaha in Madhubani district lying along metalled road also shows elongation but at some places the pattern has been disturbed by the open spaces and the construction of new buildings by the side of the main site. Majrahia in Rusera block of Samastipur district is a good example of this pattern along a linear water body. In flood affected areas this pattern occurs along rivers, oxbow lakes or old channels. Here the linear cluster usually becomes abnormally elongated along the higher river banks in the Kosi flood plains.

Grid Iron Pattern

Grid iron or the chessboard plan denotes a "right angled mesh of streets with or without central rectangular market place" (Dickinson, 1924). Hence chessboard plan is the feature of some large rectangular and square villages. In such large settlements two streets corresponding with the four gates of the village wide enough to allow the passage of bullock-carts cut each other at right angles. A few other subsidiary lanes run parallel to the main lanes, in order to provide access to other houses of the village. The four walls of the dwellings run in cardinal directions so that the grid plan is rarely disturbed. Generally the village is divided into tolas according to different castes and each grid may be occupied by one caste. This pattern also helps the poor peasants to take drinking water from a centrally located well. In this case each intersection of lanes may have masonry well and building the house is of primary consideration in accessibility to the nearest sweet water well. Sarea village in Saran district is the best example of this pattern. This village is located near the river Gandaki.

Circular or Semi-Circular Village Pattern

The circular village pattern may have several variations, which caused by an attempt to build a maximum number of houses at one site. The houses may be concentrated for the purpose of defence, or built around the mansion of the local Zamindar or around a well. It may also be necessitated by a desire to have a higher site for building purposes. In North Bihar this pattern is not the heritage of the past but this is due to the natural growth of village according to shape of the ground plan. Sometimes a semi-circular plan may develop on the crescent shape of a meander. The settlements of horse shoe pattern develop in the sharp bend of meanders or roads. At some places hollow-circular pattern also develops due to open space amidst the central site of the settlement.

The best example of circular pattern is village Gothini in Saran district which has developed in between bend of the Gandak river on the West and an unmetalled road on the East. Other examples are village Baik in Darbhanga district and Pokhra in Saran district. The village Sarea in Saran district is a fine example of semi-circular pattern on the arcuate bend of the Gandaki river.

String Pattern

The string pattern village is found in the districts of Saharsa, Katihar and Purnea in North Bihar. Such linear rural settlements develop in one line along the bank of a river or road. In this pattern houses grow in a single line in order to have an easy approach from the road or the water body. In flood affected riverine tracts of Katihar, Saharsa and Purnea where the river bluffs are suitable for settlement, the houses are built in a single line on the upper crest. Hence, this pattern is associated with the rice growing area where houses are constructed on river embankments or cart-tracks. There are two examples like Tamua in the district of Sahara along a tributary of the river Kosi and Maniakha in district Bhagalpur on the bluffs of the Ghogha rivulets. Sometimes a settlement may consist of more than one 'string' depending on the number of channels or distributaries traversing from the central site of the settlement as seen in the Kosi belt.

Star Pattern

When the circular settlement extends in several directions along the footpaths and roads, the village assumes star shape. It is common in the flood prone area where elevated sites are rare, or at nodal centres where the newer settlement project along the cart-tracks, which radiate from the central village. There is a clearcut zone of such settlements in the Tarai region of Sitamarhi and in East Champaran district. The occurrence of such settlements also takes place with the construction of new dwellings on the fringe of circular and square shaped rural settlements.

Haphazard Pattern

It is a common form of larger villages than compact settlements. In this pattern houses are huddled in irregular fashion without following any definite plan. The larger villages generally consist of several *tolas* with different farms. When compiled together these do not provide any definite pattern. This pattern is not possible in the dispersed settlements where dwellings are scattered in the whole village without any definite street. Village Haraje in Saran district is an example of this pattern. This village is located close to the river Gandak along a cart track. The influence of these two led to the emergence of irregular pattern.

Double-Nucleation

In case two settlements develop at a single site it is called 'double-dorfer' (Ahmad, 1962). In rural areas a minor *stream* is often the cause of such a pattern. Sometimes a mound, a road, a tank or a river may result in the development of twin settlements situated on eitherside of it. It is also caused by the construction of new shops at the railway station. Though the distance may be one or two kilometres from the parent village. In North Bihar such village pattern is found on the river banks, because in such places there is a struggle for water frontage and higher site on the levee. The best examples are Khanpur and Narhan in Samastipur district. These settlements have a similar sites on the bank of river Purain and the Burhi Gandak respectively.

Radial Pattern

The convergence of several and the increasing dimension of houses towards periphery of the village is the cuase of the growth of radial pattern. It also depends on the concentric growth of dwellings hence it is known as cobweb pattern. The influence of a sweet water well or the village shops in the centre of the village also causes radiating pattern of lanes. Village Baheri in Darbhanga district is a fine example of this pattern. Here from the central site of this settlement roads are radiating on all directions, which develop into the form of a radial pattern.

Amorphous Pattern

In case the village lanes are dotted with tiny hamlets all being small rectangles linked with the central site by footpaths, because dispersion of houses will result such an irregular fashion of piling of houses which is known as amorphous pattern, which leads to a scattering of dwellings over the entire area. The amorphous pattern of rural settlements are found in Saran and Champaran districts and the whole of diara belt along the Ganga, but is more common in the Kosi flood prone area in the east. Excellent examples of such villages are Gaura, Rampur, Jagdishpur and Sahebganj in Vaishali district in the diara of the river Ganga. Parhuka in Patna district is an example of S shape where the growth pattern is fully controlled by physical conditions of pynes and lowlands of paddy fields surrounding the village. In this village the burial place of Mohammedans and a tank are placed in such a manner that the villagers have forced to build their houses in a typical double arcuate form leading to the development of sigmatic pattern.

Orientation of Main Thoroughfares of Rural Settlements

A detailed study of hundreds of rural settlements in North Bihar suggests that the main thoroughfare of each and every rural settlement is oriented towards the nearby central places. For example, Baheri, Andhratharhi and Alamnagar are central places of Darbhanga, Madhubani and Saharsa districts respectively around which almost all rural settlements have unmetalled roads which led towards these central places. A short list of such rural settlements is as follows: (Fig. 15.5)

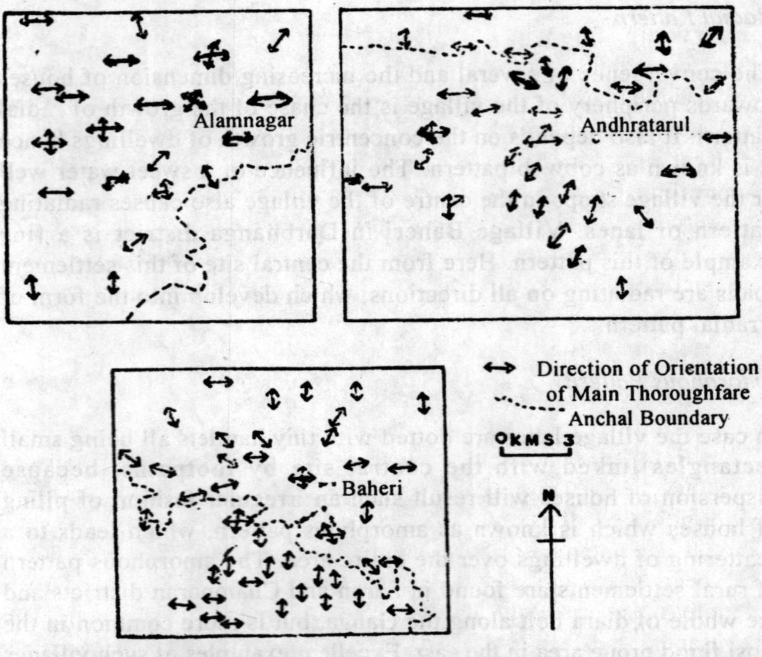

FIG. 15.5: North Bihar: Orientation of Main Throughfare of Rural settlements Around some of the central places.

The above study is helpful in demarcating the zone of influence of a central place, planning the rural settlements on new lines of residential colony or shopping centres and provides future potential lines for planned development of an advanced modern community. This is due to the over importance of the market centre for the surrounding rural inhabitants. The developed culture, commercial importance, centre for learning, source of recreation, purchase of everyday consumer goods, block development office, police station, post and telegraph office, warehousing, cold storage, banking, modes of transport and the hub of all other services at the central places give the rural settlements in their hinterland an orientation which is directed towards the nearby central places.

In rural areas of North Bihar there are some positive and negative variables, which affect or put hindrance on the "law of village anatomy and central place location" as devised by the author. Such restrictive variables are both physical and cultural. Under physical factors the presence of Chaurs, perennial lakes and pynes, intervening monticles and rivers create a hindrance for full functioning of this theory of central place location.

Under cultural parameters the low income group people and untouchables who often reside on the remote byelanes of the village present a pattern contrary to this theory. This is because they have to purchase little consumer goods due to their having meagre resources. This hypothesis may thus be fully operationalized on an isotropic plain surface having same physical and cultural characteristics in all directions.

Measurement of Shape in Rural Settlements

The ideal outer shape of a village would be a circle, and any departure from this can be measured geometrically to determine the distortion. This statement is based on the fact that if each corner of a village has same geographical landscape without any physical or cultural obstructions and is built on a favourable site, then the village should develop in a circular pattern around the central nucleus. As has been stated earlier the nucleus can consist of a tank, a tree, a temple, or a community hall, etc. Before arriving at this conclusion thousands of village patterns on topographical sheets were examined. Although it would be possible to find more extreme cause as the visual inspection indicates considerable variability among settlement patterns, three villages have been selected here to illustrate the point. These settlements resemble to varying degrees the three basic types, circular, square and rectangular.

In order to determine the shape, a circle with its circumference touching the two extreme points of a settlement was drawn. Now the pattern seems to be obvious in its geometrical perspective in comparison with the circle. The formula for the measurement of this is (Gibbs, Jack, P.: 1966):

$$S = \frac{100 \text{ x } A_a}{\pi r^2}$$

where S is the measure of circularity in shape; A is the actual area contained by the settlement and πr^2 is the area of the circle of settlement=A. The above measure that has been applied to each of the rural settlements shown in Fig. 15.4 and the results are given in the Table 15.5.

The table 15.4 shows that in North Bihar different patterns of rural settlements have clearcut tendency of expansion towards circularity. This is due to the equal chance of growth and expansion

TABLE 15.4: Orientation of Main Thoroughfare of Rural Settlements Around Some of the Central Places of North Bihar

Around Alamnagar	Around Baheri	Around Andhratharhi
Ladma EW	Baghauni EW	Katharia WE
Nathua NS, WE	Kharsam NS	Dhamaura
Saparda EW	Parsa NS	Bikramsher EW
Kunjauri WE	Daihara NS	Satghara NS
Hariharpur NW to SE	Murli NS	Rahikpur NS
Ahaon SN	Bara EW	Mahnahi A
Parail EW	Enai EW	Gonauli EW
Kishanpur SN	Sahru EW	Dhagjari EW
Bargaon NS to WE	Sarhila NS	Rajanpur A
Sanoti Chak EW	Boran EW	Gangdwar EW
Haru Dumra EW	Khanpur EW	Madna EW

Source : Compiled by the Author Through Field Investigation.

in all directions having some attractive and repulsive forces acting upon them.

The outer shape of a settlement can be best adjudged from the outer space through airphotographs and remote sensing. This can also be best visualized through bird's eye view. In this situation a sight of settlement from aeroplane may help in the identification of compactness of one settlement with the other. A sight from medium height (100 metres) may help in the identification of compactness of one settlement with the other. A sight from medium height

TABLE 15.5: Measures of the Degree of Circularity in the Shape of Some Rural Settlement Patterns in North Bihar

Some of the Settlements	Area of Circle in Square metres	Area of settlement in Square metres	% Circularity S	No. of Houses
Lagma	2,85,908	1,32,139	46	105
Muradpur	4,32,479	2,04,395	47	217
Baik	1,62,862	97,852	60	105
Bhagwatipur	6,07,525	1,70,292	28	115
Gothini	7,31,924	5,40,655	75	742
Sarea	2,85,908	1,69,966	60	112
Kaila	1,27,070	90,649	72	116

Source : Calculated by the Author

(100 metres) will give clearcut view of shape of a settlement whereas the sight of settlement from 50 metres height may highlight the internal morphology of a settlement.

The circularity values of shape are mathematically independent of the size of the entities and comparisons are also facilitated by the fact that the measure has an absolute maximum value of 100 per cent and for all practical purposes, a fixed minimum of 0.0 per cent.

The values not only expresses the degree of circularity in shape but also provides a clue to the type of geometrical figure which most closely resembles the settlement in question. Although no hard and fast rule can be applied, it appears that as the S value decreases the settlement tends to resemble first with a circular pattern, then star, square, rectangular and in the end an enlongated shape in the order mentioned.

The geometric shape of a village appears to have some relationship with its compactness. The degree of differentiation in compactness of a village pattern helps in regional planning, because problems of housing and highways become more acute as we tend to move from compact to amorphous patterns. The hierarchy of rural settlements according to shape and size shows the intensity of compactness or scattering of settlements in a region with a definite set of environment.

Jajmani System

The village communities though segregated castewise but interlinked through internal service dependency; disorganized under the banner of castism and rigging poverty but there is unity among them in social ties. Inspite of these the wide socio-cultural differences and gap based on the conception of population would not be there if there had been no Jajmani system. The Jajmani system (Wiser, 1936) has been a major factor operating as an integrating and cohesive force in rural settlements, as it is based on symbiotic relationship between various castes residing in the village. It plays a vital role in the maintenance of socio-economic patterns in the village. Hence village institution is the centre for economic and ritual mutuality and inter-dependence of various castes (Singh, 1973). Lewis (1965) observes that "it does not operate like an open market economy, and the ties between the *Jajmani* and the *Kamin* are not like those of employer and the employee in a capitalist system, though undoubtedly the importance

of money is increasing gradually with the passage of time."

In village Kharsam the perpetuation of traditional occupation indicates the existence of the jajmani system. The economic system of the village is still based on functional specialization and interdependence of different castes. Agriculture, for instance, is primarily the task of the Kurmi, but all other castes both high and low cultivate land if they have any, besides doing their traditional work. Oil crushing, hair dressing, cloth washing, drum beating and shoe making still remain the works of teli, barber, dhobi and chamar respectively. Tradition has assigned to each caste a definite position in the community structure, and this leads to specific economic and ritual function which is the staple source of livelihood of that caste. Almost all castes of Kharsam village hold a major occupation in which they have monopoly from the beginning. Although according to traditional callings there is nothing to debar them from accepting other occupations of mobility. During agricultural seasons, when there is a heavy demand on limited labour supply, the Kurmi and Bhumihar castes persuade the artisan castes to work on their fields together with womenfolk on daily wages. This sort of socio-economic system keeps lower castes in constant touch with upper castes and also untouchables with the peasants.

A closer study of the economic system and its consequent hands of mutual obligation and expectation of the village divulge these major kinds of economic dealings within the framework of caste system which have definite repurcussions on the spatial organization and morphology of rural settlements in North Bihar.

(A) The land owning caste like Bhumihar and Kurmi get their plough and equipments of agricultural use including repair work from carpenter, and in return for this the land owning castes give a fixed share in agricultural produce at the time of harvesting of Rabi and Kharif crops. The services relating to agricultural works are traditionally rendered on this basis. In case of giving such services to other people generally carpenter get their payment either in cash or kind immediately just after the work is over. In Fig. 15.6 jajmani system of carpenter has been shown with the help of different shadings and grouping of settlements. There are some of the carpenters who serve this village from times immemorial. In Kharsam proper there is no carpenter family at all but they are serving this village from the nearest neighbour village of Majrahia, Sripur, Kalwara and Sobhia.

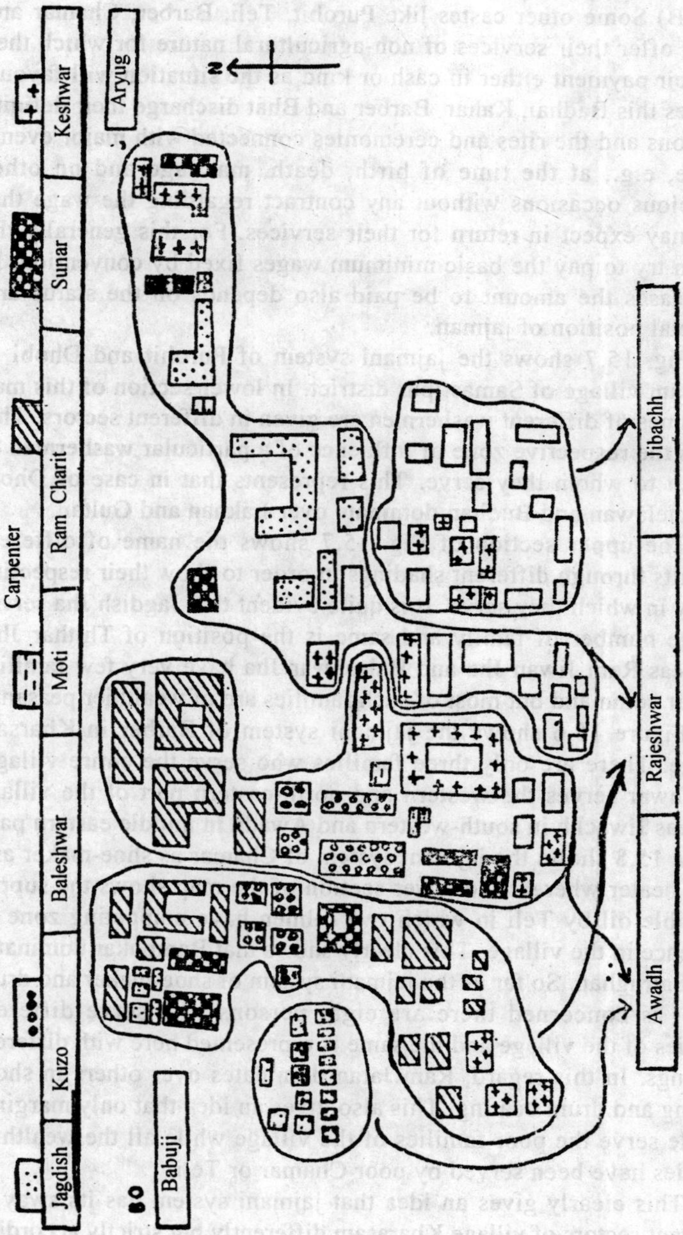

FIG.: 15.6: Kharsam: Jajmani system of Carpenter and Barbar 1991

(B) Some other castes like Purohit, Teli, Barber, Chamar and Dhobi offer their services of non-agricultural nature for which they get their payment either in cash or kind as the situation will favour. Besides this Badhai, Kahar, Barber and Bhat discharge their definite functions and the rites and ceremonies connected with major events of life, e.g., at the time of birth, death, marriage and on other auspicious occasions without any contract regarding the wage that they may expect in return for their services. For this generally the jajman try to pay the basic minimum wages fixed by convention. In most cases the amount to be paid also depends on the status and financial position of jajman.

Fig. 15.7 shows the jajmani system of Purohit and Dhobi in Kharsam village of Samastipur district. In lower section of this map the names of different washermen are given in different sectors. This shows the respective zone of influence of a particular washerman or purohit to whom they serve. This represents that in case of Dhobi Ramkhelawan and Budhan dominate over Lakhan and Gultan.

The upper section of Fig. 15.7 shows the name of different Purohits through different shadings in order to show their respective family in which they serve. It is quite evident that Jagdish Jha serves a large number of family and same is the position of Thithar Jha. Whereas Ram Jiwan Jha and Baleshwar Jha have very few families in their command but most of such families are of wealthier peasants.

Figure 15.6 shows the jajmani system of Barber in Kharsam village. There are only three families who serve the entire village. Rajeshwar serves the western and north-eastern part of the village whereas Jiwachh in south-western and Awadh in middle eastern part. Figure 15.8 shows the jajmani system of Chamar as shoe-maker and drum beater whereas the lower section of the map shows the supply of edible oil by Teli in which two oilmen have competing zone of influence in the village. This clearly shows that Rampukar dominates over Satrughan. So far as the jajmani system of shoe-maker and drum beater is concerned there are eight persons who serve different families of the village and the same is represented here with different shadings. In this regard, Ram Jatan dominates over others in shoe-making and drum beating. This also gives an idea that only marginal people serve the poor families of the village while all the wealthier families have been served by poor Chamar or Teli.

This clearly gives an idea that jajmani system has its sway in different sectors of village Kharasam differently but strictly according

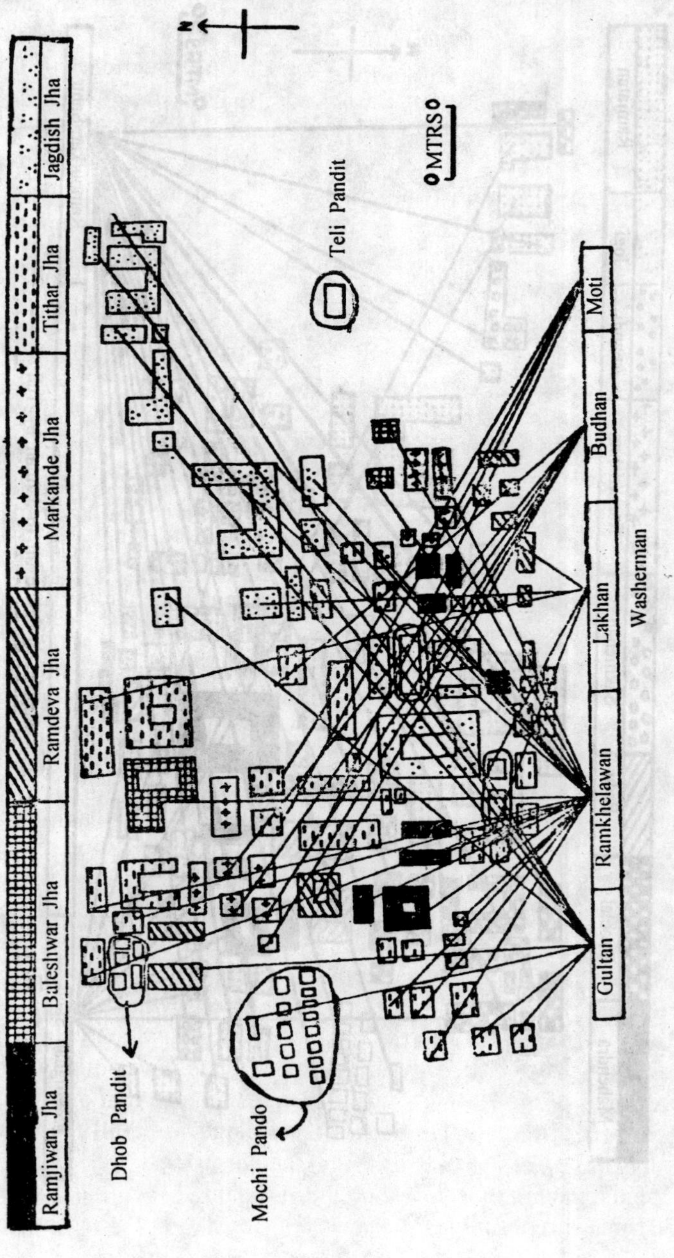

FIG.: 15.7: Kharsam: Jajmani System of Purohit and Washerman 1991.

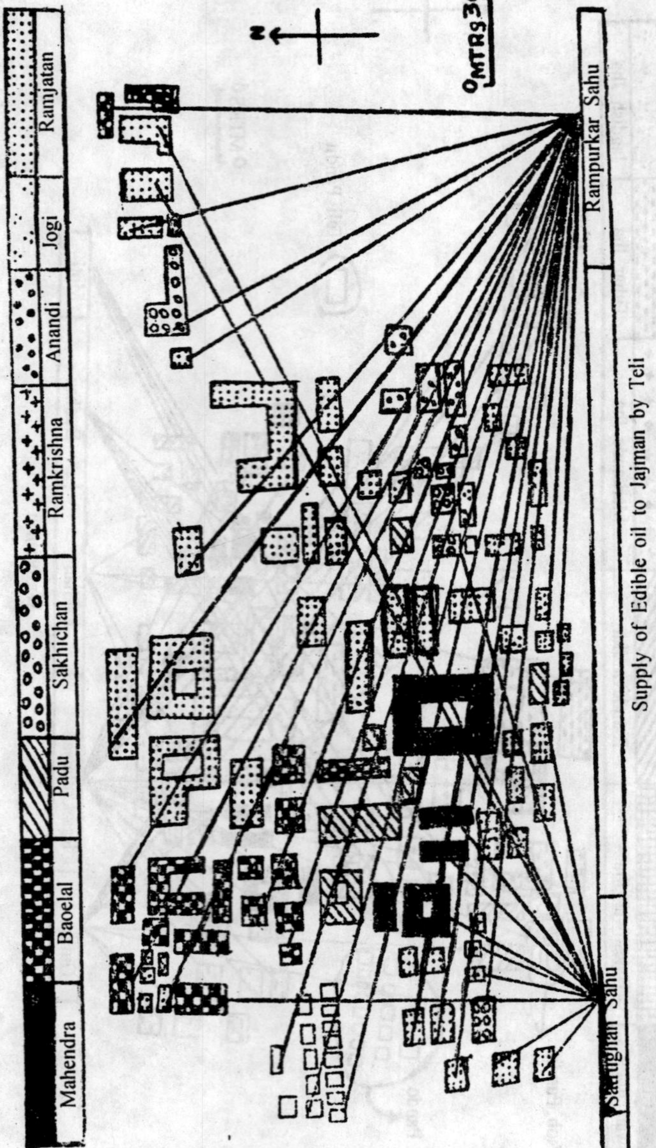

FIG.: 15.8: Kharsam: Jajmani System of Chamar and Teli, 1991

to the economic gains of both peasants and the labourers. Thus spatial variations of jajmani system have definitely shaped the social morphology of settlements not only to village Kharsam but almost all rural settlements of North Bihar.

(C) In case the services under jajmani systems are performed for the landless owning people or lower income group poor people, they instead either give their traditional services or pay in kind. Sometimes such services are performed between two or more castes on barter system also.

The above description shows how the different castes of Kharsam ritually and economically inter-linked and inter-dependent.

Spatio-Functional Organization of Rural Space

The spatio-functional organization of the countryside moving around agricultural operations and ranching of livestock which have close affiliations with the settlements, farms and the occupational structure of inhabitants.

In North Bihar the spatio-functional organization of rural settlements reveal that houses are constructed at one site which form a village. The surrounding space is occupied by agricultural fields, gardens and pasturelands. The central site of the settlement is connected with the neighbouring village through unmetalled road or footpath. Hence, the spatio-functional space of the countryside in North Bihar may be generalized into;

1. Each village has a *Central site* and satellite settlement located at some distance.
2. The Central site of the settlement has *village lanes* which connect one household with the other. Finally, these lanes have opening towards the agricultural fields and the neighbouring villages.
3. Each village consists of rectangular or square shaped fields in the surrounding space.
4. The special parts of the village are temple, school, rural health centre, block development office, thana, shops, panchayat bhawan, graveyard, cremation ground, tank, etc.

In North Bihar the occupational structure of rural population suggests the spatio-functional organization of rural settlements in general. The Census of India 1991 recorded the following categories of occupational structure of the people fo this region.

1. Cultivation,
2. Agricultural labourers,
3. Livestock, forestry, fishing, hunting, plantation, orchards and allied activities,
4. Mining and quarrying,
5. Household industry, manufacturing and repairing,
6. Construction,
7. Trade and commerce,
8. Transport, storage and communication, and
9. Other professional services.

The spatio-functional organization of some of the rural settlements are given below in order to highlight the above generalizations.

Laukahi

Laukahi is a rural settlement located in Laukahi anchal of Madhubani district. It lies 19 kilometres north-east of Nirmali railway station. Its revenue thana number is 37 and it has an area of 264.26 hectares. In 1991 this village had 393 occupied residential houses and 2,207 population. Its neighbouring rural settlements are Kakahia and Jhauri in the south, Singrahi in the west, Jamsar and Mahadeomath in the east and Atri in the north.

Settlement

In Laukahi 16 hectares of land is occupied by residential houses. Houses are systematically built on both sides of unmetalled road in western upland plains of the village. Originally the people had settled on the north-western part of the village but with the growth of population this settlement expands in the south-western upland tract. The newly constructed government offices such as the Kosi Project Office, Block Development Office, etc., are found on the southern section. At the same time the hutments of poor villagers are found on the embankment of the tank.

The chief material of wall of the house is mud due to high adhesive quality of the soil. The houses are also constructed with burnt brick and grass leaves. In Laukahi 70 per cent houses are of mud wall, 7 per cent burnt brick and the rest 23 per cent are of straw and bamboos.

Generally, the peasants of Laukahi have two compartments in their houses. One compartment is known as *angan* which is meant for kitchen, bed room, store, ladies apartment and the other is known as *bathan* for livestock and *dalan* for guests and male members. In most cases joint family system is preferred in comparison with solitary family living. The rich families of the village have separate rooms for different purposes, i.e., kitchen, bed room, etc. But the poor villagers have to accommodate in a small hutment.

Villagers of Laukahi used to take bath in the neighbouring tank. They also wash their utensils and other domestic materials in the tank. Generally ladies bring water for drinking purposes from the neighbouring tube-wells, wells and pond.

The people are hospitable to others. In the night after taking supper they go to their neighbours to smoke *(Hukka* or *Biri)*. They seat in a circular fashion arround a fire place called *Ghura* in local dialect especially during the winter season. They talk on miscellaneous topics.

Roads and Lanes

The internal morphology of Laukahi is complex one due to zig-zag lanes and insanitary village circulatory path. The main roads of the village connect all the tanks located in the north, east and south-west of the settlement. On the central site of the village all the lanes converge to form a chauk area where some shops are located besides residential houses. From this chauk the lanes again bifurcate into the eastern and western side of the village. In the middle part of agricultural fields the pastureland of Laukahi is located which is also used as road for agricultural operations in all seasons.

In Laukahi about 10 hectares of land is engaged in road and footpath. There is a District Board road which passes from Mahadeo-math in the east to Laukahi in the west. This is an unmetalled road but motorable in dry season. During rainy season the road is filled with water and mud and this makes difficult even for cycle to move. Somewhere, the road lies below the level of agricultural fields which create problems for villagers in general and passers-by in particular.

The cart-tracks in the village pass from north to south. People have settled on both sides of the track. They lead to all directions in the village. The tracks are so narrow that it is difficult for the two way bullock-cart to cross each other. There are three main footpaths which have a breadth of one to two metres. Each of them passes through the cultivable land. These footpaths are called *bandh* in local dialect. These have been made by the village to check and regulate the rain water as during rainy season water rushes from the northern higher slopes to the south.

Agricultural Land

The field pattern in Laukahi is of rectangular and square in shape. Small plots of land are found on the eastern side of settlement fringe where kitchen garden finds place. In northern side of the village plots of land are larger in size but it is medium in the southern side. The entire village is a single crop rice land but in some pockets khesari, wheat and onion are also raised. The agricultural plots are divided into different pieces separated by the *bandh* and road. Although the main occupation of the villager is cultivation but that is not a profitable business now, due to rising prices of diesel and fertilizer and relatively low production and continuously increasing number of people in each family.

Special Parts of Laukahi

The special parts of Laukahi includes Shivji temple located in the eastern side of tank near H.E. School, graveyard located in the east of the pasture land amidst agricultural fields and the other features are as follows.

The people of Laukahi have organized a library in 1951. The government of Bihar deserves thanks for giving aid to the library. It is situated in the middle of the village. The library has a good number of novels, story books and course books. There is a lower primary school situated on the embankment of the pond. The high school was established in 1948. Through the western side of this school there is a main way to enter into the village. The H.E. school has a campus of 2 hectares of land. It has three boys hostels and a good pucca building.

There is a night shool where mostly poor illiterate wage earners get education in adult education programme. There is also a drama society in this village organized by youngmen in 1947 when our country achieved independence. Later on it is renamed as 'Azad Drama Club' which had played several charity show and given money to the defence fund of India. There is also a sadachar samitee in the village which was established in 1966. Its function is to curb the corrupt practices of villagers as well as officials of the Block Development Office by means of maintaining watch against the black marketeers and bribe takers.

Laukahi thana has been established in 1964 in the northern side of H.E. School. It has a building in one hectare of land located just by the side of the main road. Laukahi Block Development Office was established in 1956 on the southern side of the District Board road. Related to this some residential quarters have established over 20 hectares of land. The Kosi Project Office was constructed for the western canal system of the Kosi river. It is situated on the western side of the District Board road covering one hectare of land.

At present in shallow ditches of the village only fish, makhanna, singarhara and purainipatta, etc., are extracted by the villagers. These ditches also serve the purpose of washing livestock of the village.

For the planned development of this village the provision of metalled road, electricity, deepening of tanks and ditches for rearing fish and the provision of underground sewage and drains are highly needed.

Mashrakh (Saran District)

Mashrakh is a large rural settlement situated on the bank of Ghogari river in Mashrakh anchal of Saran District. Its revenue thana no. is 139, latitude 26°7 N and longitude 84°48 E. It has an area of 1257.34 hectares including 1084 residential houses, 1343 households and 9197 persons in 1991. It is irregular in shape and the neighbouring rural settlements are Chakrihara Mathia and Deuria in the north, Govindpur in the east, Ghoghian in the west and Katalpur and Hanumanganj in the south.

Settlement

Mashrakh is a compact rural settlement. It is fast developing into a service centre for the surrounding rural space. The settlement area consists of 16 different units in which people of various castes reside, e.g., Rajput, Kanu, Muslim, Koeri, Teli, Brahmin etc. The chief material of wall is mud and burnt brick, while the material of roof is tile and RCC. This is due to urban influence of this settlement. Mashrakh has 400 shops of different types.

Circulatory Path

The internal pattern of village lanes are quite haphazard in which the main road runs from Kajapatti Railway Station in the north to Chapra 32 kilometres in the south. Another road comes from Tajpur in the south-west and ultimately terminates on the Mashrakh railway station. Mashrakh is a rural settlement of transformation stage whose market area expands towards railway station along the main road. The market area which lies just west of railway station has a very simple circulatory path which runs from north to south. Saturday and Sunday are market days when a big gathering can be observed on all circulatory paths of the village.

Land Use and Agricultural Practices

Agriculture and trade and commerce are the main occupations of the people of this village. Mashrakh has 750 hectares of unirrigated cultivable land, 70 hectares of irrigated land, 258 hectares of culturable wasteland and 137 hectares of land not available for cultivation. The soil is fertile and is suitable for the raising of wheat, maize, paddy, gram, pulses, oilseeds and vegetables.

In north-western part of Mashrakh mixed farming is practised, in western part bhadai and rabi crops are raised whereas southern part is meant for Aghani and Rabi, and central part for Bhadai and vegetables. Cultivable wastelands are found in the south and north of Mashrakh railway station.

Special Parts of Mashrakh

Mashrakh has a Post Office, public call telephone centre, besides 3 primary schools, 3 middle schools, one high school and one rural health centre. The people drink water from well and tubewell. It has also electricity connection besides one sugar mill.

Tamaut Parasa (Saharsa District)

Tamaut Parsa (Fig. 15.9) located in Murliganj anchal of Saharsa

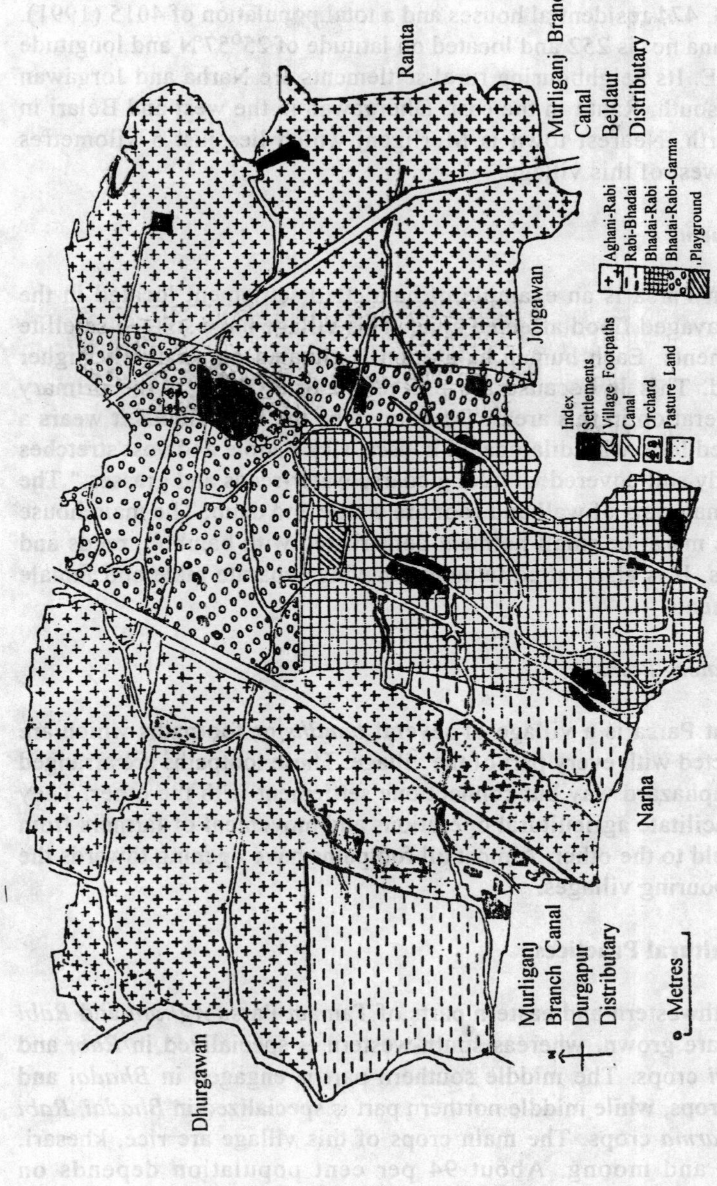

FIG.: 15.9: Spatial Organization of Tamaut Parsa: District Saharsa, 1991

district. It lies 5 kilometres east of Madhepura-Banmankhi road and represents the changing situation of the Kosi belt. It has 810 hectares of land, 474 residential houses and a total population of 4015 (1991). Its Thana no. is 252 and located on latitude of 25°57'N and longitude 84°55'E. Its neighbouring rural settlements are Narha and Jorgawan in the south, Rahta in the east, Dhurgawan in the west and Belari in the north. Nearest town is Murliganj which lies just 5 kilometres north-west of this village.

Settlement

Tamaut Parsa is an example of hamletted settlement located in the Kosi ravaged flood affected zone. This village have sixteen satellite settlements. Each human habitation is situated on relatively higher ground. This is because the protection from flood is the primary consideration in this area. "Devastated by the Kosi floods it wears a deserted look with dilapidated houses, sick people and vast stretches of sandy soil covered with long coarse water-reeds and grasses." The chief materials of wall and roof are wattle and daub. The main house type is marai or small hutment constructed with bamboo, reeds and grasses. It is also called tataughar having separate male and female apartments.

Circulatory Paths

Tamaut Parsa is a village of several *bandhs* or footpaths which are connected with every part of the village. These footpaths are arranged in a haphazard way but connect one settlement with the other. They also facilitate agricultural operations and movement of farmers from one field to the other. Almost all footpaths have opening towards the neighbouring villages.

Agricultural Practices

In northwestern and eastern parts of Tamaut Parsa *Aghani* and *Rabi* crops are grown, whereas south-western is specialized in *Rabi* and *Bhadai* crops. The middle southern part is engaged in *Bhadai* and *Rabi* crops, while middle northern part is specialized in *Bhadai, Rabi* and *Garma* crops. The main crops of this village are rice, khesari, millet and moong. About 94 per cent population depends on agriculture for their livelihood and per capita share of land is 0.32 hectare. Here 85 per cent land is net sown area and only 75 per cent of the net sown area is under double crop.

It has 342 hectares of canal irrigated land, 408 hectares of tubewell irrigated area, 12 hectares of cultivable waste and 48 hectares of land not available for cultivation.

Special Parts of Tamaut Parsa

It has one Shiva temple in the middle of the village including a play ground. It has the facility of one post office, one primary school, one middle school, 35 drinking water well, 21 bamboo boring and one tank. All footpaths are unmetalled. Thursday and Sunday are days of village hats in Tamaut Parsa. Since 1951 with the construction of eastern Kosi embankment and construction of Murliganj branch canal, Durgapur distributary and Beldaur distributary now the situations have changed a lot.

Kharsam (Samastipur District)

Kharsam is a rural settlement located in Rosera anchal of Samastipur district. It has a latitude of 25°54'N and longitude of 86°4'E. It lies north of the river Kareh in a large rural pocket being 29 kilometres south-east of the city of Darbhanga, 25 kilometres north-east of Samastipur and 19 kilometres north of Ruseraghat railway station. The population of the village is found to be 862 persons living in 450 houses in 1991. It is surrounded by Sripur in the north, Parwana in the south, Boraj in the west and Majrahia in the east. It has an area of 118 hectares of land out of which 25 hectares is irrigated and the rest is unirrigated.

Settlement

Kharsam is a settlement of rectangular shape. It is protected by the flood of the Kareh by an embankment on the south, four ditches on the north and orchards of mango on the east and west. The houses are generally placed along the village streets. The spacing between houses is not more than 2 metres. Thus it is a semi-compact settlement. The condition of houses belonging to the poor Chamars

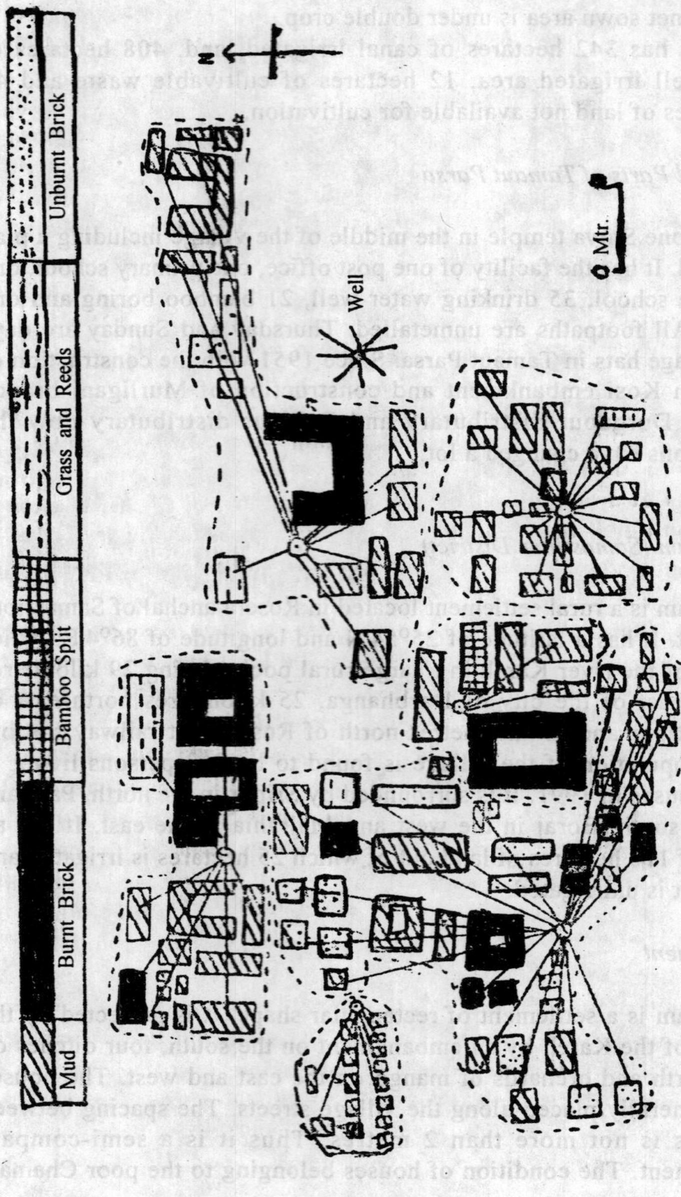

FIG.: 15.10: Kharsam Spatial Organization according to Drinking Water Well and Material Wall, 1991

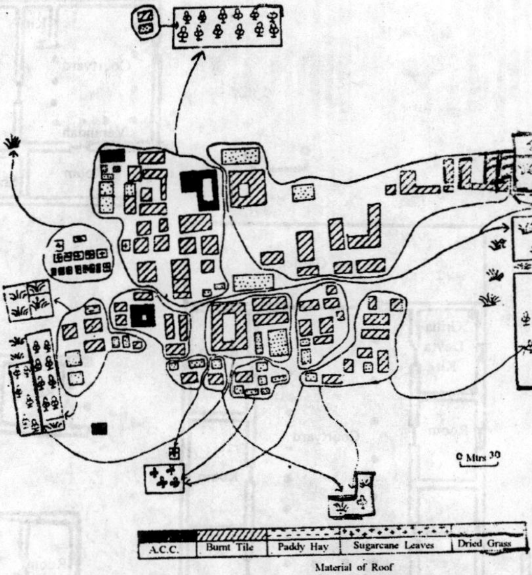

FIG.: 15.11: Kharsam: Sources of Material of roof, 1991

were not good. Now it has been converted into puca houses under Indira Awas Yojana.

The chief materials of wall are mud, burnt brick, bamboo split, grass and reeds and unburnt brick (Fig. 15.10). In this figure different houses of the village has been shaded with different shadings in order to shów the spatial variations of the material of wall. It is evident that mud and burnt brick are dominant materials of wall in this village whereas unburnt brick and grass-reeds occupy an inferior position which are generally used by the poor.

The materials of roof are RCC; burnt grass (Fig. 15.11) in Kharsam village which has shown here with different shadings. It is quite evident that burnt tile is the chief roofing material while dried grass, RCC; and sugarcane leaves have inferior position.

In spatio-functional organization of Kharsam village, the extraction of mud for the material of wall (Fig. 15.10) gives a clear picture how the residents of different sectors of the village have traditional affiliations for the extraction of mud. Similarly Fig. 15.11 represents the affiliations of different families with different mango groves not only for fruits but also for wood, dried leaves and other odd errands.

According to the four housing plans of the village Kharsam Fig.

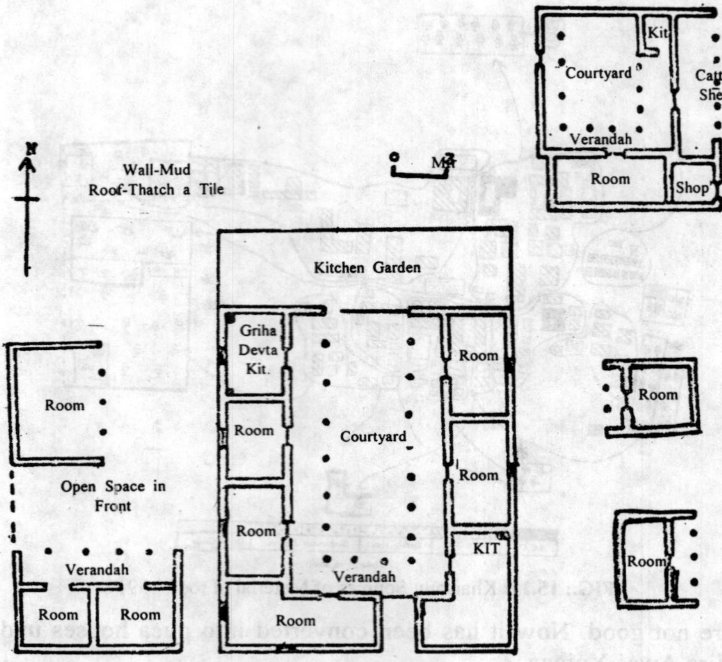

FIG.: 15.12: Kharsam: House Plans

15.12) the average living space is 4 square metres per person and the height of the house is 4 metres. An inner courtyard for women and an outer verandah or dalan for the men are common features in each and every house. Cattleshed is often located adjacent to the main house, but in some cases it may be separate structure. Each house has some banana trees at the back. Wooden windows ¼ x ½ metres size are common.

Circulatory Path

The village lanes are not so tortuous in village Kharsam. Two parallel lanes run from the Western and eastern parts of the village which connect Sripur in the north and the flood protection embankment of the river Kareh in the south. Most of the houses are clinging on the side of these two lanes. Other byelanes radiate from these two which go towards east and west. In western side these bye-lanes extend up to Lalpur and in the east up to Majrahia a neighbouring village. The main lanes have a width of just 3 metres whereas bye-lanes have a width of just one metre. In most cases the bye-lanes meet the main road almost at right angle, but there are exceptions also.

Agricultural Practices

The main occupation is cultivation of land and production of food grains of the inhabitants of Kharsam. The chief crops grown are rice, wheat, maize, millet, cheena and sweet potato. From east to west the central part of the village is a lowland where rice and khesari are mainly grown. The northern upland plain is most suitable land for sugarcane, wheat, maize, arhar and chilly cultivation. In southern and eastern part of the village sandy soil favours the cultivation of cheena and sweet potato abundantly. In this village 4 hectares of land is culturable waste and two hectares of land is the area not available for cultivation. A noticeable change is the dispersal of rural settlement with the introduction of Ganga variety of hybrid maize and the provision of tube-well irrigation in northern part of the village.

Special Parts of Kharsam

The special parts of this village are a temple dedicated to the goddess and another temple dedicated to a village deity. These are the public and religious establishments of the village.

Drinking water well also come under special parts (Fig. 15.10). In this regard it has been found that some families have permanent affiliation to fetch water from a particular well in almost all rural settlements of North Bihar. In Kharsam the wells located in the south-western and north-eastern corner of the village have wider-served areas because of the availability of sweet water throughout the year. Other wells either dry in the summer months or restricted to certain groups of people.

REFERENCES

Acharya, P.K., *Architecture of Manasara,* 1933 and Havel, E.B.: *Ancient and Medieval Architecture of India,* London, 1915.

Ahmad, E., "Indian Village Patterns", *Geographical Outlook,* Vol. 3, No. 1, 1962, pp. 5-15.

Berteille, A., *Caste, Class and Power,* Oxford University Press, Bombay, 1966.

Chatterjee, A.B. and Das, Mira, "Settlement Pattern in the Puri Chilka Coastal Tract", *Geographical Review of India,* 1964, p. 31.

Deva, K. and Mishra, V., *Vaishali Excavations,* 1950, Vaishali Sangh, Vaishali, Allahabad, 1961.

Doxiadis, C.A., *Ekistics: An Introduction to the Science of Human Settlements,* New York, Oxford University Press, 1964, p. 24.

Duggal, S.L., "Moradabad District Settlements in Relation to Land Use", *The Indian Geographers,* Vol. 6, No. 1, 1961, pp. 66-7.

Gibbs, J.P., *Urban Research Method,* New Delhi, 1966, p. 101.

Karan, P.P., *Bhutan: A Physical and Cultural Geography,* University of Kentucky Press, Lexington, 1967.

Louis Renou, *The Civilization of Ancient India,* Calcutta, 1959, p. 51.

Mandelbaum, B.G., *Society in India,* Popular Prakashan, Bombay, 1972.

Malley, O.S.S., *Bengal District Gazetteer,* Champaran, Calcutta, 1997, p. 85. The Emperial Road which Buddha Followed during his March from Rajgriha to Kushinara Had Several Villages on Either Side.

Mukerji, A.B., "Rural Settlements in the Jatakas", *Geographical Review of India,* Vol. 31, No. 4, 1969, and the Jatakas Stories, ed. by E.B. Cowell, Lazad and Co., London, 1957.

Mukherjee, Radhakamal, *Man and His Habitation,* Popular Prakashan, Bombay, 1968.

Prasad, A., Chotanagpur, *Geography of Rural Settlements,* Ranchi University, Ranchi, 1973, pp. 380-81.

Sarkar, S.S., "The Malers of the Rajmahal Hills", *Man in India,* 33, 1933.

Sharma, B.N., *Social Life in Northern India,* Munshiram Manohar Lal, Delhi, 1961, pp. 310-15.

Sharma, J., *"A Village in West Bengal, in India's Villages"* (M.N. Shrinivas, ed.), Asia Publishing House, Bombay, 1960.

Sharma, R.S., *Sudras in Ancient India,* Motilal Banarsidas, Delhi, 1958.

Singh, J.P., "Social Aspects of the Morphology of Rural Settlement", *Journal of the Indian Anthropological Society,* Vol. 12, No. 1, 1977.

Singh, K.N., "An Approach to the Study of the Morphology of the Indian Village", *Rural Settlements in Monsoon Asia* (ed. R.L. Singh), N.G.S.I.: Varanasi, 1972, pp. 203-14.

Singh, R.L., *Banaras: A Study in Urban Geography,* Banaras, 1955, p. 339.

Singh, R.L., "Evolution of Settlement in the Middle Ganga Valley", *The National Geographical Journal of India,* I, Part II, 1955.

Singh, S.J., "Habitations of Maitais", *Man in India,* 13, 1933.

16

TRANSPORTATION LINKAGES AND RURAL COMMUNITY DEVELOPMENT

Introduction

Roads, railways and caravan paths are known as transportation routes. They are considered a life line for the growth and development of rural settlements.

Thus, transportation lines play a decisive role in the location of rural community. It increases the general efficiency of the village in relation to its accessibility, morphology, health, trade and commerce, concentration of service facilities and educational institutions. Thus transportation lines have multi-lateral effects on rural communities development.

On the other hand, the long awaited transportational gap in between rural communities proved to be a great hinderance in its development. The focalization of various means of transport and better service opportunities can keep rural people mobile to get more and more food, fuel and employment. Thus, where there is a better transport linkages, the development of service centres, amenities and the increase in population size of the community have taken place.

Review of Literature

Transport Development is a strategy for rural development in developing countries: The case of Nigeria has been traced out by M.O. Filani (1992) in IGU conference in Washington.

Until very recently in Nigeria, rural transport problems had been neglected. Successive National Development Plans and Governments have emphasized intra-urban and inner-city transport linkages. The relative neglect of rural transport development could be ascribed to the absence of any clearcut policy of rural allocation of transport resources, resulting in over concentration of transport investments in inter-city linkages.

Since 1985 there has been a major shift in government policy on rural development. This policy shift is reflected in the start of the Directorate of Food, Roads and Rural Infrastructure (DFRRI) in the office of the country's President. The Directorate is expected to work closely with State governments in order to reach the various communities in each of the 453 local governments throughout the country, and to serve as an important element in the social and economic mobilization of the citizens at the grassroot level.

One of the major tasks of the Directorate is to oversee the construction and maintenance of about 60,000 km of feeder roads in the rural areas of the country. Half of a N900 million revenue, which the federal government expected from the 1986 petroleum subsidy adjustment, is earmarked for this programme. This shows government's awareness of the critical role of transport in rural development.

Therefore Filani (1992) examines the activities of DFRRI since its inception with respect to rural transport development—the strategies adopted, investment patterns and results. The extent of success is shown and the relevance of Nigeria's experience to other developing countries discussed.

In rural areas of India there is an alarming lack of service facilities and it can be solved only through providing transportational linkages to the rural community. The condition is such that in rainy season when the footpaths are filled up with water, the patients of the rural community has no way out to die because there is few road links and other means to reach the doctor. During rainy season the accumulative forces of flood and rain water, cause the damage of village footpaths to a knee to neck deep water and hence, it gravitates the problem. It is therefore, felt by the author that inspite of providing any other facilities, the provision of road linkage is prerequisite as it is economical for short hauls in comparison with waterways and railways, which are mainly suited in long hauls.[1]

Needed Research

The unbalanced growth of transport linkages over space gave rise to regional imbalances of rural community development in North Bihar e.g., railway stations and points of convergence of roads have great impact on the growth and expansion of wholesale grain markets, as both of them have conformity with each other. On different railway routes of North Bihar, the following markets are located:

(a) *Between Samastipur and Nirmali:* Mukhtapur, Kishanpur, Hayaghat, Laheria Sarai, Darbhanga, Sakuri, Jhanjharpur, Tamoria, Ghoghardiha and Nirmali.
(b) *Between Darbhanga and Narkatiaganj:* Kamtaul, Janakpur, Road, Sursand, Sitamarhi, Bairgania, Dheng, Ghorasahan, Adapur, Raxaul, Sikta and Narkatiaganj.
(c) *Between Mansi and Jogbani:* Bihpur, Kharik, Maheskhut, Karhagola, Katihar, Purnea, Kasba, Jalalgarh, Garh Banaili, Araria, Forbesganj and Jogbani.
(d) *Mairwa to Barsoi along the Ganges:* Siswan, Ekma, Revelganj, Chhapra, Dighwara, Hajipur, Desri, Mahnar, Mohiuddinagar, Sahpur Patori, Phulwaria, Teghra, Begusarai, Balia, Parbatta, Bihpur, Naugachhia, Barsoi and others.

In this way, one can easily say that "nowadays one main factor which plays the decisive role in the location of market is the proximity of the railway siding.[3]

Similarly, one another study shows that higher the transportational index higher is the community development index for a settlement. In this way, it could be said that transportation lines are the real indicator of community development. After giving proper weight for railway station, metalled and unmetalled roads, high school, middle school, college, tanks, tubewell, telephone exchange, post office, wholesale market, village market, hospital and retail market a final index for community development and transportational index has been derived separately for the purpose of comparison in between the two (Table 16.1).

According to Table 16.1 it can be said that transportation lines should be must for community development because there are several villages like Ladha, Balia, Afzala, Mahammadpur and Akbarpur in Saharsa district where due to lack of transportation the index of development is lesser.

In this way, the author want to prove his concepts with the help of some principles which are as follows:

TABLE 16.1: Summary for Transport Linkage and Community Development (1992)

Settlement	Transport Index	Development Index	Character of Community
Ujianpur	32	104	Rural Central place
Sarai Ranjan	32	334	"
Mohiuddinagar	32	382	"
Hasanpur	27	413	"
Baheri	22	301	"
Supaul	22	246	"
Ladho	2	7	Residential Village
Balia	2	77	"
Afzala	2	68	"
Mohammadpur	2	9	"
Akbarpur	7	157	Rural Central

Source: Compiled by the Author.

Morphological Principles

The Characteristic features of roads, morphology and village lanes show the areas of functional specialization of a settlement i.e.

(a) Chauk is a place for drinking well, meeting ground, Panchayat Bhawan under baniyan tree and shopping centre in case of rural service centre.

(b) Wider metalled road and brick paved roads are the main thoroughfares of the large village on commercial ribbons of rural central places. Thus good transport routes are the sign of community development.

(c) Narrow unpaved road shows the main thoroughfares of smaller villages or residential areas of rural settlements.

(d) Footpaths are generally the lanes of the village and areas of slum of poor fellows in case of rural settlements.

These principles show that better and multidirectional road links form the centre of civilization, heart of a settlement, and sign of community upliftment. Hence, the author strongly recommends the development of good road links for community development throughout India.

Orientation of Rural Community Lanes Principle

It is a very typical tendency of village roads and main thoroughfares which lead towards the neighbouring central place, as it is the life line of a particular village. With the help of this hypothesis central places of a lower order can be established on the side of potential roads having connections of several rural settlements. It is helpful in demarcating the zone of influence of a central place, planning the rural settlements on new lines of residential colony or shopping centre and provides a future potential lines for planned development of an advanced modern rural community.

The above assumption gives an idea that the market places are first originated and in case of later origin the thoroughfares of all the rural communities in its zone of influence may adjusted towards them. This is the law of village roads orientation in each and every rural central place hinterland in India.

The orientation of main village lanes towards the neighbouring market is due to the over importance of market centre for the surrounding rural inhabitants. In central villages the developed culture, commercial importance, centre for learning, source of recreation, purchase of every day consumer goods, block development office, police station, post office, warehousing, cold storage, banking, nodes of transport and the hub of all other services on the central places gives the rural community in their hinterland an orientation which is directed towards the nearby central places.

The above idea is in accordance with the central place hierarchy of Christaller (1933)[5], Losch (1954)[6], concept of range of goods, threshold relationship and ranksize rule as put forward by Zipt (1948)[7] and diffusion model of Bylund (1960)[8] and Haggerstrand[9] (1952). Thus the present concept of hinterland organization and location of central villages with the help of orientation of leading roads of the village suggests that only in that direction the future smaller potential market can grow and the planning of rural communities could be possible.

In rural areas there are some restrictive variables as "carriers and barriers[10], which affect or put hindrance on the "law of village anatomy and central place location" which is the main theme of this chapter. Such restrictive variables are physical and cultural both. Under physical factors the presence of chaurs, perennial lakes and pynes, entervening monticles and rivers are creating hindrance for the full functioning to this concept of central village location.

Under cultural parameters the low income group poor and untouchables who often reside on the remote by lanes of the village and hence it is not in accordance with this concept. This is because they have low purchasing power of consumer goods with having meagre resources. This hypothesis may be full operationalised on an isotropic plain surface.

Transportation Principle

Rural roads or foot paths are the connecting life lines of rural development and it has been delineated here in four stages in accordance with its location and future extension:

(a) The rural community of ancient times were located abnormally at greater distances and their relationship in respect of transportation lines were not multi-directional but single route location connecting distant villages, as in case of smaller tolas of the present. Thus the resultant condition is smaller settlement, single route location and poor economy.

(b) The increase in size and number of settlements two-folds, transportation lines connects that village from two directions. This forms the triangular routes as this provides greater incentive of growth and extension of settlement having better transport connections with the neighbouring villages.

(c) In the third stage residential settlements have three directional connections in general, which forms rectangular, square and diagonal connection of roads with the neighbouring rural communities.

(d) At the fourth stage rural service centres have multi-directional connection of roads with the nearby central places and other smaller rural settlements of the region on an hexagonal lattice.

Thus, the transportational linkages, cultural development, economic growth, community extension programmes and location of rural settlements have certain relationship and this may be considered as an important tools for planning the rural settlements.

Transport Network Analysis

Network analysis considers the connectivity of nodes or settlements for measuring the accessibility of a point. In this context shortest path matrix or shimbel index and Td matrices are generally calculated which could be seen in the following exercises.

Shimbel Index is a measures of accessibility of an individual node. It is the same of the shortest paths. It is the node with highest accessibility.

(a) For both 1910 and 1931 it is 5th point.

(b) The node having lowest accessibility is the one with the largest paths. In the exercise given below it is 4th, 10th and 11th point for 1910 and 10th and 11th for 1931.

Exercise

Find the β index and the α index for each time period i.e. 1910, 1932 and 1981.

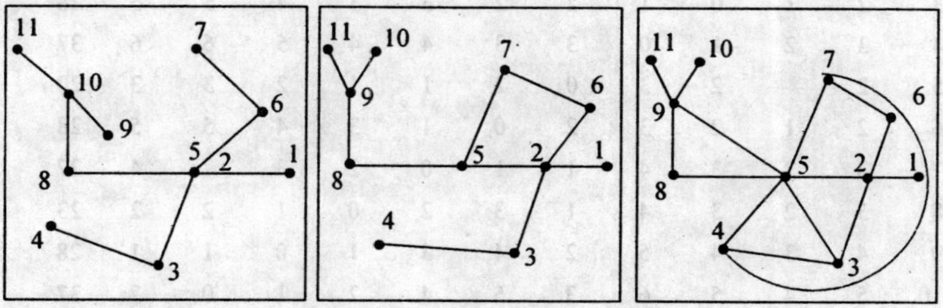

1910

$$\beta \text{ Index} = \frac{e}{\upsilon} = \frac{10}{11} = 0.909$$

$$\alpha \text{ index} = \frac{e}{3(\upsilon - 2)} = \frac{10}{3(11-2)} = \frac{10}{27} = 0.37$$

1932

$$\beta \text{ index} = \frac{e}{\upsilon} = \frac{11}{11} = 1$$

$$\alpha \text{ index} = \frac{e}{3(\upsilon - 2)} = \frac{11}{3(11-2)} = \frac{11}{27} = 0.407$$

1981

$$\beta \text{ index} = \frac{e}{\upsilon} = \frac{18}{11} = 1.64$$

$$\alpha \text{ index} = \frac{e}{3(\upsilon - 2)} = \frac{18}{3(11-2)} = \frac{18}{27} = 0.666$$

2. Has the diameter changed between the period

The diameter of:

$$1910 = 6$$

$$1932 = 6$$

$$1981 = 3$$

Between 1910 and 1932 the diameter remained the same which is 6, but in 1981 the diameter changed to 3. This is because of the circuits which has increased in 1981

3. Draw up the shortest path matrices for 1932 and 1981. Calculate the shimbel indices.

The shortest path matrix for 1932 (D-matrix)

Cell	1	2	3	4	5	6	7	8	9	10	11	
1	0	1	2	3	2	2	3	3	4	5	5	30
2	1	0	1	2	1	1	2	2	3	4	4	21
3	2	1	0	1	2	2	3	3	4	5	5	28
4	3	2	1	0	3	3	4	4	5	6	6	37
5	2		2	3	0	2	1	1	2	3	3	20
6	2	1	2	3	2	0	1	3	4	5	5	28
7	3	2	3	4	1	1	0	2	3	4	4	27
8	3	2	3	4	1	3	2	0	1	2	2	23
9	4	3	4	5	2	4	3	1	0	1	1	28
10	5	4	5	6	3	5	4	2	1	0	2	37
11	5	4	5	6	3	5	4	2	1	2	0	37
												316

The shortest Path matrix for 1981 (D - Matrix)

Cell	1	2	3	4	5	6	7	8	9	10	11	
1	0	1	2	1	2	2	1	3	2	3	3	20
2	1	0	1	2	1	1	2	2	2	3	3	18
3	2	1	0	1	1	2	3	2	2	3	3	20
4	1	2	1	0	1	3	2	2	2	3	3	20
5	2	1	1	1	0	2	1	1	1	2	2	14
6	2	1	2	3	2	0	1	3	2	3	3	22
7	1	2	2	2	1	1	0	2	1	2	2	16
8	3	2	2	2	1	3	2	0	1	2	2	20
9	2	2	2	2	1	2	1	1	0	1	1	15
10	3	3	3	3	2	3	2	2	1	0	1	23
11	3	3	3	3	2	3	2	2	1	1	0	23
												211

Calculate the accessibility surface matrix for 1981 the diameter of the Network is 3 Therefore to calculate the accessibility surface matrix is found by adding $C^1 + C^2 + C^3 = T^d$ or T^3

				C^1							x						C^1					
Cell	1	2	3	4	5	6	7	8	9	10	11	Cell	1	2	3	4	5	6	7	8	9	10	11
1	0	1	0	1	0	0	1	0	0	0	0	1	0	1	0	1	0	0	1	0	0	0	0
2	1	0	1	0	1	1	0	0	0	0	0	2	1	0	1	0	1	1	0	0	0	0	0
3	0	1	0	1	1	0	0	0	0	0	0	3	0	1	0	1	1	0	0	0	0	0	0
4	1	0	1	0	1	0	0	0	0	0	0	4	1	0	1	0	1	0	0	0	0	0	0
5	0	1	1	1	0	0	1	1	1	0	0	5	0	1	1	1	0	0	1	1	1	0	0
6	0	1	0	0	0	0	1	0	0	0	0	6	0	1	0	0	0	0	1	0	0	0	0
7	1	0	0	0	1	1	0	0	1	0	0	7	1	0	0	0	1	1	0	0	1	0	0
8	0	0	0	0	1	0	0	0	1	0	0	8	0	0	0	0	1	0	0	0	1	0	0
9	0	0	0	0	1	0	1	1	0	1	1	9	0	0	0	0	1	0	1	1	0	1	1
10	0	0	0	0	0	0	0	0	1	0	1	10	0	0	0	0	0	0	0	0	1	0	1
11	0	0	0	0	0	0	0	0	1	1	0	11	0	0	0	0	0	0	0	0	1	1	0

				$C^1 \times C^1 = C^2$							x						C^1					
Cell	1	2	3	4	5	6	7	8	9	10	11	Cell	1	2	3	4	5	6	7	8	9	10	11
1	3	0	2	0	3	2	0	0	1	0	0	1	0	1	0	1	0	0	1	0	0	0	0
2	0	4	1	3	1	0	3	1	1	0	0	2	1	0	1	0	1	1	0	0	0	0	0
3	2	1	3	1	2	1	1	1	1	0	0	3	0	1	0	1	1	0	0	0	0	0	0
4	0	3	1	3	1	0	2	1	1	0	0	4	1	0	1	0	1	0	0	0	0	0	0
5	3	1	2	1	6	2	1	1	2	1	1	5	0	1	1	1	0	0	1	1	1	0	0
6	2	0	1	0	2	2	0	0	1	0	0	6	0	1	0	0	0	0	1	0	0	0	0
7	0	3	1	2	1	0	4	2	1	1	1	7	1	0	0	0	1	1	0	0	1	0	0
8	0	1	1	1	1	0	2	2	1	1	1	8	0	0	0	0	1	0	0	0	1	0	0
9	1	1	1	1	2	1	1	1	5	1	1	9	0	0	0	0	1	0	1	1	0	1	1
10	0	0	0	0	1	0	1	1	1	2	1	10	0	0	0	0	0	0	0	0	1	0	1
11	0	0	0	0	1	0	1	1	1	1	2	11	0	0	0	0	0	0	0	0	1	1	0

$C^2 \times C^1 = C^3$

Cell	1	2	3	4	5	6	7	8	9	10	11	Total
1	0	10	3	8	3	0	9	4	3	1	1	42
2	10	2	8	2	13	7	2	2	5	1	1	53
3	3	8	4	7	8	2	6	3	4	1	1	47
4	8	2	7	2	11	5	2	2	4	1	1	49
5	3	13	8	11	8	2	13	8	10	3	3	82
6	0	7	2	5	2	0	7	3	2	1	1	30
7	9	2	6	2	13	7	2	2	9	2	2	56
8	4	2	3	2	8	3	2	2	7	2	2	37
9	3	5	4	4	10	2	9	7	6	6	6	62
10	1	1	1	1	3	1	3	2	6	2	3	24
11	1	1	1	1	3	1	2	2	6	3	2	24
Total												502

$C^1 \times C^2 + C^3 = T^3$

Cell	1	2	3	4	5	6	7	8	9	10	11	Total
1	3	11	5	9	6	2	10	4	4	1	1	56
2	11	6	10	5	15	8	5	3	6	1	1	71
3	5	10	7	9	11	3	7	4	5	1	1	63
4	9	5	9	5	13	5	4	3	5	1	1	60
5	6	15	11	13	14	4	15	10	13	4	4	109
6	2	8	3	5	4	2	8	3	3	1	1	46
7	10	5	7	4	15	8	6	4	11	3	3	76
8	4	3	4	3	10	3	4	4	9	3	3	50
9	4	6	5	5	13	3	11	9	11	8	8	83
10	1	1	1	1	4	1	3	3	8	4	5	32
11	1	1	1	1	4	1	3	3	8	5	4	32
Row Total												671

T^d or T^3 matrix gives us the point of maximum accessibility. In the present case point No. 5 has the maximum accessibility of 109 and the point having least connections are 10th and 11th.

Conclusion

The concept developed rightly entails the need for transportation linkages for rural community development. This necessitates planning like capitalist economy but India is a socialist country where people live in rural communities and they have not even resources to take his meal, due to increasing population. Thus planning is impossible in such a situation with the resource of the inhabitants but the local Government may do so in order to cope with the increasing population and sagging economy. Thus the provision of transportation linkages is to provide infrastructure for rural community development.

In this way, the above study of even a few villages of India revealed the fact that the development and orientation of metalled or unmetalled roads and railways have great impact in the creation of service facilities at one location, especially on chauk, which is the centre for varieties of shops and population concentration. Later on the provision of banks, capital formation, industrial establishments, convergence of communication lines and educational cum recretional facilities are themselves sprang up due to substantial market in the zone of influence of a central place and commercial establishments. Except lower order central places there is not even a single rural settlements in India where roads meet hexagonally related to neighbouring rural communities. Only in this situation the villages of India could be able to solve its vital problem of flood, irrigation, communication and service facilities at one time. The digging of canals and tamming of rivers are useful for irrigation and storing flood water in canals, mini-dams on different contour levels of the rivers and vast connecting underground water reservoirs to serve in drought period. The side embankments on canals can be used as road and it also solve the problem of protection from flood and the centre around which the hexagonally developed road for the location of potential service centre. In India only a few urban centres have hexagonal development of roads and the author proposes to extend this triangular connection of roads upto the entire rural communities of India so that we could except a better prospect of rural communities in the 21st century.

REFERENCES

1. Munsi, S., "Railway Network Growth in Eastern India, 1854-1910"; *Centre for Studies in Social Sciences,* Calcutta, No. 3, 1975, p. 1.
2. Mandal, R.B., "Hierarchy of Wholesale Grain Markets in North Bihar", in *Indian Geographical Studies,* 1976.
3. Singh, R.L. Bangalore, *A Urban Survey;* Varanasi, 1964, p. 72.
4. Hudson, J.C., The Vectorial Geometry of Hinterland Organisation and the Location of Towns", *Presented in the Association of American Geography,* St. Louis, 1967, pp. 1-8.
5. Christaller, W., *Central Places in Southern Germany:* Translated by C.W. Baskin; Prentice Hall; N.J. 1966.
6. Losch, A., *Economics of Location,* Translated by Wolfgang, F. Stolper, New Haven, Yale University Press, 1954.
7. Zipf, G.K., *National Unity and Disunity,* Bloominton: Principia Press, 1941.
8. Bylund, E., "Theoretical Considerations Regarding the Distribution of Settlement in Inner North Sweden, *Geografisca Annaler,* 1960, 42, pp. 225-31.
9. Hagerstrand, T., The Propagation of Innovation Waves: *Lund Studies in Geography;* series B, Human Geography, No. 4, 1952.

17

CENTRAL PLACE HIERARCHY

Central place theory is defined as the economically optimum location of services of different range and specialization both for the service provider and for the service receiver.[1] It relates to all kinds of 'Central Functions' which serve the population of surrounding 'zone of influence' besides its own population. The places where central functions are found are known as central places. The examples of central functions are retail business, medical services, repair works, schools and colleges, and small scale industrial works.

The central place theory is concerned with the number, size, spacing and arrangement of central places either urban[2] or rural[3] or urban-rural continum in character. Mark Jefferson first used the term 'Central Place'[4] in 1931 for a settlement which is necessarily a focus of various activities mostly economic and social in nature for its surrounding hinterland. The term, however become standard after the classical study of Walter Christaller in 1953.[5] The application of various theories and studies on central places has increased rapidly since Second World War. Christaller's hypothesis on the degree of 'centrality' of a place was based on the number of telephone connections at a place as the prime criterion for the respective importance of the centre. As it has turned out, this is only one of the possibilities for determination of centrality of places and the categorising of their functional importance[6], and many other parameters can be suggested for the purpose.

Much of the work relating to central place theory has been concerned with the identification of hierarchies of settlements as central places. These hierarchies were determined through the employment of a variety of criteria. But there remained the problem of a common measure of all functions. The centrality of a place, as Christaller pointed out, cannot be determined simply by the sum of its central functions[7]. He, therefore, considered the population of a place, in relation to an index calculated from the number of telephone connections in that place. But according to Ullman[8] such a measure would not seem to be valid for a country where telephones are used extensively for non-central functions. In India, where telephone connections are mostly confined to larger towns, such a study becomes particularly meaningless.

Another method would be to group the settlements in terms of the 'scale of their equipment'.[9] This measure either examines the overall facilities found within a settlement,[10] or makes use of indicator functions.[11] These methods again are largely applicable to the urban centres and it is difficult to determine their importance or their extent of impact upon the surrounding countryside. Hence, a realistic method of market area definition is based upon consumer behaviour data collected in rural areas.[12] The more complex market centres are classified on the basis of these data. Overlapping area, and the relationships between market area characteristics and the central place hierarchy are considered.

Classical Central Place Theory

The work done by Christaller and Losch regarding the spatial structure of economic development through nucleated settlements come under classical central place theory. Christaller pointed out that the number of retail establishments and total population give only the aggregate importance of a central place. According to Preston[13] "the term nodality stands for the aggregate importance of a place as a provider of central goods and services both for its own residents and for the consumers, and the term centrality will stand for the importance of a place as a provider of central goods and services in excess of the needs of its own residents". Christaller's each order of central places would be uniformly spaced in a hexagonal pattern. In marketing principle of central places (k=3 network) the frequency of occurrence of different levels of market areas follows the geometric progression of 1,3,9,27,81,243, . . . *n,* at successively lower levels of hierarchy, in transport principle of (k=4 network) the progression of occurence of market areas is 1, 4, 16, 64, 256, . . . *n;* but in administrative principle of k=7 network the frequency of the occurrence of market areas is 1, 7, 49, 343, 2401, . . . *n* (Fig. 17.1).

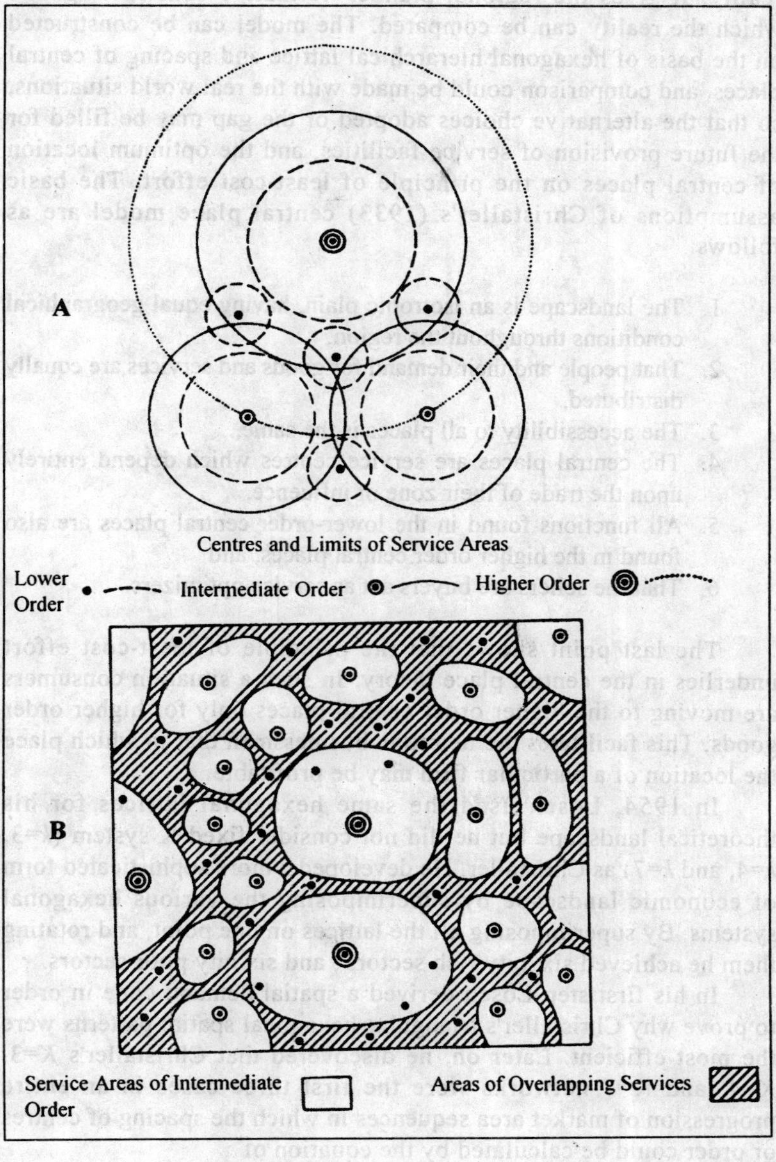

FIG. 17.1: Empirical Pattern of Centres and Service areas

Central place theory is a deductive model from abstract to reality. It gives the regional planner normative construct against which the reality can be compared. The model can be constructed on the basis of hexagonal hierarchical lattice and spacing of central places, and comparison could be made with the real world situations, so that the alternative choices adopted or the gap may be filled for the future provision of service facilities, and the optimum location of central places on the principle of least-cost effort. The basic assumptions of Christaller's (1933) central place model are as follows:

1. The landscape is an isotropic plain, having equal geographical conditions throughout the region,
2. That people and their demand for goods and services are equally distributed,
3. The accessibility to all places is the same,
4. The central places are service centres which depend entirely upon the trade of their zone of influence,
5. All functions found in the lower-order central places are also found in the higher order central places; and
6. That the sellers are buyers act as service optimizers.

The last point shows that the principle of least-cost effort underlies in the central place theory. In such a situation consumers are moving to the higher order central places only for higher order goods. This facilitates the lucrative businessmen that in which place the location of a particular firm may be profitable.

In 1954, Losch used the same hexagonal lattices for his theoretical landscape but he did not consider fixed K system (k=3, k=4, and k=7) as Christaller. He developed a more sophisticated form of economic landscape by superimposing the various hexagonal systems. By superimposing all the lattices on one point, and rotating them he achieved six 'city rich sectors', and six city poor sectors.

In his first step Losch derived a spatial demand cone in order to prove why Christaller's triangular-hexagonal spatial patterns were the most efficient. Later on, he discovered that Christaller's K=3, K=4, and K=7 networks were the first three cases in an entire progression of market area sequences in which the spacing of centres or order could be calculated by the equation of

$$dn = dn - 1\sqrt{K}$$

Where K is the hierarchy ratio and dn=1 is spacing of the next lower order of centres. The market area patterns of central places found out by Losch are shown in Fig. 17.2 Centres are located with respect to the hexagons in three possible ways: on apex K=3 and K = 12; on the middle of the edge K=4, 9, 16 and 25 and within the hexagon as K = 7, 13, 19 and 21.

Losch devised an integrated hierarchy of central places incorporating all these possible arrangements of hexagons; so that it may reflect the complexities of real world. He made his economic landscape around a single metropolitan centre using all the ten hexagonal lattices of market areas. Hence, in Losch network each place has one common place i.e., the metropolis. Then he rotates the separate patterns of network around the metropolis until the maximum coincidence of central places is achieved. The result is a division of the region into six city rich and six city-poor sectors. City-rich sectors show the functional specialization and a well developed connection of transportation routes.

Thus the contribution of Losch is mainly regarding the market areas, because his K values are variable. In making the central place hierarchy he considered the bottom-top approach. Losch also hypothesized that individual demand decreases as the distance of the consumer increases from the point where the goods are offered.

Theoretical Differences between Christaller and Losch

The theoretical bases for central place studies are given here in a nutshel. (Table 17.1)

Modern Central Place Theory

Berry and Garrison[14] emphasized that retail establishments and consumer services should be the focus of central place study. They relaxed the assumption of isotropic plain surface of Christaller by introducing the concept of range of goods and demand cone. Dacey[15] analyses the spatial aspects of central places and uses the regional method to compare the observed pattern with three expected distributions: (a) hexagonal distribution, (b) random distribution, and (c) the clustered distribution.

Recently, it has been considered that the central place theory as formulated by Christaller gives a picture of particular time period

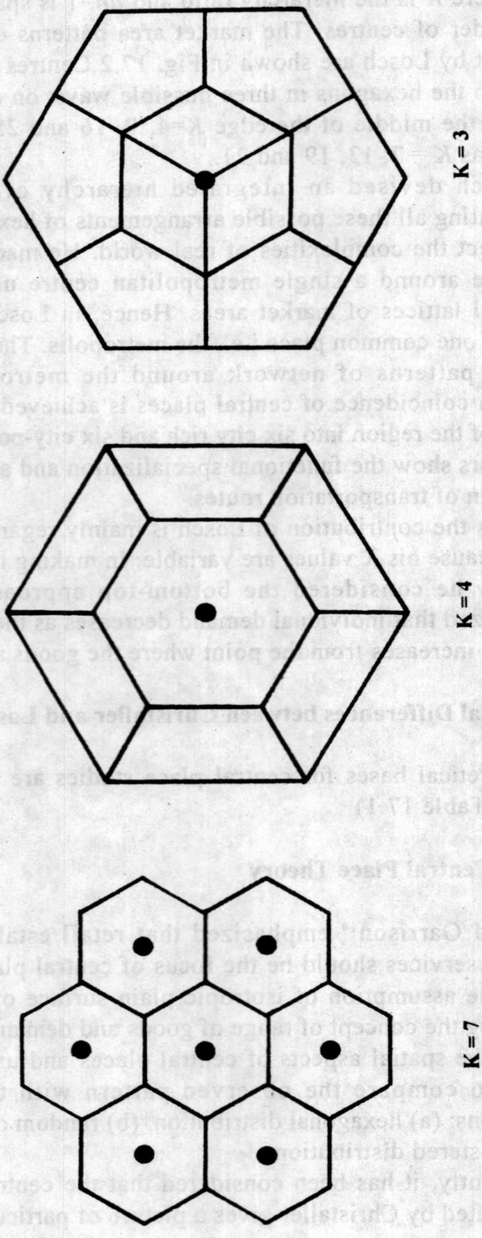

FIG. 17.2: Central Place Hierachy

TABLE 17.1: Comparative View of Christaller and Losch on Central Place Study

	View of Christaller	View of Losch
1.	Region S.W. Germany	Iowa
2.	Isotrophic plain surface	Isotropic plain surface
3.	Begin from city level centres	Begin from village level least specialized centres.
4.	Suggested hierarchy from highest order goods to the lowest	Suggested hierarchy from village level goods upwards.
5.	Considered triangular arrangement of production site retail Stores and hexagonal market areas, having uniform population density, unbounded plain and equal access in all directions.	Considered triangular arrangement of production sites, retail stores and hexagonal market area having uniform population density, unbounded plain and equal access in all directions.
6.	Christaller required that all lower-level centres locations take into account locations of larger centres	Losch derived a variety of optima and tried to assemble these into an overall pattern.
7.	Fixed *K* values of *K*-3, *K*-4 and *K*-7	No fixed *K* value
8.	Location and functions of central place obtained for one 60° sector rediating from metropolis	Location and functions of central place obtained for one 60° sector rediating from metropolis.
9.	Christaller produces central place hierarchy in which there are three levels of centres and groups of goods.	Losch derived a more diversified economic landscape in which centres specialize.
10.	Relevant for analysing retail and wholesale business	Provides a framework for analysing the spatial distribution of market oriented manufacturing.
11.	Christaller agglomerative requirement is for travel cost minimisation by rational consumers on multipurpose trips.	Not satisfied by Losch.
12.	In Germany smaller central places were larger in number relative to higher order centres.	Such a condition is not found in Iowa.
13.	All place in a particular tier are of the same function.	The same size central place need not have the same function.
14.	Number of central places minimized.	All excess profits be eliminated
15.	All higher order centres contain the functions of the smaller central places.	Larger Centres need not have the functions of lower order
16.	Different hierar..y levels have differential supply of goods.	One place may be a supply centre for all goods
17.	Model developed by the market areas of consumer behaviour pattern	Model developed by superimposition of fishets (demand cone) of different goods threshold range.

Source: Compiled from Losch (1954), Isard (1956), Christaller (1966) and Berry (1967) by R. B. Mandal, 1978.

although settlement evolved through a longer period of time, hence, Curry[16] emphasized the need to develop a dynamic central place theory and highlighted that the time factor in central place activities is the key to the understanding of geography.

From the Abstract to the Real World

Hexagonal service areas have been observed in Southern Germany by Christaller (1933), in East Anglia, Great Britain (Berry, 1967) and in parts of China before the 1950's (Skinner, 1954).[17] However, it is only in old, established and stable human landscape where central places are predominantly found. Although both trade areas and hierarchies of central functions can be distinguished in the real world, they rarely display the regular patterns described above in the real world with respect to the theoretical landscape. The reason for this is that the real world is much more complex than the theoretical landscape. The distortions of the model in the real world are caused by.

(a) The uneven distribution of population,
(b) Variations in purchasing power and spending patterns,
(c) The unequal travelling facility to different directions,
(d) The failure of consumers to act as optimizers,
(e) The non-service function of many urban settlements, and
(f) Central places of different ages provide varying technological and organizational influence.

Maximum and Minimum Trade Areas

For each central function, be it a commodity sold or service provided, there is a 'threshold'. This refers to the number of customers necessary for the central function to be viable, i.e. for the shopkeeper to make sufficient profit, or for a government service to serve sufficient people that the service providers regard their activity as worthwhile.

Suppose in planning a primary school there is a rule that the school should have at least 100 pupils to be worth the expense of construction and the provision of textbooks and teachers. This threshold of 100 pupils can be translated into a population threshold if the age structure of the surrounding population is known. For instance, 25 per cent of the total population might be between 7 to

14 years old, the primary school going age. It means to obtain 100 potential pupils there needs to be a population of 400. Using the population density figure for the area, the threshold population of 400 can be coverted into a threshold area which can be drawn as a circle. If the population density of the area is 10 persons per km^2 then the threshold area should be 40 km^2. Using the formula for the area of a circle (π^2) the radius of the threshold area of minimum trade area is found to be just over 3.5 kms.

area of circle = π radius^2

$40 = 3.14 \times r^2$

$r^2 = 40/3.4$

$r^2 = 12.4$

$r = 3.53$ km.

In the simplified, theoretical landscape these will be circular but when 'packed' to ensure that all parts of an area are served they will become hexagonal in shape. When the assumptions are relaxed and the complexities of the real world allowed to enter the model, these hexagons may become distorted.

In sparsely populated areas where the purchasing power is low, in order to accumulate sufficient demand for a commodity to make it profitable a large threshold area would have to be served because the people in such a rural or peripheral areas are beyond the range of the service. It means in order to have a profit from the sale the minimum trade area exceeds maximum trade area.

In such a situation generally the street hawkers or the suppliers of goods and services move in their trade area. This increases the service area and fulfilling the threshold demand. Throughout India such patterns have been now regularised in the form of periodic markets. Even then the hawkers are serving the area in the gap of two periodic markets especially in the off days. In this way, they move around in a cyclical way to different periodic markets in the area, and coming back to the same place once in a week. In the state of Bihar, India, the distance of one periodic market from another is hardly 5 kilometres which could easily be covered on foot. For rural townships in Zambia, the radius of the area served is about 9 kms and for the market town approximately 22 kms. It means that the distance between villages and rural townships is about 5 kms; between rural townships and market towns about 16 kms; and from village to market town not more than 22 kms.[18]

Functional Hierarchy of Central Places

Any study of central places has necessarily to include both the urban and the rural settlements, as in any scheme of hierarchy, towns, perform more central functions than villages. However, in the traditional cases consisting of rurban centres, villages may sometimes be central places of a high order than the smaller towns. The purpose of determining the hierarchy of central places would be defeated if we confine our study to rural settlements only. In the following pages, therefore, both towns and villages have been examined together to determine their centrality. The villages alone form the basis for further studies.

Most of the settlements have acquired their urban status due to their achievement in special socio-economic functions. They have grown to be the chief centres of an area because such functions are retail shops, wholesale, warehouses, banks, garrages and offices have developed to meet requirements not merely of the town's own population but of that of the surrounding area. W. Christaller explained market areas in terms of the provision of services, constructed a theory with the help of smallest units of settlements which developed in areas of uniformity. He favoured that the most efficient system of clearly defining market areas should be based upon a hexagonal lattice. This geometrical form approaches close similarity of the circle, but a circular lattice suffers from the disadvantage of allowing unsupplied or overlapping areas.

As 'the chief profession of a town is to be central to its rural surroundings' then the centre of the hexagon is the location of the 'central place'. Christaller clearly indicated that there should be mutual dependence between the central place and the supply region. In plain areas the equal spacing of settlements results in competition developing between them in the provision of services. Village shops, for example, usually stock a limited range of goods and thus villages are lower—order central places with small market area, whereas towns provide a wider range of services for a larger area and hence, they are higher order central places. In case higher order and lower-order centres are considered to be equally spaced then the hexagonal market area of higher-order is larger than that of lower-order central places and the latter areas and functions must be contained or present in the former. Hence in this model, a hierarchy of central places is conceived, ranging from small hamlets to large towns.

In Christaller's hexagonal lattice, each hamlet is located at the meeting point of three uniform market areas and hence with equal number of people having equal ease of movement and equal purchasing power, one-third of the hamlets' trade will be with each central village. Hence, the total hexagonal trade area is 2 around a village (one-third of six hexagon) plus one of its own market. Christaller used the term 'K' value to refer to the total number of settlements served by each central place. Hence, in this case $K = 3$. He also assumed that in one region the K value would be fixed ranging from hamlets, villages, small towns and so on.

In case of the establishment of third-order (K=3) centres the number of units of trade of the central place is 27 and the calculations are as follows:

(a) Six centres are located at the vertices of the hexagon each share their trade between 3 centres and therefore the central place A has 1/3 = 2 units of trade.

(b) The other 12 peripheral settlements each share their trade between 2 centres and therefore A's share is

$$\frac{12}{2} = 6$$

(c) Inside the hexagon is 18 other centres whose entire trade is directed towards *A* and therefore a further 18 units are added.

(d) The entire trade of *A* is conducted in that centre which provides 1 unit.

In this way, the total trade of *A* is found by summing up the above parts: i.e.

2 + 6 + 18 + 1 = 27

As the hierarchy of the settlements is established so the trade of each central place develops as follows:

1, 3, 9, 27, 81 ......

i.e. 1, 3, 3^2, 3^3, 3^4, ... (K = 3)

This model of central place suggests that it is possible that the function of such places controls their size of the supplying area, besides it offers a partial explanation that why settlements are scattered in the region differ in size. K = 3 hierarchy of central places in southern Germany is as follows. (Table 17.2).

TABLE 17.2: Christaller's Central Place Hierarchy in Southern Germany

(K = 3 network)

Class	Average Radius of supplying Area in K.	Typical Population Size
Market town	4.0	1,000
Central township	6.9	2,000
Country town	12.0	4,000
District city	20.7	10,000
State Capital	36.0	30,000
Provincial Capital	62.1	100,000
Regional Capital	108.0	500,000

Source: W. Christaller; The Central Places in Southern Germany, English translation by C.W. Baskin, 1966.

The K-3 Hierarchy

This represents the hierarchy of central places according to the marketing principle of Christaller. In each case the number of village-sized market areas served progression is 1, 3, 9, 27, 81 . . . Here one higher order central place area is surrounded by the two equal sized areas (one third of each) of the second order centres. (Fig. 17.2) They are called K-3 network of marketing principle.

In K-3 model of central place hierarchy the central places actually located on their original site are Bhagalpur, Munger, Khagaria, Jamui, Barahiya and Barauni. Most of the other centres have been adjusted accordingly. The presence of river Ganges does not create a barrier in the spatial distribution of central places in the Umland of Munger and Bhagalpur.

K-4 Hierarchy

This represents the hierarchy of central places according to transportation principle of Christaller. The progression of market areas in K-4 system is 1, 4, 16, 64 . . . . In K-4 network all settlements are located on the side of road leading directly away from the highest order centres. In K-4 hierarchy central places also provide a ranked order of goods and services. Here the lower order central places are located exactly halfway between place of the next highest order and lie on the boundaries separating the market areas of highest order (Fig. 17.2). Here one higher order centre area is surrounded by the three equal sized (one half area of the six surrounding centres) of the second order centres.

The K-4 central place hierarchy is based on tranportation principle which favours the actual location of Kharagpur as the biggest central place in spite of the presence of Bhagalpur and Munger city level centres in the area. This happence because the southern part of Munger and Bhagalpur are areas of low population density and the presence of lesser number of central places in the area. In case the transportation facilities are provided as transportation route set in, the region would develop properly in terms of transport whether it is the plain land or mountainous areas.

K-7 Hierarchy

The progression of market areas in K-7 central places system is 1, 7, 49, . . . Christaller and Losch both had called it administrative centres are found to be true, where one higher order centre area is equivalent to the areas associated with seven central places of the next smaller order. In this system of central places, each central place is located in the centre of the area with which it is associated and is never divided by the boundary lines of higher order places. For this fact, it is advantageous for administrative purposes. Here the centre lies in between two larger central places, the consumers can go to which ever place they choose as long as their travel costs remain unchanged.

Fig. 17.2 prepared on the basis of administrative principle shows the gradation of centres according to the level of administrative headquarters into a hexagonal lattice.

Centrality and Nodality

The centrality value incorporate the aggregate amount of services that a central place provides to its hinterland around it. In most studies this measure has been taken on the basis of functions located in the central place itself. But R.E. preston has called such central place functions as the measure of 'nodality'[19] not 'centrality'. According to him, the centrality value should be considered only after considering basic functions or city-forming services which bring capital and resources from outside the central place providing its fundamental means of sustenance and it is for this reason that geographers have paid more attention to city forming than to city serving population.[20] Thus centrality value should only be considered after measuring the intensity and amount of supply of goods and services directly to the population of a surrounding contiguous area on a regular year round basis. Only this type of analysis should be considered for measuring the centrality value in central place research. But due to lack of data the present study is based on nodality value and not centrality.

Centrality

Determination of central place importance is a universal problem in studies of space economies, and the only satisfactory model for its solution developed so far is the one offered by Christaller in 1933. His approach requires classification both in operational definition of the concept of 'centrality' and its systematic measurement. Thus the

TABLE 17.3: Weighing and Classification of Central Functions

Functional Indicators	I 20 points	II 15 points	III 10 points	IV 5 points
1. Education	University	College	High School	X
2. Medical	Medical College	X	Hospital	X
3. Communication	X	X	Telephone Exchange	X
4. Finance	X	Bank	X	X
5. Transport	Airport	Railway Junction	Railway Station	Highways
6. Administration	District Court	Sub-divisional Office	Block Development Office	X
7. Trade	X	X	Wholesale Market	X
8. Recreation	X	Cinema	X	X
9. % of total workers engaged in tertiary occupation	X	X	Over 50%	25 to 50%
10. Diversity Index	X	9 functional indicators available	7 to 8 functional indicators available	5 to 6 functional indicators available

areal distribution of the central place function was established in this study by applying the following modification of Christaller's model to places with 2500 or more inhabitants in 1960 and that appeared in the U.S. Census of Business for 1963 and 1972.[21]

$$C = R + S - \delta\, MF$$

where C = centrality, R= total sales in retail establishments, S = total sales in selected service establishment, δ = average percentage of median family income for a central place spent on retail and service goods, M = median family income in a central places, and F = the total number of families in central place. In this model $R + S$ provides an estimate of total retail and service activity in a town, or its "nodality", while $\delta\, MF$ provides an estimate of local consumption. The difference is an index of the volume of extra-local trade, or centrality. The results of this procedure were used to establish the magnitude of the central place function for places.

Criteria of Centrality

For declaring central places, only the number of persons is not a satisfactory answer to determine the centrality while Christaller has considered telephone connections. When studying the central places of Southern Germany as centrality index.

After considering telephone connections Christaller derives the degree of centrality of a place, that is, amount of services performed apart from those relating to the needs of its own inhabitants by means of the following formula.[22]

$$\text{Centrality of a place} = \text{Number of Telephone in a place} - \text{Number of inhabitants of a place} \times \frac{\text{Number of Telephone \& Area served by a place}}{\text{Number of inhabitants and area served by a place}}$$

or

$$C = T2 - E2 \text{ X } \frac{Tq}{Eq.}$$

or

$$C = (t - \frac{PT}{P})$$

where C is centrality, 't' is number of telephone in a town, 'P' is population of the town, 'T' is number of telephone in the whole region and 'P' is population of the whole region. This method has been criticised in recent years as telephones are also used for non central functions and most of the lower-order places have no connections at all.

The centrality of a centre can be measured after considering the goods and services for which the zone of influence depends on the centre. Bracey has applied this method numerically in southern England. After considering the intensity of bus services Green has measured the centrality of places in England and wales. Godlund of Sweden has selected retail trade as an index of centrality and has given the formula.[23]

$$\text{Centrality} = \frac{St.\ 10}{Pt}$$

where St is number of persons employed in retail trade and Pt is population of the region.

Kashi Nath Singh has put forward a more feasible proposition in the shape of formula as:[24]

$$C = \frac{N - 100}{P}$$

where C is centrality, N is the number of persons dependent upon commerce, and P is the total regional population in commerce.

In order to identify central places O.P. Singh (1969) covers up the functional as well as spatial gaps in the region where two types of demographic indices are distinguished. Relative Centrality Index (RCI) and Absolute Centrality Index (ACI) by the following formula.

$$RCI = \frac{50\ (CB.RT + CT.RB)}{RT.RB}$$

where CB is basic population of the centre (non-agricultural population) RB is basic population of the region. CT is commercial population of the region, and 50 is constant figure. and

$$ACI = \frac{CB}{5000}$$

where ACI is calculated hereby dividing the non-agricultural population of the centre by 5000. This figure is taken here as a norm also to lessen the size of big centres for easy calculation.

M.S. Vishwanath while studying the growth pattern and hierarchy of urban centres in Mysore has used the following formula to measure the centrality index:[26]

$$C = \frac{P \text{ X } 100}{\text{Total State Population}}$$

where *C* is centrality, and *P* is the total regional population in commerce.

V.N.P. Sinha while studying the hierarchy of urban settlements in Chhotanagpur Plateau devised the following formula to measure the centrality of a place:[27]

$$C = \frac{T \text{ X } 100}{P}$$

where *C* is centrality, *T* is the number of persons dependent upon tertiary services of a centre; *P* is the total regional tertiary population.

According to Davies[28] before deriving the centrality value for a central place, one should find out the location coefficient to shops of the region with the help of the following formula:

$$LC = \frac{t}{T} \text{ X } 100$$

where *LC* is the location coefficient of shops in a central place; t is the number of shops in that centre, and *T* is the total number of shops in the entire region under study.

Multiplying the relevant location coefficient by the centrality index (derived from the weight given to the different functions performed by a centre) will give the final degree of centrality in terms of centrality value:

$$CV = CI \text{ X } LC$$

where *CV* is centrality value, *CI* is centrality index for services, and *LC* is location coefficient for retail trade.

N.P. Saxena and R.C. Tyagi devised the following formula to measure the centrality index

$$C = A - \frac{P \text{ X } Ar}{Pr}$$

where C is centrality measure, *A* is total number of workers engaged in central functions at a centre; *P* is population of the centre; *Ar* is aggregate of workers engaged in central occupations in the region; and *Pr* is population of a region.

In measuring the centrality index O.P. Singh[30] makes use of commercial population of centres, with the following formula he calculated relative and absolute centrality index:

$$RP = \frac{PCI - P + 1 - \dfrac{RC}{Rt}}{\Sigma\, Pc - (\Sigma\, P + \dfrac{RC)}{Pt}} X\ 100$$

Where *PCI* is commercial population of the centre
P+1 is total population of the centre.
RC is regional commercial population.
Rt is total regional population.
Σ *PC* is summation of PC_1, PC_2, PC_n and
Σ *Pt* is summation of Pt_1, Pt_2, Pt_n
Absolute centrality has been calculated as

$$AC_1 = \frac{P6}{10000}$$

where *Pb* is basic population of the place.

Central Place Theory: Christaller's Model

The existence of different sized population clusters in the landscape is an inevitable feature in the spatial organisation of human activity. Settlements exist because certain activities can be carried on most efficiently if they are clustered together than dispersed. Since settlements are spatially separated from one another, the linkages between them are essential, and one framework for study is to view them as nodes or focul points in a network. About the spatial distribution of settlements, service centres and road linkages, a number of studies have been done. The contribution of Christaller and Losch is, however, outstanding which is based on scientific approach to geography.

Walter Christaller, a German Geographer, wrote his classic

Central Places in Southern Germany and he advocated a theory from a set of assumptions and principles that demonstrated that there was order in the patterns and functions of the settlements that he observed in Southern Germany. Christaller wrote his book in 1933 but his, work did not become widely known till the 1950s. It was not translated into English until 1966. For his theory Christaller borrowed the idea from Von Thunen model and Weber's model. His theoretical approach was similar to that of Von Thunen to agricultural land use- and Weber's model to industrial location.

Christaller used the term of 'threshold' for the minimum demand or size of market. Since all consumers visit their nearest centre for a good. A supplier will attempt to obtain as much larger market than the threshold so as to maximize his profit. The range of the goods defines the outer limit of the market area.

The hexagonal patterns is the most efficient method that market areas may be packed on the plain so that every possible customer is served. The market areas are of minimum size for profitable operation. There are thus the maximum number of suppliers selling the goods. Since each of these is located in a central place, there are the maximum number of central places selling the goods. From the consumer's point of view, the total distance, they travel to obtain goods, is minimized. With these properties this arrangement of central places and markets is the most efficient for the marketing of goods.

Christaller called it the 'marketing principle.'

Hamlet—Boundary of Hamlet Trading Area
Village—Boundary of Village Trading Area
Town—Boundary of Town Trading Area
City—Boundary of City Trading Area

In order to construct the whole system other goods must be considered. Each will have a different threshold range. The suppliers selling different goods will locate together in central places for the convenience of customers. The goods of similar threshold will be sold in the same central places. The lower the threshold, the greater the number of central places that will sell the goods. The goods with low thresholds and small markets are called low order goods (for example, groceries, bread, and hardware items), while goods with high thresholds are termed high order goods (for example: television, refrigerators and expensive Jewellery). The numerous centres that only sell low order goods are called low order centres. The few that offer high order goods are known as high order centres.

Christaller's model can be explained by constructing the model of the size and location of towns according to the marketing principles, those of traffic and administration. The spatial arrangements associated with these principles are described for brevity by k-values in Fig. 17.2.

The *k*-value indicates the number of centres dominated by another centre and the relationship between the number of market areas of each order. It can be seen from that lowest (lower) order centres lie on the boundaries of the market areas of lower (middle) order centres. In simplified case, people in any lower order centre may choose between three higher order centres for higher order goods, since all three are equidistant. The custom of a lower order centre may then be considered to be split into three equal ways between the three higher order centres. Each higher order centre then receives one-third of the custom of the six lower order centres which are located on the boundary of its market area. It can be considered to serve a population equivalent to two lower order centres (6 x ½). It also serves its own population.

In total, it then serves three central places (2+1). For centres of each order, it may be observed that they serve or dominate three centres of the next lower order, including themselves. This spatial arrangement, which is characterisitic of the marketing principle described above, is known as a $k - 3$ network.

The model advocated by Christaller is ideal and some of the ideals are found in the real world. But the overall spatial distribution and organisation of marketing centres, service centres and settlements are not found. Many of the assumptions he made are illogical and are not found in the complex economic structure on the earth. The assumption of a uniform distribution of population and ease of transport in all parts with the same means of transportation hardly exists in any part of the world. The hexagonal pattern of the central place theory in an uniform plain, but the physical features and physical barriers often lead to linear transport routes especially in the river valleys and mountainous areas. The assumptions made about the behaviour of suppliers and consumers is also unrealistic. In practice, consumers with their increased mobility, do not always visit their nearest market centre. The suppliers are thus unable to command a spatial monopoly and market areas overlap. The competition becomes other than spatial as suppliers become more uncertain about their market. The suppliers attempt to lure customers by the price, quality and variety of goods offered and the services provided, such as credit facilities.

In practice the distribution, size, and functions are also influenced by the government, planning and development agencies. The planning and development agencies decide where to locate different offices, including their own, which are central institutions in the theory of Christaller. Despite these distorting factors and criticisms, the Christaller's model is more applicable to the retailing. The theory has, however, great economic and social significance and many have attributed it as geography's finest intellectual product. Moreover, the theory has stimulated much work on retailing and consumer behaviour, not only between settlements but also within them. Such work has permitted geographers to advise on planning of settlements and retail centres and has given geographers a commercial role in market research.

Losch Model

Losch was an economist. He elaborated and extended the Christaller's model of central place theory, adopting the hexagonal based model and modifying it into complex hexagonal shape which gives more realistic patterns of the real world. He based his model on the following assumptions:

1. That the population is not evenly distributed.
2. That the central places and service centres are not located in a uniform plain.
3. He assumed that the people are living is isolated, evenly spaced farmstead.
4. That no supplier is allowed to earn excess profit, i.e., more profit than to sustain the firm.
5. That each goods has its own distinct threshold and size of market area.
6. He assumed that there are more k-functions than the k-3,4,7 as advocated by Christaller.
7. He assumed that the cost of transportation increases with distance, so that toward the edges of a market area the price asked is higher and the demand lower.

Losch Model has been shown in Fig. 17.1

The basic features of horizontal arrangement of settlement in the Losch model area:

1. Concentration of settlement into sectors separated by interstitial area wherein settlement is less dense.
2. Settlement increase in size with distance from the central metropolis.
3. Small settlements are located "about half way" between two larger ones.

Losch Model about the central places like that of Christaller, however, does not lead to larger market areas containing all the activities of the smaller, or to identical activities in all settlements of the same size. The system is much less rigid, because Losch does not immediately assume a fixed *k*. Thus, a restricted but greater number of possible market areas exists. Losch considers Christaller's fixed k hierarchies later and only as special cases.

Losch also tried to introduce economic equilibrium conditions, but Beckmann has found them to be inadequate. In addition, Losch presents a critical review of previous work and makes the selling point about location theory which must consider maximization of profits. For an overall settlements model, still a lot of research has to be done to arrive at a model which is nearer to the reality.

The Contributions of Central Place Study in Regional Planning

1. It guides the planner in identifying the existing hinterlands of localized or mobile services.
2. It helps in identifying the planner that which areas and which people are out of the reach of individual service or service centres.
3. It shows the planner that which centres are stronger in terms of available services and so could cater either for an increased local demand or for a demand in a larger hinterland.
4. It helps the regional planner to reorganise the central places in such a way so that they can combine hinterlands covering all people in that area.
5. It requires from the planner to keep up-to-date information for

each district level systems of central places on the following headlines:

(a) Population distribution,
(b) Location of all government and private services,
(c) Threshold values for individual service under different forms of management as for example mobile versus fixed businessmen, part-time versus full-time health worker, and
(d) The real trade areas of various services demarcated on the basis of consumer behaviour pattern as against the assumed ones demarcated on the basis of gravity potential model.

The Values of Central Place Theory

1. It enables a comparative analysis of regional centres to be made.
2. It shows the interdependence of town and region.
3. A hierarchy of functions and settlements is devised.
4. The idea of competition between centres is stressed.
5. The intensity and spacing of centres suggests further investigation as to how these service centres have evolved and are changing their character at present.
6. On the basis of a theoretical structure it is possible to make a number of predictions about the pattern of future settlement location.

Criticisms of Central Place Theory

1. Christaller's Central Place Theory is concerned only with one central place activity, that of the service functions for the hinterland. Other aspects such as places of residence or industrial centres are not considered besides the sites of availability of mineral resources, favourable climate, strategic position, growth of a part, railway expansion and urban 'overspill' requirements.
2. Central place theory may have played a significant part in the development of a settlement in an agricultural area, but works less well in industrial areas.
3. There may be planned delay in establishing full services in 'New Towns' until increased their populations.
4. The theory does not work well in areas where the industries are expanding or retarding.

REFERENCES

1. L.M. Vanden Berg, Central Place Theory and the Planning of Rural Service Centre in Africa; *Zambia Geographical Association: Occasional Study No. 11,* 1981, p. 1.
2. W.A.V. Clark, "Consumer Travel Patterns and the Concept of Range", *Annals of the Association of American Geographers,* Vol. 58, June 1968, p. 386.
3. Om Prakash Singh: "Functions and Functional Classes of Central Places in Uttar Pradesh", *The National Geographical Journal of India,* Vol. XIV, 1968, pp. 1-2.
4. M. Jefferson, "The Distribution of World's City's Folks", *Geographical Review;* Vol. XXI, 1931, p. 453.
5. Walter Christaller, *Central Places in Southern Germany* (translated by C.W. Baskin); Prentice Hall, New Jersey, 1966.
6. G. Kulucka, "Central Places and Their Functional Areas in the Federal Republic of Germany", *Paper read at the 21st International Geographical Congress,* India, 1968, (unpublished)
7. Scot Peter, "The Hierarchy of Central Places in Tasmania", *The Australian Geographer,* 1968, p. 13.
8. E. Ullman, "A Theory of Location for Cities", *American Journal of Sociology;* Vol. 6, 1940-41, p. 858.
9. H.E. Bracy, "Towns as Rural Service Centres", *Transactions and Papers, Institute of British Geographers,* Vol. 49, 1953, pp. 95-105.
10. H.E. Bracy, English Central Places, Identification, Distribution and Functions", in *Lund Symposium on Problems of Urban Geography,* 19th International Geographical Congress, 1960.
11. A.E. Smailes, "The Urban Hierarchy in England and Wales", *Geography,* Vol. 29, 1944, pp. 51-55.
12. G. Rowley, "Central Places in Rural Wales", *Annals of the Association of American Geographers,* Vol. 61, No. 3, 1971, pp. 537-50.
13. R. E. Preston, "Two Centrality Models", *Yearbook Association of Pacific Coast Geographers;* Vol. 32, 1970, p. 62.
14. B.J.L. Berry and W.L. Garrison: "Recent Developments of Central Place Theory", *Papers and Proceedings of Regional Science Association;* No. 4, 1958, p. 107.
15. M.F. Dacey, "Analysis of Central Place and Point Patterns by a Nearest Neighbour Method", *Lund Studies in Geography,* Service B, *Human Geography,* Vol. 24, 1962, pp. 55-75.
16. L. Curry, "A Classical Approach to Central Place Dynamics", *Geographical Analysis,* Vol. 1, 1969, pp. 272-82.
17. G.W. Skinner, "Marketing and Social Structure in Rural China," *Journal of Asian Studies,* Vol. 24, 1954, pp. 3-43.
18. Doxiadis Associates, Consultants on Development and Ekistics; Rural Townships in Zambia, *General Report,* Athens, 1967, p. 51.
19. R.E. Preston, *Op. cit.*
20. W.K. Davies, "Centrality and the Central Place Hierarchy", *Urban Studies,* Vol. 4, 1967, p. 65.

21. B.J.L. Berry, *Geography of Market Centres and Retail Distribution,* Prentice Hall, New Jersey, 1967, p. 65.
22. W.K.D. Davies, *Op.cit.,* p. 77.
23. Godlund, S., "The Functions and Growth of Bus Traffic within the Sphere of urban influence", *Lund Studies in Geography,* Series B, *Human Geography,* No. 18, 1956. p. 12.
24. Singh, K.N., *Rural Markets and Rurban Centres in Uttar Pradesh,* Ph.D. Thesis, Banaras Hindu University, 1962, p. 187.
25. Singh, O.P., "Towards Determining Hierarchy of Service Centres: A Methodology for Central Place Studies", *The National Geographical Journal of India;* Vol. XVII; Part-4, 1971, pp. 165-77.
26. Vishwanath, M.S., "Growth Pattern and Hierarchy of Urban Centres in Mysore", *The Indian Geographical Journal,* Vol. XLVII, 1972, Vol. 1 & 2, pp. 1-11.
27. Sinha, V.N.P., *Chotanagpur Plateau: A Study in Settlement Geography,* K.B. Publications, New Delhi, 1976, p. 177.
28. Davies, W.K.D.; "Centrality and the Central Place Hierarchy", *Urban Studies,* Vol. 4, No. 1, 1967, p. 63.
29. Saxena, N.P. and Tyagi, R.G.; "Criteria for Determining Centrality in a Mac. O. Region", *The Geographical Observer,* Vol. II, March 1975, pp. 55-64.
30. Singh, *Op.cit.*

18

RURAL URBAN DIVIDE

The areas having dominance of agricultural operations are known as rural whereas areas having predominance of non-agriculture function are known as urban. Recently with the concentration of wealth in urban areas due to exodus of people from rural areas a hiatus gap has been created in the form of rural-urban divide. On the whole urban is a glitter and rural is a gloom.

The survival of rural-urban divide is a function of the interactions of rural and urban areas in their zone of influence or the hinterland. These interactions could be observed in the form of flow of people in the form of migrant, food and raw materials for running industries in urban areas. On the other hand, urban areas as core centres provide ideas, finance and industrial product to the rural areas. Hence, Friedmans mode of core-periphery model operates in the form of dichotomy between rural and urban areas.[1]

Economic Variations

The economic structure of the countryside is quite different in comparison with urban areas. This is known as rural economy and the urban economy. The rural economy is made of agriculture and allied activities e.g. tethering of cattle wealth and they still practice bartar system for the exchange of goods at least to some extent (Table 18.1). On the other hand, urban economy is based on non-agricultural activities which include organized manufacturing but also a large number of small scale industrial units along with the service sector economic activities.[2]

Income Differential

In rural area per capita income is just half of the urban area. In villages

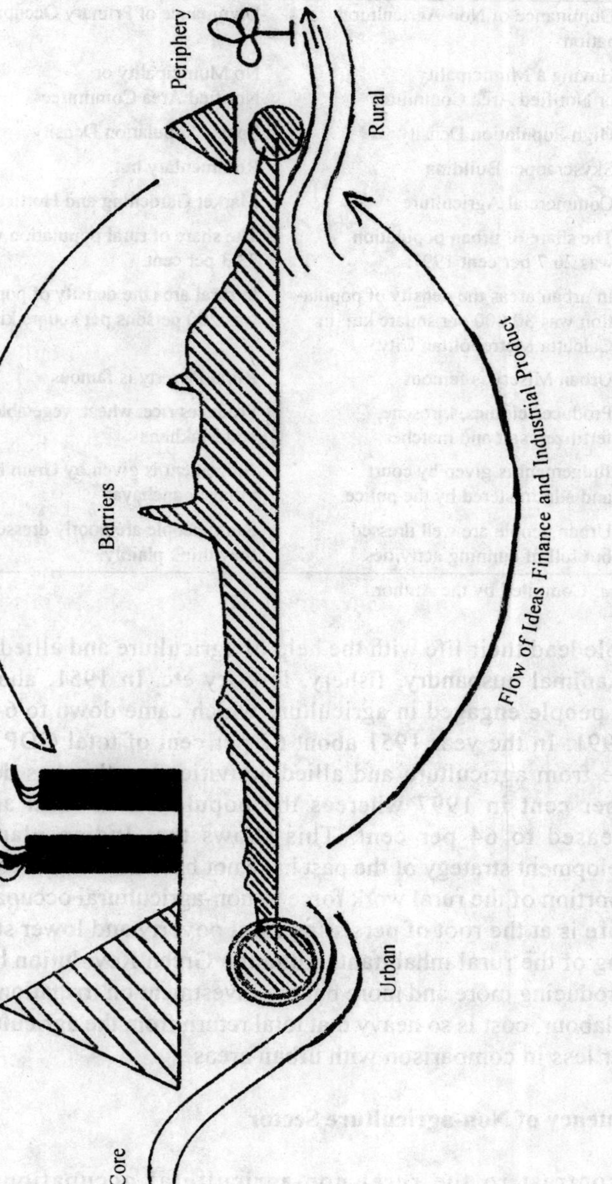

FIG.: 18.1: Rural Urban Divide: A Core-Periphery Model

TABLE 18.1: Distinction Between Rural and Urban Areas

	Urban	Rural
1.	Dominance of Non-Agricultural Occupation	Dominance of Primary Occupation
2.	Having a Municipality or Notified Area Committee	No Municipality or Notified Area Committee
3.	High Population Density	Sparse Population Density
4.	Skyscrapper Building	Rudimentary hut.
5.	Commercial Agriculture	Market Gardening and Horticulture
6.	The share of urban population was 26.7 per cent 1991.	The share of rural population was 73.3 per cent.
7.	In urban areas the density of population was 30,000 per square km. in Calcutta Metropolitan City.	In rural area the density of population was 200 persons per square kilometre.
8.	Urban Misery is famous	Rural Poverty is famous
9.	Produces clothes, kirosene, fertilizer, salt and matches.	Produces rice, wheat, vegetable, milk, ghee and Makhana
10.	Judgement is given by court and administered by the police.	Judgement is given by Gram Kutchhery in village panchayat.
11.	Urban people are well dressed but full of cunning activities	Rural people are poorly dressed and they think plainly.

Source: Compiled by the Author.

people lead their life with the help of agriculture and allied activities like animal husbandry, fishery, forestry etc. In 1951, about 85 per cent people engaged in agriculture which came down to 64 per cent in 1991. In the year 1951 about 62 per cent of total GDP produced came from agriculture and allied activities but this has declined to 26 per cent in 1997 whereas the population in rural areas have increased to 64 per cent. This shows that Indian planning and development strategy of the past have not been able to shift substantial proportion of the rural work force to non-agricultural occupation. This failure is at the root of persisting rural poverty and lower standard of living of the rural inhabitant. Although Green Revolution has helped in producing more and more but the investment on irrigation, fertilizer and labour, cost is so heavy that total return from the agriculture sector is far less in comparison with urban areas.

Affluency of Non-agriculture Sector

In contrast to the rural non-agricultural occupations include manufacturing, construction, electricity and service sector which grow fast because of their rising demand and technological advancement. The manufacturing is also exposed to the law of diminishing return. In agriculture sector it is only possible with the introduction of new tecchnology and new products. The urban areas are more affluent as the computers and business sectors provide more attractive income potential in comparison with rural areas. In developed countries of the world people are now less dependent on agriculture (Table 18.2).

TABLE 18.2: Share of Poverty in Rural and Urban Areas of India

Year	Rural Area		Urban Areas	
	% of people below Poverty line	Persons in crore	% of people below poverty line	Persons in crore
1973-74	56.44	26.13	49.01	6.00
1977-78	53.07	26.43	45.24	6.47
1983-84	45.65	25.20	40.79	7.09
1987-88	40.09	23.19	38.20	7.52
1993-94	37.27	24.40	32.36	7.63

Source: Kurukshetra, November 1997.

On the basis of Table 18.2 it could be said that the poverty is increasing in India because the people who are deciding how to tackle it know absolutely nothing about the poor. It is vested interest of the urban expert that poverty continues to grow in the rural areas. The ruralising urban areas and urbanizing rural areas is not the way to lessen the divide. The villagers should start building from scratch. Narrating the tremendous success of the barefoot approach the problem could be tackled only by those living in the rural areas.

In solving the rural problems no urban trained persons qualified expert is required. The college in rural areas provide the mental and physical space for the dropouts, the rejects and the weak to acquire skills, develop self confidence with some self-respect and eventually become respectable citizens in their own society.

The income generated by villagers is a tiny fraction of the income generated by the urban areas. The disparities between the urban and rural areas are increasing with every passing day. The gap is widening even into newer areas in a various form. There is no Indian who left untouched with differentiation, stratification and inequalities. The cleavages have resulted not from the isolation of rural areas but from the nature of rural-urban interface as a specific manifestation of the basic non-egalitarian nature of our economy, society and polity.[3] It has been also maintained that "the scourage of widespread, painful and inhuman poverty of an overwhelming majority of Indians gives an especially unacceptable, abnoxious order to the growing disparities in India."

The 1991 census indicates that the literacy gap between rural and urban was 23 per cent where as the same is 33.3 per cent for female. The urban female is 63.9 per cent literate but this figure is 30.3 per cent only for rural female. The infant mortality was 82 per thousand live births in rural areas but only 45 per thousand live births in urban areas.

The distribution of medical facility is also unequal throughout India. With 75 per cent of total population, the rural areas has less than one third of hospitals, 50 per cent dispensaries and less than 20 per cent hospitals beds and dispensaries of the country. In urban areas 80 per cent population avail medical facilities within less than 2 kms of distance but in rural areas the medical facility is available to less than 3 per cent population. So far as the availability of electricity is concerned in urban areas 76 per cent houses are electrified but in rural area only 31 per cent people have acquired this facility.

Need for Agrarian Reform

Land to the tiller is a far cry as nothing has been done in the majority of our villages in this regard. A large scale investment is needed for the socio-economic rejuvenation of our rural settlements and whatever money has been invested in this regard does not produce the expected results due to institutional constraints and corruption. Thus agrarian reform has been considered as the foundation of the development of rural economy and this is an unfinished agenda in rural India. This is the root problem that make the rural-urban divide more visible.

Model to Reduce Rural-Urban Divide

Fig. 18.2 clearly states that the programmes are of an all India character whereas the strategy to tackle the issue are different in different parts of the country. While in rural areas of Bihar, Madhya Pradesh, Rajasthan and Uttar Pradesh have lagged behind in all respects, but the states like Kerala, Punjab, Haryana and West Bengal

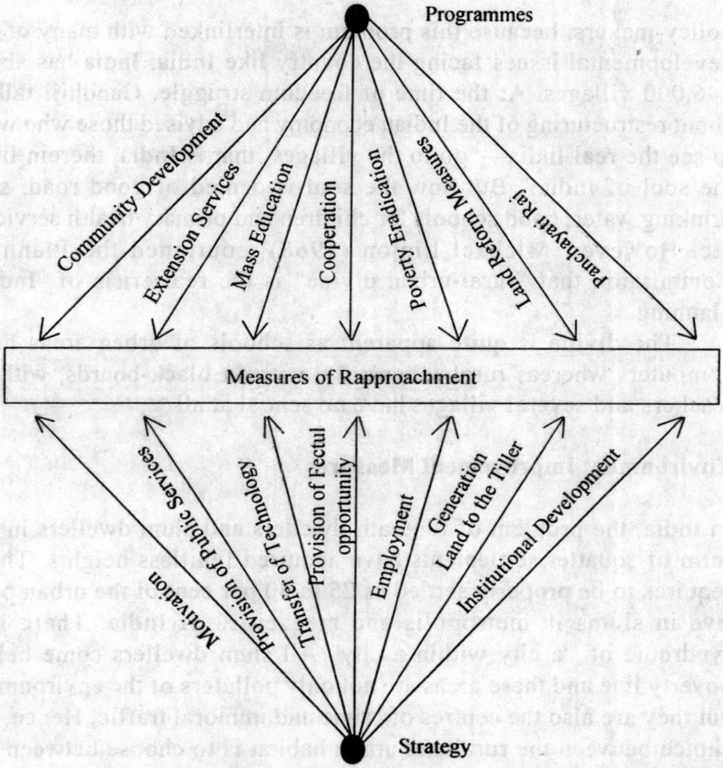

FIG.: 18.2: Programmes and Strategy to Reduce Rural Urban divide

have forged different strategies for the success of rural development programmes which are under different stages of development.[4]

The Role of Panchayati Raj

The problem of rural-urban divide can be effectively tackled through transfer of economic and political power to the people through Panchayati Raj. The initiative of the centre and the State government towards grass-root democracy is loudable to remove the lacunae in the new set up to make democratic decentralization and effective tool of change in order to remove imbalances in rural-urban development.

There is a long list of unfinished tasks in the national agenda, rural-urban divide is one of the serious issue to be tackled by the policy-makers, because this problem is interlinked with many of the developmental issues facing the country like India. India has about 646,000 villages. At the time of freedom struggle, Gandhiji talked about restructuring of the Indian economy and advised those who want to see the real India—"go to the villages; that is India, therein lives the soul of India." But now the soul is denied of good road, safe drinking water, good schools for children and primary health services, etc. However, Michael Lipton (1968)[5] coutioned the Planning Commission that "rural-urban divide" is the real crisis of Indian planning.

The divide is quite apparent as schools of urban areas have computers whereas rural schools are without black-boards, without teachers and several villages have no school at all.[6]

Environment Improvement Measures

In India, the problem of footpath-dwellers and slum dwellers in the form of squatter settlements have acquired limitless heights. These requires to be properly settled as 25 to 40 per cent of the urban poor live in slums in metropolis and megacities of India. There is a syndrome of 'a city within a city'. All slum dwellers come below poverty line and these areas are not only polluters of the environment but they are also the centres of crime and immoral traffic. Hence, the choice between the rural and urban habitat is to choose between the devil and the deep blue sea.

Neglect of Small Towns

India lacks to have an unambiguously articulated urban policy even after 50 years of its Independence. The four mega-cities of India—Bombay, Calcutta, Delhi and Chennai together account for more than one sixth of the total urban population of India. This is because the neglect of small towns. In fact, most of the small and medium sized towns are devoid of anything described as planning. The infrastructure of these towns remains primitive forcing the inhabitants to migrate to urban areas in search of livelihood. Both the service and industrial sectors of these small towns are not developed enough to provide enough employment potential to the growing number of unemployed youth.

Glaring Disparities

With the help of Table 18.3 Rural-Urban disparities could be seen in India.

TABLE 18.3: Rural-Urban Sectors and Disparities in India (1995-96)

Sectors	Unit	Rural	Urban
Population	Lakh	629	218
Settlements	Number	627,000	3768
Workers	Lakh	241.7	64.3
Work Participation Rate	%	40.1	30.2
Poverty Ratio	%	33.4	20.1
Housing Shortage	Number	13.7	4.8
Safe Drinking Water	% Pop.	56	82
Toilet Facility	%	9	64
GNP	%	30	70

Source: Statistical Outline of India, 1995-96, Tata Services, Bombay.

The rural sector of India gives sustenance to 629 lakhs people whereas urban area provide sustenance to only 218 lakh people. The rural population is growing at the rate of 2 per cent per annum. However, the greatest disparity in rural-urban divide so as to say is that 75 per cent rural population produce about 113 of GNP only. All other disparities and divide spring from this alarming disparity.

Conclusion

The undergoing rural-urban divide needs to be bridged and it cannot be left on the market forces alone. The market forces may concentrate on disparities like regional and social infra-structure build up, provision of basic minimum services and bridging the income differentials. In improving the productivity and diversification of agriculture the assistance of the government is also needed especially in the field of establishing agro-based industries. It is quite essential to generate employment. Urbanizing rural area is not the solution of rural-urban divide but the problem should be tackled separately.

The defective policies and planning of the government is responsible for the plight of millions of people in rural areas. This happens as rural areas are predominantly agricultural consisting of farm land, agricultural labourers along with small non-viable land holdings, struggling artisans, tribals and displaced persons. All these left far behind in comparison with luxurious and glitered urban-areas where the majority of people earn big money from business and have soaked the money from rural people. This has created rural-urban divide in a hiatus manner.

The growing rural-urban divide due to short-sighted policies and administrative make up have proven disastrous to both the areas. The problem of villages and towns are interrelated and integrated approach is needed to the solution of related issues through short and long-term planning.

The real transfer of power through Panchayati Raj to the people who have been deprived for centuries is considered to be one of the significant solutions to resolve the problem of rural-urban divide.

REFERENCES

1. Friedman, J., *Regional Development Policy: A Case Study of Venezuela,* MIT Press, Cambridge, 1966.
2. Thimmaiah, G., "Rural Urban Divide in India", *Kurukshetra,* Oct-Nov. 1997, p. 3.
3. Kabra, K.N., "Contextualizing Rural-Urban Divide", *Kurukshetra,* Oct-Nov. 1997; p. 11.
4. Dreze, J. and Sen, A., *Indian Development–Selected Regional Perspectives;* Oxford University Press, 1997.
5. Lipton, M., *The Crisis of Indian Planning,* New Delhi, 1968.
6. Naganathan, M. and Sivagnanam, K. J., "Rural-Urban Divide: Role of Panchayati Raj Institutions", *Kurukshetra,* Oct. - Nov. 1997, p. 89.

19

STRATEGY FOR GROWTH OF RURAL SETTLEMENTS

As a development approach, rural settlement has emerged as a distinctive field of policy and practice and of research in 1970's and 1980's especially since the inception of the 'new strategy' for development planning by World Bank and United Nations Agencies. This strategy came to be formulated as a result of the general disagreement with previous approaches to development planning at national, regional and sectoral levels. It's concern was with the equity objectives of various kinds–especially motivating people to live in compact villages for the reduction of inequalities in income, employment, access to public goods and services and the alleviation of poverty.

It is this focus on distributional issues which has marked out 'rural development' as a distinct field, because an overwhelming majority of poor people in the Third World countries and especially in India and Tanzania live in rural areas. The World Bank, indeed, recently defined rural development as "a strategy designed to improve the economic and social life of a specific group of people—the rural poor."[1]

This chapter aims to investigate the patterns, growth and distribution of rural settlements in Tanzania with special reference to villagization programme.

Trends of Development

In Tanzania before Independence in 1961 most of the people in rural area, did not have a fixed abode from one generation to another as they practised shifting cultivation. Hence, it created a tendency of scattered, frequently moving households and not settled village communities. Neither the provision of basic services e.g., health, education, pure water or economic infrastructure such as roads, godowns, small scale irrigation and forestation, nor of inputs such as improved seeds, extension services and fertilizer could go very far within the limits of household and the shifting residence imposed by the pre-colonial long cycle rotation agricultural system. Hence, unless "we shall be able to develop our land and to raise our standard of living, we shall not be able to use tractors, provide schools for our children, build hospitals, or have clean drinking water. If we do not start living in proper village communities than all our attempts to develop the country side will be just so much waste of effort."[2]

A blueprint for human settlement in Tanzania was a policy booklet on socialism and Rural Development–published after the Arusha Declaration in February, 1967. The three important principles which evolve from the booklet are:[3]

1. To explain the philosophy of Ujamaa to villagers and encourage compliance by them with the principle thereof.
2. To train villagers in management and leadership.
3. To provide crucially important technical support in the form of extension services, health, education and communication services; and
4. To give priority to Ujamaa villagers in the distribution of land, education and health facilities and the construction and maintenance of feeder roads.

Hence, in order to provide good service facilities in a planned way Nyerere noted that: Before we can bring any benefits of modern development to the farmers of Tanzania, the very first step is to make it possible for them to start living in village communities.

After independence, in order to change the aforesaid situations the government of Tanzania started 'village settlement schemes' in the name of 'Ujamaa village' in Five Year Plans. This scheme was a self-help programme under which people residing in dispersed settlement and practising shifting cultivation should settle at selected housing site in the form of compact and semi-compact villages. This scheme of rural housing development is more or less the Ghana's roof loan scheme, the Sudan's cooperative and comprehensive rural development projects in al jezirah; the rebuilding of villages through self-help in Liberia; Kenya's site and service scheme; India's many projects such as village redevelopment on the model of Shamspur, homesteading and rural housing lots; and Pakistan's recent 'five marlas' scheme of house lots for rural poor. These are only some of the examples that can be cited to substantiate the point about the variety of ongoing programmes in different parts of the world like villagization in Tanzania.

Hence, it has been felt that "Ujamaa villages have come to pursue not only the path of Ruvuma schemes but also that of all the earlier rural development policies."[4] It can be said that the Ujamaa village conception is a combination of the 'improvement approach,' the 'transformation approach' and 'the cooperative scheme of Ruvuma'. The transformation approach for its part has contributed its villagisation dimension and in implementation the Ujamaa village has in many cases been seen as a 'resettlement project'.

Methodology of Villagisation

In Tanzania, in the last few years emphasis has shifted away from communal production to block farming in which peasants cultivate their own plots within an overall block of land allocated to the village and on individual holdings within a village framework. This should be seen in terms of a sequence of stages eventually leading upto fully cooperative villages. In reality, such a "step-by-step transformation" was explicitly foreseen individuals. Nyerere's *Socialism and Rural Development.* (1967):

> "Where necessary then, progress can be made in three stages. The first may be to persuade people to move their houses into a single village, if possible near water, and to plant their next year's food crops within easy reach of the area where the houses will be . . . For another step is to persuade a group of people perhaps the members of a ten-house cell—to start a small communal plot on which they work cooperatively, sharing the proceeds at harvest time according to the work they each have done . . . Once these two steps had been effected, the final stage would come when the people have confidence in a community farm, so that they are willing to invest all their effort in it, simply keeping gardens around their own houses for special vegetable, etc. Then the socialist village would be really established and other productive community activities can get underway".[5]

Hence "almost all the help which government can give in the way of tractors, improved houses, and rural water supplies, will be concentrated on these new village settlement schemes (Smith, 1966, p. 361).[6] This means that farming would be done by groups of people who live as a community and work as a community. 'They would live together in a village, to cultivate farm together, market together and undertake the provision of local services and small local requirements as a community" (Nyerere, 1968, 351).[7]

Ujamaa Villages: An Integrated Rural Development Approach

In terms of development from below, Ujamaa (familyhood) policy has multipurpose objectives comprising political, social and economic aims. From economic consideration, the "Village and Ujamaa Act" of 1975 indicated about two types of rural settlements in Tanzania: the traditional African villages and the Ujamaa villages. The latter in some places called "registered Ujamaa Villages" and in others 'permanent', 'planned' or 'development' villages.[8] According to 1975 Act, one village will house at least 250 families within specific boundary. The villagers would be organised under a cooperative with self-government by a village council elected by a village assembly of all adult members of the villages. The council's duty is to see day-today administration, promote development, encourage cooperation, undertake village planning besides coordinating various activities of the village. In these villages although cooperative communal farming will be encouraged but the council will guide private ownership of production also. The supply of machinery, the development of small-scale industry and other major service such as distributing loan through cooperative chain, purchase and supply of inputs and the provision of local shopping/ marketing centres will be provided communally.

For the integrated development of Ujamaa village it is necessary to have sufficient land for cultivation by the peasants so that they can raise both subsistence and cash crops. Hence, after leaving aside the traditional mode of living and agricultural practices, now peasants are adopting modern technological innovations, fertilizers, insecticides and irrigation for good agricultural produce. But the high yields of crops depend on other factors such as seeds, correct methods and suitable time of planting, weeding and harvesting. All these require the proper analysis of ecological conditions in order to select the variety of seeds, fertilizer besides other factors. Hence, at this juncture farmers require the assistance of agriculture extension workers. As for example Ilonga Research station experiments with maize, Iyamungo does coffee research, Ukiluguru does work with cotton and Mlingano for sisal. The research stations for animal husbandry are Uyole and Mpwapwa which aim at better animal husbandry.

In this way, the formation of new compact rural settlements become the keynote of Tanzania's agrarian development. The bases of such a considerations are the desire to reduce population pressure from high density areas of the Kilimanjaro, the Pare, the Usambara mountains' and some parts of the Southern Highlands by the shifting of some villages in low land areas. It has been felt essential in order to provide social services and infrastructure facilities cheaply to a large number of people.

Luttrell[9] argues that the Ujamaa village policy stresses three interlinked facts:

(a) New settlements to introduce modern techniques of production;
(b) New permanent compact planned villages to conform to a grid iron pattern streets, and
(c) Ideal social relations of production which are based upon community property holdings. In this way, the Ujamaa Vijijini programme is regarded as a vehicle for socialist rural transformation.

Village Settlement Scheme

In Tanzania, the unsuccessful operation of the 'land development' and 'soil conservation shcemes' as well as 'focal point approach' from which only the rich large scale farmers benefited paved the way for the World Bank recommendation in 1962 to transform peasant agriculture through settlement schemes. It would involve a change to mechanized methods and a break with traditional social structures. But the main beneficiaries were spatially concentrated privileged group of farmers who intended to get success through the roads of transformation to modernization.

In Tanzania, some areas have developed Ujamaa living spontaneously by people who adhered to socialist principles. Other old settlement schemes were 'taken over' by the government, and third group of villages were established under 'Ruvuma Development Association' in southern Tanzania. In many cases old settlement schemes were rebaptised between 1968-1969, such as upper Kitete and Kerege. In other areas some progressive farmers established cooperative system in agricultural development and marketing of their produce such as in Bukoba, Kilimanjaro, Arusha, Tukuyu and Lushoto. In some literature they have been termed 'Kulak-Ujamaa'.[10]

This is because it has been stated that if farmers could not be forced or persuaded, the only alternative is to ignore them altogether and go for mechanized agriculture with the help of outsiders as 'groundnut scheme' and 'settler farms' by Europeans or to take them away from the traditional surroundings to settlement schemes where in return for receiving land they might agree to follow the instructions of the agricultural staff. As with the 'Meru Land Case when the authorities tried to resettle the landless Meru peasants, the first settlement scheme by the Government of Tanzania was started on the abandoned land cleared for the groundnut scheme at Urambo and Nachingwea. Successively about 23 schemes were started with high capital investment, paid high wages in order to have close supervision and to learn modern farming practices. Apart from these projects, most of the unofficial settlements were established as cooperative farms by members of TANU Youth League in the spirit of 'building a nation.'[11]

The First Five Year Plan (1964-1969) proposed the establishment of 74 model village settlement schemes of about 250 families. The execution of the programme was the concern of the Village Settlement Agency. In 1965 the Agency was working on 23 settlements, whereby 8 schemes were designed as pilot projects so to gain experience in planned resettlement and developing modern agricultural techniques. The three schemes financed by Israel were located around Mwanza, and seven other by the Tanganyika Agricultural Corporation were distributed in different parts of Tanzania. The Five Year Plan suggested two model layouts for the villages: "either in a single, large village around a service centre or two to three smaller satellite villages grouped around a common service centre".[12]

Growth and Development of Villagisation

The decisive impetus to the villagisation movement came from the

TABLE 19.1: Trends of the Growth of Ujamaa Villages in Tanzania

Year	Number of Ujamaa villages	Population
1967	48	5,000
1969	809	10,000
1970	1,956	531,200
1971	4,644	1,545,240
1972	5,556	1,980,962
1973	5,628	2,028,164
1981	7,750	14,874,522
1983	8,187	15,060,926
1984	8,200	15,869,205
1992	8,250	20,025,250

Source : Prime Minister of Tanzania Office, Dodoma, 1975 and 1983. 1992 figure is estimated.

Arusha Declaration and the ideological foundations laid down in Nyerere's "Socialism and Rural Development" in 1967. Uptil now the progress towards villagisation has been uneven but the recent shift is truly encouraging (Table 19.1).

The progress in villagisation after 1965 Arusha Declaration was slow, as for example in 1967 the number of Ujamaa villages were only 48 with a total population of 5,000. But in 1968 with the call to 'go to Ujamaa' raised the number of villages to 809 in 1969, 5,556 in 1972 and 8,187 in 1983 representing over 90 per cent of the rural population. The average number of residents per village increased from 272 in 1970 to 511 in 1974, and 1,919 in 1980-81. So far as the regional variations in villagisation is concerned highest number of villages 643 is found in Mwanza Region and the lowest 47 in Dar es Salaam Region due to its urban characteristics (Table 19.2).

Table 19.2 shows that 98 per cent rural settlements of Tanzania have already come into the fold of Ujamaa living upto 1992. This also highlights that the progress of villagisation programme is quite satisfactory.

Density and Size of Settlements

In Tanzania, the density of rural population per square kilometre varies from 66 in Mwanza region to 6 in Tabora. On the basis of Quartile and Median the country has been divided into four regions.

TABLE 19.2: Number of Ujamaa Villages in Tanzania upto December, 1993

Sr. No.	Region	Total Number of villages	Number of Ujamaa Villages	% of Total
1.	Arusha	463	457	99
2.	Dar es Salaam	47	47	100
3.	Dodoma	423	423	100
4.	Iringa	593	593	100
5.	Kagera	505	505	100
6.	Kigoma	222	218	99
7.	Kilimanjaro	372	349	94
8.	Lindi	362	362.	100
9.	Mara	348	340	97
10.	Mbeya	577	571	99
11.	Morogoro	459	425	93
12.	Mtwara	489	489	100
13.	Mwanza	643	643	100
14.	Pwani	355	352	99
15.	Rukwa	304	304	100
16.	Ruvuma	313	312	99
17.	Shinyanga	628	589	93
18.	Singida	323	311	96
19.	Tabora	375	365	98
20.	Tanga	538	536	99
	Total	8339	8187	98

Source: Principal Secretary, Prime Minister's Office Dodoma, September, 1993.

The high population density regions are found around lake Victoria, Kilimanjaro, Central mountains besides Dar es Salaam lake Mtwara. Medium High density areas are found around lake regions of Kigoma, Shinyanga, Mara, Coastal region of Tanga, capital region of Dodoma besides the highland of Mbeya.

In all these areas, population density varies from 33 to 16 persons per km^2. Entire central parts of Tanzania except mountainous regions come under low density below 16 persons per km^2. It includes Morogoro, Iringa, Singida, Lindi, Ruvuma, Rukwa and Tabora. The factors which generally affect the density of population are agricultural and industrial development, availability of drinking water, suitable landscape available for settlement siting and the salubrious climatic conditions for the growth of plants and promoting habitable environment to the people.

In Tanzania, the population progressions (Table 19.3) show that the growth of urban population would be more rapid than rural. This is due to the massive natural growth and increased dimension of rural-urban migration. It means the growth and expansion of urban areas shall continuously reduce the spatial dimension of rural areas, but on the other hand urban centres may diffuse urban economic and social components to rural areas. Hence, the population supporting capacity of the rural area will improve automatically. Hence, there is a desire on national level to enhance the construction of planned rural communities so that in future it may match up with the urban environment without any physical obstructions.

In Tanzania, average population size of rural settlements varies

TABLE 19.3: Estimated Rural and Urban Population in Tanzania in Thousands (1978-2000)

Years	Total	Rural	Urban	Urban as % of Total
1978				
Actual				
Estimated	17,512.6	15,095.7	2,412.9	13.8
1980	18,178.0	15,413.0	2,763.0	15.2
1981	18,778.0	15,822.0	2,956.0	15.7
1982	19,398.0	16,235.0	3,163.0	16.3
1983	20,038.0	16,654.0	3,384.0	16.9
1984	20,699.0	17,078.0	3,621.0	17.5
1985	21,341.0	17,466.0	3,875.0	18.2
1990	25,114.0	19,680.0	5,434.0	21.6
1995	29,684.0	22,062.0	7,622.0	25.7
2000	34,815.0	24,125.0	10,690.0	30.7

Source: Derived from 1978 Census assuming total population growing at 3.3% per annum and urban population at 7 per cent per annum.

from 2,633 the bigger one to 1,314 the smaller. The median value is 1,736 persons per village. In high population size areas of Mwanza and Kigoma regions are flood affected; Kilimanjaro is mountainous whereas Dodoma lies in semi-desert environment. The low population size regions are Lindi, Mtwara, Iringa and Rukwa. Areas having occasional floods and drought may have bigger rural settlements size,

TABLE 19.4: Distribution and Size of Villages* by Region in Tanzania (1978)

Region	Less than 200	200 to 499	500 to 999	1000 to 1999	2000 to 4999	5000 to 9999	Total
Dododoma	—	4	54	178	184	5	425
Arusha	—	3	48	220	154	2	427
Kilimanjaro	—	3	26	143	192	3	367
Tanga	—	23	135	250	127	—	535
Morogoro	—	16	99	217	128	4	464
Coast	2	21	108	149	51	3	334
Dar es Salaam	1	5	15	27	4	1	53
Lindi	—	2	52	131	85	—	270
Mtwara	—	6	116	263	76	—	461
Ruvuma	—	—	54	141	96	4	295
Iringa	—	18	138	292	115	—	563
Mbeya	—	3	80	326	166	—	575
Singida	—	3	23	185	92	—	303
Tabora	—	7	61	176	123	3	370
Rukwa	—	5	42	120	47	2	216
Kigoma	—	3	6	53	149	6	217
Shinyanga	—	11	62	270	276	4	623
Mwanza	1	1	30	276	192	2	502
Kagera	—	-	53	320	269	2	644
Mara	—	2	25	193	123	3	346
Mainland (Total)	4	136	1227	3930	2649	44	7990
North	—	—	22	16	13	—	51
Central	—	1	31	19	1	—	52
West	—	—	11	9	2	1	23
Pemba North	—	—	1	3	13	6	23
Pemba South	—	—	4	5	12	6	27
Zanzibar (Total	—	1	69	52	41	13	176

Source: Bureau of Statistics.

* As defined under the 1975 villages Act.

whereas the areas having excessive flood and drought are more prone to scattered and lower population size settlements.

Table 19.4 shows that in Tanzania, the majority of villages lie in the size categories of 500 to 5,000 population in 1978. The highest number of villages is 3,930 lie in the size category of 1,000 to 2,000 persons per village. The Zanzibar and Pemba islands of Tanzania also denote the same population size distribution of villages. Villages are more evenly scattered in Pemba than on Zanzibar Island. Even in the tiny villages there is a mosque, a school and a shop or two.

In any region, the density of rural settlements is governed by four factors e.g. agricultural development, availability of drinking water in the nearby areas, development of road transport and productive defensible terrain with more equable climatic conditions. On the basis of quartile and Median, the rural settlements of Tanzania have been divided into four categories: high density areas, medium high density areas, medium low density areas and low density areas. It shows that above median value of .010 rural settlements per square kilometre, the areas are relatively more dense in terms of rural settlements and comprises areas around lake victoria, Tanga, Kilimanjaro, Dar es Salaam and Mtwara. The road leading to Morogoro, Dodoma, besides the centrally located mountains of Uluguru and Ushambara's are comparatively densely settled due to cooler climate and healthy mountainous environment.

Conclusions

It can be concluded that most of the dispersed household in Tanzania have been moved into nucleated Ujamaa villages in between 1965-85. This is considered as a dramatic change in comparison with the situation in 1965 when 86 per cent people were living in scattered homesteads–outside nucleated village and urban centres. This process of change from scattered to nucleated living is known as villagisation programme and the major thrust were resettlement and agricultural development besides a wide range of benefits such as management of schools, health facilities, transport and water supply for the majority of people. The strategy of villagisation programme has been considered by the Tanzanian policy makers as a sufficient condition for rural development.

Although the density of rural settlements and thier population size vary according to population supporting capacity of the region i.e. agricultural or industrial development but Tanzanian villagisation programme is unique in nature where little attention has been given on fertility of land in favour of health, transportation and schooling facilities.

Like traditional settlement, the success of Ujamaa policy is highly dependent on the availability and supply of water for both agricultural and domestic use. The supply of water is essential in order to utilise women labour force in more productive work than devoting much time in collecting water for domestic use.

Similarly the integrated control of crop vermin is quite essential in rural development process. As the existence of a certain pest follows ecological zones, the peasants of those areas will be in a better position to fight against them communally when they live in social groups of Ujamaa.

In this way, the planning and implementation of rural development strategies that will be effective in expanding opportunities for productive employment and raising the income of families in the village sector of Tanzania is an extremely demanding task. For rural settlements, the programmes of rural development need to be supplemented by the provision of rural transport services; the construction of crop storage facilities; the development of processing and marketing facilities; the establishment of rural service centres; the organization of wholesale and retail trade; the distribution of farm inputs and implements; the provision of health services, education, training and enhancing the opportunities for cultural activities.

The Tanzanian idea of socialism and rural development may be applied to other developing countries of the world but the characteristics and mode of application may be different because in Tanzania all land belong to the government which facilitates the movement of people from one place to another either for settling or practising communal agriculture. This is because private ownership of land has no place in national settlement policy of Tanzania.

REFERENCES

1. Harris, J., (1982): *Rural Development Theories of Peasant Economy and Agrarian Change*, Hutchinson University Library, London, p. 1.
2. Nyerere, J.K., (1966): *Freedom and Unity: A Selection from Writings and Speeches 1952-65:* Oxford Press. Dar es Salaam, p. 183.
3. *National Report on Human Settlements Policy in Tanzania,* 1976; pp. 3-4.
4. Mapolu, H., (1973): *The Social and Economic Organization of Ujamaa Villages,* M.A. Thesis, University of Dar es Salaam.
5. Nyerere, J.K., (1967): *Socialism and Rural Development,* Dar es Salaam.

6. Smith, H.E., (1966): *Readings on Economic Development and Administration in Tanzania,* Oxford University Press, London, p. 361.
7. Nyerere, J.K., (1968): *Freedom and Socialism: A Selection from Writings and Speeches 1965-67;* Oxford University Press, Dar es Salaam, p. 351.
8. Omari, C.K., (1977): "Ujamaa Cooperative Farming the Way Ahead", *Journal of Rural Cooperation;* Vol. V; No. 1; pp. 25-26.
9. Luttrell, W., (1971): "Villagisation, Cooperative Production and Rural Cadres: Strategies and Tactics in Tanzanian Socialism Development", *Economic Research Bureau,* University of Dar es Salaam.
10. Raikes, P.L., (1972): "Village Planning for Ujamaa", *Economic Research Bureau,* University of Dar es Salaam.
11. Schuler, U., (1984): *Rural Development Strategies and Land use and Settlement Planning in Tanzania,* Ardhi Institute, Dar es Salaam, Part I, p. 77.
12. Newigor, N., (1968): "Village Settlement Schemes" (H. Ruthernberg Edt.); *Smallholder Farming and Smallholder Development in Tanzania,* Munchen.

20

QUESTIONNAIRE ON SPATIAL ORGANIZATION AND PLANNING OF RURAL SETTLEMENTS

All questions are to be completed either by the author or by investigators except those questions relating to consumer behaviour which would be filled in by the shop-keepers and consumers of different central places.

Settlement as a Whole

1. Name of the Village ______________________
2. Block/Anchal ______________________
3. District ______________________
4. Number and Name of the Satellite Settlements ______________________
5. Number of household units in the Settlements ______________________
6. Chief materials of wall ______________________
7. Chief Materials of roof ______________________
8. Problems of flood ______________ Yes or no __________
9. Total % of area flooded ______________________
10. Location of Village Diety ______________________
11. Distance of village from the nearest Market ______________
12. Distance of village from the nearest metalled road ______________
13. Does the settlement have a school ______________
    Health Centre ______________________
14. Distance of the nearest river in relation to the village ______________________

15. Sources of irrigation available in the village

    ____

16. Total irrigated area of the village ______________
17. Agricultural implements used in the village:

    Improved *Traditional*

18. Per Hectare input of Fertilizers
19. Different classes of soil available in the village and the resulting crop dominance:

    Classes of soil *Dominant crop*

Satellite Settlements

Name	*No. of Houses*	*Population*	*No. of Different Castes*	*Distance from the Parent village*

Individal Households of a Family

1. Name of the House owner ______________
2. Caste Affiliation ______________
3. Siting condition ______________
4. Materials of wall ______________
5. Materials of Roof ______________
6. Total annual income in the family ______________
7. Total No. of Family Members ______________
8. Materials of door ______________
9. Total No. of rooms ______________
10. No. of rooms for men ______________
11. No. of rooms for women ______________
12. Location of Kitchen ______________
13. Location of House Diety ______________
14. Location of Cattleshed ______________
15. Height of the House ______________
16. Length and Breadth of the House ______________
17. No. of windows and their height of placing on the wall

    ____

18. Floor materials of the house ______________
19. Housing Problems if any ______________

Agricultural Information

How far is it from your house to the farm(s) (in terms of kms/ walking hours)

(a) *Nearest Plots:*

(1) less than 15 minutes ____________

(2) 15 to 30 minutes ____________

(3) 30 to 45 minutes ____________

(4) 45 to 1 hours ____________

(5) Not applicable ____________

(b) *Farthest Plot:* ____________

(1) Less than 15 minutes ____________

(2) 15 to 30 minutes ____________

(3) 30 to 45 minutes ____________

(4) 45 to 1 hours ____________

(5) Not applicable ____________

(c) *What crops do you grow in your nearest plots* (in order of importance)

	Crop	Output	Area	Income
(1)				
(2)				
(3)				
(4)				
(5)				
(6)				
(7)				
(8)				
(9)	Not applicable.			

(d) *Progress made in land consolidation:*

Facilities Available in the Village

1. No. of Drinking Water Well ____________

No. of Hand Pump ____________

No. of Tap ____________

No. of Pond ____________

No. of Pumping Set ____________

No. of rivers ____________

No. of Natural or man-made Ditch ____________

2. Health Centre:
   Available in the village ____________
   Available in Nearest village ____________
   Town ____________
   No. of Dispensary ____________
   Maternity Home ____________
   Family Planning Centres ____________
   No. of Allopathic Doctor ____________
   No. of Homeopathic Doctor ____________
   No. of Ayurvedic Doctor ____________
   No. of Unani Hakim ____________
   No. of Naturalopath Doctor ____________
3. Transport and Communication:
   (a) Distance from metalled road ____________
   (b) Distance from unmetalled road ____________
   (c) Nature of road length:
   metalled Unmetalled Footpath

(d) *Telephone Facility:* Distance:
   Available in the village ____________
   Available in the Neighbouring village ____________
   Available in the Town ____________

(e) *Electricity:*
   Available ____________
   Not Available ____________
   Entermittantly coming ____________

(f) Sources of entertainment ____________

4. Education

Primary School	Middle School	High School	Inter College	Training College	Degree College	University

5. Finance:
   Cooperative Society:
   Cooperative Bank ____________
   Rural Bank ____________
   Village Lenders ____________
   Nearest urban Bank ____________
6. Functional Activities:
   % of population engaged in Agriculture ____________
   % of population engaged in Transport ____________

% of population engaged in Industry ________________

Agricultural Processing	Crafts	Machine Tools	Jewelleries	Bangles Making

% of people engaged in Trade and Commerce ____________
% of people engaged in Mining & Quarrying ____________
% of people engaged in Fishing ____________
% of people engaged in Basket Weaving ____________
No. of saw mills ____________
No. of carpenters ____________
No. of Hair Dressers ____________
No. of Drum Beaters ____________
No. of Shoe Makers ____________
No. of Purohit ____________
No. of flour mills ____________
No. of oil preparing machine ____________
No. of Washerman ____________
No. of Temples ____________
No. of Mosques ____________
No. of Churches ____________

Diffusion of Houses in the village

1. Where in the village construction of new houses taken place ____
2. No. of new houses built each year ____________
3. No. of planned or unplanned houses ____________
4. Difference between old and new structure:

Building Materials	Style of constructions	Living condition	Sanitaion

5. Perception about living conditions:

very good	medium	poor	Not at all congenial

6. No.of houses used as shops: ________
7. Under which circumstances new houses constructed and where:
   Circumstances Location in the village
8. Caste barrier in the diffusion of houses:
9. Defence Barriers:

Poor Siting	Thieves	Flooding	Lowland

Caste structure in the village
No. of castes living in the village

Name of the Caste	Families	Population	Female	Male

Land Values in Rs. in the villages:

(a) Central Part of the settlement ______
(b) Mid-Part of the settlement ______
(c) Fringe of the settlement ______
(d) Satellite settlement ______
(e) Kitchen garden ______
(f) Treble cropped land ______
(g) Double cropped land ______
(h) Single cropped land ______
(i) Outer Fringe of the village ______
(j) Land value of unconsolidated Land
1- Acre:
(k) Land value of consolidated land
1 - Acre:-

Migration Family Level

1. How many years ago migrated to the present place of living ______
2. From where migrated ______
3. What were the causes of such a migration ______
4. What were the attractions to the place of arrival ______
5. What were the problems faced in migration ______
6. How many family members involved in such a migration ______
7. Occupation of the peasant at the time of migration ______
8. Ownership of landed property:
   Before migration ______
   At the time of migration ______
   After migration ______
9. Mobility of the people if any ______
10. Present income from agriculture ______
11. Income from other sources ______

Central Place Study

Types of Shops *No. of Shops*

Edible:

Backery-Store __________

Hotel __________

Motel __________

Pan-Bidi shop __________

Sattu-shop __________

Butchery shop __________

Parched Grain shop __________

Fish shop __________

Vegetable shop __________

Tea store __________

Fruits shop __________

Sweets shop __________

Grain shop __________

Wine + Bear shop __________

Toddy shop __________

Ganja-Affim shop __________

Sebai House __________

Ice-Cream shop __________

Tobacco shop __________

Milk stall __________

Tea Stall __________

Grain wholesalers __________

Clothes:

Cloth General __________

Ready Made Garments __________

Woollen cloth __________

Baniyan __________

Wool House __________

Sari shop __________

Cap shop __________

Cloth wholesalers __________

Dry cleaners shop __________

Laundary ______________________________
Cloth colouring shop ____________________
Tailor General __________________________
Embroidary Tailor _______________________

Art + Recreation:

Sports Goods Shop ______________________
Hair Dressing Saloon ____________________
Radio shop _____________________________
Radio repairing shop _____________________
Photo Frame shop _______________________
Musical Instrument shop __________________
Jewellery shop __________________________
Photo Studio ___________________________
X-Ray shop _____________________________
Cinema House ___________________________
Theatre ________________________________
Club __________________________________
Dancing Girls shop _______________________
Band Party shop _________________________
No. of Play grounds ______________________
Beauty shop ____________________________
Loudspeaker Hiring Shop __________________

Medicine & Health:

Allopathic Medicine ______________________
Homeopathic Medicine ____________________
Ayurvedic Medicine ______________________
Unani Hakim ____________________________
Dentist shop ____________________________
Pen Hospital ____________________________
Hospital ________________________________
Optical shops ___________________________
Phermacist shop _________________________

Sources of Energy:

Coal Depot ____________________
Petrol Tank ____________________
Gas Filling Station ________________
Fuelwood Selling ________________
Stove and Fitters shop ______________
Industries and Machinery:
Sewing Machine Shop ______________
Carpenters shop __________________
Typing Centre ___________________
Barbars shop ____________________
Book Binding Shop _______________
Shoe-makers shop
Bicycle Repairing Shop _____________
Autoparts shop __________________
Furniture shop ___________________
Motor + Cycle Air filing shop ________
Printing Press ___________________
Engineering Industries ______________ Gun shop __________
Flour milks _____________________
Motor + Motor Repairing shop ________
Iron Grill Industry ________________
Watch shop _____________________
Book Publishing House ____________
News Paper Publishing House ________
Rice Mills _______________________
Sugar Mills ______________________
Jute Mills _______________________
Saw Mills _______________________
Thathera shop ____________________
Watch Repairing shop ______________
Bicycle shop _____________________
Flax and string shop _______________
Bamboo Basket shop ______________
Auto-Service shop _________________

Others:

Scientific Instruments and chemicals:
Book stall ____________________
Bangles shop ____________________
Fishing Net and Zewra shop ________
Tin utensils shop ________________
Brass utensils shop ______________
Stainless steel utensils shop ________
Potteries shop __________________
Earthen jars shop ________________
Fertilizer shop __________________
Shoe store ____________________
Glass House ___________________
Merchandise shop ________________
Leather shop ___________________
Papers shop ____________________
Lime shop _____________________
Tyre shop _____________________
Super market ___________________
Gadda shar ____________________
Plastic store ___________________
Almirah shop ___________________
Grill Cement Store _______________
Stationery Shop _________________
Cement shop ___________________
Bamboo shop ___________________
Utensil and Saṃiyana Hiring shop _______
Paper cards shop ________________

Consumer Behaviour

1. Name of the control place ___________
2. District ____________________
3. From which villages do people come for the purchase of clothes:
   East-West North South
4. From which village do people come for the purchase of medicine:
   East West North South

5. From which villages do the consumers come for the purchase of books, merchandise and stationary goods.
East West North South

Problems: Village Level

1. Flood-Annual-Occasional months
2. Fire problem
3. Robbery-Stealing-Pick-pocket
4. Problems of Material of Wall-roof.
   Rust on wall ____________
5. Fragmented small land holdings _____ Yes ______ No. ______
6. Wild Beasts ____________
7. Cattle Disease ____________
8. Crow-monkey's as menace of Tile roofs
9. Storms ____________
10. Supersticious Beliefs:
11. Problems of water drains ______
12. Frost ____________
13. Kind of Diseases ________ Human Animal
14. Water losses ________
15. Sanitary problem ________
16. Problem of garbage disposal ______
17. Problems of suitable drainage lines __
18. Problems of pastureland ________
19. Problems of playing ground ______
20. Problem of the disposal of
   (a) Dead body __________ Hindu _____ Muslim _____
   (b) Dead Animals ________
21. Problems of Drinking Water ______
   Laaking ____________ No Laaking
22. Problems of sugar ____________
   Salt ____________
   Kerosene Oil ____________
   Coal ____________
   Diesel ____________
   Fertiliser ____________

Credit facilities ________________

Fuel ________________

23. Lack of living space for animals

No. ________________ Lack ________________

24. Village politics ________________

Yes ________________ No. ________________

25. Quarrel among Villagers ________

26. Lighting problems:

Electricity __________ Lamp ________ Hurricane ______

27. Illiteracy Among women ________

Men ________________

Adult ________________

Children ________________

28. Water erosion ________________

Wind erosion ________________

River embankment erosion ________

Integrated Planning

1. Raising village site ________________
2. Village Reorganization needed ______
3. Straightening of roads needed ______
4. Caste separation in planned house required or not ____________
5. Remodelling and relocation of house needed ________________
6. Provision of light required ________
7. Drinking Water required ________
8. Playground needed ________________
9. Health Centre needed ____________
10. Educational Institution of which level required ____________
11. Bathing Place required

    Pond River well Handpump
12. Worshipping place required

    Temple-church-mosque-Idgah
13. Place of Dead Body Disposal ________

    Graveyard Cremation ground
14. Provision of Transporation lines required ________________

15. Provision of community hall ________
16. Provision of Panchayat Bhawan ________
17. Provision of marriage platform ________
18. Provision of rathering cattle ________ Barns ________
19. Irrigation Facilities ________
20. Facilities of Grain bans ________
21. Provision of safety latrine ________
22. Sewage disposal ________
23. Provision of Bee-keeping and kitchen garden ________
24. Need of adult education to irradicate illiteracy ________
25. Child welfare scheme desired ________
26. Women Welfare scheme desired ____
27. Whether the location of following items are required in the village: Police Station ________
    Fire Brigade ________
    Post-Office ________
    Bank ________
    Bus Station ________
    Village-Market ________
28. Consolidation of land required: ____

BIBLIOGRAPHY

Books

Acharya, P.K.; *Architecture of Mansara,* 1933.

Ahmad, E.; *Geographical Essays on India,* Patna, 1951.

Ahmad, E.; *Bihar: A Physical, Economic and Regional Geography,* Ranchi, 1965.

Alam, M. & K.N. Gopi; *Settlement System of India;* Oxford and IBH Publishing Co., New Delhi, 1982.

Altekar, A.S.; *A History of Village Community in India;* Hind Kitab, Bombay, 1927.

Ambak, S.G.P.; *Bihar Ke Darsniya Asthan,* Patna, 1917.

Ayyar, N.P.; *Rural Population and Settlements of Jabalpore District: An essay in Agricultural Geography,* Ed., B. Banerjee, Calcutta, 1967.

Baden Powell, B.H.; *The Indian Village Community,* London, 1897.

Baden Powell, B.H.; *Land System of British India,* London, 1892, Vol. I.

Ball, V.; *Travels in India by Jean Baptiste Tavernier,* London, 1889, Vol. I.

Beal, S.; *Budhist Record of the Western World,* 1884, Vol. I.

Berry, Brian, J.L.; *Geography of Market Centres and Retail Distribution,* Prentice Hall, 1965.

Bhattacharya, N.D.; *A Study in Settlement Geography in Murshidabad* District, Census of India, Handbook on Murshidabad District, 1967.

Blache, Vidal de La; *Principles of Human Geography,* London, 1962.

Bohman, Carter V.; *The English Village: A Pelican Book,* New York, 1951.

Borchert, John R.; *Upper Midwest Urban Change in the 1960's,* Minneapolis, 1968.

Bracy, H.E.; *English Central Places Identification, Distribution and Functions,* Lund, 1960.

Brunhes, J.; *Human Geography,* Paris, 1952.

Bryn, P.W.; *Man's Adaptation of Nature,* London, 1933.

Cowell, E.B. (Ed.); *The Jataka Stories,* Published by Luzac and Co., London, 1957.

Chatterjee, S.C.; *Magadh Architecture and Culture,* University of Calcutta, 1942.

Chisholon, M.; *Rural Settlement and Landuse,* London, 1952.

Choudhary, R.K.; *Early History of Vaishali, Vaishali Visesank,* Muzaffarpur, 1960.

Christaller, W.; *Central Places in Southern Germany,* N.J. Prentice Hall, 1966.

Davis, K.; *The Population of India and Pakistan,* Princeton University Press, 1951.

Dayal, P.; *Bihar in Maps,* Patna, 1953.

Demangeon, A.; *The Origins and Census of Settlement Types, Readings in Cultural Geography* (Ed.) Wegener, Chicago, 1962.

Despande, R.S.; *Cheap and Healthy Houses for Middle Classes of India,* Bombay, 1954.

Dicken, S.N. & Pitts, F.R.; *Introduction to Human Geography,* New York, 1963.

Dickinson, R.E.; *City Region and Regionalism,* London, 1960.

Diwakar, R.R.; *Bihar Through the Ages,* Calcutta, 1960.

Dumont, Rene; *Types of Rural Economy, Studies in World Agriculture,* Methuen & Co. London, 1964.

Dube, S.C.; *Indian Villages,* London, 1955.

Dube, S.C.; *India's Changing Villages,* Ithoca, New York, 1958.

Duggal, S.L. & Gaur, K.; *Rural House Types; Human Geography,* Merath, 1958.

Fergusson, J.; *Bihar Caves, History of Architecture,* London, 1867.

Finch, V.C. & Trewartha, G.T.; *Elements of Geography, Physical and Cultural,* New York, 1949.

Folke, S.; *Central Place Systems and Spatial Interaction in Nilgiris and Coorg (South India),* Denmark, (Edited by Jacobse, N.K. and Jensen, R.H.), Copenhagen, 1968.

Forde, C.D.; *Habitat, Economy and Society,* Methuen & Co. London, 1966.

Galpin, C.G.; *The Social Anatomy of Agricultural Community,* Research Bulletin 34, Wisconsin, 1915.

Ghosal, H. & J.K.; *Buddhism and Vaishali,* Patna, 1987.

Ghosh, Manoranjan; *The Pataliputra,* Patna, 1919.

Grierson, G.A.; *Bihar Peasant Life,* Patna, 1926.

Hagget, P.; *Locational Analysis in Geography,* London, 1965.

Hand, J.R.; *Early English Administration of Bihar,* Calcutta, 1894.
Harper, J.; *Final Report on Settlement of Basti,* Allahabad, 1891.
Havel, E.B.; *Ancient and Medieval Architecture of India,* London, 1915.
Houston, J.M.; *A Social Geography of Europe,* London, 1953.
Isard, W.; *Location and Space Economy,* New York, 1956.
Isard, W.; *Methods of Regional Analysis: An Introduction to Regional Science,* New York, 1960.
Jayaswal, K.P.; *Hindu Polity,* Calcutta, 1924.
Jayaswal, P.K; *Itihas Anushilan* (Hindi), December, 1967, Ank-2.
John, E.D.; *Village Life in Modern Thailand,* Chicaco, 1955.
Jones, Emrys; *Human Geography,* Chottu Windus, London, 1964.
Karve, I.; *Some Aspects of the Organisation of Caste System of the Hindus,* (Eds.) H.W. Sovani and V.M. Dandekar, Changing India, London, 1961.
Kayastha, S.L.; *The Himalayan Beas Basin,* Varanasi, 1964.
Lefevre, M.A., X; *L. Habitat Rural in Belgique,* Liege, 1926.
Lefevre, M.A.; *Classification Generale des types d, Habitat,* Second Report of the Commission on Types of Rural Habitat, Florence, Italy, 1930.
Lewis, Oscar; *Village Life in Northern India,* Urbana III, Illinois, 1958.
Lovis, Renon; *The Civilization of Ancient India,* Calcutta, 12, 1959.
Mandal, R.B.; *Introduction to Rural Settlements,* Concept Publishing Company, New Delhi, 1979.
Mandal, R.B.; *Systems of Rural Settlements in Developing Countries,* Concept Publishing Company, New Delhi, 1989.
Mandan, S.R.; *Changing Pattern of Indian Villages,* S. Chand & Co., Delhi, 1959.
Mathur, C.C.; *Rural Housing and Village Planning,* National Building Organization, New Delhi, 1964.
Mayer, H.M. & Kohn, C.F.; *Readings in Urban Geography,* Ind. Ed. Allahabad, 1967.
Monkhouse, F.J. & Wilkinson, H.R.; *Maps and Diagrams,* London, 1952.
Murthy, K.K.; *Antiquities of Forts in India,* Archaeological Survey of India, Annual Report, 1912-13, New Delhi.
Mukerjee, L.; *History of India, Hindu Period,* Calcutta, 1968.
Mukerji, R.; *The Changing Face of Bengal,* Calcutta, 1938.
Mukerji, R.; *Man and His Habitation,* London, 1940.
Mukerji, R.; *Hindu Civilization,* Bombay, 1950.
Nath, V.; *The Village and the Community India's Urban Future,* (Eds. Roy and Turner), 1962.

Oldham, C.E. A.W.; *Journal of Francis,* Buchanan, Patna, 1930.

Pandey, M.S.; *Historical Geography and Topography of Bihar,* Patna, 1954.

Padhye, S.S.; *A Formation of Settlement Terminology,* Bombay, 1964.

Prasad, A.; *Geography of Rural Settlement,* Ranchi University, Ranchi, 1973.

Ramchandran, A.; *Habitat News;* United Nations Centre for Human Settlements; Nairobi, 1982 to 1993.

Reilly, W.J.; *The Law of Retail Gravitation,* New York, 1931.

Rhys, T.W. & Davides; *Buddhist India,* Calcutta, 12, 1959.

Richard, D.L.; *The Impact of Urban Soceity Upon Village Life, Indias Urban Future,* (Eds. Roy & Turner), Allahabad, 1962.

Smaddar, J.N.; *Aryan Settlement, The Clories of Magadha,* Patna, 1927.

Sarkar, J.; *The Mughal Administration,* Lecture IV, Patna, 1920.

Shankar, B.; *Welcome Address to the 20th Sub-school Inspectors Conference,* Arrah, 1971.

Sharp, T.; *Anatomy of Village,* Manchester, 1946.

Shastri, A.P.B.; *Asura India,* Patna, 1926.

Shastri, A.P.B.; *Early Inscriptions of Bihar and Orissa,* Patna, 1927.

Singh, L.R.; *The Terai Region of U.P.,* Allahabad, 1965.

Singh, R.L.; *Rural Settlements in Monsoon Asia,* NGSI, Varanasi, 1972.

Singh, R.L.; *et al; Readings in Rural Settlement Geography,* NGSI, Varanasi, 1975.

Singh, R.L.; *et. al; Geographic Dimensions of Rural Settlements;* NGSI, Varanasi, 1976.

Singh, R.L.; *et. al.; Approach to Rural Settlement Geography;* NGSI, Varanasi, 1978.

Singh, S.N.; *History of Tirhut,* Calcutta, 1922.

Sinha, B.P.; *The Decline of the Kingdom of Magadha,* Patna, 1954.

Sinha, V.N.P.; *Chhotanagpur, Plateau: A Study in Settlement Geography,* Rajesh Publications, New Delhi, 1980.

Smith, T.L.; *The Sociology of Rural Life,* New York, 1947.

Spate, O.H.K.; *India and Pakistan,* London, Methuen & Co. London, 1967.

Srinivas; *India's Villages,* London, 1960.

Stone, K.H.; *Geographic Aspects of Planning for New Rural Settling in the Free World's Northern Lands in 'Problems and Trends in American Geography* (Ed.S.C. Cohen), New York, 1967.

Tarachand; *Short History of the Indian People,* Calcutta, 1934.

Thakur, U.; *History of Mithila,* Mithila Institute, Darbhanga, 1956.

Thomas, A.; *Rural Planning and Development, Commission of Conservation,* Ottawa, 1917.

Trewartha, G.T.; *Settlements and Houses of Japan: A Physical, Cultural and Regional Geography,* Wisconsin, 1947.

Victor, Olygyay; *Design with Climate,* Princeton, New Jersey, 1963.

Waddell, L.A.; *Report on the Excavations at Pataliputra, (Patna),* Calcutta 1903.

Wagle, N.; *Indian Antiquity* (Edt. G.V. Deva), Rastogi Vol. I, 1964.

Wilson, W.H.; *Evolution of the Country Community,* New York, 1912.

Articles in Journals

Abiodun, J.O.; Central Place Study in Abiokuta Province, South-Western Nigeria, *Jour. of Regional Sc.* Vol. 8, No. 1, 1968.

Agrawala, V.S.; Geographical Data in Panini, *The Ind. Histo. Quaterly,* Vol. XXIX, 1953.

Ahmad, E.; Rural Settlement Types in the U.P., *Annals As. Am. Geog.* Vol. XLII, No. 3, 1952.

Ahmad, E.; Village Survey, *Ind. Geog. Jour,* Vol. 28, Nos. 1 & 2, 1953.

Ahmad, E.; Rural Population of Bihar, *The Geog. Rev.,* Vol. 51, 1961.

Ahmad, E.; Indian Village Patterns, *Geog. Out. Look,* Vol. 3, No. 1, 1962.

Ahmad, E.; Human Settlement in Indian Desert; a Historical Perspective, *The Geographer,* 1965.

Ahmad, N.; The Pattern of Rural Settlement in East Pakistan, *The Geog. Rev.* Vol. 58, 1968.

Alan, R.H.B.; Reversal of Rank Size Rule, *The Professional Geographer,* Vol. XXI, No. 6, 1969.

Anas, M.; The Pattern of Rural Settlements in the Sub-Himalayan Regions, *The Geographer,* Vol. VI, No. 2, 1954.

Arthur & Getis, J.; Christaller's Central Place Theory, *Jour. of Geog.,* Vol. XIV, No. 5, 1966.

Aurousseau, M.; The Arrangement of Rural Population, *Geog. Rev.,* Vol. 10, 1920.

Ayyar, T.S.S.; Place Names of the Tirnne-Valley District, *Jour. Mad. Geog. Asso.,* Vol. 15, No. 4, 1940.

Bailay, P.J.M.; The Geography of Settlement in Stanstend Township Province of Quebec, *Geography*, Vol. XLII, No. 19, Part I, 1956.

Bandopadhyay, P.; Settlement Patterns of Eastern Kolhan, *Geog. Rev. of Ind.,* Vol. 19, No. 1, 1957.

Barnes, J.A. & Robinson, A.H.; A New Method for the Representation of Dispersed Rural Population, *Geog. Rev.,* Vol. 30, 1940.

Baterford, H.; Types and Materials of Houses in England, *The Geographical Teacher,* Vol. XII, No. 65, Part I, 1923.

Berry, B.J.L. & Garrison, W.L.; Alternative Explanations of Urban Rank Size Relationships, *Annals Asso. Ame. Geogs.,* Vol. 48, 1958.

Berry, B.J.L. & Garrison, W.L.; The Functional Bases of the Central Place Hierarchy, *Eco. Geog.* Vol. 34, 1958.

Bharati, S.S.; Place Names in Pandinad, *Jour., of Mad. Geog. Asso.* Vol. 7, No. 3, 1932.

Bhattacharya, A.N.; Effect of Tribal and Caste Factor on Rural Settlements in U.P., *India Geog. Journ,* Vol. 31, Nos. 3&4, 1956.

Bhattacharya, A.N. & Verma, L.N.; Rural Settlements Forms in the Sone Valley, *Indian Geographer,* Vol. 2, No. 2, 1957.

Bhattacharya, N.D.; Rural Settlements of Murshidabad, West Bengal, *N.G.J.I.,* Vol. 12, Part 4, 1966.

Bobland, J.; The Influence of Kinship Ties on the Settlement Pattern of Northeast Georgia, *The Professional Geographer,* Vol. XXII, No. 5, 1970.

Birch, B.P.; The Measurement of Dispersed Patterns of Settlement, Tej, Voor, *Econo. en Socio. Geog.* Vol. 58, 1967.

Boal, F.W. & Johnson, D.B.; The Rank Size Rule, *The Professional Geographers,* Vol. XVII, No. 5, 1965.

Bohland, J.R.; A Classification for the Spatial Arrangement of Rural Setling Projects, Piedmont Homestead Project, Georgia, *The Professional Geographer,* Vol. XX, No. 3, 1968.

Bose, A.B. & Malhotra, S.P.; The Form of Settlement in a Desert Village, *Indian Geographer,* Vol. 6, No. 1, 1961.

Bowen, E.G.; A Study of Rural Settlements in South-west Wales, *The Geographical Teacher,* Vol. XIII, Part 4, No. 74, 1926.

Bowmen, I.; The Scientific Study of Settlement, *Geographical Review,* Vol. 16, 1926.

Brooke, Clark; The Rural Village in Ethopian Highlands, *The Geog. Rev.* Vol. 50, 1950.

Bracy, H.E.; Towns as Rural Service Centres, *Transactions and Papers of the Ins. of Bri. Geogs.,* Vol. 19, 1953.

Brown, R.L.; Changing Rural Settlements Patterns in Arctic Alaska, *The Professional Geographer,* Vol. XXI, No. 5, 1969.

Brush, J.E.; The Urban Hierarchy in Europe, *Geographical Reviews,* Vol. 43, 1953.

Brush, J.E.; The Hierarchy of Central Places in South-Western Wisconsin, *Goeg. Rev.*, Vol. 43, 1953.

Buschman, K.H.; Settlements and Habitations in India I, *Geog. Rev.* Ind. Vol. 16, No. 3, 1954.

Bushchman, K.H.; Settlements and Habitations in India II, *Geog. Rev. Ind.* Vol. 16, No. 4, 1954.

Carol, H.; *The City Centred Region: A Proposed Base for Regional Planning and Regional Government in Ontario, Terra, (Helsinki),* Vol. 81, 1969.

Caruthers, I.; A Classification of Service Centres in England and Wales, *The Geog Jour.* Vol. CXXIV, Part I, 1958.

Charles, B.E.; Path of the Settlement and Distribution of Population of Mains, *Eco.Geog.*, Vol. 20, 1944.

Chauhan, V.S.; Rural Settlements in the Upland Region of Jamuna Hindan Doab, U.P. *Trans. of the Ind. Con. of Geog.,* Vol. V, 1968.

Chatterji, A.B. & Das M.; Settlement Patterns in the Puri-Chilka Coastal Tract, *Geog. Rev. India,* Vol. 26, No. 4, 1964.

Chatterji, A.B.; A Village on the Hooghly Side 1970; *Geog. Rev. Ind.*, Vol. 28, 1966.

Chettiar, C.M.R.; The Place Names in Salem District, *Jour. Md. Geog. Ass.*, Vol. II, No. 2, 1936.

Chettiar, C.M.R.; A Study of Place Names in Tanjor District, *Jour. Mad. Geog. Assó.*, Vol. 12, No. 2, 1937.

Chettiar, C.M.R.; Place Names in Tamilnad, *Jour. Mad. Geog. Ass.*, Vol. 8, No. 1, 1938.

Chettiar, C.M.R.; Place Names in South Karnatak District; *Jour. Mad. Geog. Ass* Vol. 13, no. 4, 1938.

Chettiar, C.M.R.; Place Names in North Arcot Distirct, *Jour. Mad. Geog. Ass.,* Vol. 18, No. 2, 1943.

Clark, P.J. & Evans, F.C.; Distance to Nearest Neighbour as a Measure of Spatial Relationship in Populations, *Ecology,* Vol. 35, 1954.

Clark, W.A.V.; Consumer Travel Patterns and the Concept of Range; *Annals Ass. Amr. Geogs.*, Vol. 58, no. 2, 1968.

Cozens, A.B.; The Geographic Background of Some Mexican House Types, *Annals. Ass. Amer. Geogs.*, Vol. 28, 1938.

Davies, W.K.D.; The Ranking of Service Centres; *Trans. Ins. Bri. Geogs.*, No. 40, 1966.

Davies, W.K.D.; Centrality and the Central Place Hierarchy, *Urban Studies,* Vol. 4, No. 1, 1967.

Datta, J.M.; Daha Village in Howrah, *Geog. Rev. Ind.*, Vol. 19, No. 4, 1957.

Despande, C.D.; Settlement Types of Bombay Karnatak, *Ind. Geog. Jour,* Vol. 17, No. 2, 1942.

Devi, M.N.V.; Edakkad, The Socio-Geographic Survey of a Village, *Ind. Geog. Jour.,* Vol. 37, 1962.

Dickinson, R.C.; The Regional Functions and Zones of Influence of Leeds and Bradford, *Geography,* Vol. 15, 1930.

Dickinson, R.E.; The Distribution and Functions of the Smaller Urban Settlements of East Anglia, *Geography,* Vol. XVII, No. 95, Part I, 1932.

Dickinson, R.E.; Rural Settlements in German Lands, *Annals Ass. Amer. Geographers,* Vol. 39, 1949.

Dikshit, R.D.; Rural House Types in Dehradun Valley, *The Deccan Geographer,* Vol. 3, no. 1, 1965.

Dikshit, R.D.; Evolution of Settlements in the Dun Valley of U.P., *The Deccan Geographer,* Vol. 7, No. 1, 1969.

Dobby; Settlement Patterns in Malaya, *Geog., Rev.,* Vol. 32, 1942.

Duggal, S.L.; Moradabad District, Settlements in Relation to Landuse, *Indian Geographer,* Vol. 6, No. 1, 1961.

Dutt, A.K. & Banerji, S.; Transportation Index in West Bengal, A means to Determine Central Place Hierarchy, *N.G.J.I.,* Vol. XVI, part 3-4, 1970.

Edward, U.; A Theory of Location for Cities, *Amer Jour. Sec.,* Vol. 46, 1940.

Eugene, V.C.; Finnish Settlement in Canada, *The Geog. Rev.,* Vol. 42, 1952.

Fairhurst, H.; Types of Settlement in Spain, *Scott. Geog. Mag.,* Vol. 51, 1935.

Fawcett, C.B.; The Distribution of Rural Settlements, *Geog. Jour.,* Vol. XCIII, No. 2, 1939.

Fuller, M.L. & Clapp, F.G. ; Rural Dwellings of Shensi China, *The Geog. Rev.,* Vol. 14, 1924.

Gleave, M.B.; Hill Settlements and their Abondonment in Tropical Africa, *Trans. Inst. Bri. Geogs.* No. 40, 1966.

Golledge, R.G., Rushton, G. and Clark, W.A.V.; Some Spatial Characteristics of Iowa's Dispersed Farm Population and their Implications for the Grouping of Central Place Functions, *Economic Geog.,* Vol. 42, 1966.

Gonothinayagam, V.; Housing: A Sociological Analysis, *Social Welfare,* 1969.

Gorni, O.; Problems of Rural Settlement in Spain, *International Labour Review,* 1929.

Green, F.H.W.; Rural and Coastal Settlement in the Moray Firth Lowlands, *The Scott. Geog. Mag.,* Vol. 52, No. 2, 1936.

Guha, B.; The Rural Service Centres of Hooghly District, *Geog. Rev. Ind.,* Vol. 29, No. 4, 1967.

Hall, R.B.; Some Rural Settlement Forms in Japan, *Geog. Rev.,* Vol. XXI, No. 1, 1931.

Hall, R.B.; A Map of Settlement Agglomeration and Dispersion in Japan, *Papers of the Michigan Academy of Science,* 1936.

Hance, W.A.; Crofting Settlements and Housing in the Outer Hebrides, *Annals Ass. Amer. Geogs.* Vol. XLI, no. 1, 1951.

Hirst, M.A.; Rural Settlement and Landuse, A Note on Tanzania, *The Professional Geographer,* Vol. XXII, No. 5, 1970.

Hobson, P.M.; Population and Settlement in Novascotia, *The Scott. Geog. Mag,* Vol. 70, No. 2, 1954.

Hoffman, G.W.; Transformation of Rural Settlement in Bulgaria, *The Geog. Rev.,* Vol. 54, 1964.

Hopkins, E.W.; Position of the Ruling Caste in Ancient India, *Jour. Ame. Ori. Soci.,* Vol. 13, 1883.

Janaki, V.A., Geographical Basis for the Distribution and Pattern of Rural Settlement in Kerala, *Jour. M.S. University,* Baroda, Vol. 2, No. 2, 1953.

Janaki, V.A.; Historical Development of Settlements of Kerala, *Jour. of Baroda Univ.,* Vol. 6, 1987.

Jayaswal, S.N.P.; Bindki' A Study in Evolution of a Trade Centre, *N.G.J.I.,* Vol. 9, Part 3 & 4 1963.

Jayaswal, S.N.D.; Sachendi—A Study of Rural Service Centre, *Geog. Rev. Ind.,* Vol. 24, No. 1, 1962.

Jay, L.J.; Pioneer Settlement on the Darling Downs, *Scott, Geog. Mag.,* Vol. 72, 1956.

Jefferson, M.; The Distribution of the World's Cities Folks, *Geog. Rev.,* Vol. XXI, 1931.

Jha, B.; Village in Ancient India, *Journ. Bi. Res. Soci,* Vol. 41, Part-I, 1955.

Jha, B.N.; River Problem of North Bihar, *Geog. Rev. Ind.,* Vol. XVIL, No. 2, 1955.

Johnson, L.J.; The Spatial Uniformity of a Central Place Distribution in New England, *Eco. Geog.,* Vol. 47. no. 2, 1971.

Johnson, J.H.; Studies of Irish Rural Settlement, *The Geog. Rev.,* Vol. 48, 1958.

Johnson, R.J.; Central Places and the Settlement Pattern, *Annals Ass. of*

Ame. Geogs, Vol. 56, No. 3, 1966.

Jones, E.; Settlement Pattern in the Middle Theify Valley, *Geography,* Vol. XXX, Part 4, No. 150, 1945.

Kanaujia, L.R.S. The Terai Region of U.P.: A Study in Human Geography, *The National Geographer,* Vol. 1, No. 1, 1958.

Kapadia, K.M. Rural Family Patterns; *Sociological Bulletin,* Bombay 5, September, 1956.

Kaushic, S.D.; Types of Human Settlements in Jaunsar Himalaya, *Geog. Rev. Ind.,* Vol. 121, Nos. 2, 3 and 4, 1959.

Kaushic, S.D.; Climatic Zones and Their Related Socio-Economy in the Garhwal Himalaya, *Geog. Rev. Ind.,* Vol. 24, Nos. 3-4, 1962.

Kayastha, S.L.; Human Habitation in the Himalayan Beas Basin, *The Ind. Geog. Jour.,* Vol. 6, No. 2, 1961.

Keating, H.M.; Village Types and Their Distribution in the Plains of Nottingham, *Geography* Vol. XX, 1935.

Korsok, A.J.; Rural Dwelling Characteristics and Distribution in Ceylon, *Jour. of Geog.,* Vol. LXX, No. 1, 1971.

Krishnan, G.; Spatial Analysis of Vegetable Supply of a Planned City, Chandigarh, *Ind. Geog. Jour.,* Vol. 38, 1963.

Kniffen, F.B.; Louisiana House Types, *Annals Ass. Ame. Geogs.,* Vol. 26, 1936.

Kulkarni, A.R.; Village Life in the Deccan in the 17th Century, *The Ind. Eco. and Soci. His. Rev.,* Vol. IV, No. 1, 1967.

Lahiri, R.; Settlement Types in Ajay-Barakar Basin, *Cal. Geog. Rev.* Vol. 12, No. 4, 1950.

Lahiri, J.B.; Urbanisation Potential of Villages, *Geog. Rev. of India,* Vol. 28, No. 2, 1966.

Lal, Rama Shanker; Demographic Features of Lower Ghaghra-Gandak Doab, *Transactions of the Council of Indian Geographers,* Vol. 5, 1968.

Learmonth, A.T.A.; Learmonth, A.M.; Aspects of Village Life in Indo-Pakistan, *Geography,* Vol. 40, 1955.

Lee, D.H.K.; Thoughts on Housing for the Humid Tropics, *Geog. Rev.,* Vol. 41, 1951.

Malaviya, H.D.; Economy of the Vedic Village, *Eco. Rev.,* Sept. 15, 1954.

Mikesell, Marvin, W.; Market Centres of Northeastern Spain, *The Geographical Review,* Vol. 1, no. 2, April, 1960.

Mophail, I.R.; The Character of the Ruralshire in New South Wales, *The Australian Geographer,* Vol. X, No. 6, Sept. 1968.

McKay, J.; A Review of Rural Settlement Studies for Tanzania, *The East African Geographical Review,* No. VI, April, 1968.

Mc Carty, H.H.; A Functional Analysis of Population Distribution, *Geographical Review,* Vol. 32, 1942.

McKim, Marriet; *Village India, The American Anthropological Association Memoir,* Vol. 57, No. 88, 1965.

Mishra, S.D.; Population and Settlement in Himachal Pradesh, *The Deccan Geographer,* Vol. 3, No. 1, 1965.

Mishra, S.D.; Settlements in a Zone of Transition, *Pak. Geog. Rev.,* Vol. 17, No. 1, 1963.

Mishra, S.N.; Human Dwellings in Sonpar Region' U.P.: A Geographical Analysis, *N.G.J.I.,* Vol. 15, Part I, 1969.

Mitra, A.; House Types in India, *The Illustrated Weekly of India,* Bombay, November 10, 1968.

Moodie, A.E.; Fuller, G. Joan; Cole, M.M.; Duttand, G.J., *Settlement and Population, Geog. Studies,* Vol. 2, no. 2, 1955.

Mukerji, A.B.; Jat Settlements and Habitations I, *Ind. Geog. Journ.* Vol. 31, Nos. 3-4, 1956.

Mukerji, A.B.; Nomenclature of the Jat Villages, *Geographer,* 1956.

Mukerji, A.B.; Jat Settlements and Habitations II, *Ind, Geog. Jour.,* Vol. 32, Nos, 1-2, 1957.

Mukerji, A.B.; Bhawanti House Type in Andhra Pradesh, *Geog. Outlook,* Vol. 3, No. 1, 1962.

Mukerji, A.B.; Jat House Types, *Geografia,* No. 1, 1962.

Mukerji, A.B.; Succession of Culture Landscapes in Telengana Reddi Villages, *Ind. Geog. Jour.* Vol. 39, No. 1&2, 1964.

Mukerji, A.B.; Cultural Landscape of a Telengana Village, *Geographia,* Vol. 3, No. 1, 1964.

Mukerji, A.B.; Musalman House Type in Meerut Rural Area, *Folklore,* Vol. 8, No. 4, 1967

Mukerji, A.B.; Rural Settlements in the Jatakas, *Geog. Rev. Ind.,* Vol. 31, No. 4, 1969.

Mukerji, A.B.; Spacing of Rural Settlements in Andhra Pradesh, A Spatial Interpretation, *Geographical Outlook* (Ranchi), Vol. VI, 1969.

Mukerji, A.B.; Spacing of Rural Settlements in Rajasthan: A Spatial Analysis, *Geographical Outlook* (Agra), Vol. 1, No. 1, 1970.

Mukerji, S.; The Influence of the Architecture of Rural Houses in Maharashtra, *The Ind. Geog. Jour,* Vol. XLVI, No. 1-2, 1971.

Mukhopadhyay, C.; Growth Pattern of a Rural Town (1851-1961), *The Ind. Eco. and Soci. Hist. Rev.,* Vol. IV, no. 4, 1967.

Munshi, S.K.; Case Study of Isolated Indian Mining Settlement, *Ind. Geog. Jour.,* Vol. 40, Nos. 1-2, 1965.

Nath, N.; Kautilyakalin Gramya Byabastha (Hindi), *Bihar Samachar,* No. 18, Nov. 1968.

Natesan, S.; Place Names of Coimbatore District, *Jour. Mad. Geog. Ass.,* Vol. 5, No. 2-3, 1930.

Natesan, S.; A Study of the Place Names of the Tanjore District, *Jour. Mad. Geog. Ass.,* Vol. 12, No. 2, 1937.

Neolithic Culture Found at Chirand, *The Indian Nation,* Patna, May 6, 1970.

Niddrie, D.L.; Eighteenth Century Settlement in the British Caribbean, *Trans. Ins. Bri. Geogs,* 1966.

Nirmala. C.; Vittalam Village, *Ind. Geog. Jour.,* Vol. 35, Nos. 3&4, 1960.

Nityanand; Types of Rural Settlements in East Rajasthan, *Agra Univ. Jour.* Vol. 8, Part 2, 1960.

Nityanand; Site, Morphology and Classification of Rural Settlements in East Rajasthan, *All, Geog. Jour.* Vol. 3, 1961.

Nityanand; Distribution and Spatial Arrangement of Rural Population in East Rajasthan, India, *Annals Ass. Amer. Geogs.,* Vol. 56, 1966.

Nits, H.J.; Studies in the Field Patterns of Northern India and Germany, *The Geographer,* Vol. 13, 1966.

Nobb., W.A.; Approaches Towards An Understanding of Traditional South Asian Peasant Dwelling, *The Professional Geographer,* Vol. 21, No. 4, 1969.

Nobb, W.A.; Toda Dwellings and Temples, *Anthropos,* Vol. 61, 1966.

Pag. W.; Forms of Medieval Settlement in England, *The Geographical Teacher,* Vol. XI, No. 59, Part I, 1921.

Padhye, S.S.; Tribal People of the Melighat, *Ind. Geog. Jour.,* Vol. 37, No. 3, 1962.

Padhye, S.S.; Dessertation of Villages in the Deccan Trap Region of Vidarbha, *Bombay Geog. Magazine,* Vol. 13, No. 1, 1965.

Parsons, James J.; The Settlement of the Sinn Valley of Colombia, *The Geographical Review,* Vol. 42, 1952.

Peter Scott; The Hierarchy of Central Places in Tasmania, *The Australian Geographer,* 1968.

Pillai, J.H.V.; The Badagas, *Jour. of Mad. Geog. Asso.,* Vol. 12, 1937.

Preston, E. James; Expanding Frontiers of Settlement in Latin America, *The Hispanic American Historical Review,* Vol. 21, 1941.

Preston, Richard E.; The Structure of Central Place Systems, *Economic Geography,* Vol. 47, No. 2, April, 1971.

Pryor, Robin J.; Problems of Rural Land Development, Frinders Island, Jashmania, *The Australian Geographer,* Vol. X, No. 3, March, 1962.

Rahman, G.; Village Housing in East Pakistan, *Oriental Geographer*, Dacca, Vol. XII, No. 1, 1968.

Ramchandran, R.; Mohammadpuram, *Ind. Geog. Jour.*, Vol. 35, No. 3-4, 1960.

Rao, C.N.; A Study of Place Names in the Anantpur District, *Journal of Mad. Geog. Asso.*, Vol. 10, No. 1, 1935.

Rasalpuri, Ramrijhan; "Kumhar' (Hindi) *Bihar Samachar*, Patna, October, 1969.

Savory, H.S.; Settlement in the Glamocko Polje, *The Geog Jour.*, Vol. 123-24, 1957-58.

Scott, P.; Areal Variation in the Class Structure of the Central Place Hierarchy, *Aus. Geog. Stu.*, Vol. 11, No. 2, 1964.

Scofield, E.; The Origin of Settlement Patterns in Rural New England, *Geog. Rev.* Vol. 28, 1938.

Sen. A.K.; Settlements Pattern in Rajasthan, *Man in India*, Vol. 46, No. 3, 1966.

Sen.V & Guha H.; Landuse and Settlements Characters in Bankura, *Geog. Rev. Ind.*, Vol. 22, no. 4, 1960.

Shrivastava, K.N.; Bhils of Mewar, *Ind. Geog Jour.*, Vol. 21, No. 2, 1946.

Sharma, R.C.; Western Rajasthan, A Study of House Types, *The National Geographer*, Vol. 3, 1960.

Singh, B.; Nalanda Plate of Samudra Gupta, A Reconsideration, *The Jour. of Bihar Res. Socie.* Vol. XLVII, Part 1-4, 1961.

Singh, C.; Chirand, *Bihar Samachar*, Patna, 1971.

Singh, O.P.; Functions and Functional Classes of Central Places in U.P., *The N.G.J.I.*, Vol. XIV, Part 2-3, 1968.

Singh, R.B.; Historical Geography, Place Names and Settlements, *The N.G.J.I.*, Vol. 11, Part II, 1965.

Singh, R.B.; Cultural Geography of Varanasi District during Pre-Rajput Period, The *N.G.J.I.*, Vol. II, Part 3-4, 1965.

Singh, R.B.; Rural Settlement Types and Their Distribution, *The N.G.J.I.*, Vol. XV, No. 2, 1969.

Singh, S.M.; The Ancient Bhars and Their Ruined Settlements in the Ganga-Ghaghra Doab-West, The *N.G.J.I.*, Vol. 8, Part 3&4, 1962.

Singh, S.M.; Failure of Land Settlements in the South Australian Arid Lands, *The N.G.J.I.*, Vol. 10, No. 2, 1964.

Singh, S.M.; The Stability Theory of Rural Central Place Development, *The N.G.J.I.*, Vol. II, Part I, 1965.

Singh, S.M.; Thrrufs Bhawanti and Raotar in Ganga-Ghaghra Doab West, A Study in Land Settlement and Social Geography, *The N.G.J.I.*,

Vol. II, Nos. 3 & 4, 1965.

Singh, K.N.; Changes in the Functional Structure of Some Small Towns in Eastern U.P., *Indian Geographer,* Vol. VI, No. 1, 1961.

Singh, K.N.; Spatial Pattern of Central Places in the Middle Ganga Valley, *The N.G.J.I.,* Vol. 12, Part 4, 1966.

Singh, K.N.; The Territorial Basis of Medieval Town and Village Settlement in Eastern U.P., *Annals Ass. Amer. Geogs.,* Vol. 158, No. 2, 1968.

Singh, R.L.; Evolution of Settlements in the Middle Ganga Valley, *The N.G.J.I.,* Vol. I, Part 2, 1955.

Singh, R.L.; Typical Rural Dwellings in the Umland of Banaras, *The N.G.J.I.,* Vol. 3, Part 2, 1957.

Singh, R.L. and Singh, S.M.; Mungra Badshahpur: A Rural Settlemet in the Ganga-Ghaghra Doab West, *The N.G.J.I.,* Vol. VI, Part IV, 1960.

Singh, R.L.; Meaning, Objectives and Scope of Settlement Geography, *The N.G.J.I.,* Vol. 7, part I, 1961.

Singh, R.L.; "Evolution of Clan Territorial Units through land Occupance in the Middle Ganga Valley" *National Geographical Journal of India,* Vol. 20, No. 1, 1974. pp. 1-19.

Singh, R.L. and Singh, R.B.; "Spatial Diffusion of Rajput Clan Settlements in a part of Middle Ganga Valley" Rural Settlement in Monsoon Asia, Varanasi, 1972, pp. 152-170.

Singh, R.L. & Singh, R.P.B.; "Shape Analysis in Rural Settlement Geography" in Readings in Rural Settlement Geography, *National Geographical Society of India,* 1975, pp. 444-452.

Singh, S.C.; Changes in the Course of the Kosi, The *N.G.J.I.,* Vol. XVI, Part 3&4, 1970.

Singh, T.; A Case Study of House Types in Village Kurali, *Meerut Geog. Observer,* No. 1, 1965.

Sinha, S.; A Village in Singhbhum, *Cal. Geog. Rev.,* Vol. 12, No. 1, 1950.

Sinha, C.R.P.; Buxar in Archaeological Perspectives, *The Jour. Bih, Reas. Soci.,* Patna. Vol. XLIX, 1963.

Sinha, K.K.; The Growth of Towns Along the Ganga in Bihar, *Trans. of the Coun. of Ind. Geogs.,* Vol. 5, 1968.

Sinha, V.N.P.; Rural settlement in Barakar Basin, *Trans. Coun. Ind. Geog.,* Vol. 5, 1968.

Sinha, V.N.P., Houses and House Types of the Chota Nagpur Plateau, *The Geog. Know,* Vol. 2, No. 2, 1969.

Spate, O.H.K.; The Burmese Village, *Geog. Rev.,* Vol. 35, 1945.

Spate, O.H.K.& Despande, C.D.; The Indian Village, *Geography,* Vol. 37, 1952.

Spenor, J.E.; The House of the Chinese, *Geog. Rev.,* Vol. 37, No. 2, 1947.

Stone, K.H.; Swedish Fringes of Settlement, *Annals Ass. Amer. Geogs.,* Vol. 52, 1962.

Stone, K.H.; The Development of a Focus for the Geography of Settlement, *Eco. Geog.,* Vol. 41, 1965.

Stone, K.H.; Multiple Scale Classifications for Rural Settlement Geography, *Acta Geographica* (Helsinki), Vol. 20, 1968.

Subrahmanyam, K.M.; Four Main House Types in South India, *Jour. Mad. Geog. Asso.,* Vol. 8, No. 2, 1938.

Subrahmanyam, N.; Rural Geography, *Jour. Mad. Geog. Asso.* Vol. 1, No. 1, 1925.

Swainson, R.M.; Dispersion and Agglomeration of Rural Settlement in Somerset, *Geography,* Vol. XXX, 1945.

Tamaskar, B.G.; Geographical Data in the Jatakas Tales, *Qur. Rev. of His. Stud,* Vol. 7, No. 2, 1967-68.

Thakur, B.; Types of Rural Settlement in North Bihar, *Trans. Coun. Ind. Geogs.,* Vol. V, 1968.

Tiwari, A.K. A House Type in Janusar Himalaya, *The Australian Geographer,* Vol. 10, No. 1, 1966.

Thomas, N.E.; Some Comments on the Functional Basis for Small Iowa Towns, *Iowa Business Digest,* 1960.

Trewartha, G.T.; The Unincorporated Hamlet, One Element of the American Settlement Fabric, *Annals Ass. Amer. Geogs.,* Vol. 33, 1943.

Trewartha, G.T.; Types of Rural Settlement in Colonial America, *The Geog. Rev.,* Vol. 36, 1946.

Udo, R.K.; Disintegration of Nucleated Settlement in Eastern Nigeria, *The Geg. Rev.* Vol. 55, 1965.

Ullman, E.L.; Trade Centres and Tributary Areas of the Philippines, *The Geog. Rev.,* Vol. 1, No. 2, 1960.

Vandarhill, B.G.; The Direction of Settlement in the Prairie Provinces of Canada, *Journal of Geography,* Vol. LVIII, No. 7, 1959.

Verma, B.S.; Archaeological Remains of Mithila, *The Jour. of Bihar Research Society,* Vol. XLVIII, 1962.

INDEX